Ford Fairmont Mercury Zephyr Automotive Repair Manual

by Larry Warren and John H Haynes Member of the Guild of Motoring Writers

Models covered

Ford Fairmont and Mercury Zephyr 2-door, 4-door and Station Wagon with 140 cu in (2.3 liter), 140 cu in (2.3 liter) Turbo, 200 cu in (3.3 liter), 255 cu in (4.2 liter) and 302 cu in (5.0 liter) engines. 1978 thru 1983

ISBN 0 85696 958 3

ABCDE
FGHIJ

2

"Ford" and the Ford logo are registered trademarks of Ford Motor Company. Ford Motor Company is not a sponsor or affiliate of Haynes Publishing Group or Haynes North America, Inc. and is not a contributor to the content of this manual.

Haynes Publishing Group
Sparkford Nr Yeovil
Somerset BA22 7JJ England

Haynes North America, Inc
861 Lawrence Drive
Newbury Park
California 91320 USA

About this manual

Its aim

The aim of this manual is to help you get the best from your car. It can do so in several ways. It can help you decide what work must be done (even should you choose to get it done by a garage), provide information on routine maintenance and servicing, and give a logical course of action and diagnosis when random faults occur. However, it is hoped that you will use the manual by tackling the work yourself. On simpler jobs it may even be quicker than booking the car into a garage and going there twice to leave and collect it. Perhaps most important, a lot of money can be saved by avoiding the costs the garage must charge to cover its labour and overheads.

The manual has drawings and descriptions to show the function of the various components so that their layout can be understood. Then the tasks are described and photographed in a step-by-step sequence so that even a novice can do the work.

Its arrangement

The manual is divided into twelve Chapters, each covering a logical sub-division of the vehicle. The Chapters are each divided into Sections, numbered with single figures, eg 5; and the Sections into paragraphs (or sub-sections), with decimal numbers following on from the Section they are in, eg 5.1. 5.2 etc.

It is freely illustrated, especially in those parts where there is a detailed sequence of operations to be carried out. There are two forms of illustration: figures and photographs. The figures are numbered in sequence with decimal numbers, according to their position in the Chapter – Fig. 6.4 is the fourth drawing/illustration in Chapter 6. Photographs carry the same number (either individually or in related groups) as the Section or sub-section to which they relate.

There is an alphabetical index at the back of the manual as well as a contents list at the front. Each Chapter is also preceded by its own individual contents list.

References to the 'left' or 'right' of the vehicle are in the sense of a person in the driver's seat facing forwards.

Unless otherwise stated, nuts and bolts are removed by turning anti-clockwise, and tightened by turning clockwise.

Vehicle manufacturers continually make changes to specifications and recommendations, and these, when notified, are incorporated into our manuals at the earliest opportunity.

While every care is taken to ensure that the information in this manual is correct, no liability can be accepted by the authors or publishers for loss, damage or injury caused by any errors in, or omissions from, the information given.

Introduction to the Ford Fairmont and Mercury Zephyr

Body styles include a fastback coupe, 2 and 4 door sedans and a station wagon. Engine options range from the 140 cubic inch (2.3 liter) four-cylinder (also available with turbocharging) to the 200 cubic inch (3.3 liter) inline six to the 255 (4.2 liter) and 302 (5.0 liter) cubic inch V8s.

Chassis layout is conventional with the engine mounted at the front with the power being transmitted through either manual or automatic transmissions by driveshaft to the solid rear axle.

Front suspension is a modified McPherson coil spring design and the rear suspension features coil springs and the axle is located by four links. Steering is manual rack and pinion with power assist optional.

Brakes are disc at the front and drum at the rear with vacuum assist as an option.

Contents

1

2A

2B

2C

3

4

5

6

7A

7B

8

9

10

11

12

13

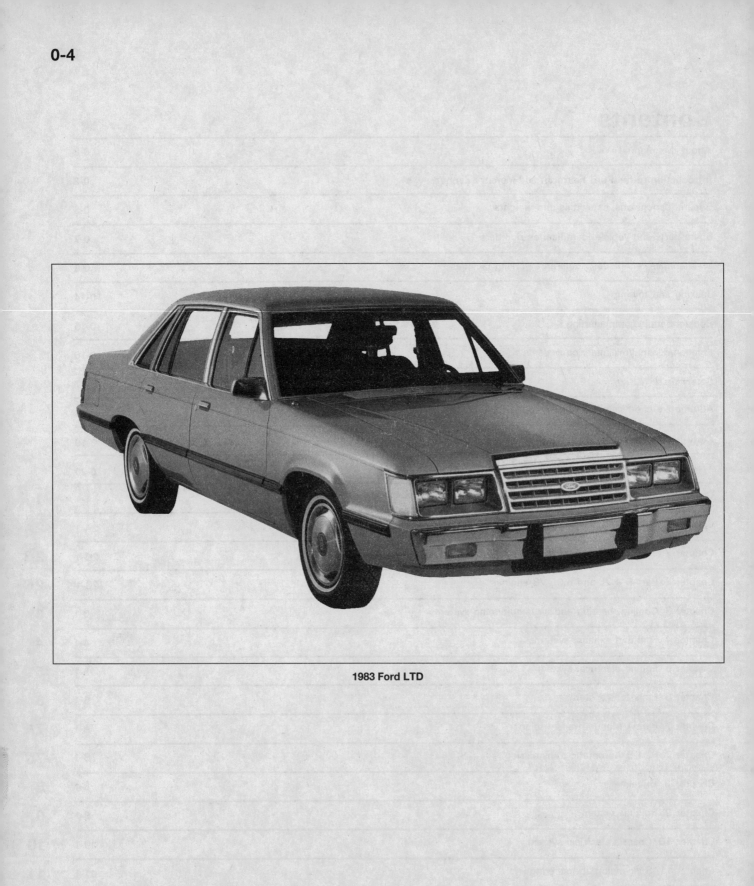

1983 Ford LTD

General dimensions, capacities and weights

Dimensions
Overall length
Coupe .... 197.4 in
2-door, 4-door and station wagon .... 195.5 in
Overall height
Coupe .... 52.3 in
2- and 4-door .... 53.5 in
Station wagon .... 54.2 in
Wheelbase .... 105.5 in

Capacities
Engine oil
All models .... 4.0 US qts*
Add 1 quart extra if the filter is replaced
Cooling system

1978 and 1979	w/air conditioning US qts	Standard US qts
2.3L	10.2	8.6
3.3L	9.0	9.0
5.0L	14.0	13.9
1980		
2.3L	10.2	10.2
3.3L	9.0	9.0
4.2L	14.3	14.2
1981		
2.3L	9.2	8.6
3.3L	8.5	8.4
4.2L	15.2	14.8

Fuel tank (approximate) — US gallons
1978 and 1979 .... 16.0
1980 .... 14.0 (Turbo 12.7)
1981 .... 16.0 (2.3L 14.0)
Manual transmission lubricant — US pints
3-speed 3.5
4-speed ET-type 2.8
4-speed RUG-type 4.5
Automatic transmission fluid
1978
C-3 (2.3L and 3.3L) 8.0
C-4 (3.3L) 8.25
C-4 (5.0L) 10.0
1979
C-3 (2.3L and 3.3L) 8.0
C-4 (3.3L) 7.6
C-4 (5.0L) 10.1
1980 and 1981
C-3 (2.3L and 3.3L) 8.0
C-4 (3.3L) 7.7
C-4 (4.2L) 10.0

Rear axle   **US pints**
6¾ in ring gear 2.50
7½ in ring gear 3.50

Curb weights (with base 4-cylinder engine)

1978   **lbs**
Coupe 2609
2-door 2572
4-door 2614
Station wagon 2722

1979
Coupe 2551
2-door 2516
4-door 2580
Station wagon 2681

1980
Coupe 2644
2-door 2605
4-door 2647
Station wagon 2769

1981
Coupe 2729
2-door 2677
4-door 2723
Station wagon 2831

Spare parts and
vehicle identification numbers

Buying spare parts

Spare parts are available from many sources, which generally fall into one of two categories — authorized dealer parts departments and independant retail auto parts stores. Our advice concerning spare parts is as follows:

Authorized dealer parts department: This is the best source for parts which are peculiar to your vehicle and not generally available elswhere (i.e. major engine parts, transmission parts, trim pieces, etc.). It is also the only place you should buy parts if your vehicle is still under warranty, as non-factory parts may invalidate the warranty. To be sure of obtaining the correct parts, have your vehicle's engine and chassis numbers available and, if possible, take the old parts along for positive identification.

Retail auto parts stores: Good auto parts stores will stock frequently needed components which wear out relatively fast (i.e. clutch components, exhaust systems, brake parts, tune-up parts, etc.). These stores often supply new or reconditioned parts on an exchange basis, which can save a considerable amount of money. Discount auto parts stores are often very good places to buy materials and parts needed for general vehicle maintenance (i.e. oil, grease, filters, spark plugs, belts, touch-up paint, bulbs, etc.). They also usually sell tools and general accessories, have convenient hours, charge lower prices, and can often be found not far from your home.

Vehicle identification numbers

Regardless from which source parts are obtained, it is essential to provide correct information concerning the vehicle model and year of manufacturer plus the engine serial number and the vehicle identification number (VIN). The accompanying illustrations show where these important numbers can be found.

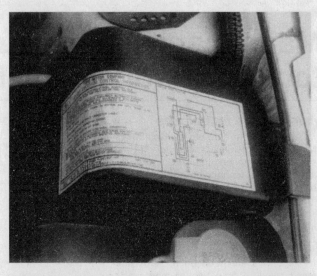

The vehicle emission control label is located under the hood

The vehicle certification label can be found on the door pillar or door, depending on the model

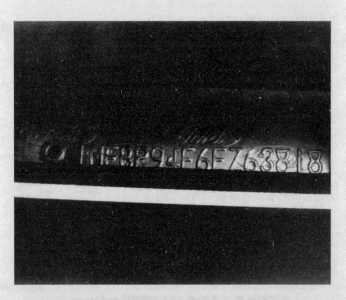

The vehicle identification number is attached to the dashboard and can be seen through the driver's side of the windshield

Maintenance techniques, tools and working facilities

Maintenance techniques

There are a number of techniques involved in maintenance and repair that will be referred to throughout this manual. Application of these techniques will enable the home mechanic to be more efficient, better organized and capable of performing the various tasks properly, which will ensure that the repair job is thorough and complete.

Fasteners

Fasteners are nuts, bolts, studs and screws used to hold two or more parts together. There are a few things to keep in mind when working with fasteners. Almost all of them use a locking device of some type, either a lockwasher, locknut, locking tab or thread adhesive. All threaded fasteners should be clean and straight, with undamaged threads and undamaged corners on the hex head where the wrench fits. Develop the habit of replacing all damaged nuts and bolts with new ones. Special locknuts with nylon or fiber inserts can only be used once. If they are removed, they lose their locking ability and must be replaced with new ones.

Rusted nuts and bolts should be treated with a penetrating fluid to ease removal and prevent breakage. Some mechanics use turpentine in a spout-type oil can, which works quite well. After applying the rust penetrant, let it work for a few minutes before trying to loosen the nut or bolt. Badly rusted fasteners may have to be chiseled or sawed off or removed with a special nut breaker, available at tool stores.

If a bolt or stud breaks off in an assembly, it can be drilled and removed with a special tool commonly available for this purpose.

Most automotive machine shops can perform this task, as well as other repair procedures, such as the repair of threaded holes that have been stripped out.

Flat washers and lockwashers, when removed from an assembly, should always be replaced exactly as removed. Replace any damaged washers with new ones. Never use a lockwasher on any soft metal surface (such as aluminum), thin sheet metal or plastic.

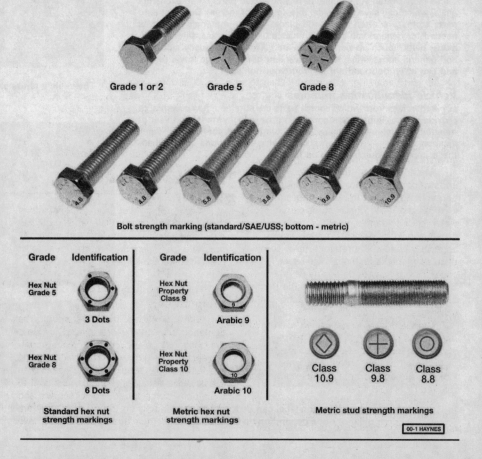

Bolt strength marking (standard/SAE/USS; bottom - metric)

Grade	Identification	Grade	Identification
Hex Nut Grade 5	3 Dots	Hex Nut Property Class 9	Arabic 9
Hex Nut Grade 8	6 Dots	Hex Nut Property Class 10	Arabic 10
Standard hex nut strength markings		**Metric hex nut strength markings**	

Class 10.9   Class 9.8   Class 8.8

Metric stud strength markings

00-1 HAYNES

Fastener sizes

For a number of reasons, automobile manufacturers are making wider and wider use of metric fasteners. Therefore, it is important to be able to tell the difference between standard (sometimes called U.S. or SAE) and metric hardware, since they cannot be interchanged.

All bolts, whether standard or metric, are sized according to diameter, thread pitch and length. For example, a standard 1/2 - 13 x 1 bolt is 1/2 inch in diameter, has 13 threads per inch and is 1 inch long. An M12 - 1.75 x 25 metric bolt is 12 mm in diameter, has a thread pitch of 1.75 mm (the distance between threads) and is 25 mm long. The two bolts are nearly identical, and easily confused, but they are not interchangeable.

In addition to the differences in diameter, thread pitch and length, metric and standard bolts can also be distinguished by examining the bolt heads. To begin with, the distance across the flats on a standard bolt head is measured in inches, while the same dimension on a metric bolt is sized in millimeters (the same is true for nuts). As a result, a standard wrench should not be used on a metric bolt and a metric wrench should not be used on a standard bolt. Also, most standard bolts have slashes radiating out from the center of the head to denote the grade or strength of the bolt, which is an indication of the amount of torque that can be applied to it. The greater the number of slashes, the greater the strength of the bolt. Grades 0 through 5 are commonly used on automobiles. Metric bolts have a property class (grade) number, rather than a slash, molded into their heads to indicate bolt strength. In this case, the higher the number, the stronger the bolt. Property class numbers 8.8, 9.8 and 10.9 are commonly used on automobiles.

Strength markings can also be used to distinguish standard hex nuts from metric hex nuts. Many standard nuts have dots stamped into one side, while metric nuts are marked with a number. The greater the number of dots, or the higher the number, the greater the strength of the nut.

Metric studs are also marked on their ends according to property class (grade). Larger studs are numbered (the same as metric bolts), while smaller studs carry a geometric code to denote grade.

It should be noted that many fasteners, especially Grades 0 through 2, have no distinguishing marks on them. When such is the case, the only way to determine whether it is standard or metric is to measure the thread pitch or compare it to a known fastener of the same size.

Standard fasteners are often referred to as SAE, as opposed to metric. However, it should be noted that SAE technically refers to a non-metric fine thread fastener only. Coarse thread non-metric fasteners are referred to as USS sizes.

Since fasteners of the same size (both standard and metric) may have different strength ratings, be sure to reinstall any bolts, studs or nuts removed from your vehicle in their original locations. Also, when replacing a fastener with a new one, make sure that the new one has a strength rating equal to or greater than the original.

Metric thread sizes	Ft-lbs	Nm
M-6	6 to 9	9 to 12
M-8	14 to 21	19 to 28
M-10	28 to 40	38 to 54
M-12	50 to 71	68 to 96
M-14	80 to 140	109 to 154

Pipe thread sizes		
1/8	5 to 8	7 to 10
1/4	12 to 18	17 to 24
3/8	22 to 33	30 to 44
1/2	25 to 35	34 to 47

U.S. thread sizes		
1/4 - 20	6 to 9	9 to 12
5/16 - 18	12 to 18	17 to 24
5/16 - 24	14 to 20	19 to 27
3/8 - 16	22 to 32	30 to 43
3/8 - 24	27 to 38	37 to 51
7/16 - 14	40 to 55	55 to 74
7/16 - 20	40 to 60	55 to 81
1/2 - 13	55 to 80	75 to 108

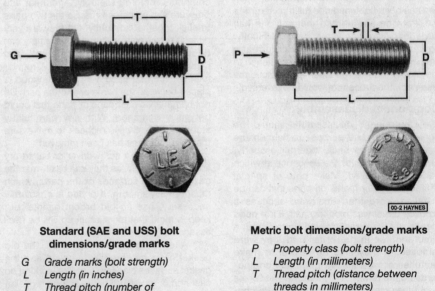

Standard (SAE and USS) bolt dimensions/grade marks

G   Grade marks (bolt strength)
L   Length (in inches)
T   Thread pitch (number of threads per inch)
D   Nominal diameter (in inches)

Metric bolt dimensions/grade marks

P   Property class (bolt strength)
L   Length (in millimeters)
T   Thread pitch (distance between threads in millimeters)
D   Diameter

Tightening sequences and procedures

Most threaded fasteners should be tightened to a specific torque value (torque is the twisting force applied to a threaded component such as a nut or bolt). Overtightening the fastener can weaken it and cause it to break, while undertightening can cause it to eventually come loose. Bolts, screws and studs, depending on the material they are made of and their thread diameters, have specific torque values, many of which are noted in the Specifications at the beginning of each Chapter. Be sure to follow the torque recommendations closely. For fasteners not assigned a specific torque, a general torque value chart is presented here as a guide. These torque values are for dry (unlubricated) fasteners threaded into steel or cast iron (not aluminum). As was previously mentioned, the size and grade of a fastener determine the amount of torque that can safely be applied to it. The figures listed here are approximate for Grade 2 and Grade 3 fasteners. Higher grades can tolerate higher torque values.

Fasteners laid out in a pattern, such as cylinder head bolts, oil pan bolts, differential cover bolts, etc., must be loosened or tightened in sequence to avoid warping the com-

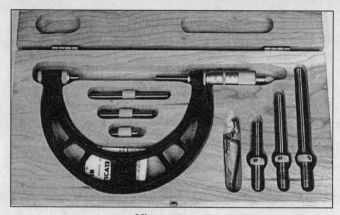

Micrometer set

Dial indicator set

ponent. This sequence will normally be shown in the appropriate Chapter. If a specific pattern is not given, the following procedures can be used to prevent warping.

Initially, the bolts or nuts should be assembled finger-tight only. Next, they should be tightened one full turn each, in a criss-cross or diagonal pattern. After each one has been tightened one full turn, return to the first one and tighten them all one-half turn, following the same pattern. Finally, tighten each of them one-quarter turn at a time until each fastener has been tightened to the proper torque. To loosen and remove the fasteners, the procedure would be reversed.

Component disassembly

Component disassembly should be done with care and purpose to help ensure that the parts go back together properly. Always keep track of the sequence in which parts are removed. Make note of special characteristics or marks on parts that can be installed more than one way, such as a grooved thrust washer on a shaft. It is a good idea to lay the disassembled parts out on a clean surface in the order that they were removed. It may also be helpful to make sketches or take instant photos of components before removal.

When removing fasteners from a component, keep track of their locations. Sometimes threading a bolt back in a part, or putting the washers and nut back on a stud, can prevent mix-ups later. If nuts and bolts cannot be returned to their original locations, they should be kept in a compartmented box or a series of small boxes. A cupcake or muffin tin is ideal for this purpose, since each cavity can hold the bolts and nuts from a particular area (i.e. oil pan bolts, valve cover bolts, engine mount bolts, etc.). A pan of this type is especially helpful when working on assemblies with very small parts, such as the carburetor, alternator, valve train or interior dash and trim pieces. The cavities can be marked with paint or tape to identify the contents.

Whenever wiring looms, harnesses or connectors are separated, it is a good idea to identify the two halves with numbered pieces of masking tape so they can be easily reconnected.

Gasket sealing surfaces

Throughout any vehicle, gaskets are used to seal the mating surfaces between two parts and keep lubricants, fluids, vacuum or pressure contained in an assembly.

Many times these gaskets are coated with a liquid or paste-type gasket sealing compound before assembly. Age, heat and pressure can sometimes cause the two parts to stick together so tightly that they are very difficult to separate. Often, the assembly can be loosened by striking it with a soft-face hammer near the mating surfaces. A regular hammer can be used if a block of wood is placed between the hammer and the part. Do not hammer on cast parts or parts that could be easily damaged. With any particularly stubborn part, always recheck to make sure that every fastener has been removed.

Avoid using a screwdriver or bar to pry apart an assembly, as they can easily mar the gasket sealing surfaces of the parts, which must remain smooth. If prying is absolutely necessary, use an old broom handle, but keep in mind that extra clean up will be necessary if the wood splinters.

After the parts are separated, the old gasket must be carefully removed and the gasket surfaces cleaned. If you're working on cast iron or aluminum parts, stubborn gasket material can be soaked with rust penetrant or treated with a special chemical to soften it so it can be easily scraped off. **Caution:** *Never use gasket removal solutions or caustic chemicals on plastic or other composite components.* A scraper can be fashioned from a piece of copper tubing by flattening and sharpening one end. Copper is recommended because it is usually softer than the surfaces to be scraped, which reduces the chance of gouging the part. Some gaskets can be removed with a wire brush, but regardless of the method used, the mating surfaces must be left clean and smooth. If for some reason the gasket surface is gouged, then a gasket sealer thick enough to fill scratches will have to be used during reassembly of the components. For most applications, a non-drying (or semi-drying) gasket sealer should be used.

Hose removal tips

Warning: *If the vehicle is equipped with air conditioning, do not disconnect any of the A/C hoses without first having the system depressurized by a dealer service department or a service station.*

Hose removal precautions closely parallel gasket removal precautions. Avoid scratching or gouging the surface that the hose mates against or the connection may leak. This is especially true for radiator hoses. Because of various chemical reactions, the rubber in hoses can bond itself to the metal spigot that the hose fits over. To remove a hose, first loosen the hose clamps that secure it to the spigot. Then, with slip-joint pliers, grab the hose at the clamp and rotate it around the spigot. Work it back and forth until it is completely free, then pull it off. Silicone or other lubricants will ease removal if they can be applied between the hose and the outside of the spigot. Apply the same lubricant to the inside of the hose and the outside of the spigot to simplify installation.

As a last resort (and if the hose is to be replaced with a new one anyway), the rubber can be slit with a knife and the hose peeled from the spigot. If this must be done, be careful that the metal connection is not damaged.

If a hose clamp is broken or damaged, do not reuse it. Wire-type clamps usually weaken with age, so it is a good idea to replace them with screw-type clamps whenever a hose is removed.

Tools

A selection of good tools is a basic requirement for anyone who plans to maintain and repair his or her own vehicle. For the owner who has few tools, the initial investment might seem high, but when compared to the spiraling costs of professional auto maintenance and repair, it is a wise one.

To help the owner decide which tools are needed to perform the tasks detailed in this manual, the following tool lists are offered: *Maintenance and minor repair, Repair/overhaul* and *Special.*

The newcomer to practical mechanics should start off with the *maintenance and*

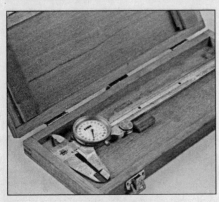

Dial caliper

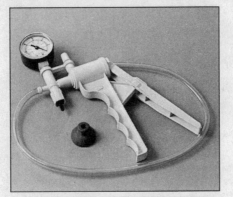

Hand-operated vacuum pump

Timing light

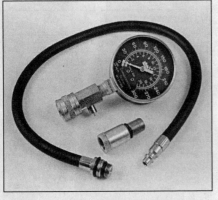

Compression gauge with spark plug hole adapter

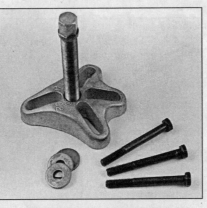

Damper/steering wheel puller

General purpose puller

Hydraulic lifter removal tool

Valve spring compressor

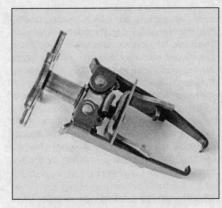

Valve spring compressor

Ridge reamer

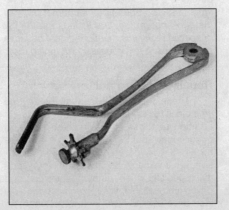

Piston ring groove cleaning tool

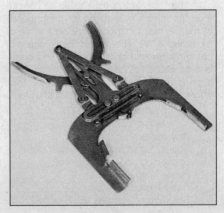

Ring removal/installation tool

Ring compressor

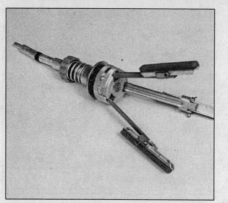

Cylinder hone

Brake hold-down spring tool

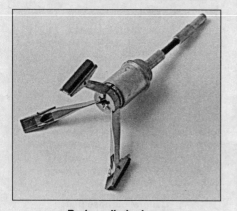

Brake cylinder hone

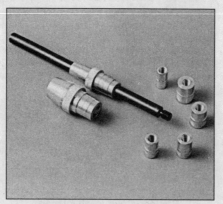

Clutch plate alignment tool

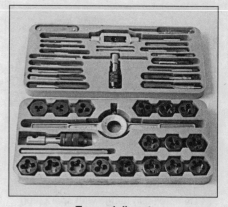

Tap and die set

minor repair tool kit, which is adequate for the simpler jobs performed on a vehicle. Then, as confidence and experience grow, the owner can tackle more difficult tasks, buying additional tools as they are needed. Eventually the basic kit will be expanded into the *repair and overhaul* tool set. Over a period of time, the experienced do-it-yourselfer will assemble a tool set complete enough for most repair and overhaul procedures and will add tools from the special category when it is felt that the expense is justified by the frequency of use.

Maintenance and minor repair tool kit

The tools in this list should be considered the minimum required for performance of routine maintenance, servicing and minor repair work. We recommend the purchase of combination wrenches (box-end and open-end combined in one wrench). While more expensive than open end wrenches, they offer the advantages of both types of wrench.

Combination wrench set (1/4-inch to 1 inch or 6 mm to 19 mm)
Adjustable wrench, 8 inch
Spark plug wrench with rubber insert
Spark plug gap adjusting tool
Feeler gauge set
Brake bleeder wrench
Standard screwdriver (5/16-inch x 6 inch)

Phillips screwdriver (No. 2 x 6 inch)
Combination pliers - 6 inch
Hacksaw and assortment of blades
Tire pressure gauge
Grease gun
Oil can
Fine emery cloth
Wire brush
Battery post and cable cleaning tool
Oil filter wrench
Funnel (medium size)
Safety goggles
Jackstands (2)
Drain pan

Note: *If basic tune-ups are going to be part of routine maintenance, it will be necessary to purchase a good quality stroboscopic timing light and combination tachometer/dwell meter. Although they are included in the list of special tools, it is mentioned here because they are absolutely necessary for tuning most vehicles properly.*

Repair and overhaul tool set

These tools are essential for anyone who plans to perform major repairs and are in addition to those in the maintenance and minor repair tool kit. Included is a comprehensive set of sockets which, though expensive, are invaluable because of their versatility, especially when various extensions and drives are available. We recommend the 1/2-inch drive over the 3/8-inch drive. Although the larger drive is bulky and more expensive,

it has the capacity of accepting a very wide range of large sockets. Ideally, however, the mechanic should have a 3/8-inch drive set and a 1/2-inch drive set.

Socket set(s)
Reversible ratchet
Extension - 10 inch
Universal joint
Torque wrench (same size drive as sockets)
Ball peen hammer - 8 ounce
Soft-face hammer (plastic/rubber)
Standard screwdriver (1/4-inch x 6 inch)
Standard screwdriver (stubby - 5/16-inch)
Phillips screwdriver (No. 3 x 8 inch)
Phillips screwdriver (stubby - No. 2)
Pliers - vise grip
Pliers - lineman's
Pliers - needle nose
Pliers - snap-ring (internal and external)
Cold chisel - 1/2-inch
Scribe
Scraper (made from flattened copper tubing)
Centerpunch
Pin punches (1/16, 1/8, 3/16-inch)
Steel rule/straightedge - 12 inch
Allen wrench set (1/8 to 3/8-inch or 4 mm to 10 mm)
A selection of files
Wire brush (large)
Jackstands (second set)
Jack (scissor or hydraulic type)

Note: *Another tool which is often useful is an electric drill with a chuck capacity of 3/8-inch and a set of good quality drill bits.*

Special tools

The tools in this list include those which are not used regularly, are expensive to buy, or which need to be used in accordance with their manufacturer's instructions. Unless these tools will be used frequently, it is not very economical to purchase many of them. A consideration would be to split the cost and use between yourself and a friend or friends. In addition, most of these tools can be obtained from a tool rental shop on a temporary basis.

This list primarily contains only those tools and instruments widely available to the public, and not those special tools produced by the vehicle manufacturer for distribution to dealer service departments. Occasionally, references to the manufacturer's special tools are included in the text of this manual. Generally, an alternative method of doing the job without the special tool is offered. However, sometimes there is no alternative to their use. Where this is the case, and the tool cannot be purchased or borrowed, the work should be turned over to the dealer service department or an automotive repair shop.

Valve spring compressor
Piston ring groove cleaning tool
Piston ring compressor
Piston ring installation tool
Cylinder compression gauge
Cylinder ridge reamer
Cylinder surfacing hone
Cylinder bore gauge
Micrometers and/or dial calipers
Hydraulic lifter removal tool
Balljoint separator
Universal-type puller
Impact screwdriver
Dial indicator set
Stroboscopic timing light (inductive pick-up)
Hand operated vacuum/pressure pump
Tachometer/dwell meter
Universal electrical multimeter
Cable hoist
Brake spring removal and installation tools
Floor jack

Buying tools

For the do-it-yourselfer who is just starting to get involved in vehicle maintenance and repair, there are a number of options available when purchasing tools. If maintenance and minor repair is the extent of the work to be done, the purchase of individual tools is satisfactory. If, on the other hand, extensive work is planned, it would be a good idea to purchase a modest tool set from one of the large retail chain stores. A set can usually be bought at a substantial savings over the individual tool prices, and they often come with a tool box. As additional tools are needed, add-on sets, individual tools and a larger tool box can be purchased to expand the tool selection. Building a tool set gradually allows the cost of the tools to be spread over a longer period of time and gives the mechanic the freedom to choose only those tools that will actually be used.

Tool stores will often be the only source of some of the special tools that are needed, but regardless of where tools are bought, try to avoid cheap ones, especially when buying screwdrivers and sockets, because they won't last very long. The expense involved in replacing cheap tools will eventually be greater than the initial cost of quality tools.

Care and maintenance of tools

Good tools are expensive, so it makes sense to treat them with respect. Keep them clean and in usable condition and store them properly when not in use. Always wipe off any dirt, grease or metal chips before putting them away. Never leave tools lying around in the work area. Upon completion of a job, always check closely under the hood for tools that may have been left there so they won't get lost during a test drive.

Some tools, such as screwdrivers, pliers, wrenches and sockets, can be hung on a panel mounted on the garage or workshop wall, while others should be kept in a tool box or tray. Measuring instruments, gauges, meters, etc. must be carefully stored where they cannot be damaged by weather or impact from other tools.

When tools are used with care and stored properly, they will last a very long time. Even with the best of care, though, tools will wear out if used frequently. When a tool is damaged or worn out, replace it. Subsequent jobs will be safer and more enjoyable if you do.

How to repair damaged threads

Sometimes, the internal threads of a nut or bolt hole can become stripped, usually from overtightening. Stripping threads is an all-too-common occurrence, especially when working with aluminum parts, because aluminum is so soft that it easily strips out.

Usually, external or internal threads are only partially stripped. After they've been cleaned up with a tap or die, they'll still work. Sometimes, however, threads are badly damaged. When this happens, you've got three choices:

1) *Drill and tap the hole to the next suitable oversize and install a larger diameter bolt, screw or stud.*
2) *Drill and tap the hole to accept a threaded plug, then drill and tap the plug to the original screw size. You can also buy a plug already threaded to the original size. Then you simply drill a hole to the specified size, then run the threaded plug into the hole with a bolt and jam nut. Once the plug is fully seated, remove the jam nut and bolt.*
3) *The third method uses a patented thread repair kit like Heli-Coil or Slimsert. These easy-to-use kits are designed to repair damaged threads in straight-through holes and blind holes. Both are available as kits which can handle a variety of sizes and thread patterns. Drill the hole, then tap it with the special included tap. Install the Heli-Coil and the hole is back to its original diameter and thread pitch.*

Regardless of which method you use, be sure to proceed calmly and carefully. A little impatience or carelessness during one of these relatively simple procedures can ruin your whole day's work and cost you a bundle if you wreck an expensive part.

Working facilities

Not to be overlooked when discussing tools is the workshop. If anything more than routine maintenance is to be carried out, some sort of suitable work area is essential.

It is understood, and appreciated, that many home mechanics do not have a good workshop or garage available, and end up removing an engine or doing major repairs outside. It is recommended, however, that the overhaul or repair be completed under the cover of a roof.

A clean, flat workbench or table of comfortable working height is an absolute necessity. The workbench should be equipped with a vise that has a jaw opening of at least four inches.

As mentioned previously, some clean, dry storage space is also required for tools, as well as the lubricants, fluids, cleaning solvents, etc. which soon become necessary.

Sometimes waste oil and fluids, drained from the engine or cooling system during normal maintenance or repairs, present a disposal problem. To avoid pouring them on the ground or into a sewage system, pour the used fluids into large containers, seal them with caps and take them to an authorized disposal site or recycling center. Plastic jugs, such as old antifreeze containers, are ideal for this purpose.

Always keep a supply of old newspapers and clean rags available. Old towels are excellent for mopping up spills. Many mechanics use rolls of paper towels for most work because they are readily available and disposable. To help keep the area under the vehicle clean, a large cardboard box can be cut open and flattened to protect the garage or shop floor.

Whenever working over a painted surface, such as when leaning over a fender to service something under the hood, always cover it with an old blanket or bedspread to protect the finish. Vinyl covered pads, made especially for this purpose, are available at auto parts stores.

Jacking and towing

Jacking

The jack supplied with the vehicle should only be used for raising the car for changing a tire or placing jackstands under the frame. Under no circumstances should work be performed beneath the vehicle or the engine started while this jack is being used as the only means of support.

All vehicles are supplied with a scissors-type jack which fits into a notch in the vertical rocker panel flange nearest to the wheel being changed.

The car should be on level ground with the wheels blocked and the transmission in Park (automatic) or Reverse (manual). Loosen the wheel nuts one half turn and leave them in place until the wheel is raised off the ground. Remove the hubcap, using the tapered end of the lug wrench.

Place the jack under the side of the car in the jacking notch. Use the supplied wrench to turn the jackscrew clockwise until the wheel is raised off the ground. Remove the wheel nuts, pull off the wheel and replace it with the spare.

With the beveled side in, replace the wheel nuts and tighten them until snug. Lower the vehicle by turning the jackscrew counter-clockwise. Remove the jack and tighten the nuts in a diagonal fashion. Replace the hubcap by placing it into position and using the heel of your hand or a rubber mallet to seat it.

Towing

The vehicle can be towed with all four wheels on the ground provided speeds do not exceed 35 mph and the distance is not over 50 miles, otherwise transmission damage can result.

Towing equipment specifically designed for this purpose should be used and should be attached to the main structural members of the car and not the bumper or brackets.

Safety is a major consideration when towing and all applicable state and local laws mus be obeyed. A safety chain system must be used for all towing.

While towing, the parking brake should be fully released and the transmission should be in Neutral. The steering must be unlocked (ignition switch in the Off position). Remember that power steering and power brakes will not work with the engine off.

Front and rear jacking points

Booster battery (jump) starting

Observe these precautions when using a booster battery to start a vehicle:

a) *Before connecting the booster battery, make sure the ignition switch is in the Off position.*

b) *Turn off the lights, heater and other electrical loads.*

c) *Your eyes should be shielded. Safety goggles are a good idea.*

d) *Make sure the booster battery is the same voltage as the dead one in the vehicle.*

e) *The two vehicles MUST NOT TOUCH each other!*

f) *Make sure the transaxle is in Neutral (manual) or Park (automatic).*

g) *If the booster battery is not a maintenance-free type, remove the vent caps and lay a cloth over the vent holes.*

Connect the red jumper cable to the positive (+) terminals of each battery (**see illustration**).

• Connect one end of the black jumper cable to the negative (-) terminal of the booster battery. The other end of this cable should be connected to a good ground on the vehicle to be started, such as a bolt or bracket on the body.

Start the engine using the booster battery, then, with the engine running at idle speed, disconnect the jumper cables in the reverse order of connection.

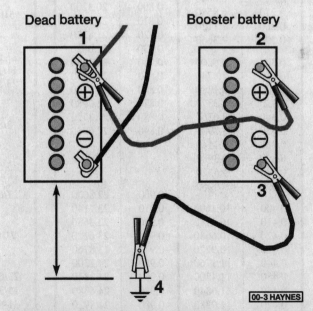

Make the booster battery cable connections in the numerical order shown (note that the negative cable of the booster battery is NOT attached to the negative terminal of the dead battery)

DECIMALS to MILLIMETERS

Decimal	mm	Decimal	mm
0.001	0.0254	0.500	12.7000
0.002	0.0508	0.510	12.9540
0.003	0.0762	0.520	13.2080
0.004	0.1016	0.530	13.4620
0.005	0.1270	0.540	13.7160
0.006	0.1524	0.550	13.9700
0.007	0.1778	0.560	14.2240
0.008	0.2032	0.570	14.4780
0.009	0.2286	0.580	14.7320
		0.590	14.9860
0.010	0.2540		
0.020	0.5080		
0.030	0.7620		
0.040	1.0160	0.600	15.2400
0.050	1.2700	0.610	15.4940
0.060	1.5240	0.620	15.7480
0.070	1.7780	0.630	16.0020
0.080	2.0320	0.640	16.2560
0.090	2.2860	0.650	16.5100
		0.660	16.7640
0.100	2.5400	0.670	17.0180
0.110	2.7940	0.680	17.2720
0.120	3.0480	0.690	17.5260
0.130	3.3020		
0.140	3.5560		
0.150	3.8100		
0.160	4.0640	0.700	17.7800
0.170	4.3180	0.710	18.0340
0.180	4.5720	0.720	18.2880
0.190	4.8260	0.730	18.5420
		0.740	18.7960
0.200	5.0800	0.750	19.0500
0.210	5.3340	0.760	19.3040
0.220	5.5880	0.770	19.5580
0.230	5.8420	0.780	19.8120
0.240	6.0960	0.790	20.0660
0.250	6.3500		
0.260	6.6040		
0.270	6.8580	0.800	20.3200
0.280	7.1120	0.810	20.5740
0.290	7.3660	0.820	21.8280
		0.830	21.0820
0.300	7.6200	0.840	21.3360
0.310	7.8740	0.850	21.5900
0.320	8.1280	0.860	21.8440
0.330	8.3820	0.870	22.0980
0.340	8.6360	0.880	22.3520
0.350	8.8900	0.890	22.6060
0.360	9.1440		
0.370	9.3980		
0.380	9.6520		
0.390	9.9060		
		0.900	22.8600
0.400	10.1600	0.910	23.1140
0.410	10.4140	0.920	23.3680
0.420	10.6680	0.930	23.6220
0.430	10.9220	0.940	23.8760
0.440	11.1760	0.950	24.1300
0.450	11.4300	0.960	24.3840
0.460	11.6840	0.970	24.6380
0.470	11.9380	0.980	24.8920
0.480	12.1920	0.990	25.1460
0.490	12.4460	1.000	25.4000

FRACTIONS to DECIMALS to MILLIMETERS

Fraction	Decimal	mm	Fraction	Decimal	mm
1/64	0.0156	0.3969	33/64	0.5156	13.0969
1/32	0.0312	0.7938	17/32	0.5312	13.4938
3/64	0.0469	1.1906	35/64	0.5469	13.8906
1/16	0.0625	1.5875	9/16	0.5625	14.2875
5/64	0.0781	1.9844	37/64	0.5781	14.6844
3/32	0.0938	2.3812	19/32	0.5938	15.0812
7/64	0.1094	2.7781	39/64	0.6094	15.4781
1/8	0.1250	3.1750	5/8	0.6250	15.8750
9/64	0.1406	3.5719	41/64	0.6406	16.2719
5/32	0.1562	3.9688	21/32	0.6562	16.6688
11/64	0.1719	4.3656	43/64	0.6719	17.0656
3/16	0.1875	4.7625	11/16	0.6875	17.4625
13/64	0.2031	5.1594	45/64	0.7031	17.8594
7/32	0.2188	5.5562	23/32	0.7188	18.2562
15/64	0.2344	5.9531	47/64	0.7344	18.6531
1/4	0.2500	6.3500	3/4	0.7500	19.0500
17/64	0.2656	6.7469	49/64	0.7656	19.4469
9/32	0.2812	7.1438	25/32	0.7812	19.8438
19/64	0.2969	7.5406	51/64	0.7969	20.2406
5/16	0.3125	7.9375	13/16	0.8125	20.6375
21/64	0.3281	8.3344	53/64	0.8281	21.0344
11/32	0.3438	8.7312	27/32	0.8438	21.4312
23/64	0.3594	9.1281	55/64	0.8594	21.8281
3/8	0.3750	9.5250	7/8	0.8750	22.2250
25/64	0.3906	9.9219	57/64	0.8906	22.6219
13/32	0.4062	10.3188	29/32	0.9062	23.0188
27/64	0.4219	10.7156	59/64	0.9219	23.4156
7/16	0.4375	11.1125	15/16	0.9375	23.8125
29/64	0.4531	11.5094	61/64	0.9531	24.2094
15/32	0.4688	11.9062	31/32	0.9688	24.6062
31/64	0.4844	12.3031	63/64	0.9844	25.0031
1/2	0.5000	12.7000	1	1.0000	25.4000

Safety first!

Regardless of how enthusiastic you may be about getting on with the job at hand, take the time to ensure that your safety is not jeopardized. A moment's lack of attention can result in an accident, as can failure to observe certain simple safety precautions. The possibility of an accident will always exist, and the following points should not be considered a comprehensive list of all dangers. Rather, they are intended to make you aware of the risks and to encourage a safety conscious approach to all work you carry out on your vehicle.

Essential DOs and DON'Ts

DON'T rely on a jack when working under the vehicle. Always use approved jackstands to support the weight of the vehicle and place them under the recommended lift or support points.

DON'T attempt to loosen extremely tight fasteners (i.e. wheel lug nuts) while the vehicle is on a jack - it may fall.

DON'T start the engine without first making sure that the transmission is in Neutral (or Park where applicable) and the parking brake is set.

DON'T remove the radiator cap from a hot cooling system - let it cool or cover it with a cloth and release the pressure gradually.

DON'T attempt to drain the engine oil until you are sure it has cooled to the point that it will not burn you.

DON'T touch any part of the engine or exhaust system until it has cooled sufficiently to avoid burns.

DON'T siphon toxic liquids such as gasoline, antifreeze and brake fluid by mouth, or allow them to remain on your skin.

DON'T inhale brake lining dust - it is potentially hazardous (see *Asbestos* below).

DON'T allow spilled oil or grease to remain on the floor - wipe it up before someone slips on it.

DON'T use loose fitting wrenches or other tools which may slip and cause injury.

DON'T push on wrenches when loosening or tightening nuts or bolts. Always try to pull the wrench toward you. If the situation calls for pushing the wrench away, push with an open hand to avoid scraped knuckles if the wrench should slip.

DON'T attempt to lift a heavy component alone - get someone to help you.

DON'T rush or take unsafe shortcuts to finish a job.

DON'T allow children or animals in or around the vehicle while you are working on it.

DO wear eye protection when using power tools such as a drill, sander, bench grinder, etc. and when working under a vehicle.

DO keep loose clothing and long hair well out of the way of moving parts.

DO make sure that any hoist used has a safe working load rating adequate for the job.

DO get someone to check on you periodically when working alone on a vehicle.

DO carry out work in a logical sequence and make sure that everything is correctly assembled and tightened.

DO keep chemicals and fluids tightly capped and out of the reach of children and pets.

DO remember that your vehicle's safety affects that of yourself and others. If in doubt on any point, get professional advice.

Asbestos

Certain friction, insulating, sealing, and other products - such as brake linings, brake bands, clutch linings, torque converters, gaskets, etc. - may contain asbestos. Extreme care must be taken to avoid inhalation of dust from such products, since it is hazardous to health. If in doubt, assume that they do contain asbestos.

Fire

Remember at all times that gasoline is highly flammable. Never smoke or have any kind of open flame around when working on a vehicle. But the risk does not end there. A spark caused by an electrical short circuit, by two metal surfaces contacting each other, or even by static electricity built up in your body under certain conditions, can ignite gasoline vapors, which in a confined space are highly explosive. Do not, under any circumstances, use gasoline for cleaning parts. Use an approved safety solvent.

Always disconnect the battery ground (-) cable at the battery before working on any part of the fuel system or electrical system. Never risk spilling fuel on a hot engine or exhaust component. It is strongly recommended that a fire extinguisher suitable for use on fuel and electrical fires be kept handy in the garage or workshop at all times. Never try to extinguish a fuel or electrical fire with water.

Fumes

Certain fumes are highly toxic and can quickly cause unconsciousness and even death if inhaled to any extent. Gasoline vapor falls into this category, as do the vapors from some cleaning solvents. Any draining or pouring of such volatile fluids should be done in a well ventilated area.

When using cleaning fluids and solvents, read the instructions on the container carefully. Never use materials from unmarked containers.

Never run the engine in an enclosed space, such as a garage. Exhaust fumes contain carbon monoxide, which is extremely poisonous. If you need to run the engine, always do so in the open air, or at least have the rear of the vehicle outside the work area.

If you are fortunate enough to have the use of an inspection pit, never drain or pour gasoline and never run the engine while the vehicle is over the pit. The fumes, being heavier than air, will concentrate in the pit with possibly lethal results.

The battery

Never create a spark or allow a bare light bulb near a battery. They normally give off a certain amount of hydrogen gas, which is highly explosive.

Always disconnect the battery ground (-) cable at the battery before working on the fuel or electrical systems.

If possible, loosen the filler caps or cover when charging the battery from an external source (this does not apply to sealed or maintenance-free batteries). Do not charge at an excessive rate or the battery may burst.

Take care when adding water to a non maintenance-free battery and when carrying a battery. The electrolyte, even when diluted, is very corrosive and should not be allowed to contact clothing or skin.

Always wear eye protection when cleaning the battery to prevent the caustic deposits from entering your eyes.

Household current

When using an electric power tool, inspection light, etc., which operates on household current, always make sure that the tool is correctly connected to its plug and that, where necessary, it is properly grounded. Do not use such items in damp conditions and, again, do not create a spark or apply excessive heat in the vicinity of fuel or fuel vapor.

Secondary ignition system voltage

A severe electric shock can result from touching certain parts of the ignition system (such as the spark plug wires) when the engine is running or being cranked, particularly if components are damp or the insulation is defective. In the case of an electronic ignition system, the secondary system voltage is much higher and could prove fatal.

Automotive chemicals and lubricants

A number of automotive chemicals and lubricants are available for use during vehicle maintenance and repair. They include a wide variety of products ranging from cleaning solvents and degreasers to lubricants and protective sprays for rubber, plastic and vinyl.

Cleaners

Carburetor cleaner and choke cleaner is a strong solvent for gum, varnish and carbon. Most carburetor cleaners leave a dry-type lubricant film which will not harden or gum up. Because of this film it is not recommended for use on electrical components.

Brake system cleaner is used to remove brake dust, grease and brake fluid from the brake system, where clean surfaces are absolutely necessary. It leaves no residue and often eliminates brake squeal caused by contaminants.

Electrical cleaner removes oxidation, corrosion and carbon deposits from electrical contacts, restoring full current flow. It can also be used to clean spark plugs, carburetor jets, voltage regulators and other parts where an oil-free surface is desired.

Demoisturants remove water and moisture from electrical components such as alternators, voltage regulators, electrical connectors and fuse blocks. They are non-conductive and non-corrosive.

Degreasers are heavy-duty solvents used to remove grease from the outside of the engine and from chassis components. They can be sprayed or brushed on and, depending on the type, are rinsed off either with water or solvent.

Lubricants

Motor oil is the lubricant formulated for use in engines. It normally contains a wide variety of additives to prevent corrosion and reduce foaming and wear. Motor oil comes in various weights (viscosity ratings) from 0 to 50. The recommended weight of the oil depends on the season, temperature and the demands on the engine. Light oil is used in cold climates and under light load conditions. Heavy oil is used in hot climates and where high loads are encountered. Multi-viscosity oils are designed to have characteristics of both light and heavy oils and are available in a number of weights from 5W-20 to 20W-50.

Gear oil is designed to be used in differentials, manual transmissions and other areas where high-temperature lubrication is required.

Chassis and wheel bearing grease is a heavy grease used where increased loads and friction are encountered, such as for wheel bearings, balljoints, tie-rod ends and universal joints.

High-temperature wheel bearing grease is designed to withstand the extreme temperatures encountered by wheel bearings in disc brake equipped vehicles. It usually contains molybdenum disulfide (moly), which is a dry-type lubricant.

White grease is a heavy grease for metal-to-metal applications where water is a problem. White grease stays soft under both low and high temperatures (usually from -100 to +190-degrees F), and will not wash off or dilute in the presence of water.

Assembly lube is a special extreme pressure lubricant, usually containing moly, used to lubricate high-load parts (such as main and rod bearings and cam lobes) for initial start-up of a new engine. The assembly lube lubricates the parts without being squeezed out or washed away until the engine oiling system begins to function.

Silicone lubricants are used to protect rubber, plastic, vinyl and nylon parts.

Graphite lubricants are used where oils cannot be used due to contamination problems, such as in locks. The dry graphite will lubricate metal parts while remaining uncontaminated by dirt, water, oil or acids. It is electrically conductive and will not foul electrical contacts in locks such as the ignition switch.

Moly penetrants loosen and lubricate frozen, rusted and corroded fasteners and prevent future rusting or freezing.

Heat-sink grease is a special electrically non-conductive grease that is used for mounting electronic ignition modules where it is essential that heat is transferred away from the module.

Sealants

RTV sealant is one of the most widely used gasket compounds. Made from silicone, RTV is air curing, it seals, bonds, waterproofs, fills surface irregularities, remains flexible, doesn't shrink, is relatively easy to remove, and is used as a supplementary sealer with almost all low and medium temperature gaskets.

Anaerobic sealant is much like RTV in that it can be used either to seal gaskets or to form gaskets by itself. It remains flexible, is solvent resistant and fills surface imperfections. The difference between an anaerobic sealant and an RTV-type sealant is in the curing. RTV cures when exposed to air, while an anaerobic sealant cures only in the absence of air. This means that an anaerobic sealant cures only after the assembly of parts, sealing them together.

Thread and pipe sealant is used for sealing hydraulic and pneumatic fittings and vacuum lines. It is usually made from a Teflon compound, and comes in a spray, a paint-on liquid and as a wrap-around tape.

Chemicals

Anti-seize compound prevents seizing, galling, cold welding, rust and corrosion in fasteners. High-temperature ant-seize, usually made with copper and graphite lubricants, is used for exhaust system and exhaust manifold bolts.

Anaerobic locking compounds are used to keep fasteners from vibrating or working loose and cure only after installation, in the absence of air. Medium strength locking compound is used for small nuts, bolts and screws that may be removed later. High-strength locking compound is for large nuts, bolts and studs which aren't removed on a regular basis.

Oil additives range from viscosity index improvers to chemical treatments that claim to reduce internal engine friction. It should be noted that most oil manufacturers caution against using additives with their oils.

Gas additives perform several functions, depending on their chemical makeup. They usually contain solvents that help dissolve gum and varnish that build up on carburetor, fuel injection and intake parts. They also serve to break down carbon deposits that form on the inside surfaces of the combustion chambers. Some additives contain upper cylinder lubricants for valves and piston rings, and others contain chemicals to remove condensation from the gas tank.

Miscellaneous

Brake fluid is specially formulated hydraulic fluid that can withstand the heat and pressure encountered in brake systems. Care must be taken so this fluid does not come in contact with painted surfaces or plastics. An opened container should always be resealed to prevent contamination by water or dirt.

Weatherstrip adhesive is used to bond weatherstripping around doors, windows and trunk lids. It is sometimes used to attach trim pieces.

Undercoating is a petroleum-based, tar-like substance that is designed to protect metal surfaces on the underside of the vehicle from corrosion. It also acts as a sound-deadening agent by insulating the bottom of the vehicle.

Waxes and polishes are used to help protect painted and plated surfaces from the weather. Different types of paint may require the use of different types of wax and polish. Some polishes utilize a chemical or abrasive cleaner to help remove the top layer of oxidized (dull) paint on older vehicles. In recent years many non-wax polishes that contain a wide variety of chemicals such as polymers and silicones have been introduced. These non-wax polishes are usually easier to apply and last longer than conventional waxes and polishes.

Conversion factors

Length (distance)

Inches (in)	X	25.4	= Millimeters (mm)	X 0.0394	= Inches (in)
Feet (ft)	X	0.305	= Meters (m)	X 3.281	= Feet (ft)
Miles	X	1.609	= Kilometers (km)	X 0.621	= Miles

Volume (capacity)

Cubic inches (cu in; in³)	X	16.387	= Cubic centimeters (cc; cm³)	X 0.061	= Cubic inches (cu in; in³)
Imperial pints (Imp pt)	X	0.568	= Liters (l)	X 1.76	= Imperial pints (Imp pt)
Imperial quarts (Imp qt)	X	1.137	= Liters (l)	X 0.88	= Imperial quarts (Imp qt)
Imperial quarts (Imp qt)	X	1.201	= US quarts (US qt)	X 0.833	= Imperial quarts (Imp qt)
US quarts (US qt)	X	0.946	= Liters (l)	X 1.057	= US quarts (US qt)
Imperial gallons (Imp gal)	X	4.546	= Liters (l)	X 0.22	= Imperial gallons (Imp gal)
Imperial gallons (Imp gal)	X	1.201	= US gallons (US gal)	X 0.833	= Imperial gallons (Imp gal)
US gallons (US gal)	X	3.785	= Liters (l)	X 0.264	= US gallons (US gal)

Mass (weight)

Ounces (oz)	X	28.35	= Grams (g)	X 0.035	= Ounces (oz)
Pounds (lb)	X	0.454	= Kilograms (kg)	X 2.205	= Pounds (lb)

Force

Ounces-force (ozf; oz)	X	0.278	= Newtons (N)	X 3.6	= Ounces-force (ozf; oz)
Pounds-force (lbf; lb)	X	4.448	= Newtons (N)	X 0.225	= Pounds-force (lbf; lb)
Newtons (N)	X	0.1	= Kilograms-force (kgf; kg)	X 9.81	= Newtons (N)

Pressure

Pounds-force per square inch (psi; lbf/in²; lb/in²)	X	0.070	= Kilograms-force per square centimeter (kgf/cm²; kg/cm²)	X 14.223	= Pounds-force per square inch (psi; lbf/in²; lb/in²)
Pounds-force per square inch (psi; lbf/in²; lb/in²)	X	0.068	= Atmospheres (atm)	X 14.696	= Pounds-force per square inch (psi; lbf/in²; lb/in²)
Pounds-force per square inch (psi; lbf/in²; lb/in²)	X	0.069	= Bars	X 14.5	= Pounds-force per square inch (psi; lbf/in²; lb/in²)
Pounds-force per square inch (psi; lbf/in²; lb/in²)	X	6.895	= Kilopascals (kPa)	X 0.145	= Pounds-force per square inch (psi; lbf/in²; lb/in²)
Kilopascals (kPa)	X	0.01	= Kilograms-force per square centimeter (kgf/cm²; kg/cm²)	X 98.1	= Kilopascals (kPa)

Torque (moment of force)

Pounds-force inches (lbf in; lb in)	X	1.152	= Kilograms-force centimeter (kgf cm; kg cm)	X 0.868	= Pounds-force inches (lbf in; lb in)
Pounds-force inches (lbf in; lb in)	X	0.113	= Newton meters (Nm)	X 8.85	= Pounds-force inches (lbf in; lb in)
Pounds-force inches (lbf in; lb in)	X	0.083	= Pounds-force feet (lbf ft; lb ft)	X 12	= Pounds-force inches (lbf in; lb in)
Pounds-force feet (lbf ft; lb ft)	X	0.138	= Kilograms-force meters (kgf m; kg m)	X 7.233	= Pounds-force feet (lbf ft; lb ft)
Pounds-force feet (lbf ft; lb ft)	X	1.356	= Newton meters (Nm)	X 0.738	= Pounds-force feet (lbf ft; lb ft)
Newton meters (Nm)	X	0.102	= Kilograms-force meters (kgf m; kg m)	X 9.804	= Newton meters (Nm)

Vacuum

Inches mercury (in. Hg)	X	3.377	= Kilopascals (kPa)	X 0.2961	= Inches mercury
Inches mercury (in. Hg)	X	25.4	= Millimeters mercury (mm Hg)	X 0.0394	= Inches mercury

Power

Horsepower (hp)	X	745.7	= Watts (W)	X 0.0013	= Horsepower (hp)

Velocity (speed)

Miles per hour (miles/hr; mph)	X	1.609	= Kilometers per hour (km/hr; kph)	X 0.621	= Miles per hour (miles/hr; mph)

Fuel consumption*

Miles per gallon, Imperial (mpg)	X	0.354	= Kilometers per liter (km/l)	X 2.825	= Miles per gallon, Imperial (mpg)
Miles per gallon, US (mpg)	X	0.425	= Kilometers per liter (km/l)	X 2.352	= Miles per gallon, US (mpg)

Temperature

Degrees Fahrenheit = (°C x 1.8) + 32

Degrees Celsius (Degrees Centigrade; °C) = (°F - 32) x 0.56

*It is common practice to convert from miles per gallon (mpg) to liters/100 kilometers (l/100km), where mpg (Imperial) x l/100 km = 282 and mpg (US) x l/100 km = 235

Troubleshooting

Contents

Engine

1 Engine will not rotate when attempting to start

1   Battery terminal connections loose or corroded. Check the cable terminals at the battery; tighten or clean corrosion as necessary.
2   Battery discharged or faulty. If the cable connectors are clean and tight on the battery posts, turn the key to the 'On' position and switch on the headlights and/or windshield wipers. If these fail to function, the battery is discharged.
3   Automatic transmission not fully engaged in 'Park' or manual transmission clutch not fully depressed.
4   Broken, loose or disconnected wiring in the starting circuit. Inspect all wiring and connectors at the battery, starter solenoid (at lower right side of engine) and ignition switch (on steering column).
5   Starter motor pinion jammed on flywheel ring gear. If manual transmission, place gearshift in gear and rock the car to manually turn the engine. Remove starter (Chapter 10) and inspect pinion and flywheel (Chapter 10) at earliest convenience.
6   Starter solenoid faulty (Chapter 10).
7   Starter motor faulty (Chapter 10).
8   Ignition switch faulty (Chapter 10).

2 Engine rotates but will not start

1   Fuel tank empty.
2   Battery discharged (engine rotates slowly). Check the operation of electrical components as described in previous Section (see Chapter 1).
3   Battery terminal connections loose or corroded. See previous Section.
4   Carburetor flooded and/or fuel level in carburetor incorrect. This will usually be accompanied by a strong fuel odor from under the hood. Wait a few minutes, depress the accelerator pedal all the way to the floor and attempt to start the engine.
5   Choke control inoperative (Chapter 4).
6   Fuel not reaching carburetor. With ignition switch in 'Off' position, open hood, remove the top plate of air cleaner assembly and observe the top of the carburetor (manually move choke plate back if necessary). Have an assistant depress accelerator pedal fully and check that fuel spurts into carburetor. If not, check fuel filter (Chapters 1 and 3), fuel lines and fuel pump (Chapter 4).
7   Excessive moisture on, or damage to, ignition components (Chapter 5).
8   Worn, faulty or incorrectly adjusted spark plugs (Chapter 5).
9   Broken, loose or disconnected wiring in the starting circuit (see previous Section).
10 Distributor loose, thus changing ignition timing. Turn the distributor body as necessary to start the engine, then set ignition timing as soon as possible (Chapter 5).
11 Ignition condenser faulty (Chapter 5).
12 Broken, loose or disconnected wires at the ignition coil, or faulty coil (Chapter 5).

3 Starter motor operates without rotating engine

1   Starter pinion sticking. Remove the starter (Chapter 5) and inspect.
2   Starter pinion or engine flywheel teeth worn or broken. Remove the inspection cover at the rear of the engine and inspect.

4 Engine hard to start when cold

1   Battery discharged or low. Check as described in Section 1.
2   Choke control inoperative or out of adjustment (Chapter 4).
3   Carburetor flooded (see Section 2).
4   Fuel supply not reaching the carburetor (see Chapter 4).
5   Carburetor worn and in need of overhauling (Chapter 4).

5 Engine hard to start when hot

1   Choke sticking in the closed position (Chapter 4).
2   Carburetor flooded (see Section 2).
3   Air filter in need of replacement (Chapter 4).
4   Fuel not reaching the carburetor (see Section 2).

6 Starter motor noisy or excessively rough in engagement

1   Pinion or flywheel gear teeth worn or broken. Remove the inspection cover at the rear of the engine and inspect.
2   Starter motor retaining bolts loose or missing.

7 Engine starts but stops immediately

1   Loose or faulty electrical connections at distributor, coil or alternator.
2   Insufficient fuel reaching the carburetor. Disconnect the fuel line at the carburetor and remove the filter (Chapter 4). Place a container under the disconnected fuel line. Observe the flow of fuel from the line. If little or none at all, check for blockage in the lines and/or replace the fuel pump (Chapter 4).
3   Vacuum leak at the gasket surfaces or the intake manifold and/or carburetor. Check that all mounting bolts (nuts) are tightened to specifications and all vacuum hoses connected to the carburetor and manifold are positioned properly and are in good condition.

8 Engine 'lopes' while idling or idles erratically

1   Vacuum leakage. Check mounting bolts (nuts) at the carburetor and intake manifold for tightness. Check that all vacuum hoses are connected and are in good condition. Use a doctor's stethoscope or a length of fuel line hose held against your ear to listen for vacuum leaks while the engine is running. A hissing sound will be heard. A soapy water solution will also detect leaks. Check the carburetor and intake manifold gasket surfaces.
2   Leaking EGR valve or plugged PCV valve (see Chapter 6).
3   Air cleaner clogged and in need of replacement (Chapter 4).
4   Fuel pump not delivering sufficient fuel to the carburetor (see Section 7).
5   Carburetor out of adjustment (Chapter 4).
6   Leaking head gasket. If this is suspected, take the car to a repair shop or dealer where this can be pressure checked without the need to remove the heads.
7   Timing chain or gears worn and in need of replacement (Chapter 2).
8   Camshaft lobes worn, necessitating the removal of the camshaft for inspection (Chapter 2).

9 Engine misses at idle speed

1   Spark plugs faulty or not gapped properly (Chapter 5).
2   Faulty spark plug wires (Chapter 4).
3   Carburetor choke not operating properly (Chapter 4).
4   Sticking or faulty emissions systems (see Chapter 6).
5   Clogged fuel filter and/or foreign matter in fuel. Remove the fuel filter (Chapter 4) and inspect.
6   Vacuum leaks at carburetor, intake manifold or at hose connections. Check as described in Section 8.
7   Incorrect idle speed (Chapter 5) or idle mixture (Chapter 4).
8   Incorrect ignition timing (Chapter 5).
9   Uneven or low cylinder compression. Remove plugs and use compression tester as per manufacturer's instructions.

10 Engine misses throughout driving speed range

1   Carburetor fuel filter clogged and/or impurities in the fuel system (Chapter 4). Also check fuel output at the carburetor (see Section 7).

2   Faulty or incorrectly gapped spark plugs (Chapter 5).
3   Incorrectly set ignition timing (Chapter 5).
4   Check for a cracked distributor cap, disconnected distributor wires, or damage to the distributor components (Chapter 5).
5   Leaking spark plug wires (Chapter 5).
6   Emission system components faulty (Chapter 6).
7   Low or uneven cylinder compression pressures. Remove spark plugs and test compression with gauge.
8   Weak or faulty EEC ignition system (see Chapter 5).
9   Vacuum leaks at carburetor, intake manifold or vacuum hoses (see Section 8).

11 Engine stalls

1   Carburetor idle speed incorrectly set (Chapter 4).
2   Carburetor fuel filter clogged and/or water and impurities in the fuel system (Chapter 4).
3   Choke improperly adjusted or sticking (Chapter 4).
4   Distributor components damp, points out of adjustment or damage to distributor cap, rotor, etc. (Chapter 5).
5   Emission system components faulty, Chapter 6.
6   Faulty or incorrectly gapped spark plugs. (Chapter 5). Also check spark plug wires (Chapter 5).
7   Vacuum leak at the carburetor, intake manifold or vacuum hoses. Check as described in Section 8.
8   Valve lash incorrectly set (Chapter 2).

12 Engine lacks power

1   Incorrect ignition timing (Chapter 5).
2   Excessive play in distributor shaft. At the same time check for worn or maladjusted contact rotor, faulty distributor cap, wires, etc. (Chapter 5).
3   Faulty or incorrectly gapped spark plugs (Chapter 5).
4   Carburetor not adjusted properly or excessively worn (Chapter 4).
5   Weak coil or condensor (Chapter 5).
6   Faulty EEC system coil (Chapter 5).
7   Brakes binding (Chapter 9).
8   Automatic transmission fluid level incorrect, causing slippage (Chapter 7).
9   Manual transmission clutch slipping (Chapter 7).
10   Fuel filter clogged and/or impurities in the fuel system (Chapter 4).
11   Emission control system not functioning properly (Chapter 6).
12   Use of sub-standard fuel. Fill tank with proper octane fuel.
13   Low or uneven cylinder compression pressures. Test with compression tester, which will also detect leaking valves and/or blown head gasket.

13 Engine backfire

1   Emission system not functioning properly (Chapter 6).
2   Ignition timing incorrect (Section 3).
3   Carburetor in need of adjustment or worn excessively (Chapter 4).
4   Vacuum leak at carburetor, intake manifold or vacuum hoses. Check as described in Section 8.
5   Valve lash incorrectly set, and/or valves sticking (Chapter 2).

14 Pinging or knocking engine sounds on hard acceleration or uphill

1   Incorrect grade of fuel. Fill tank with fuel of the proper octane rating.
2   Ignition timing incorrect (Chapter 5).
3   Carburetor in need of adjustment (Chapter 4).
4   Improper spark plugs. Check plug type with that specified on tune-up decal located inside engine compartment. Also check plugs and wires for damage (Chapter 5).
5   Worn or damaged distributor components (Chapter 5).
6   Faulty emission system (Chapter 6).
7   Vacuum leak (Check as described in Section 8).

15 Engine 'diesels' (continues to run) after switching off

1   Idle speed too fast (Chapter 5).
2   Electrical solenoid at side of carburetor not functioning properly (not all models, see Chapter 4).
3   Ignition timing incorrectly adjusted (Chapter 5).
4   Air cleaner valve not operating properly (Chapter 4).
5   Excessive engine operating temperatures. Probable causes of this are: malfunctioning thermostat, clogged radiator, faulty water pump (See Chapter 3).

Engine electrical

16 Battery will not hold a charge

1   Alternator drivebelt defective or not adjusted properly (Chapter 5).
2   Electrolyte level too low or too weak (Chapter 10).
3   Battery terminals loose or corroded (Chapter 10).
4   Alternator not charging properly (Chapter 10).
5   Loose, broken or faulty wiring in the charging circuit (Chapter 10).
6   Short in vehicle circuitry causing a continual drain on battery.
7   Battery defective internally.

17 Ignition light fails to go out

1   Fault in alternator or charging circuit (Chapter 5).
2   Alternator drivebelt defective or not properly adjusted (Chapter 5).

18 Ignition light fails to come on when key is turned

1   Ignition light bulb faulty (Chapter 10).
2   Alternator faulty (Chapter 5).
3   Fault in the printed circuit, dash wiring or bulb holder (Chapter 10).

Engine fuel system

19 Excessive fuel consumption

1   Dirty or choked air filter element (Chapter 4).
2   Incorrectly set ignition timing (Chapter 5).
3   Choke sticking or improperly adjusted (Chapter 4).
4   Emission system not functioning properly (not all cars, see Chapter 6).
5   Carburetor idle speed and/or mixture not adjusted properly (Chapter 4).
6   Carburetor internal parts excessively worn or damaged (Chapter 4).
7   Low tire pressure or incorrect tire size (Chapter 11).

20 Fuel leakage and/or fuel odor

1   Leak in a fuel feed or vent line (Chapter 4).
2   Tank overfilled. Fill only to automatic shut-off.
3   Emission system filter in need of replacement (Chapter 6).
4   Vapor leaks from system lines (Chapter 4).
5   Carburetor internal parts excessively worn or out of adjustment (Chapter 4).

Engine cooling system

21 Overheating

1   Insufficient coolant in system (Chapter 3).
2   Fan belt defective or not adjusted properly (Chapter 2).
3   Radiator core blocked or radiator grille dirty and restricted (Chapter 3).

4 Thermostat faulty (Chapter 3).
5 Fan blades broken or cracked (Chapter 3).
6 Radiator cap not maintaining proper pressure. Have cap pressure tested by gas station or repair shop.
7 Ignition timing incorrect (Chapter 5).

22 Overcooling

1 Thermostat faulty (Chapter 3).
2 Inaccurate temperature gauge (Chapter 10).

23 External water leakage

1 Deteriorated or damaged hoses. Loose clamps at hose connections (Chapter 3).
2 Water pump seals defective. If this is the case, water will drip from the 'weep' hole in the water pump body (Chapter 3).
3 Leakage from radiator core or header tank. This will require the radiator to be professionally repaired (see Chapter 3 for removal procedures).
4 Engine drain plugs or water jacket freeze plugs leaking.

24 Internal water leakage

Note: *Internal coolant leaks can usually be detected by examining the oil. Check the dipstick and inside of valve cover for water deposits and an oil consistency like that of a milkshake.*
1 Faulty cylinder head gasket. Have the system pressure-tested professionally or remove the cylinder heads (Chapter 2) and inspect.
2 Cracked cylinder bore or cylinder head. Dismantle engine and inspect (Chapter 2).

25 Water loss

1 Overfilling system (Chapter 3).
2 Coolant boiling away due to overheating (see causes in Section 21).
3 Internal or external leakage (see Sections 22 and 23).
4 Faulty radiator cap. Have the cap pressure tested.

26 Poor coolant circulation

1 Inoperative water pump. A quick test is to pinch the top radiator hose closed with your hand while the engine is idling, then let loose. You should feel a surge of water if the pump is working properly (Chapter 3).
2 Restriction in cooling system. Drain, flush and refill the system (Chapter 3). If it appears necessary, remove the radiator (Chapter 3) and have it reverse-flushed or professionally cleaned.
3 Fan drivebelt defective or not adjusted properly (Chapter 3).
4 Thermostat sticking (Chapter 3).

Clutch

27 Fails to release (pedal pressed to the floor – shift lever does not move freely in and out of reverse)

1 Improper linkage adjustment (Chapter 8).
2 Clutch fork off ball stud. Look under the car, on the left side of transmission.
3 Clutch disc warped, bent or excessively damaged (Chapter 8).

28 Clutch slips (engine speed increases with no increase in road speed)

1 Linkage in need of adjustment (Chapter 8).

2 Clutch disc oil soaked or facing worn. Remove disc (Chapter 8) and inspect.
3 Clutch disc not seated in. It may take 30 or 40 normal starts for a new disc to seat.

29 Grabbing (juddering) on take-up

1 Oil on clutch disc facings. Remove disc (Chapter 8) and inspect. Correct any leakage source.
2 Worn or loose engine or transmission mounts. These units may move slightly when clutch is released. Inspect mounts and bolts.
3 Worn splines on clutch gear. Remove clutch components (Chapter 8) and inspect.
4 Warped pressure plate or flywheel. Remove clutch components and inspect.

30 Squeal or rumble with clutch fully engaged (pedal released)

1 Improper adjustment; no lash (Chapter 8).
2 Release bearing binding on transmission bearing retainer. Remove clutch components (Chapter 8) and check bearing. Remove any burrs or nicks, clean and relubricate before reinstallation.
3 Weak linkage return spring. Replace the spring.

31 Squeal or rumble with clutch fully disengaged (pedal depressed)

1 Worn, faulty or broken release bearing (Chapter 8).
2 Worn or broken pressure plate springs (or diaphragm fingers) (Chapter 8).

32 Clutch pedal stays on floor when disengaged

1 Bind in linkage or release bearing. Inspect linkage or remove clutch components as necessary.
2 Linkage springs being over-traveled. Adjust linkage for proper lash. Make sure proper pedal stop (bumper) is installed.

Manual transmission

Note: *All the following Sections contained within Chapter 7 unless noted.*

33 Noisy in neutral with engine running

1 Input shaft bearing worn.
2 Damaged main drive gear bearing.
3 Worn countergear bearings.
4 Worn or damaged countergear anti-lash plate.

34 Noisy in all gears

1 Any of the above causes, and/or:
2 Insufficient lubricant (see checking procedures in Chapter 7).

35 Noisy in one particular gear

1 Worn, damaged or chipped gear teeth for that particular gear.
2 Worn or damaged synchronizer for that particular gear.

36 Slips out of high gear

1 Transmission loose on clutch housing.
2 Shift rods interfering with engine mounts or clutch lever.
3 Shift rods not working freely.
4 Damaged mainshaft pilot bearing.

5 Dirt between transmission case and clutch housing, or misalignment of transmission (Chapter 8).
6 Worn or improperly adjusted linkage (Chapter 8).

37 Difficulty in engaging gears

1 Clutch not releasing fully (see clutch adjustment, Chapter 8).
2 Loose, damaged or maladjusted shift linkage. Make a thorough inspection, replacing parts as necessary. Adjust as described in Chapter 8.

38 Fluid leakage

1 Excessive amount of lubricant in transmission (see Chapter 7 for correct checking procedures. Drain lubricant as required).
2 Side cover loose or gasket damaged.
3 Rear oil seal or speedometer oil seal in need of replacement (Section 6).

Automatic transmission

Note: *Due to the complexity of the automatic transmission, it is difficult for the home mechanic to properly diagnose and service this component. For problems other than the following, the vehicle should be taken to a reputable mechanic.*

39 Fluid leakage

1 Automatic transmission fluid is a deep red color, and fluid leaks should not be confused with engine oil which can easily be blown by air flow to the transmission.
2 To pinpoint a leak, first remove all built-up dirt and grime from around the transmission. Degreasing agents and/or steam cleaning will achieve this. With the underside clean, drive the car at low speeds so the air flow will not blow the leak far from its source. Raise the car and determine where the leak is coming from. Common areas of leakage are:
   a) Fluid pan: tighten mounting bolts and/or replace pan gasket as necessary (see Chapter 7B).
   b) Rear extension: tighten bolts and/or replace oil seal as necessary (Chapter 7B).
   c) Filler pipe: replace the rubber oil seal where pipe enters transmission case.
   d) Transmission oil lines: tighten connectors where lines enter transmission case and/or replace lines.
   e) Vent pipe: transmission over-filled and/or water in fluid (see checking procedures, Chapter 7B).
   f) Speedometer connector: replace the O-ring where speedometer cable enters transmission case.

40 General shift mechanism problems

1 Chapter 7B deals with checking and adjusting the shift linkage on automatic transmissions. Common problems which may be attributed to maladjusted linkage are:
   a) Engine starting in gears other than 'P' (Park) or 'N' (Neutral).
   b) Indicator on quadrant pointing to a gear other than the one actually being used.
   c) Vehicle will not hold firm when in 'P' (Park) position.
   Refer to Chapter 7B to adjust the manual linkage.

41 Transmission will not downshift with accelerator pedal pressed to the floor

1 Chapter 7B deals with adjusting the downshift cable or downshift switch to enable the transmission to downshift properly.

42 Engine will start in gears other than 'P' (Park) or 'N' (Neutral)

1 Chapter 7B deals with adjusting the neutral start switches used with automatic transmissions.

43 Transmission slips, shifts rough, is noisy or has no drive in forward or reverse gears

1 There are many probable causes for the above problems, but the home mechanic should concern himself only with one possibility: fluid level.
2 Before taking the vehicle to a specialist, check the level of the fluid and condition of the fluid as described in Chapter 7B. Correct fluid level as necessary or change the fluid and filter if needed. If problem persists, have a professional diagnose the probable cause.

Driveshaft

44 Leakage of fluid at front of driveshaft

1 Defective transmission rear oil seal. See Chapter 7 for replacing procedures. While this is done, check the splined yoke for burrs or a rough condition which may be damaging the seal. If found, these can be dressed with crocus cloth or a fine dressing stone.

45 Knock or clunk when transmission is under initial load (just after transmission is put into gear)

1 Loose or disconnected rear suspension components. Check all mounting bolts and bushings (Chapter 11).
2 Loose driveshaft bolts. Inspect all bolts and nuts and tighten to torque specifications (Chapter 8).
3 Worn or damaged universal joint bearings. Test for wear (Chapter 8).

46 Metallic grating sound consistent with road speed

1 Pronounced wear in the universal joint bearings. Test for wear (Chapter 8).

47 Vibration

Note: *Before it can be assumed that the driveshaft is at fault, make sure the tires are perfectly balanced and perform the following test.*
1 Install a tachometer inside the car to monitor engine speed as the car is driven. Drive the car and note the engine speed at which the vibration (roughness) is most pronounced. Now shift the transmission to a different gear and bring the engine speed to the same point.
2 If the vibration occurs at the same engine speed (rpm) regardless of which gear the transmission is in, the driveshaft is NOT at fault since the driveshaft speed varies.
3 If the vibration decreases or is eliminated when the transmission is in a different gear at the same engine speed, refer to the following probable causes.
4 Bent or dented driveshaft. Inspect and replace as necessary (Chapter 8).
5 Undercoating or built-up dirt, etc, on the driveshaft. Clean the shaft thoroughly and test.
6 Worn universal joint bearings. Remove and inspect (Chapter 8).
7 Driveshaft and/or companion flange out of balance. Check for missing weights on the shaft. Remove driveshaft (Chapter 8) and reinstall 180° from original position. Retest. Have driveshaft professionally balanced if problem persists.

Rear axle

48 Noise – same when in drive as when vehicle is coasting

1 Road noise. No corrective procedures available.
2 Tire noise. Inspect tires and tire pressures (Chapter 11).
3 Front wheel bearings loose, worn or damaged (Chapter 11).

49 Vibration

1 See probable causes under 'Driveshaft'. Proceed under the guide-lines listed for the driveshaft. If the problem persists, check the rear wheel bearings by raising the rear of the car and spinning the wheels by hand. Listen for evidence of rough (noisy) bearings. Remove and inspect (Chapter 8).

50 Oil leakage

1 Pinion oil seal damaged (Chapter 8).
2 Axle shaft oil seals damaged (Chapter 8).
3 Differential inspection cover leaking. Tighten mounting bolts or replace the gasket as required (Chapter 8).

Brakes

Note: *Before assuming a brake problem exists, check: that the tires are in good condition and are inflated properly (see Chapter 11); the front end alignment is correct; and that the vehicle is not loaded with weight in an unequal manner.*

51 Vehicle pulls to one side under braking

1 Defective, damaged or oil contaminated disc pad on one side. Inspect as described in Chapter 9.
2 Excessive wear of brake pad material or disc on one side. Inspect and correct as necessary.
3 Loose or disconnected front suspension components. Inspect and tighten all bolts to specifications (Chapter 11).
4 Defective caliper assembly. Remove caliper and inspect for stuck piston or damage (Chapter 9).

52 Noise (high pitched squeak without brake applied)

1 Front brake pads worn out. This noise comes from the wear sensor rubbing against the disc. Replace pads with new ones immediately (Chapter 9).

53 Excessive brake pad travel

1 Partial brake system failure. Inspect entire system (Chapter 9) and correct as required.
2 Insufficient fluid in master cylinder. Check (Chapter 9) and add fluid and bleed system if necessary.
3 Rear brakes not adjusting properly. Make a series of starts and stops while the vehicle is in 'R' (Reverse). If this does not correct the situation remove drums and inspect self-adjusters (Chapter 9).

54 Brake pedal appears spongy when depressed

1 Air in hydraulic lines. Bleed the brake system (Chapter 9).
2 Faulty flexible hoses. Inspect all system hoses and lines. Replace parts as necessary.
3 Master cylinder mountings insecure. Inspect master cylinder bolts (nuts) and torque-tighten to specifications.
4 Master cylinder faulty (Chapter 9).

55 Excessive effort required to stop vehicle

1 Power brake servo not operating properly (Chapter 9).
2 Excessively worn linings or pads. Inspect and replace if necessary (Chapter 9).
3 One or more caliper pistons (front wheels) or wheel cylinders (rear wheels) seized or sticking. Inspect and rebuild as required (Chapter 9).
4 Brake linings or pads contaminated with oil or grease. Inspect and replace as required (Chapter 9).
5 New pads or linings fitted and not yet 'bedded in'. It will take a while for the new material to seat against the drum (or rotor).

56 Pedal travels to floor with little resistance

1 Little or no fluid in the master cylinder reservoir caused by: leaking wheel cylinder(s); leaking caliper piston(s); loose, damaged or discon-nected brake lines. Inspect entire system and correct as necessary.

57 Brake pedal pulsates during brake application

1 Wheel bearings not adjusted properly or in need of replacement (Chapter 11).
2 Caliper not sliding properly due to improper installation or obstruc-tions. Remove and inspect (Chapter 9).
3 Rotor not within specifications. Remove the rotor (Chapter 9) and check for excessive lateral run-out and parellelism. Have the rotor professionally machined or replace it with a new one.

Suspension and steering

58 Car pulls to one side

1 Tire pressures uneven (Chapter 11).
2 Defective tire (Chapter 11).
3 Excessive wear in suspension or steering components (Chapter 11.
4 Front end in need of alignment. Take car to a qualified specialist.
5 Front brakes dragging. Inspect braking system as described in Chapter 9.

59 Shimmy, shake or vibration

1 Tire or wheel out of balance or out of round. Have professionally balanced.
2 Loose, worn or out of adjustment wheel bearings (Chapter 11.
3 Shock absorbers and/or suspension components worn or damag-ed (Chapter 11).

60 Excessive pitching and/or rolling around corners or during braking

1 Defective shock absorbers. Replace as a set (Chapter 11).
2 Broken or weak springs and/or suspension components. Inspect as described in Chapter 11.

61 Excessively stiff steering

1 Lack of lubricant in steering box (manual) or power steering fluid reservoir (Chapter 11).
2 Incorrect tire pressures (Chapter 11).
3 Lack of lubrication at steering joints (Chapter 11).
4 Front end out of alignment.
5 See also Section 62 'Lack of power assistance'.

62 Excessive play in steering

1   Loose wheel bearings (Chapter 11).
2   Excessive wear in suspension or steering components (Chapter 11).
3   Steering gear out of adjustment (Chapter 11).

63 Lack of power assistance

1   Steering pump drivebelt faulty or not adjusted properly (Chapter 11).
2   Fluid level low (Chapter 11).
3   Hoses or pipes restricting the flow. Inspect and replace parts as necessary.
4   Air in power steering system. Bleed system (Chapter 11).

64 Excessive tire wear (not specific to one area)

1   Incorrect tire pressures (Chapter 11).
2   Tires out of balance. Have professionally balanced.
3   Wheels damaged. Inspect and replace as necessary.
4   Suspension or steering components excessively worn (Chapter 11).

65 Excessive tire wear on outside edge

1   Inflation pressures not correct (Chapter 11).
2   Excessive speed on turns.
3   Front end alignment incorrect (excessive toe-in). Have professionally aligned.
4   Suspension arm bent or twisted.

66 Excessive tire wear on inside edge

1   Inflation pressures incorrect (Chapter 11).
2   Front end alignment incorrect (toe-out). Have professionally aligned.
3   Loose or damaged steering components (Chapter 11).

67 Tire tread worn in one place

1   Tires out of balance. Balance tires professionally.
2   Damaged or buckled wheel. Inspect and replace if necessary.
3   Defective tire.

Chapter 1 Tune-up and routine maintenance

Contents

Specifications

Note: *Additional specifications and torque settings are given in each individual Chapter.*

Oil filter type .... Disposable cartridge

Engine crankcase oil capacity .... 4 US qts (5 US qts with new (dry) filter)

Crankcase PCV valve type .... See Emissions label in engine compartment

Radiator pressure cap rating
All models except 2.3L without air conditioning .... 16.0 psi
2.3L without air conditioning .... 13.0 psi

Thermostat type .... Wax pellet

Thermostat rating .... See Chapter 3

Ignition system

Spark plug type and gap*	Type (Motorcraft)	Gap
2.3L engine (non-turbo)	AWSF42C or equivalent	.034 inch
2.3L engine (turbo)	AWSF32C or equivalent	.034 inch
3.3L engine	BSF82C or equivalent	.044 inch
4.2L and 5.0L engines	ASF52C or equivalent	.050 inch

* Refer to the *Vehicle Emission Control Information* label in the engine compartment; use the information there if it differs from that listed here.

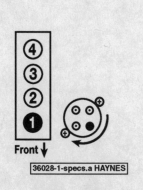

2.3L engine
Firing order 1-3-4-2

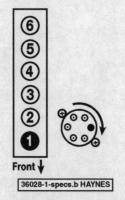

3.3L engine
Firing order 1-5-3-6-2-4

4.2L and 5.0L engines
Firing order 1-5-4-2-6-3-7-8

Cylinder location and distributor rotation

Torque specifications

	ft-lb	Nm
Oil pan drain plug		
2.3L	5 to 10	7 to 13
3.3L, 4.2L and 5.0L	10 to 15	13 to 20
Carburetor mounting nuts	12 to 15	16 to 20
Fuel filter inlet nut	7 to 10	10 to 14
Rear axle cover bolts	24 to 35	34 to 47
Wheel nuts	80 to 105	109 to 142

Recommended lubricants and fluids

Component	Description	Factory Specification
Hinges, hinge check, and pivots	Polyethylene grease	ESB-M1C106-B
Brake master cylinder	Extra Heavy Duty Brake Fluid (or DOT 3 fluid)	ESA-M6C25-A
Front suspension balljoints, front wheel bearings, and clutch linkage	Balljoint and Multi-purpose grease	ESA-M1C75-B
Hood latch and auxiliary catch	Polyethylene grease	ESB-M1C106-B
Lock cylinders	Lock lubricant	ESB-M2C20-A
Rear axle and differential:		
Standard	Hypoid Gear Oil	ESW-M2C-154-A
Limited slip	Hypoid Gear Oil	ESW-M2C-119-A
Power steering pump reservoir	Automatic Transmission Fluid	ESW-M2C33-F, Type F
Automatic transmission	Automatic Transmission Fluid	ESW-M2C33-F, Type F
Manual transmission	Hypoid Transmission Gear Oil	ESW-M2C83-C
Engine	Engine oil* (type SE or SF)	ESE-M2C101C
Engine coolant	Ford Cooling System Fluid	ESE-M97B18-C
Door weatherstrip	Silicone Lubricant	ESR-M1314-A

Viscosity of the oil used depends on ambient temperature in your area. Check your Owner's Manual, supplied with the car, for further information.

1 Introduction

This Chapter was designed to help the home mechanic maintain his (or her) car for peak performance, economy, safety and longevity.

On the following pages you will find a maintenance schedule along with sections which deal specifically with each item on the schedule. Included are visual checks, adjustments and item replacements.

Servicing your car using the time/mileage maintenance schedule and the sequenced section will give you a planned program of maintenance. Keep in mind that it is a full plan, and maintaining only a few items at the specified intervals will not give you the same results.

You will find as you service your car that many of the procedures can, and should, be grouped together, due to the nature of the job at hand. Examples of this are as follows:

If the car is fully raised for a chassis lubrication, for example, this is the ideal time for the following checks: manual transmission fluid, rear axle fluid, exhaust system, suspension, steering and the fuel system.

If the tires and wheels are removed, as during a routine tire rotation, go ahead and check the brakes and wheel bearings at the same time.

If you must borrow or rent a torque wrench, you will do best to service the spark plugs and/or repack (or replace) the wheel bearings all in the same day to save time and money.

The first step of this or any maintenance plan is to prepare yourself before the actual work begins. Read through the appropriate Sections for all work that is to be performed before you begin. Gather together all necessary parts and tools. If it appears you could have a problem during a particular job, don't hesitate to ask advice from your local parts man or dealer service department.

Basic maintenance intervals

Every 250 miles (400 km), weekly and before long trips

Steering
    Check tire pressures (cold)
    Check steering for smooth and accurate operation
    Inspect tires for wear and damage
Brakes
    Check the brake fluid reservoir level. If the amount of fluid has dropped noticeably since the last check, inspect all brake lines and hoses for leakage and condition
    Check for satisfactory brake condition
Other
    Check the operation of the windshield wipers and washers
    Check the windshield wiper blade condition
    Check the operation of the horn
    Check the operation of all instruments
    Check the radiator coolant level and add coolant as required
    Check the battery electrolyte level and add distilled water as required

5000 miles (8000 km) or 5 months

Check engine drive belt condition and tension
Check engine idle speed
Change engine oil and oil filter (see Turbo notes)
Check and adjust automatic transmission bands as required (Chapter 7)

10 000 miles (16 000 km) or 10 months

Change engine oil and oil filter (see Turbo notes)
Check and adjust automatic transmission bands as required (Chapter 7)
Check engine drive belt condition and tension
Check clutch pedal freeplay and adjust as required
Check and adjust engine idle speed as required
Inspect exhaust system and shields

15 000 (24 000 km) or 15 months

Check and adjust automatic transmission bands as required (Chapter 7)
Change engine oil and oil filter (see Turbo notes)
Replace spark plugs
Check clutch pedal freeplay and adjust as required
Check engine drivebelt condition and tension

20 000 miles (32 000 km) or 20 months

Drain and refill automatic transmission fluid (see Chapter 7)
Change engine oil and oil filter (see Turbo notes)
Check clutch pedal freeplay and adjust as required
Inspect exhaust system and shields
Check engine drivebelt condition and tension

25 000 miles (40 000 km) or 25 months

Change engine oil and oil filter (see Turbo notes)
Check and adjust automatic transmission bands as required (Chapter 7)
Check clutch pedal freeplay and adjust as required
Check engine drivebelt condition and tension

30 000 miles (48 000 km) or 30 months

Check the choke system for freedom of movement and adjust and lubricate as necessary
Inspect exhaust system and shields
Lubricate front suspension and steering linkage
Check and adjust automatic transmission bands as required (Chapter 7)
Change engine oil and oil filter
Replace spark plugs
Check engine drivebelt condition and tension
Replace PCV valve (3.3L engine)
Replace carburetor air cleaner element
Replace crankcase filter in air cleaner
Check thermactor delay valve and replace if necessary
Inspect brake lining, lines and hoses
Inspect front wheel bearing lubrication
Check master cylinder fluid level
Check clutch pedal freeplay

35 000 miles (56 000 km) or 35 months

Change engine oil and oil filter (see Turbo notes)
Check and adjust automatic transmission bands as required (Chapter 7)
Check clutch pedal freeplay and adjust as required
Check engine drivebelt condition and tension

40 000 miles (80 000 km) or 40 months

Drain and refill automatic transmission (Chapter 7)
Change engine oil and oil filter (see Turbo notes)
Check clutch pedal freeplay and adjust as required
Check and adjust automatic transmission bands as required (Chapter 7)
Check engine drivebelt tension and condition

45 000 miles (72 000 km) or 45 months

Change engine oil and oil filter
Check and adjust automatic transmission bands as required (Chapter 7)

1

Check clutch pedal freeplay and adjust as required
Check engine drivebelt condition and tension

---

50 000 (80 000 km) or 50 months

Check and adjust automatic transmission band as required (Chapter 7)
Change engine oil and oil filter (see Turbo notes)
Replace coolant
Check cooling system hoses and clamps
Check clutch pedal freeplay and adjust as required
Replace PCV filter
Replace carburetor air cleaner element
Check engine drivebelt condition and tension

Severe operating conditions

Severe operating conditions are defined as vehicles operating under the following conditions:

    a)   Extended periods of idling or low speed operation
    b)   Towing any trailers up to 1000 lb (450 kg) for long distances
    c)   Operation when outside temperature remains below +10°F (-12° C) for 60 days or more and most trips are less than 10 miles (16 km)
    d)   Operation in severe dust conditions
    e)   The automatic transmission is also considered to be part of the systems under severe operating conditions and must be serviced at closer time intervals on vehicles with no auxiliary coolers or vehicles which accumulate 2000 miles (3200 km) per month

If your vehicle falls into the severe operating conditions category, the maintenance schedule must be amended as follows:

    a)   Change engine oil every 3 months or 3000 miles (4800 km) and oil filter every other oil change
    b)   Check, clean and regap spark plugs every 6000 miles (9600 km)
    c)   Service the automatic transmission bands every 5000 miles (8000 km) (Chapter 7) and drain and refill the transmission with fresh fluid every 20 000 miles (32 000 km)

Annual checks

Check coolant levels and coolant protection just prior to the onset of freezing weather. If the coolant appears to be dirty or rusty, the system must be drained and flushed, then filled with new coolant
Check all coolant system hoses and clamps
Change coolant every three years or at the required mileage interval
Change coolant hoses and clamps every three years or at the required mileage interval, whichever occurs first

---

Additional instructions

Change engine oil and filter every 10 000 miles (16 000 km) or 12 months, whichever occurs first
Checking of all engine idle speeds at 10 000 miles (16 000 km) need only be repeated to correct unusual engine operation thereafter
Checking of engine idle fuel mixture at 30 000 miles (48 000 km) need only be repeated to correct unusual operation thereafter

---

Turbo – special operation and maintenance notes

Change engine oil and filter every 3000 miles (4800 km)
The manufacturer recommends that turbocharged cars not be used for pulling trailers greater than light duty load (Class 1).

---

2   Fluid levels check

---

1   There are a number of components on a vehicle which rely on the use of fluids to perform their job. Through the normal operation of the car, these fluids are used up and must be replenished before damage occurs. See the *Recommended Lubricants* Section for the specific fluid to be used when adding is required. When checking fluid levels it is important that the car is on a level surface.

Engine oil

2   The engine oil level is checked with a dipstick which is located at the side of the engine block. This dipstick travels through a tube and into the oil pan at the bottom of the engine.
3   The oil level should be checked preferably before the car has been driven, or about 15 minutes after the engine has been shut off. If the oil is checked immediately after driving the car, some of the oil will remain in the upper engine components, thus giving an inaccurate reading on the dipstick.
4   Pull the dipstick from its tube and wipe all the oil from the end with a clean rag. Insert the clean dipstick all the way back into the oil pan and pull it out again. Observe the oil at the end of the dipstick. At its highest point, the level should be between the 'Add' and 'Full' marks.
5   It takes approximately 1 quart of oil to raise the level from the 'Add' mark to the 'Full' mark on the dipstick. Do not allow the level to drop below the 'Add' mark as this may cause engine damage due to oil starvation. On the other hand, do not overfill the engine by adding oil above the 'Full' mark as this may result in oil-fouled spark plugs, oil leaks or oil seal failures.
6   Oil is added to the engine after removing a twist-off cap located either on the rocker arm cover or through a raised tube near the front of the engine. The cap should be duly marked 'Engine oil' or similar wording. An oil can spout or funnel will reduce spills as the oil is poured in.
7   Checking the oil level can also be a step towards preventative maintenance. If you find the oil level dropping abnormally, this is an indication of oil leakage or internal engine wear which should be corrected. If there are water droplets in the oil, or it is milky looking, this also indicates component failure and the engine should be checked immediately. The condition of the oil can also be checked along with the level. With the dipstick removed from the engine, take your thumb and index finger and wipe the oil up the dipstick, looking for small dirt particles or engine filings which will cling to the dipstick (photo). This is an indication that the oil should be drained and fresh oil added (Section 4).

Engine coolant

8   All vehicles are equipped with a pressurized coolant recovery system which makes coolant level checks very easy. A clear or white coolant reservoir attached to the inner fender panel is connected by a hose to the radiator cap. As the engine heats up during operation, coolant is forced from the radiator, through the connecting tube and into the reservoir. As the engine cools, this coolant is automatically drawn back into the radiator to keep the correct level.
9   The coolant level should be checked when the engine is cold. Merely observe the level of fluid in the reservoir, which should be at or near the 'Full cold' mark on the side of the reservoir. If the system is completely cooled, also check the level in the radiator by removing the cap. On crossflow radiators the coolant level should be $1\frac{1}{2}$ to 4 inches below the filler neck and on downflow radiators (2.3L only) $\frac{3}{4}$ to $1\frac{1}{2}$ inches. Some systems also have a 'Full hot' mark to check the level when the engine is hot.
10   If your particular vehicle is not equipped with a coolant recovery system, the level should be checked by removing the radiator cap. However, the cap should not under any circumstances be removed while the system is hot, as escaping steam could cause serious injury. Wait until the engine has completely cooled, then wrap a thick cloth around the cap and turn it to its first stop. If any steam escapes from the cap, allow the engine to cool further. Then remove the cap and check the level in the radiator. It should be about 2 to 3 inches below the bottom of the filler neck.
11   If only a small amount of coolant is required to bring the system up to the proper level, regular water can be used. However, to maintain the proper antifreeze/water mixture in the system, both should be mixed together to replenish a low level. High-quality antifreeze offering protection to -20° should be mixed with water in the proportion specified on the container. Do not allow antifreeze to come in contact with your skin or painted surfaces of the car. Flush contacted areas immediately with plenty of water.

12 On systems with a recovery tank, coolant should be added to the reservoir after removing the cap at the top of the reservoir. Coolant should be added directly into the radiator on systems without a coolant recovery tank.

13 As the coolant level is checked, observe the condition of the coolant. It should be relatively clear. If the fluid is brown or a rust color, this is an indication that the system should be drained, flushed and refilled (Section 28).

14 If the cooling system requires repeated additions to keep the proper level, have the pressure radiator cap checked for proper sealing ability. Also check for leaks in the system (cracked hoses, loose hose connections, leaking gaskets, etc.).

Windshield washer

15 The fluid for the windshield washer system is located in a plastic reservoir. The level inside the reservoir should be maintained at the 'Full' mark.

16 The proper washer solvent solution should be added through the plastic cap whenever replenishing is required. Do not use plain water alone in this system, especially in cold climates where the water could freeze.

Battery

Note: *There are certain precautions to be taken when working on or near the battery: a) Never expose a battery to open flame or sparks which could ignite the hydrogen gas given off by the battery; b) Wear protective clothing and eye protection to reduce the possibility of the corrosive sulfuric acid solution inside the battery harming you (if the fluid is splashed or spilled, flush the contacted area immediately with plenty of water); c) Remove all metal jewelry which could contact the positive terminal and another grounded metal source, thus causing a short circuit; d) Always keep batteries and battery acid out of the reach of children.*

17 Maintenance-free batteries require no maintenance as the battery case is sealed and has no removal caps for adding water.

18 If a maintenance-type battery is installed, the caps on the top of the battery should be removed periodically to check for a low water level. This check will be more critical during the warm summer months.

19 Remove each of the caps and add distilled water to bring the level of each cell to the split ring in the filler opening.

20 At the same time the battery water level is checked, the overall condition of the battery and its related components should be inspected. If corrosion is found on the cable ends or battery terminals, remove the cables and clean away all corrosion using a baking soda/water solution or a wire brush cleaning tool designed for this purpose. See Chapter 5 for complete battery care and servicing.

Brake master cylinder

21 The brake master cylinder is located on the left side of the engine compartment firewall and has a cap which must be removed to check the fluid level.

22 Before removing the cap, use a rag to clean all dirt, grease, etc. from around the cap area. If any foreign matter enters the master cylinder with the cap removed, blockage in the brake system lines can occur. Also make sure all painted surfaces around the master cylinder are covered, as brake fluid will ruin paintwork.

23 Release the clip(s) securing the cap to the top of the master cylinder. In most cases, a screwdriver can be used to pry the wire clip(s) free.

24 Carefully lift the cap off the cylinder and observe the fluid level. It should be approximately ¼-inch below the top edge of each reservoir.

25 If additional fluid is necessary to bring the level up to the proper height, carefully pour the specified brake fluid into the master cylinder. Be careful not to spill the fluid on painted surfaces. Be sure the specified fluid is used, as mixing different types of brake fluid can cause damage to the system. See *Recommended Lubricants* or your Owner's manual.

26 At this time the fluid and master cylinder can be inspected for contamination. Normally, the braking system will not need periodic draining and refilling, but if rust deposits, dirt particles or water droplets are seen in the fluid, the system should be dismantled, drained and refilled with fresh fluid.

27 Reinstall the master cylinder cap and secure it with the clip(s). Make sure the lid is properly seated to prevent fluid leakage and/or system pressure loss.

Fig. 1.1 Checking brake fluid in the master cylinder (Sec 2)

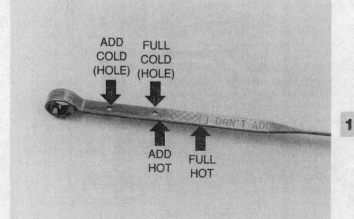

Fig. 1.2 Automatic transmission dipstick and markings (Sec 2)

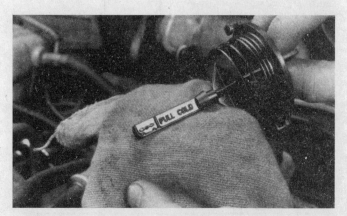

Fig. 1.3 Power steering pump and built-in dipstick (Sec 2)

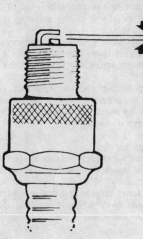

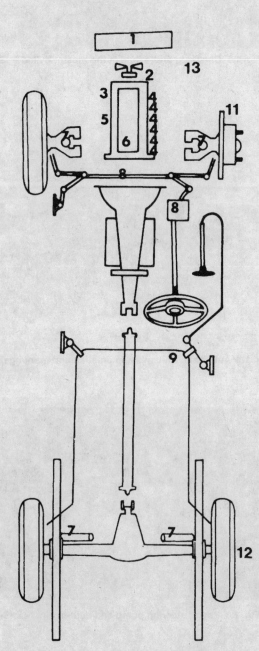

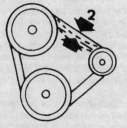

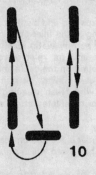

MAINTENANCE KEY

1. Radiator.
2. Fan drive belt and tension checking point.
3. Distributor cap and rotor
4. Spark plugs and plug gap measuring point.
5. Carburettor and air cleaner assembly.
6. PCV valve.
7. Shock absorbers.
8. Steering gear and linkage.
9. Handbrake cable adjusting point.
10. Diagram for tyre rotation.
11. Front brakes.
12. Rear brakes.
13. Battery.

36028-1-1.4 HAYNES/G

Fig. 1.4 3.3L engine service points (Sec 2)

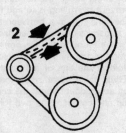

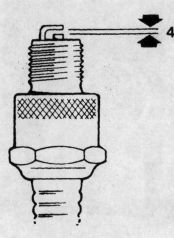

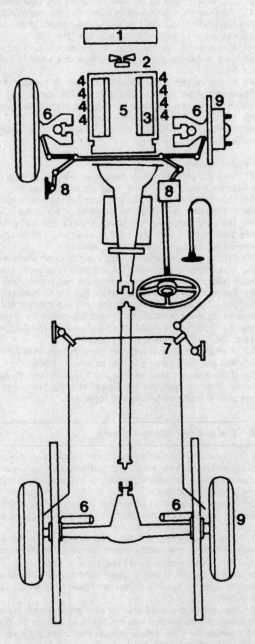

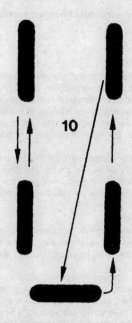

MAINTENANCE KEY.

1. Radiator.
2. Fan drive belt and tension checking point.
3. PCV valve.
4. Spark plugs and plug gap measuring point.
5. Carburetor and air cleaner assembly.
6. Shock absorbers.
7. Handbrake adjustment point.
8. Steering gear and linkage.
9. Brake inspection points.
10. Tire rotation diagram.

36028-1-1.5 HAYNES/G

Fig.1.5 V8 engine service points (Sec 2)

Fig. 1.6 Typical windshield washer reservoir (Sec 2)

28 The brake fluid in the master cylinder will drop slightly as the brake shoes or pads at each wheel wear down during normal operation. If the master cylinder requires repeated replenishing to keep it at the proper level, this is an indication of leakage in the brake system which should be corrected immediately. Check all brake lines and their connections, along with the wheel cylinders and booster (see Chapter 9 for more information).

29 If upon checking the master cylinder fluid level you discover one or both reservoirs empty or nearly empty, the braking system should be bled (Chapter 9). When the fluid level gets low, air can enter the system and should be removed by bleeding the brakes.

Manual transmission

30 Manual shift transmissions do not have a dipstick. The fluid level is checked by removing a plug in the side of the transmission case. Locate this plug and use a rag to clean the plug and the area around it.

31 With the vehicle components cold, remove the plug. If fluid immediately starts leaking out, thread the plug back into the transmission because the fluid level is alright. If there is no fluid leakage, completely remove the plug and place your little finger inside the hole. The fluid level should be just at the bottom of the plug hole.

32 If the transmission needs more fluid, use a syringe to squeeze the appropriate lubricant into the plug hole to bring the fluid up to the proper level.

33 Thread the plug back into the transmission and tighten it securely. Drive the car and check for leaks around the plug.

Automatic transmission

34 The fluid inside the transmission must be at normal operating temperature to get an accurate reading on the dipstick. This is done by driving the car for several miles, making frequent starts and stops to allow the transmission to shift through all gears.

35 Park the car on a level surface, place the selector lever in 'Park' and leave the engine running at an idle.

36 Remove the transmission dipstick (located on the right side, near the rear of the engine) and wipe all the fluid from the end of the dipstick with a clean rag.

37 Push the dipstick back into the transmission until the cap seats firmly on the dipstick tube. Now remove the dipstick again and observe the fluid on the end. The highest point of fluid should be between the 'Full' mark and $\frac{1}{4}$ inch below the 'Full' mark.

38 If the fluid level is at or below the 'Add' mark on the dipstick, add sufficient fluid to raise the level to the 'Full' mark. One pint of fluid will raise the level from 'Add' to 'Full'. Fluid should be added directly into the dipstick guide tube, using a funnel to prevent spills.

39 It is important that the transmission not be overfilled. Under no circumstances should the fluid level be above the 'Full' mark on the dipstick, as this could cause internal damage to the transmission. The best way to prevent overfilling is to add fluid a little at a time, driving the car and checking the level between additions.

40 Use only transmission fluid specified by the manufacturer. This information can be found in the *Recommended Lubricants* Section.

41 The condition of the fluid should also be checked along with the level. If the fluid at the end of the dipstick is a dark reddish-brown color, or if the fluid has a 'burnt' smell, the transmission fluid should be changed. If you are in doubt about the condition of the fluid, purchase some new fluid and compare the two for color and smell.

Rear axle

42 Like the manual transmission, the rear axle has an inspection and fill plug which must be removed to check the fluid level.

43 Remove the plug which is located in the removable cover plate. The lubricant should be $\frac{3}{8}$ in below the bottom of the plug hole. Use a clean piece of wire to make a gauge (Fig. 1.8).

44 If this is not the case, add the proper lubricant into the rear axle carrier through the plug hole. A syringe or a small funnel can be used for this.

45 Make certain the correct lubricant is used, as regular and Positraction rear axles require different lubricants. You can ascertain which type of axle you have by reading the stamped number affixed to the tag bolted to the differential cover.

46 Tighten the plug securely and check for leaks after the first few miles of driving.

Power steering

47 Unlike manual steering, the power steering system relies on fluid which may, over a period of time, require replenishing.

48 The reservoir for the power steering pump will be located near the front of the engine, and can be mounted on either the left or right side.

49 The power steering fluid level should be checked only after the car has been driven, with the fluid at operating temperature. The front wheels should be pointed straight ahead.

50 With the engine shut off, use a rag to clean the reservoir cap and the areas around the cap. This will help to prevent foreign material from falling into the reservoir when the cap is removed.

51 Twist off the reservoir cap which has a built-in dipstick attached to it. Pull off the cap and clean the fluid at the bottom of the dipstick with a clean rag. Now reinstall the dipstick/cap assembly to get a fluid level reading. Remove the dipstick/cap and observe the fluid level. It should be at the 'Full hot' mark on the dipstick.

52 If additional fluid is required, pour the specified lubricant directly into the reservoir using a funnel to prevent spills.

53 If the reservoir requires frequent fluid additions, all power steering hoses, hose connections, the power steering pump and the steering box should be carefully checked for leaks.

3   Tire and tire pressure checks

1   Periodically inspecting the tires can not only prevent you from being stranded with a flat tire, but can also give you clues as to possible problems with the steering and suspension systems before major damage occurs.

2   Proper tire inflation adds miles to the lifespan of the tires, allows the car to achieve maximum miles per gallon figures, and helps the overall riding comfort of the car.

3   When inspecting the tire, first check the wear on the tread. Irregularities in the tread pattern (cupping, flat spots, more wear on one side than the other) are indications of front end alignment and/or balance problems. If any of these conditions are found you would do best to take the car to a competent repair shop which can correct the problem.

4   Also check the tread area for cuts or punctures. Many times a nail or tack will embed itself into the tire tread and yet the tire will hold its air pressure for a short time. In most cases, a repair shop or gas station can repair the punctured tire.

5   It is also important to check the sidewalls of the tire, both inside and outside. Check for the rubber being deteriorated, cut or punctured. Also inspect the inboard side of the tire for signs of brake fluid leakage, indicating a thorough brake inspection is needed immediately (Section 25).

6   Incorrect tire pressure cannot be determined merely by looking at the tire. This is especially true for radial tires. A tire pressure gauge must be used. If you do not already have a reliable gauge, it is a good idea to purchase one and keep it in the glove box. Built-in pressure gauges at gas stations are often unreliable. If you are in doubt as to the accuracy of your gauge, many repair shops have 'master' pressure gauges which you can use for comparison purposes.

7   Always check tire inflation when the tires are cold. Cold, in this case, means the car has not been driven more than one mile after sitting for three hours or more. It is normal for the pressure to increase 4 to 8 pounds or more when the tires are hot.

8   Unscrew the valve cap protruding from the wheel or hubcap and firmly press the gauge onto the valve stem. Observe the reading on the gauge and check this figure against the recommended tire pressure listed on the tire placard. This tire placard is usually found attached to the rear portion of the driver's door.

9   Check all tires and add air as necessary to bring all tires up to the recommended pressure levels. Do not forget the spare tire. Be sure to reinstall the valve caps which will keep dirt and moisture out of the valve stem mechanism.

Fig. 1.7 Tread wear indicators which run across the tread when the tire is in need of replacement (Sec 3)

4   Engine oil and filter change

1   Frequent oil changes may be the best form of preventative maintenance available for the home mechanic. When engine oil ages, it gets diluted and contaminated which ultimately leads to premature parts wear.

2   Although some sources recommend oil filter changes every other oil change, we feel that the minimal cost of an oil filter and the relative ease with which it is installed dictates that a new filter be used whenever the oil is changed.

3   The tools necessary for a normal oil and filter change are: a wrench to fit the drain plug at the bottom of the oil pan; an oil filter wrench to remove the old filter; a container with at least a six-quart capacity to drain the old oil into; and a funnel or oil can spout to help pour fresh oil into the engine.

4   In addition, you should have plenty of clean rags and newspapers handy to mop up any spills. Access to the underside of the car is greatly improved if the car can be lifted on a hoist, driven onto ramps or supported by jack stands. Do not work under a car which is supported only by a bumper, hydraulic or scissors-type jack.

5   If this is your first oil change on the car, it is a good idea to crawl underneath and familiarize yourself with the locations of the oil drain plug and the oil filter. Since the engine and exhaust components will be warm during the actual work, it is best to figure out any potential problems before the car and its accessories are hot.

6   Allow the car to warm up to normal operating temperature. If the new oil or any tools are needed, use this warm-up time to gather everything necessary for the job. The correct type of oil to buy for your application can be found in Recommended Lubricants near the front of this Chapter.

7   With the engine oil warm (warm engine oil will drain better and more built-up sludge will be removed with the oil), raise the vehicle for access beneath. Make sure the car is firmly supported. If jack stands are used they should be placed towards the front of the frame rails which run the length of the car.

8   Move all necessary tools, rags and newspaper under the car. Position the drain pan under the drain plug. Keep in mind that the oil will initially flow from the pan with some force, so place the pan accordingly.

9   Being careful not to touch any of the hot exhaust pipe components, use the wrench to remove the drain plug near the bottom of the oil pan. Depending on how hot the oil has become, you may want to wear gloves while unscrewing the plug the final few turns.

10   Allow the old oil to drain into the pan. Some models have 2 drain plugs and it will be necessary to remove both to completely drain the oil pan. It may be necessary to move the pan further under the engine as the oil flow reduces to a trickle.

11   After all the oil has drained, clean the drain plug thoroughly with a clean rag. Small metal filings may cling to this plug which could immediately contaminate your new oil.

12   Clean the area around the drain plug opening and reinstall the drain plug. Tighten the plug securely with your wrench. If a torque wrench is available, the torque setting is 20 ft-lb.

4.14 Using an oil filter wrench to loosen the filter

13   Move the drain pan in position under the oil filter.

14   Now use the filter wrench to loosen the oil filter (photo). Chain or metal band-type filter wrenches may distort the filter canister, but don't worry too much about this as the filter will be discarded anyway.

15   Sometimes the oil filter is on so tight it cannot be loosened, or it is positioned in an area which is inaccessible with a filter wrench. As a last resort, you can punch a metal bar or long screwdriver horizontally through the bottom of the canister and use this as a T-bar to turn the filter. If this must be done, be prepared for oil to spurt out of the canister as it is punctured.

16   Completely unscrew the old filter. Be careful, it is full of oil. Empty the old oil inside the filter into the drain pan.

17   Compare the old filter with the new one to make sure they are of the same type.

18   Use a clean rag to remove all oil, dirt and sludge from the area where the oil filter mounts to the engine (photo). Check the old filter to make sure the rubber gasket is not stuck to the engine mounting surface. If this gasket is stuck to the engine (use a flashlight if necessary), remove it.

19   Open one of the cans of new oil and fill the new filter with fresh

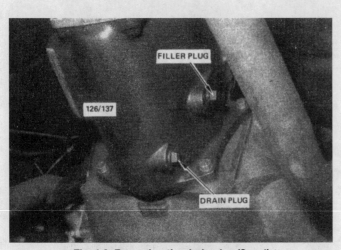

Fig. 1.8 Removing the drain plug (Sec 4)

FILLER PLUG

126/137

DRAIN PLUG

oil. Also smear a light coat of this fresh oil onto the rubber gasket of the new oil filter (photo).

20 Screw the new filter to the engine following the tightening directions printed on the filter canister or packing box (photo). Most filter manufacturers recommend against using a filter wrench due to possible overtightening or damage to the canister.

21 Remove all tools, rags, etc. from under the car, being careful not to spill the oil in the drain pan. Lower the car off its support devices.

22 Move to the engine compartment and locate the oil filler cap on the engine. In most cases there will be a screw-off cap on the rocker arm cover (at the side of the engine) or a cap at the end of a fill tube at the front of the engine. In any case, the cap will most likely be labeled 'Engine Oil' or something similar.

23 If an oil can spout is used, push the spout into the top of the oil can and pour the fresh oil through the filler opening. A funnel placed into the opening may also be used.

24 Pour about 3 qts. of fresh oil into the engine. Wait a few minutes to allow the oil to drain to the pan, then check the level on the oil dipstick (see Section 2 if necessary). If the oil level is at or near the lower 'Add' mark, start the engine and allow the new oil to circulate.

25 Run the engine for only about a minute and then shut it off. Immediately look under the car and check for leaks at the oil pan drain plug and around the oil filter. If either is leaking, tighten with a bit more force.

26 With the new oil circulated and the filter now completely full, recheck the level on the dipstick and add enough oil to bring the level to the 'Full' mark on the dipstick.

27 During the first few trips after an oil change, make a point to check for leaks and also the oil level.

28 The old oil drained from the engine cannot be reused in its present state and should be disposed of. Oil reclamation centers, auto repair shops and gas stations will normally accept the oil which can be refined and used again. After the oil has cooled, it can be drained into a suitable container (capped plastic jugs, topped bottles, milk cartons, etc.) for transport to one of these disposal sites.

5 Chassis lubrication

1 A grease gun and a cartridge filled with the proper grease (see *Recommended Lubricants)* are usually the only equipment necessary to lubricate the chassis components. Occasionally on later model vehicles, plugs will be installed rather than grease fittings, in which case grease fittings will have to be purchased and installed.

2 Carefully look over Fig. 1.11 which shows where the various

grease fittings are located. Look under the car to find these components and ascertain if grease fittings or solid plugs are installed. If there are plugs, remove them with the correct wrench and buy grease fittings which will thread into the component. A Ford dealer or auto parts store will be able to find replacement fittings. Straight, as well as angled, fittings are available for easy greasing.

3 For easier access under the car, raise the vehicle with a jack and place jack stands under the frame. Make sure the car is firmly supported by the stands.

4 Before you do any greasing, force a little of the grease out the nozzle to remove any dirt from the end of the gun. Wipe the nozzle clean with a rag.

5 With the grease gun, plenty of clean rags and the location diagram, go under the car to begin lubricating the components.

6 Wipe the grease fitting nipple clean and push the nozzle firmly over the fitting nipple. Squeeze the trigger on the grease gun to force grease into the component (photo).

Note: *The balljoints should be lubricated until the rubber reservoir is firm to the touch.* Do not pump too much grease into these fittings as this could rupture the reservoir. For all other suspension and steering fittings, continue pumping grease into the nipple until grease seeps out of the joint between the two components. If the grease seeps out around the grease gun nozzle, the nipple is clogged or the nozzle is not fully seated around the fitting nipple. Re-secure the gun nozzle to the fitting and try again. If necessary, replace the fitting.

7 Wipe the excess grease from the components and the grease fitting. Follow these procedures for the remaining fittings.

8 Check the universal joints on the driveshaft; some have fittings, some are factory sealed. About two pumps is all that is required for grease type universal joints. While you are under the car, clean and lubricate the parking brake cable along with its cable guides and levers. This can be done by smearing some of the chassis grease onto the cable and its related parts with your fingers. Place a few drops of light engine oil on the transmission shifting linkage rods and swivels.

9 Lower the car to the ground for the remaining body lubrication process.

10 Open the hood and smear a little chassis grease on the hood latch mechanism. If the hood has an inside release, have an assistant pull the release knob from inside the car as you lubricate the cable at the latch.

11 Lubricate all the hinges (door, hood, trunk) with a few drops of light engine oil to keep them in proper working order.

12 Finally, the key lock cylinders can be lubricated with spray-on graphite which is available at auto parts stores.

5.6 Pumping grease into the lower suspension grease fitting

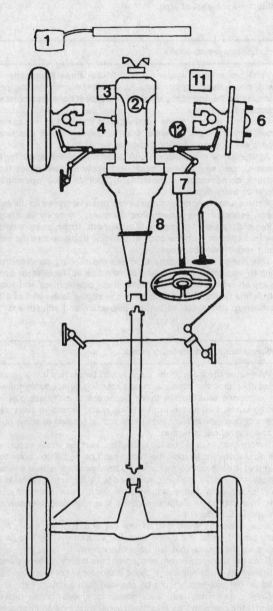

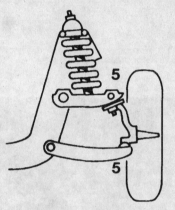

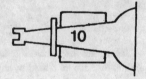

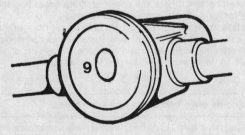

LUBRICATION KEY

1. Radiator expansion tank.
2. Oil filler.
3. Oil filter.
4. Engine oil dipstick.
5. Front suspension ball joints.
6. Front hub bearings.
7. Manual steering gear.
8. Manual transmission filler plug.
9. Rear axle filler plug.
10. Automatic transmission.
11. Battery.
12. Brake master cylinder.

208 LD2/G HAYNES

1.9 Chassis lubrication points

6.3 Inspecting the radiator pressure cap

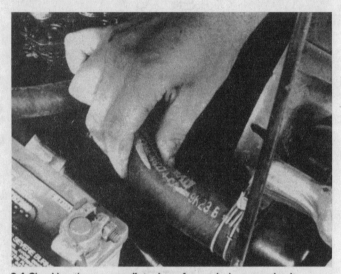

6.4 Checking the upper radiator hose for cracks by squeezing it

6   Cooling system check

1   Many major engine failures can be attributed to a faulty cooling system. If equipped with an automatic transmission, the cooling system also plays an integral role in transmission longevity.
2   The cooling system should be checked with the engine cold. Do this before the car is driven for the day or after it has been shut off for one or two hours.
3   Remove the radiator cap and thoroughly clean the cap (inside and out) with clean water (photo). Also clean the filler neck on the radiator. All traces of corrosion should be removed.
4   Carefully check the upper and lower radiator hoses along with the smaller diameter heater hoses. Inspect their entire length, replacing any hose which is cracked, swollen or shows signs of deterioration. Cracks may become more apparent if the hose is squeezed (photo).
5   Also check that all hose connections are tight. A leak in the cooling system will usually show up as white or rust colored deposits on the areas adjoining the leak.
6   Use compressed air or a soft brush to remove bugs, leaves, etc. from the front of the radiator or air conditioning condenser. Be careful not to damage the delicate cooling fins, or cut yourself on the sharp fins.
7   Finally, have the cap and system tested for proper pressure. If you

do not have a pressure tester, most gas stations and repair shops will do this for a minimal charge.

7   Exhaust system check

1   With the exhaust system cold (at least three hours after being driven), check the complete exhaust system from its starting point at the engine to the end of the tailpipe. This is best done on a hoist where full access is available.
2   Check the pipes and their connections for signs of leakage and/or corrosion indicating a potential failure. Check that all brackets and hangers are in good condition and are tight.
3   At the same time, inspect the underside of the body for holes, corrosion, open seams, etc. which may allow exhaust gases to enter the trunk or passenger compartment. Seal all body openings with silicone or body putty.
4   Rattles and other driving noises can often be traced to the exhaust system, especially the mounts and hangers. Try to move the pipes, muffler and catalytic converter (if equipped). If the components can come into contact with the body or driveline parts, secure the exhaust system with new mountings.
5   This is also an ideal time to check the running condition of the engine by inspecting the very end of the tailpipe. The exhaust deposits here are an indication of engine tune. If the pipe is black and sooty, or bright white deposits are found here, the engine is in need of a tune-up including a thorough carburetor inspection and adjustment.

8   Suspension and steering check

1   Whenever the front of the car is raised for service it is a good idea to visually check the suspension and steering components for wear.
2   Indications of a fault in these systems are: excessive play in the steering wheel before the front wheels react; excessive sway around corners or body movement over rough roads; binding at some point as the steering wheel is turned.
3   Before the car is raised for inspection, test the shock absorbers by pushing downward to rock the car at each corner. If you push the car down and it does not come back to a level position within one or two bounces, the shocks are worn and need to be replaced. As this is done, check for squeaks and strange noises from the suspension components. Information on shock absorber and suspension components can be found in Chapter 11.
4   Now raise the front end of the car and support firmly by jack stands placed under the frame rails. Because of the work to be done, make sure the car cannot fall from the stands.
5   Grab the top and bottom of the front tire with your hands and rock the tire/wheel on its spindle. If there is movement of more than 0.005 in, the wheel bearings should be serviced (see Section 23).
6   Crawl under the car and check for loose bolts, broken or disconnected parts and deteriorated rubber bushings on all suspension and steering components. Look for grease or fluid leaking from around the steering box. Check the power steering hoses and their connections for leaks. Check the balljoints for wear.
7   Have an assistant turn the steering wheel from side to side and check the steering components for free movement, chafing or binding. If the steering does not react with the movement of the steering wheel, try to determine where the slack is located.

9   Engine drive belt check and adjustment

1   The drive belts, or V-belts as they are sometimes called, at the front of the engine play an important role in the overall operation of the car and its components. Due to their function and material make-up, the belts are prone to failure after a period of time and should be inspected and adjusted periodically to prevent major engine damage.
2   The number of belts used on a particular car depends on the accessories installed. Drive belts are used to turn: the generator (alternator); A.I.R. smog pump; power steering pump; water pump; fan; and air conditioning compressor. Depending on the pulley arrangement, a single belt may be used for more than one of these ancillary components.

3   With the engine off, open the hood and locate the various belts at the front of the engine. Using your fingers (and a flashlight if necessary), move along the belts checking for cracks or separation. Also check for fraying and for glazing which gives the belt a shiny appearance. Both sides of the belts should be inspected, which means you will have to twist the belt to check the underside.

4   The tension of each belt is checked by pushing on the belt at a distance halfway between the pulleys. Push firmly with your thumb and see how much the belt moves downward (deflects). A rule of thumb, so to speak, is that if the distance (pulley center to pulley center) is between 7 inches and 11 inches the belt should deflect $\frac{1}{4}$ inch. If the belt is longer and travels between pulleys spaced 12 inches to 16 inches apart, the belt should deflect $\frac{3}{8}$ in.

5   If it is found necessary to adjust the belt tension, either to make the belt tighter or looser, this is done by moving the belt-driven accessory on its bracket.

6   For each component there will be an adjustment or strap bolt and a pivot bolt. Both bolts must be loosened slightly to enable you to move the component.

7   After the two bolts have been loosened, move the component away from the engine (to tighten the belt) or toward the engine (to loosen the belt). Hold the accessory in this position and check the belt tension. If it is correct, tighten the two bolts until snug, then recheck the tension. If it is alright, fully tighten the two bolts.

8   It will often be necessary to use some sort of pry bar to move the accessory while the belt is adjusted. If this must be done to gain the proper leverage, be very careful not to damage the component being moved, or the part being pried against.

10 Fuel system check

1   There are certain precautions to take when inspecting or servicing the fuel system components. Work in a well ventilated area and do not allow open flames (cigarettes, appliance pilot lights, etc.) to get near the work area. Mop up spills immediately and do not store fuel-soaked rags where they could ignite.

2   The fuel system is under some amount of pressure, so if any fuel lines are disconnected for servicing, be prepared to catch the fuel as it spurts out. Plug all disconnected fuel lines immediately after disconnection to prevent the tank from emptying itself.

3   The fuel system is most easily checked with the car raised on a hoist where the components under the car are readily visible and accessible.

4   If the smell of gasoline is noticed while driving, or after the car has sat in the sun, the system should be thoroughly inspected immediately.

5   Remove the gas filler cap and check for damage, corrosion and a proper sealing imprint on the gasket. Replace the cap with a new one if necessary.

6   With the car raised, inspect the gas tank and filler neck for punctures, cracks or any damage. The connection between the filler neck and the tank is especially critical. Sometimes a rubber filler neck will leak due to loose clamps or deteriorated rubber; problems a home mechanic can usually rectify.

7   Do not under any circumstances try to repair a fuel tank yourself (except rubber components) unless you have considerable experience. A welding torch or any open flame can easily cause the fuel vapors to explode if the proper precautions are not taken.

8   Carefully check all rubber hoses and metal lines leading away from the fuel tank. Check for loose connections, deteriorated hose, crimped lines or damage of any kind. Follow these lines up to the front of the car, carefully inspecting them all the way. Repair or replace damaged sections as necessary.

9   If a fuel odor is still evident after the inspection, refer to Section 16 for carburetor adjustment.

11 Positive Crankcase Ventilation (PCV) valve replacement

1   The PCV valve can usually be found pushed into one of the rocker arm covers at the side of the engine. There will be a hose connected to the valve which runs to either the carburetor or the intake manifold.

2   When purchasing a replacement PCV valve, make sure it is for your particular vehicle, model year and engine size.

3   Pull the valve (with the hose attached) from its rubber grommet in the rocker arm cover.

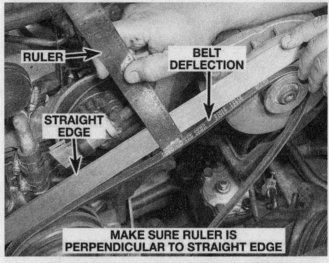

Fig. 1.10 Measuring drive belt deflection (Sec 9)

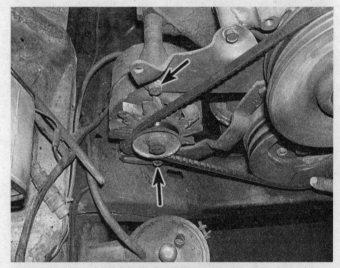

Fig. 1.11 Drive belt adjustment (Sec 9)

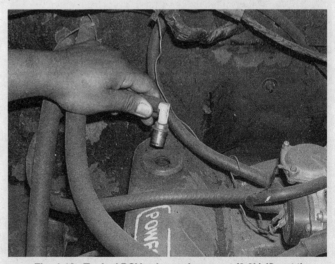

Fig. 1.12 Typical PCV valve replacement (3.3L) (Sec 11)

4   Now pull the PCV valve from the end of the hose, noting its installed position and direction.
5   Compare the old valve with the new one to make sure they are the same.
6   Push the new valve into the end of the hose until it is fully seated.
7   Inspect the rubber grommet in the cover for damage and replace it with a new one if faulty.
8   Push the PCV valve and hose securely into the rocker arm cover.
9   More information on the PCV system can be found in Chapter 6.

---

12 Air filter and crankcase emission filter replacement

1   At the specified intervals, the air filter and crankcase emission filter should be replaced with new ones. A thorough program of preventative maintenance would call for the two filters to be inspected periodically between changes.
2   The air filter is located inside the air cleaner housing on the top of the engine. To remove the filter, unscrew the wing nut at the top of the air cleaner and lift off the top plate. If there are vacuum hoses connected to this plate, note their positions and disconnect them.
3   While the top plate is off, be careful not to drop anything down into the carburetor.
4   Lift the air filter out of the housing (photo).
5   To check the filter, hold it up to strong sunlight, or place a flashlight or droplight on the inside of the ring-shaped filter. If you can see light coming through the paper element, the filter is alright. Check all the way around the filter.
6   Wipe the inside of the air cleaner clean with a rag.
7   Place the old filter (if in good condition) or the new filter (if specified interval has elapsed) back into the air cleaner housing. Make sure it seats properly in the bottom of the housing.
8   Connect any disconnected vacuum hoses to the top plate and reinstall the top plate with the wing nut.

12.4 With the top plate removed, the air cleaner element can be lifted out

9   On nearly all cars the crankcase emission filter is also located inside the air cleaner housing. Remove the top plate as described previously and locate the filter on the side of the housing.
10 Loosen the hose clamp at the end of the filter hose leading to the filter. Disconnect the hose from the filter.
11 Remove the metal locking clip which secures the filter holder to the air cleaner housing. Pliers can be used for this.
12 Remove the filter and plastic holder from the inside of the air cleaner.
13 Remove the old filter pad from the container and wash the container in a suitable solvent. Lightly oil the new filter pad.

Fig. 1.13 Typical air cleaner assembly (Sec 12)

14 Place the new filter assembly into position and install the metal locking clip on the outside of the air cleaner.
15 Connect the filter hose and tighten the clamp around the end of the hose.
16 Reinstall the air cleaner top plate and any vacuum hoses which were disconnected.
17 For more information on these filters and the systems they are a part of, see Chapter 4 and Chapter 6.

13 Clutch pedal free travel check

1 Clutch pedal free travel must be periodically measured and adjusted to compensate for wear or when new clutch parts or linkage have been installed.
2 On 1981 models, clutch pedal travel adjustment is self-compensating by an automatic adjustment device.
3 A description of clutch pedal travel measurement and adjustment as well as a description of the self-adjusting mechanism can be found in Chapter 8.

14 Tire rotation

1 The tires should be rotated at the specified intervals and whenever uneven wear is noticed. Since the car will be raised and the tires removed anyway, this is a good time to check the brakes (Section 25) and/or repack the wheel bearings (Section 23). Read over these Section if this is to be done at the same time.
2 The locations for each tire in the rotation sequence depends on the type of tire used on your car. Tire type can be determined by reading the raised printing on the sidewall of the tire. Fig. 1.7 shows the rotation sequence for each type of tire.
3 See the information in *Jacking and Towing* at the front of this manual for the proper procedures to follow in raising the car and changing a tire; however, if the brakes are to be checked do not apply the parking brake as stated. Make sure the tires are blocked to prevent the car from rolling.
4 Preferablty, the entire car should be raised at the same time. This can be done on a hoist or by jacking up each corner of the car and then lowering the car onto jack stands placed under the frame rails. Always use four jack stands and make sure the car is firmly supported all around.
5 After rotation, check and adjust the tire pressures as necessary and be sure to check wheel nut tightness.

15 Thermo controlled air cleaner check

1 All models are requipped with a thermostatically controlled air cleaner which draws air to the carburetor from different locations depending upon engine temperature.
2 This is a simple visual check; however, if access is tight, a small mirror may have to be used.

Fig. 1.14 Crankcase filter installation (Sec 12)

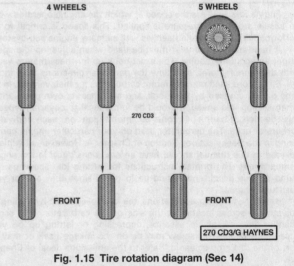

Fig. 1.15 Tire rotation diagram (Sec 14)

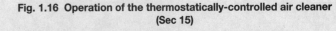

Fig. 1.16 Operation of the thermostatically-controlled air cleaner (Sec 15)

3   Open the hood and find the vacuum flapper door on the air cleaner assembly. It will be located inside the long 'snorkel' of the metal air cleaner. Check that the flexible air hose(s) are securely attached and are not damaged.

4   If there is a flexible air duct attached to the end of the snorkel, leading to an area behind the grille, disconnect it at the snorkel. This will enable you to look through the end of the snorkel and see the flapper door inside.

5   The testing should preferably be done when the engine and outside air are cold. Start the engine and look through the snorkel at the flapper door which should move to a closed position. With the door closed, air enters the air cleaner through the flexible duct attached to the exhaust manifold.

6   As the engine warms up to operating temperature, the door should open to allow air through the snorkel end. Depending on ambient temperature, this may take 10 to 15 minutes. To speed up this check you can reconnect the snorkel air duct, drive the car and then check that the door is fully open.

7   If the thermo controlled air cleaner is not operating properly, see Chapter 6 for more information.

16 Engine idle speed adjustment

1   Engine idle speed is the speed at which the engine operates when no accelerator pedal pressure is applied. This speed is critical to the performance of the engine itself, as well as many engine sub-systems.

2   A hand-held tachometer must be used when adjusting idle speed to get an accurate reading. The exact hook-up for these meters varies with the manufacturer, so follow the particular directions included.

3   Since Ford used many different carburetors for their vehicles in the time period covered by this book, and each has its own peculiarities when setting idle speed, it would be impractical to cover all types in this Section. Chapter 4 contains information on each individual carburetor used. The carburetor used on your particular engine can be found in the Specifications Section of Chapter 4. However, all vehicles covered in this manual should have an emissions decal in the engine compartment. The printed instructions for setting idle speed can be found on this decal, and should be followed since they are for your particular engine.

4   Basically, for most applications, the idle speed is set by turning an adjustment screw located at the side of the carburetor. This screw changes the linkage, in essence, depressing or letting up on your accelerator pedal. This screw may be on the linkage itself or may be part of the idle stop solenoid. Refer to the emissions decal or Chapter 4.

5   Once you have found the idle screw, experiment with different length screwdrivers until the adjustments can be easily made, without coming into contact with hot or moving engine components.

6   Follow the instructions on the emissions decal of in Chapter 4, which will probably include disconnecting certain vacuum or electrical connections. To plug a vacuum hose after disconnecting it, insert a properly-sized metal rod into the opening, or thoroughly wrap the open end with tape to prevent any vacuum loss through the hole.

7   If the air cleaner is removed, the vacuum hose to the snorkel should be plugged.

8   Make sure the parking brake is firmly set and the wheels blocked to prevent the car from rolling. This is especially true if the transmission is to be in 'Drive'. An assistant inside the car pushing on the brake pedal is the safest method.

9   For all applications, the engine must be completely warmed-up to operating temperature, which will automatically render the choke fast idle inoperative.

17 Fuel filter replacement

1   Fuel filters are of the paper replacement type and either screw into the carburetor fuel inlet or are located in the fuel line.

2   This job should be done with the engine cold (after sitting at least 3 hours). You will need the proper replacement filter, wrenches for removing the flare nut fittings on carburetor-mounted filters or screwdriver and pliers to remove the clamps on in-line type filters. Also gather together some clean rags to catch spilled fuel.

3   Remove the air cleaner assembly. If vacuum hoses must be disconnected, make sure you note their positions and/or tag them to help during the reassembly process.

4   Follow the fuel hose from the fuel pump and locate the filter.

5   Place some rags under the fuel inlet fittings to catch any fuel as the filter is connected.

Carburetor – mounted types

6   On carburetor-mounted filters, use the proper size wrench to hold the nut immediately next to the carburetor body. Loosen the fitting and the end of the fuel line. A flare nut wrench on this fitting will help prevent slipping and possible damage. However, an open-end or adjustable wrench should do the job. Make sure the larger nut next to the carburetor is held firmly while the fuel line is disconnected.

7   With the fuel line disconnected, move it slightly for better access to the inlet filter nut. Do not crimp the fuel line.

8   Unscrew the fuel inlet filter nut which was previously held steady. As this fitting is drawn away from the carburetor body, remove the filter, gasket and spring.

Fig. 1.17 Carburetor-mounted fuel filter installation (Sec 17)

9   Install the spring, new filter and gasket and hand tighten the fuel inlet fitting into the carburetor. Hand start the fuel line into the fitting and then fully tighten (using two wrenches) to 15 to 18 ft-lbs (20 to 24 Nm).
10 On screw-in type carburetor filters, remove the spring clamps and rubber connector hose. Unscrew the filter from the carburetor and remove and discard the filter, hose and clamps.
11 Hand start the filter into the carburetor and once in place, fully tighten to 7 to 10 ft-lbs (10 to 14 Nm).
12 Cut a new fuel hose of the proper length, position the spring clamps and push one end of the hose onto the fuel filter inlet and the other end on the steel fuel supply line.
13 Install the spring clamps with pliers.

In-line type
14 To install an in-line type fuel filter, remove the spring type clamps and rubber hoses and discard.
15 Cut new hoses to the proper length, install the clamps and push one end of the hose to the filter inlet and the other on the outlet. Push the inlet side on the metal supply line and the other on carburetor inlet fitting.
16 Install the spring-type clamps with pliers.
17 Run the engine, check for leaks and reinstall the air cleaner assembly, connecting all hoses to their original positions.

18 Ignition timing – adjustment

1   An emissions label, located under the hood, gives important information for adjusting ignition timing as well as other information.
2   At specified intervals or whenever the distributor has been changed the ignition timing must be adjusted.
3   Chapter 5 contains information on the ignition system as well as the procedures for doing so.

19 Carburetor choke check

1   The choke only operates when the engine is cold, and thus this check can only be performed before the car has been started for the day.
2   Open the hood and remove the top plate of the air cleaner assembly. It is held in place by a wing-nut at the center. If any vacuum hoses must be disconnected, make sure you tag the hoses for reinstallation to their original positions. Place the top plate and wing nut aside, out of the way of moving engine components.
3   Look at the top of the carburetor at the center of the air cleaner housing. You will notice a flat plate at the carburetor opening.
4   Have an assistant press the accelerator pedal to the floor. The plate should close fully. Start the engine while you observe the plate at the carburetor. Do not position your face directly over the carburetor, as the engine could backfire, causing serious burns. When the engine starts, the choke plate should open slightly.
5   Allow the engine to continue running at an idle speed. As the engine warms up to operating temperature, the plate should slowly open, allowing more cold air to enter through the top of the carburetor.
6   After a few minutes, the choke plate should be fully open to the vertical position.
7   You will notice that the engine speed corresponds with the plate opening. With the plate fully closed, the engine should run at a fast idle speed. As the plate opens, the engine speed will decrease.
8   If during the above checks a fault is detected, refer to Chapter 4 for specific information on adjusting and servicing the choke components.

20 Exhaust Gas Recirculation (EGR) valve check

1   The EGR valve is located on the intake manifold, adjacent to the carburetor. The majority of the time, when a fault develops in this emissions system it is due to a stuck or corroded EGR valve.
2   With the engine cold to prevent burns, remove the EGR valve as described in Chapter 6.
3   Using moderate pressure, manually push the valve diaphragm up and down within the housing.
4   If the diaphragm does not move or moves only with much effort, replace the EGR valve with a new one. If you are in doubt about the condition of the valve, obtain a new valve and compare the free movement between the two.
5   Further information on EGR system can be found in Chapter 6.

21 Rear axle fluid change

1   To change the fluid in the rear axle it is necessary to remove the cover plate on the differential housing. These rear axles use silicone

Fig. 1.18 Carburetor choke plate (Sec 19)

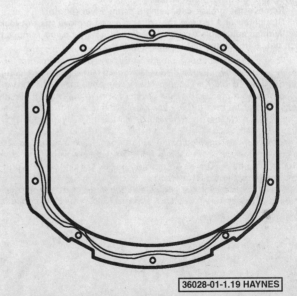

36028-01-1.19 HAYNES

Fig. 1.19 Differential cover silicone sealant installation (Sec 21)

sealant instead of a gasket so it will be necessary to obtain a tube of sealant.

2   Move a drain pan (at least 5 pint capacity), rags, newspapers and wrenches under the rear of the car. Thoroughly clean the area around the differential cover so that no dirt can enter when the cover is removed.

3   With the drain pan under the differential cover, remove the bolts on the lower half of the cover, keeping the upper half of the cover loosely attached with the bolts. Allow the fluid to drain into the drain pan, then completely remove the cover.

4   Using a lint-free rag, clean the inside of the cover and accessible areas of the differential housing. As this is done, check for chipped gears or metal filings in the fluid indicating the differential should be thoroughly inspected and repaired. See Chapter 8 for more information.

5   Clean the mating surface on the cover and differential housing of any traces of old silicone sealant, using a gasket scraper or putty knife.

6   Apply a bead of silicone sealant and install the cover on the differential housing. Install the securing bolts, tightening a little at a time in a diagonal fashion working across the cover. If a torque wrench is available, tighten to specifications.

7   Fill the housing with the proper lubricant to a level ⅜ in below the plug hole as described in Section 2.

8   Securely install the plug.

22   Spark plug replacement

1   The spark plugs should be inspected and/or replaced periodically in accordance with the maintenance schedule or if a fault is suspected. The procedure for spark plug inspection and replacement can be found in Chapter 5.

23   Wheel bearing check and adjustment

1   In most cases, the front wheel bearings will not need servicing until the brake pads are changed. However, these bearings should be checked whenever the front wheels are raised for any reason.

2   With the vehicle securely supported on jack stands, spin the wheel and check for noise, rolling resistance or free play. Grasp the top of the tire with one hand and the bottom of the tire with the other. Move the tire in and out on the spindle. If it moves more than 0.005 in, the bearing should be checked, then repacked with grease or replaced as necessary.

3   To remove the bearings for replacing or repacking, begin by removing the hub cap and wheel.

4   Remove the grease cap, using a screwdriver (photo).

5   Straighten and remove the cotter pin and remove the nut lock.

6   With an adjustable wrench or channel-lock-type pliers, remove the lock nut. Remove the flat washer (photo).

7   Grasp the brake rotor firmly and with a slight rocking motion, withdraw the hub from the spindle (photo).

8   Inspection and packing procedures for the wheel bearings can be found in Chapter 9.

9   Installing is the reversal of removal but the wheel bearings must be adjusted before the nut lock and cotter pin are fitted.

10 Install the lock nut finger tight and then rock the hub assembly in and out several times to push the brake pads away from the rotor.

11 Install the wheel. While rotating the wheel and hub assembly, tighten the nut to 17 to 25 ft-lb (10 to 15 Nm) to seat the bearings.

12 Loosen the nut one-half turn and then retighten to 10 to 15 lb-in (1.1 to 1.7 Nm).

13 Install the nut lock on the nut so that the castellations on the lock align with the spindle cotter pin hole.

14 Install the cotter pin, bending the ends around the flange of the nut lock.

15 Spin the wheel and hub assembly to check for proper operation. Reinstall the grease cap, using a punch to lock it in position (photo).

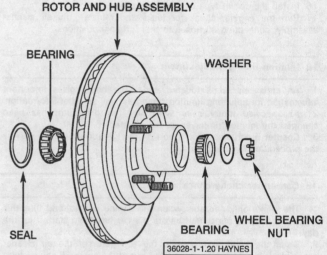

Fig. 1.20 Wheel bearing components (Sec 23)

23.4 Removing the front hub

23.6 Removing the adjusting nut

23.7 Withdrawing hub from spindle

23.15 Lock grease cap in place using punch

24 Automatic transmission fluid change

1   At the specified time intervals, the transmission fluid should be changed and also the filter replaced with a new one. Since there is no drain plug, the transmission oil pan must be removed from the bottom of the transmission to drain the fluid. The procedure for changing automatic transmission fluid can be found in Chapter 7.

25 Brakes check

1   The brakes should be inspected every time the wheels are removed or whenever a fault is suspected. Indication of a potential braking system fault are: the car pulls to one side when brake pedal is depressed; noises coming from the brakes when they are applied; excessive brake pedal travel; pulsating pedal; and leakage of fluid, usually seen on the inside of the tire or wheel.

Disc brakes
2   Disc brakes can be visually checked without the need to remove any parts except the wheels.
3   Raise the vehicle and place securely on jack stands. Remove the front wheels (See *Jacking and Towing* at the front of this manual if necessary).
4   Now visible is the disc brake caliper which contains the pads. There is an outer brake pad and an inner pad. Both should be inspected.
5   Most later model vehicles come equipped with a 'wear sensor' attached to the inner pad. This is a small, bent piece of metal which is visible from the inboard side of the brake caliper. When the pads wear to a danger limit, the metal sensor rubs against the disc and makes a screeching sound (photo).
6   Inspect the pad thickness by looking at each end of the caliper and through the cut-out inspection hole in the caliper body. If the wear sensor clip is very close to the rotor, or the lining material is $\frac{1}{32}$ in or less in thickness, the pads should be replaced. Keep in mind that the lining material is riveted or bonded to a metal backing shoe and the metal portion is not included in this measuring.
7   Since it will be difficult, if not impossible, to measure the exact thickness of the remaining lining material, if you are in doubt as to the pad quality, remove the pads for further inspection or replacement. See Chapter 9 for disc brake pad replacement.
8   Before installing the wheels, check for any leakage around the brake hose connections leading to the caliper or damage (cracking, splitting etc.) to the brake hose. Replace the hose or fittings as necessary, referring to Chapter 9.
9   Also check the condition of the disc for scoring, gouging or burnt spots. If these conditions exist, the hub/rotor assembly should be removed for servicing (Chapter 9).

25.5 Location of the 'wear sensor'

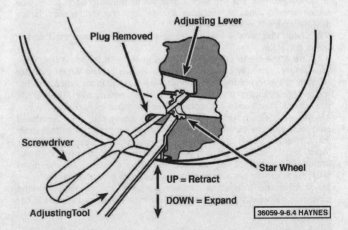

Fig. 1.21 Backing off the drum brake adjustment (Sec 25)

Plug Removed

Adjusting Lever

Screwdriver

Star Wheel

Adjusting Tool

UP = Retract

DOWN = Expand

36059-9-6.4 HAYNES

25.15 Measuring thickness of brake linings

Drum brakes (rear)

10 Raise the vehicle and support firmly on jack stands. Block the front tires to prevent the car from rolling; however, do not apply the parking brake as this will lock the drums into place.

11 Remove the wheels, referring to *Jacking and Towing* at the front of this manual if necessary.

12 Mark the hub so it can be reinstalled in the same place. Use a scribe, chalk, etc. on drum and center hub and backing plate.

13 Pull the brake drum off the axle and brake assembly. If this proves difficult, make sure the parking brake is released, then squirt some penetrating oil around the center hub area. Allow the oil to soak in and try again to pull the drum off. Then, if the drum cannot be pulled off, the brake shoes will have to be adjusted inward. This is done by first removing the rubber plug in the drum or backing plate. With this rubber plug removed, rotate the drum until the opening lines up with adjuster wheel. Pull the lever off the sprocket and then use a small screwdriver to turn the sprocket wheel which will move the linings away from the drums.

14 With the drum removed, carefully brush away any accomulations of dirt and dust. Do not blow this out with compressed air or in any similar fashion. Make an effort not to inhale this dust as it contains asbestos and is harmful to your health.

15 Observe the thickness of the lining material on both the front and rear brake shoes (photo). If the material has worn away to within $\frac{1}{32}$ in of the recessed rivets or metal backing, the shoes should be replaced. If the linings look worn, but you are unable to determine their exact thickness, compare them with a new set at the auto parts store. The shoes should also be replaced if they are cracked, glazed (shiny surface), or wet with brake fluid.

16 Check that all the brake assembly springs are connected and in good condition.

17 Check the brake components for any signs of fluid leakage. With your finger, carefully pry back the rubber cups on the wheel cylinder located at the top of the brake shoes. Any leakage is an indication that the wheel cylinders should be overhauled immediately (Chapter 9). Also check fluid hoses and connections for signs of leakage.

18 Wipe the inside of the drum with a clean rag, and denatured alcohol. Again, be careful not to breathe the dangerous asbestos dust.

19 Check the inside of the drum for cracks, scores, deep scratches or 'hard spots' which will appear as small discolorations. If these imperfections cannot be removed with fine emery cloth, the drum must be taken to a machine shop equipped to turn the drums.

20 If after the inspection process all parts are in good working condition, reinstall the brake drum. Install the wheel and lower the car to the ground.

Parking brake

21 The easiest way to check the operation of the parking brake is to park the car on a steep hill, with the parking brake set and the transmission in 'Neutral'. If the parking brake cannot prevent the car from rolling, it is in need of adjustment (see Chapter 9).

26 Carburetor mounting

1 The carburetor is attached to the top of the intake manifold by two or four nuts. These fasteners can sometimes work loose through normal engine operation and cause a vacuum leak.

2 To properly tighten the carburetor mounting nuts, a torque wrench is necessary. If you do not own one, they can usually be rented on a daily basis.

3 Remove the air cleaner assembly, tagging each hose to be disconnected with a piece of numbered tape to make reassembly easier.

4 Locate the mounting nuts at the base of the carburetor. Decide what special tools or adapters will be necessary, if any, to tighten the nuts with a properly sized socket an the torque wrench.

5 Tighten the nuts to a torque of about 12 ft-lbs. Do not overtighten the nuts, as this may cause the threads to strip.

6 If you suspect a vacuum leak exists at the bottom of the carburetor, get a length of spare hose about the diameter of fuel hose. Start the engine and place one end of the hose next to your ears as you probe around the base of the carburetor with the other end. You will be able to hear a hissing sound if a leak exists. A soapy water solution brushed around the suspect area can also be used to pinpoint pressure leaks.

7 If, after the nuts are properly tightened, a vacuum leak still exists, the carburetor must be removed and a new gasket used. See Chapter 4 for more information.

8 After tightening nuts, reinstall the air cleaner, connecting all hoses to their original positions.

27 Spark plug wires check

1 The spark plug wires should be checked at the recommended intervals or whenever new spark plugs are installed.

2 The wires should be inspected one at a time to prevent mixing up the order which is essential for proper engine operation.

3 Disconnect the plug wire from the spark plug. A removal tool can be used for this, or you can grab the rubber boot, twist slightly and then pull the wire free. Do not pull on the wire itself, only on the rubber boot.

4 Inspect inside the boot for corrosion which will look like a white, crusty powder. Use a screwdriver blade to apply a thin coat of silicone lubricant to the inside of the spark plug boot.

5 Now push the wire and boot back onto the end of the spark plug. It should be a tight fit on the plug end. If not, remove the wire and use a pair of pliers to carefully crimp the metal connector inside the wire boot until the fit is secure.

6 Now using a clean rag, clean the wire its entire length. Remove all built-up dirt and grease. As this is done, inspect for burns, cracks or any other form of damage. Bend the wires in several places to ensure the conductive inside wire has not hardened.

7 Disconnect the wire at the distributor (again, pulling and twisting only on the rubber boot). Check for corrosion and a tight fit in the same manner as the spark plug end. Any time an ignition wire is disconnected, silicone lubricant must be reapplied to the area of contact.

8 Reinstall the wire boot onto the top of the distributor.

9 Check the remaining spark plug wires in the same way, making sure they are securely fastened at the distributor and spark plug.

10 A visual check of the spark plug wires can also be made. In a darkened garage (make sure there is ventilation) start the engine and observe each plug wire. Be careful not to come into contact with any moving engine parts. If there is a break or fault in the wire, you will be able to see arcing or a small spark at the damaged area.

11 If it is decided the spark plug wires are in need of replacement, purchase a new set for your specific engine model. Wire sets can be purchased which are pre-cut to the proper size and with the rubber boots already installed. HEI ignition systems use a different type of plug wire from conventional systems. Remove and replace each wire individually to prevent mix-ups in the firing sequence.

28 Cooling system servicing (draining, flushing and refilling)

1 Peridoically, the cooling system should be drained, lfushed and refilled. This is to replenish the antifreeze mixture and prevent rust and corrosion which can impair the performance of the cooling system and ultimately cause engine damage.

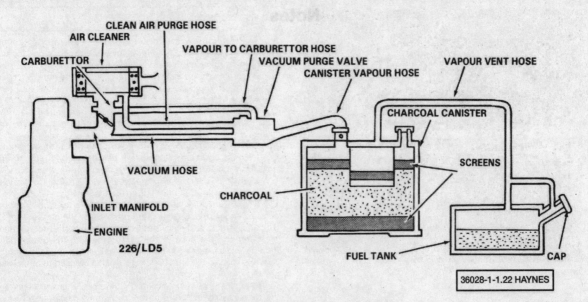

Fig. 1.22 Typical ECS diagram (Sec 29)

2   At the same time the cooling system is serviced, all hoses and the fill cap should be inspected and replaced if faulty (see Section 6).

3   As antifreeze is a poisonous solution, take care not to spill any of the cooling mixture on the vehicle's paint or your own skin. If this happens, rinse immediately with plenty of clear water, Also, it is advisable to consult your local authorities about the dumping of antifreeze before draining the cooling system. In many areas reclamation centers have been set up to collect automobile oil and drained antifreeze/water mixtures rather than allowing these liquids to be added to the sewage and water facilities.

4   With the engine colt, remove the radiator pressure fill cap.

5   Move a large container under the radiator to catch the water/antifreeze mixture as it is drained.

6   Drain the radiator. Most models are equipped with a drain plug at the bottom of the radiator which can be oepned using a wrench to hold the fitting while the petcock is turned to the open position. If this drain has excessive corrosion and cannot be turned easily, or the radiator is not equipped with a drain, disconnect the lower radiator hose to allow the coolant to drain. Be careful that none of the solution is splashed on your skin or in your eyes.

7   If accessible, remove the two engine drain plugs. There is one plug on each side of the engine, about halfway back and on the lower edge near the oil pan rail. These will allow the coolant to drain from the engine itself.

8   On systems with an expansion reservoir, disconnect the overflow pipe and remove the reservoir. Flush it out with clean water.

9   Place a cold water hose (a common garden hose is fine) in the radiator filler neck at the top of the radiator and flush the system until the water runs clean at all drain points.

10 In severe cares of contamination or clogging of the radiator, remove it (see Chapter 3) and reverse flush it. This involves simply inserting the cold pressure hose in the bottom radiator outlet to allow the clear water to run against the normal flow, draining through the top. A radiator repair shop should be consulted if further cleaning or repair is necessary.

11 Where the coolant is regularly drained and the system refilled with the correct antifreeze/inhibitor mixture there should be no need to employ chemical cleaners or descalers.

12 To refill the system, reconnect the radiator hoses and indtall the drain plugs securely in the engine. Special thread sealing tape (available at auto parts stores) should be used on the drain plugs going into the engine block. Install the expansion reservoir and the overflow hose where applicable.

13 On crossflow radiators, fill to within $1\frac{1}{2}$ to 4 inches below the filler neck and on downflow radiators (2.3L only) to between $\frac{3}{4}$ to $1\frac{1}{2}$ inches.

14 On vehicles with an expansion reservoir, fill the radiator to the base of the filler neck and then add more coolant to the expansion reservoir so that it reaches the 'FULL COLD' mark.

15 Run the engine until normal operating temperature is reached and with the engine idling, add coolant up to the correct level (see Section 2), then fit the radiator cap so that the arrows are in alignment with the overflow pipe. Install the reservoir cap.

16 Always refill the system with a mixture of high quality antifreeze and water in the proportion called for on the antifreeze container or in your Owner's manual. Chapter 3 also contains information on anti-freeze mixtures.

17 Keep a close watch on the coolant level and the various cooling hoses during the first few miles of driving. Tighten the hose clamps and/or add more coolant mixture as necessary.

29 Evaporative Control System (ECS) checking

1   The function of the ECS emissions system is to draw fuel vapors from the fuel tank and carburetor, store them in the charcoal canister and then burn these fumes during normal engine operation.

2   If a strong fuel odor is detected, the canister, purge control valve and system hoses should be inspected for faults.

3   The purge control valve controls the flow of fuel vapors into and out of the charcoal canister. If the control valve malfunctions or becomes clogged, the vapors will back up in the canister.

4   The purge control valve is difficult to test without special equipment, so if a fault is suspected replace the valve with a new one.

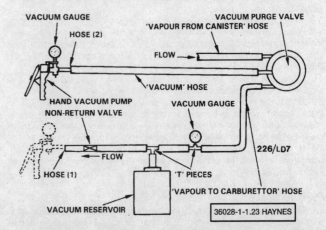

Fig. 1.23 Purge control valve and ECS canister (Sec 29)

Notes

Chapter 2A 2.3L 4-cylinder engine

Refer to Chapter 13 for specifications and information on later models

Contents

2A

Specifications

Engine, general

Displacement	2.3L
Number of cylinders	4
Bore and stroke	3.780 x 3.126 in
Firing order	1 – 3 – 4 – 2
Oil pressure (hot at 2000 rpm)	40 to 60 psi

④
③
②
①

**Firing order
1 - 3 - 4 - 2**

Front ↓

36028-2a-specs HAYNES

2.3L engine
Firing order 1-3-4-2
Cylinder location and distributor rotation

Drivebelt tension

All, except $\frac{1}{4}$ in
  new (A) .... 120 to 160 lb
  used .... 75 to 120 lb (B)
$\frac{1}{4}$ in, only
  new (A) .... 50 to 80 lb
  used .... 40 to 60 lb (C)
Ribbed belt W/O tensioner
  new (A) .... 140 to 170 lb
  used .... 140 to 160 lb (D)
Ribbed belt with tensioner
  new (A) .... 105 to 155 lb
  used .... 105 to 155 lb (E)

(A) tension measured after belt is installed and before it stretches or seats.
(B) if less than 75 lb, adjust to 90 to 120 lb
(C) if less than 40 lb, adjust to 40 to 60 lb
(D) if less than 110 lb, adjust to 140 to 160 lb
(E) if less than 105 lb, replace tensioner

Cylinder head and valve train

Combustion chamber volume .... 59.8 to 62.8 cc

Valve guide bore diameter .... 0.3433 to 0.3443 in

Valve seats
Width – Intake .... 0.060 to 0.080 in
Width – Exhaust .... 0.070 to 0.090 in
Angle .... 45°

Runout limit .... 0.0016 in

Valve arrangement (front to rear) .... E-I-E-I-E-I-E-I

Valve lash adjuster bore diameter .... 0.8430 to 0.9449 in

Valve stem-to-guide clearance
Intake .... 0.0010 to 0.0027 in
Exhaust .... 0.0015 to 0.0032 in
Service clearance limit .... 0.0055 in max.

Valve head diameter
Intake .... 1.73 to 1.74 in
Exhaust .... 1.49 to 1.51 in

Valve face runout limit .... 0.002 in max.

Valve face angle limit .... 44°

Valve stem diameter (standard)
Intake .... 0.3416 to 0.3423 in
Exhaust .... 0.3411 to 0.3418 in
0.015 oversize
Intake .... 0.3566 to 0.3573 in
Exhaust .... 0.3561 to 0.3568 in
0.030 oversize
Intake .... 0.3716 to 0.3723 in
Exhaust .... 0.3711 to 0.3718 in

Valve springs
Compression pressure (lb. @ spec. length)
Intake .... 71 to 79 @ 1.56 in
Exhaust .... 159 to 175 @ 1.16 in
Free length (approximate) .... 1.89 in
Assembled height .... $1\frac{17}{32}$ in to $1\frac{19}{32}$ in
Service limit .... 10% pressure loss @ specified length
Out-of-square limit .... $\frac{5}{64}$ (0.078) in

Rocker arm (cam follower)
Ratio 1.64:1

2A

Valve tappet, lifter or adjuster

Diameter (standard)	0.8422 to 0.8427 in
Clearance to bore	0.0007 to 0.0027 in
Service limit	0.005 in max.
Hydraulic leakdown rate	2 to 8 seconds. Time required for plunger to leak down $\frac{1}{8}$ in of travel with 50 lb load leakdown fluid in lash adjuster

Collapsed tappet gap
Allowable	0.035 to 0.055 in at cam
Desired	0.040 to 0.050 in at cam

Camshaft

Lobe lift

Intake	0.2437 in
Exhaust	0.2437 in
Allowable lobe lift loss	0.005 in max.

Theoretical valve lift @ zero lash

Intake	0.3997 in
Exhaust	0.3997 in

Endplay

	0.001 to 0.007 in
Service limit	0.009 in

Journal-to-bearing clearance

	0.001 to 0.003 in
Service limit	0.006 in

Journal diameter

No. 1	1.7713 to 1.7720 in
No. 2	1.7713 to 1.7720 in
No. 3	1.7713 to 1.7720 in
No. 4	1.7713 to 1.7720 in
Runout limit	0.005 in
Out-of-round limit	0.005 in
Front bearing location	0.000 to 0.010. Distance in inches that front bearing is installed below front face of bearing tower.

Cylinder block

Head gasket surface flatness

	0.003 in for any 6 in span to 0.006 overall

Cylinder bore

Diameter	3.7795 to 3.7831 in
Out-of-round limit	0.0015 in
Out-of-round service limit	0.005 in
Taper service limit	0.010 in

Main bearing bore diameter

	2.5902 to 2.5910 in

Distributor shaft bearing bore diameter

	0.5155 to 0.5170 in

Crankshaft and flywheel

Main bearing journal diameter

	2.399 to 2.3982 in
Out-of-round limit	0.0006 in max.
Taper limit	0.0006 per inch
Journal runout limit	0.002 in max.
Surface finish (RMS)	12 max.
Runout service limit	0.005 in

Thrust bearing journal

Length	1.201 to 1.199 in

Connecting rod journal

Diameter	2.0462 to 2.0472 in
Out-of-round limit	0.0006 in max.
Taper limit	0.0006 per inch max.

Main bearing thrust face

Runout limit	0.001 in max.

Flywheel clutch face

Runout limit	0.005 in

Flywheel ring gear lateral runout
Standard transmission .... 0.025 in
Automatic transmission .... 0.060 in

Crankshaft free endplay limit .... 0.004 to 0.008 in
Service limit .... 0.012 in

Auxiliary shaft endplay .... 0.001 to 0.007 in

Connecting rod bearings
Clearance to crankshaft
    Desired .... 0.0008 to 0.0015 in
    Allowable .... 0.0008 to 0.0026 in
Bearing wall thickness (standard) .... 0.0619 to 0.0624 in
    0.002 in undersize = add 0.001 in to standard thickness.

Main bearings
Clearance to crankshaft
    Desired .... 0.0008 to 0.0015 in
    Allowable .... 0.0008 to 0.0026 in
Bearing wall thickness (standard) .... 0.0008 to 0.0015 in
    0.002 in undersize = add 0.001 in to standard thickness.

Auxiliary shaft bearings
Clearance to shaft .... 0.0006 to 0.0026 in

Connecting rod, pistons and rings

Connecting rod
Piston pin bore diameter .... 0.9123 to 0.9126 in – Non-Turbo
    0.9124 to 0.9127 in – Turbo
Crankshaft bearing bore diameter .... 2.1720 to 2.1728 in
    Out-of-round limit .... 0.0004 in
    Taper limit .... 0.0004 in
Length (center-to-center) .... 5.2031 to 5.2063 in
    Twist .... 0.024 in
    Bend .... 0.012 in
Side clearance (assembled to crank)
    Standard .... 0.0035 to 0.0105 in
    Service limit .... 0.014 in

Piston
Diameter
    Coded red .... Non-Turbo 3.7780 to 3.7786 in
    Turbo 3.7760 to 3.7766 in
    Coded blue .... Non-Turbo 3.7792 to 3.7798 in
    Turbo 3.7772 to 3.7778 in
    0.003 in oversize .... Non-Turbo 3.7804 to 3.7810 in
    Turbo 3.7784 to 3.7790 in
Piston-to-bore clearance .... Non-Turbo 0.0014 to 0.0022 in
    Turbo 0.0034 to 0.0042 in
Pin bore diameter .... Non-Turbo 0.9123 to 0.9126 in
    Turbo 0.9124 to 0.9127 in
Ring groove width
    Compression (top) .... 0.080 to 0.081 in
    Compression (bottom) .... 0.080 to 0.081 in
    Oil .... 0.188 to 0.189 in

Piston pin
Length .... 3.010 to 3.040 in
Diameter
    Standard .... 0.9119 to 0.9124 in
    0.001 oversize .... 0.9130 to 0.9133 in
    0.002 oversize .... 0.9140 to 0.9143 in
Piston-to-pin clearance .... 0.0002 to 0.0004 in
Pin-to-rod clearance .... Interference fit

Piston rings
Ring width
    Compression (top) .... 0.077 to 0.078 in
    Compression (bottom) .... 0.077 to 0.078 in

Side clearance
  Compression (top) .... 0.002 to 0.004 in
  Compression (bottom) .... 0.002 to 0.004 in
  Oil ring .... Snug fit
  Service limit .... 0.006 in max.
Ring gap
  Compression (top) .... 0.010 to 0.020 in
  Compression (bottom) .... 0.010 to 0.020 in
  Oil (steel rail) .... 0.015 to 0.055 in

Lubrication system

Oil pump
Relief valve spring tension (lbs at spec. length) .... 15.2 to 17.2 at 1.20 in
Driveshaft-to-housing bearing clearance .... 0.0015 to 0.0030 in
Relief valve-to-bore clearance .... 0.0015 to 0.0030 in
Rotor assembly end clearance (assembled) .... 0.004 in max.
Outer race-to-housing clearance .... 0.001 to 0.013 in
Oil capacity (quarts U.S) .... 4 – add one pint with filter change

Fuel pump

Static pressure .... 5.0 to 7.0 psi

Minimum volume flow .... 1 pint in 25 seconds

Eccentric total lift .... 0.304 to 0.326 in

Torque specifications

	ft-lb	Nm
Auxiliary shaft gear bolt	28 to 40	38 to 54
Auxiliary shaft thrust plate bolt	6 to 9	8 to 12
Belt tensioner (timing pivot bolt)	28 to 40	38 to 54
Belt tensioner (timing) adjusting bolt	14 to 21	19 to 28
Camshaft gear bolt	50 to 71	68 to 96
Camshaft thrust plate bolt	6 to 9	8 to 12
Carburetor-to-spacer stud	7.5 to 15	10 to 20
Carburetor-to-spacer nut	10 to 14	14 to 19
Carburetor spacer to manifold bolt	14 to 21	19 to 28
Connecting rod nut	30 to 36	41 to 49
Torque in sequence in two steps:		
Step 1	25 to 30	34 to 41
Step 2	30 to 36	41 to 49
Crankshaft damper bolt	100 to 120	136 to 162
Cylinder head bolt	80 to 90	108 to 122
Torque cylinder head bolts in sequence in two steps:		
Step 1	50 to 60	68 to 81
Step 2	80 to 90	108 to 122
Distributor clamp bolt	14 to 21	19 to 28
Distributor vacuum tube-to-manifold adapter	5 to 8	7 to 11
Exhaust manifold-to-cylinder head bolt, stud or nut	16 to 23	22 to 31
Torque in sequence in two steps:		
Step 1	5 to 7	7 to 9
Step 2	16 to 23	22 to 31
Flywheel-to-crankshaft bolt	56 to 64	73 to 87
Fuel pump-to-cylinder block	14 to 21	19 to 28
Intake manifold-to-cylinder head bolt/nut – Non-Turbo	14 to 21	19 to 28
Torque in sequence in two steps:		
Step 1	5 to 7	7 to 9
Step 2 – Non-Turbo	14 to 21	19 to 28
Step 2 – Turbo	13 to 18	18 to 24
Intake manifold-to-cylinder head bolt/nut – Turbo	13 to 18	18 to 24
Main bearing cap bolt	80 to 90	108 to 122
Torque in sequence in two steps:		
Step 1	50 to 60	68 to 81
Step 2	80 to 90	108 to 122
Oil pressure sending wire-to-block	8 to 18	11 to 24
Oil pump pick-up tube-to-pump	14 to 21	19 to 28
Oil pump-to-block	14 to 21	19 to 28
Oil pan drain plug-to-pan	15 to 25	21 to 33
Oil pan-to-block	8 to 10	11 to 13
	8 to 10	11 to 13
Oil filter insert-to-cylinder block	20 to 25	28 to 33
Oil filter-to-engine	$\frac{1}{2}$ turn after gasket contacts surface – oil gasket	
Rocker arm cover-to-cylinder head	6 to 8	8 to 11

2A

Spark plug-to-cylinder head	5 to 10	7 to 13
Temperature sending unit-to-block	8 to 18	11 to 24
Water jacket drain plug-to-block	23 to 28	32 to 37
Water pump-to-block bolt	14 to 21	19 to 28
EGR valve-to-spacer bolt	14 to 21	19 to 28
EGR tube-to-exhaust manifold conn.	9 to 11	13 to 14
EGR tube nut	9 to 11	13 to 14
Auxiliary shaft cover bolt	6 to 9	9 to 12
Water outlet connection bolt	14 to 21	19 to 28
Cylinder front cover bolt	6 to 9	9 to 12
Inner timing belt cover bolt	6 to 9	9 to 12
Rocker arm cover shield bolt	28 to 40	38 to 54
Thermactor check valve-to-manifold	17 to 20	24 to 27
(After tightening rotate to position)		
Fuel filter-to-carburetor	80 to 100 in. lb	9 to 11
Compressor housing bolt (Turbo)	145 to 165 in. lb	16 to 19
Housing bolt (Turbo)	164 to 181 in. lb	19 to 20
Outlet elbow and wastegate assembly — bolt (Turbo)	164 to 181 in. lb	19 to 20

1   General information

The 2.3 and 2.3 liter Turbo engines described in this Chapter are of in-line configuration and constructed of lightweight cast iron.

The valves are actuated by a single overhead camshaft and hydraulic valve lash adjusters.

The camshaft of the 2.3 liter engine is driven from the crankshaft by a toothed belt, which also operates the auxiliary shaft. The auxiliary shaft drives the oil pump, distributor, and fuel pump. Tension on the belt is maintained by a preloaded idler pulley which runs on the outside of the belt.

The water pump, fan, and alternator are driven from separate V-belts. V-belts are also used to provide motion to the engine-driven accessories.

2   Methods of engine removal

1   The engine may be lifted out either on its own or in unit with the transmission. On models fitted with automatic transmission, it is recommended that the engine be lifted out on its own, unless a substantial crane or overhead hoist is available, because of the weight factor. If the engine and transmission are removed as a unit they have to be lifted out at a very steep angle, so make sure that there is sufficient lifting height available.

3   Engine – removal (without transmission)

Note: *If equipped with air conditioning have a specialist discharge the system.*

1   Providing a good set of tools and lifting tackle is available, the home mechanic should be able to remove the engine without encountering any major problems. Make sure that a set of metric sockets and wrenches is available in addition to a hydraulic jack and a pair of axle stands. An assistant will make the task easier.
2   First raise the car hood and disconnect the battery leads.
3   Mark the position of the hood hinges with a pencil. Undo the retaining bolts and remove the hood.
4   Remove the air cleaner and exhaust manifold shroud.
5   If air conditioning is fitted remove the compressor unit from the engine mounting bracket but **do not** disconnect the refrigerant hoses. Position the pump out of the way without straining the hoses.
6   Remove the plug and drain the crankcase oil into a suitable container.
7   Remove the bottom radiator hose and drain the coolant.
8   Remove the top hose and transmission oil cooler hoses (if fitted) from the radiator, undo and remove the mounting bolts and remove the radiator.
9   Undo the four bolts and remove the fan.
10   Jack up the front of the car and support it on axle stands.
11   Where applicable, remove the engine shield.

12   Remove the starter motor. Further details will be found in Chapter 5, if required.
13   *On automatic transmission models:* remove the torque converter bolt access plug. Remove the three flywheel-to-converter bolts. Remove the converter housing cover and disconnect the converter from the flywheel.
14   *On manual transmission models:* remove the flywheel cover.
15   Remove the flywheel or converter housing cover, as applicable.
16   Detach the exhaust pipe from the exhaust manifold. Remove the packing washer.
17   Remove the nuts from the engine mountings, and remove the nuts and through bolts retaining the rear engine support crossmember.
18   Detach the fuel lines from the fuel pump, plugging the lines to prevent fuel spillage.
19   Where applicable, remove the power steering pump drivebelt and draw off the pulley. The drivebelt arrangement is shown in Chapter 3; refer to Chapter 11 for further information on the pump.
20   Remove the lower bolt securing the power steering pump to the bracket.
21   Lower the car to the ground.
22   Disconnect the heater and vacuum hoses from the engine. It is recommended that a sketch be made showing the various connections to avoid confusion when refitting.
23   Disconnect the power brake hose.
24   Remove the oil pressure union from the connection on the rear left-hand side of the cylinder head.
25   Detach the carburetor cable(s).
26   Disconnect the wire to the throttle solenoid and choke heater.
27   Detach the wire from the water temperature sender on the rear left-hand side of the cylinder block.
28   Disconnect the lines from the vacuum amplifier.
29   From the distributor, disconnect the coil wire and vacuum line.
30   Pull off the multi-plug from the alternator, followed by the ground wire.
31   Remove the bolt from the alternator adjusting arm.
32   Remove the remaining power steering pump-to-bracket bolts, and remove the pump, (if fitted).
33   Support the weight of the transmission on a suitable jack, with a wood block interposed between the jack head and the transmission.
34   Attach the hoist hooks to the engine lifting brackets and lift the engine a little.
35   Draw the engine forward to disengage the transmission, ensuring that the transmission is still satisfactorily supported.
36   Lift the engine out, ensuring that no damage occurs to the hoses etc, in the engine compartment or to the engine mounting equipment. Transfer the engine to a suitable working area and detach the accessories. These will vary according to the engine, but would typically be:

Alternator
Thermactor pump
Air conditioning compressor
Clutch

37   Clean the outside of the engine using a water soluble solvent, then transfer it to where it is to be dismantled. On the assumption that engine overhaul is to be carried out, remove the fuel pump, oil filter (unscrew), spark plugs, distributor (index mark the distributor body and block to assist with installation), fan, water pump, thermostat, oil pressure and water temperature senders, emission control ancillaries, etc. Refer to the appropriate Sections in this and other Chapters for further information.

4   Engine – removal (with manual transmission)

1   The procedure for removing the engine and transmission together is basically similar to that described in the previous Section. However, the following differences should be noted:

   a)   *Disconnect the gearshift linkage from the transmission, referring to Chapter 7, as necessary.*

   b)   *Detach the propeller shaft following the procedure given in Chapter 8.*

   c)   *Disconnect the clutch operating cable from the release arm.*

   d)   *Do not remove the clutch housing bolts. These items are removed after the assembly has been removed from the car. Further information on this will be found in Chapter 8.*

   e)   *Remove the speedometer drive cable, and the transmission electrical connections. If there is any possibility of their being mixed up, suitably label them or make a sketch showing their installed positions.*

   f)   *Support the weight of the transmission in a similar manner to that described in the previous Section, paragraph 33, while the rear mounting is being detached.*

   g)   *It is a good idea to do the preliminary cleaning of the engine with the transmission still attached.*

5   Engine – dismantling (general)

1   It is best to mount the engine on a dismantling stand, but if this is not available, stand the engine on a strong bench at a comfortable working height. Failing this, it can be stripped down on the floor.

2   During the dismantling process, the greatest care should be taken to keep the exposed parts free from dirt. As an aid to achieving this, thoroughly clean down the outside of the engine, first removing all traces of oil and dirt.

3   A good grease solvent will make the job much easier, for, after the solvent has been applied and allowed to stand for a time, a vigorous jet of water will wash off the solvent and grease with it. If the dirt is thick and deeply embedded, work the solvent into it with a strong stiff brush.

4   Finally wipe down the exterior of the engine with a rag and only then, when it is quite clean, should the dismantling process begin. As the engine is stripped, clean each part in a bath of solvent. Clean oil passages with a small brush or, preferably, air pressure.

5   Re-use of old gaskets is false economy. To avoid the possibility of trouble after the engine has been reassembled always use new gaskets throughout.

6   Do not throw away the old gaskets, for sometimes it happens that an immediate replacement cannot be found and the old gasket is then very useful as a template. Hang up the gaskets as they are removed.

7   To strip the engine, it is best to work from the top down. When the stage is reached where the crankshaft must be removed, the engine can be turned on its side and all other work carried out with it in this position.

8   Wherever possible, refit nuts, bolts and washers finger-tight from wherever they were removed; this helps to avoid loss and confusion.

9   Before dismantling begins it is important that a special tool is obtained for compressing the lash adjusters. This has the Ford number T74P-6565-A.

6   Cylinder head removal – engine out of the car

1   Remove the carburetor from the intake manifold using a suitable wrench.

2   Take off the gasket. Remove the EGR spacer, followed by the second gasket.

3   Remove any emission control system hoses and fittings from the intake manifold, carefully noting their installed positions to assist in reassembly later.

4   Loosen the intake manifold securing bolts by about $\frac{1}{2}$ turn each, in the reverse order to that shown. Then remove the bolts completely and lift away the manifold. Note the lifting eye on the No. 7 bolt.

5   Remove the timing belt outer cover (4 bolts). Note the spacers used with two of the bolts adjacent to the auxiliary shaft sprocket.

6   If major engine dismantling is going to be carried out, remove the nut and washer retaining the crankshaft pulley. If this is found difficult because the engine tends to turn over, either wedge a screwdriver in the flywheel teeth or lock the pulley using a suitable bar in the slots.

7   Draw off the pulley using a suitable puller (or carefully pry it off using a large screwdriver), then remove the belt guide.

8   Loosen the timing belt tensioner adjustment bolt to relieve the belt tension.

9   Remove the timing belt by drawing it off the sprockets.

10 Remove the timing belt tensioner from the front end of the cylinder head (2 bolts).

11 Remove the single stud and washer from the upper attachment point of the inner timing belt cover.

12 Loosen the 8 screws from around the rocker cover and the 2 screws at the front end. Remove the screws, lift off the cover and remove the gasket.

13 Loosen each cylinder head bolt slightly in the reverse order to that shown. Then remove all the bolts with the exception of Nos. 7 and 8 which should be unscrewed so that only about two threads are engaged.

14 Using the exhaust manifold for leverage, lift it up to break the cylinder head/gasket seal.

15 Loosen the exhaust manifold retaining bolts in the reverse order to that shown. Remove the bolts while supporting the manifold, then remove the manifold from the engine. Note the lifting eye on the rear bolt.

16 Remove the two remaining cylinder head bolts and lift off the head. Transfer it to a suitable workbench for further dismantling. Remove the old gasket from the block.

7   Cylinder head removal – engine in the car

1   Removal of the cylinder head with the engine in the car is very similar to the procedure given in the previous Section. However, the following points should be noted:

   a)   *First remove the engine compartment hood for improved access.*

   b)   *Disconnect the battery ground lead.*

   c)   *Drain the engine coolant and remove the hoses connected to the cylinder head. Refer to Chapter 3, if necessary.*

   d)   *Remove the air cleaner, carburetor and emission control system items attached to the carburetor and manifolds. Refer to Chapter 4 if necessary. It is recommended that a sketch be made showing the various connections to avoid confusion when refitting.*

   e)   *The camshaft drivebelt need not be completely removed unless it is to be replaced. This means that the crankshaft pulley and belt guide need not be removed.*

   f)   *Remove the appropriate drivebelts from the engine driven accessories as necessary to permit the drivebelt outer cover to be removed.*

   g)   *If air conditioning refrigerant lines need to be disconnected, this must be carried out by a qualified air conditioning specialist.*

   h)   *Detach the spark plug leads and the oil pressure gauge connection.*

2A

8   Auxiliary shaft – removal

1   Using a metal bar to lock the auxiliary shaft sprocket, remove the sprocket retaining bolt and washer.
2   Pull off the sprocket using a universal puller, and remove the sprocket locking pin from the shaft.
3   Remove the auxiliary shaft cover (3 screws).
4   Remove the auxiliary shaft retaining plate (2 screws).
5   Withdraw the auxiliary shaft. If this is tight, refit the bolt and washer, then use a pry bar and a spacer block to pry out the shaft.

9   Flywheel and rear cover plate – removal

1   With the clutch removed, as described in Chapter 8, lock the flywheel using a screwdriver in mesh with the starter ring gear and undo the 6 bolts that secure the flywheel to the crankshaft in a diagonal and progressive manner. Lift away the bolts.
2   Mark the relative position of the flywheel and crankshaft and then lift away the flywheel.
3   Undo the remaining engine rear cover plate securing bolts and ease the rear cover plate from the 2 dowels. Lift away the rear cover plate.

10   Oil pan, oil pump and strainer – removal

1   Undo and remove the bolts that secure the oil pan to the underside of the crankcase.
2   Lift away the oil pan and its gasket.
3   Undo and remove the screw and spring washer that secures the oil pump pick-up pipe support bracket to the crankcase.
4   Using special tool 21 - 020 available at tool/rental shops, undo the two special bolts that secure the oil pump to the underside of the crankcase. Unfortunately there is no other tool suitable to slot into the screw head so do not attempt to improvise; this will only cause damage to the screw.
5   Lift away the oil pump and strainer assembly.
6   Carefully lift away the oil pump making a special note of which way round it is fitted.

11   Crankshaft sprocket, drivebelt inner cover and cylinder front cover – removal

1   Having already removed the crankshaft pulley (Section 6), very carefully pry off the crankshaft sprocket using 2 large screwdrivers.
2   Remove the remaining bolt and take off the belt inner cover.
3   Remove the two bolts and take off the cylinder front cover.
4   Remove the gasket.
5   If the crankshaft key is not a tight fit in the keyway, remove it at this stage to prevent it from being lost.

12   Pistons, connecting rods and connecting rod bearings – removal

1   Note that the pistons have a notch marked on the crown showing the forward facing side. Inspect the connecting rod bearing caps and connecting rods to make sure identification marks are visible. This is to ensure that the correct caps are fitted to the correct connecting rods and the connecting rods placed in their respective bores.
2   Undo the connecting rod nuts and place to one side in the order in which they were removed.
3   Remove the connecting rod caps, taking care to keep them in the right order and the correct way round. Also ensure that the shell bearings are kept with their correct connecting rods unless the rods are to be replaced.
4   If the connecting rod caps are difficult to remove, they may be gently tapped free with a soft-headed mallet.
5   To remove the shell bearings, press the bearing opposite the groove in both the connecting rod and its cap, and the bearing will slide out easily.
6   Withdraw the pistons and connecting rods upwards and ensure

they are kept in the correct order for replacement in the same bore as they were originally fitted.

13   Crankshaft and main bearings – removal

1   Make sure that identification marks are visible on the main bearing caps, so that they may be refitted in their original positions and also the correct way round.
2   If the bearing caps are not already marked, mark them as they are removed to ensure correct installation.
3   Undo by one turn at a time the bolts which hold the 5 bearing caps.
4   Lift away each main bearing cap and the bottom half of each bearing shell, taking care to keep the bearing shells in the right caps.
5   When removing the rear main bearing caps note that this also retains the crankshaft rear oil seal.
6   When removing the center main bearing cap, note the bottom semi-circular halves of the thrust washers, one half lying on each side of the cap. Lay them with the main bearing cap on the correct side.
7   As the center and rear bearing caps are accurately located by dowels it may be necessary to gently tap the caps to release them.
8   Slightly rotate the crankshaft to free the upper halves of the bearing shells and thrust washers which can be extracted and placed over the correct bearing caps.
9   Remove the two halves of the rear crankcase oil seal.
10   Remove the crankshaft by lifting it away from the crankcase.

14   Camshaft drivebelt – removal (engine in the car)

1   It is possible to remove the camshaft drivebelt with the engine in place but experience shows that this type of belt is very reliable and unlikely to break or stretch considerably. However, during a major engine overhaul it is recommended that a new belt is fitted. To replace the belt, engine in the car:
2   Refer to Chapter 3, and drain the cooling system. Loosen the top hose securing clips and remove the top hose.
3   Loosen the alternator mounting bolts and push the unit towards the engine. Remove the drivebelt(s). **Note**: *On cars equipped with a thermactor pump and air conditioning compressor these drivebelts will have to be removed first* (see Chapter 3).
4   Undo and remove the bolts that secure the drivebelt outer cover to the front of the engine. Lift away the cover.
5   Loosen the belt tensioner mounting plate securing bolt and release the tension on the belt.
6   Place the car in gear (manual gearbox only), and apply the brakes firmly. Undo and remove the bolt and plain washer that secures the crankshaft pulley to the nose of the crankshaft. On vehicles fitted with automatic transmission, the starter must be removed and the ring gear jammed to prevent the crankshaft from rotating.
7   Using a suitable extractor (or even a large screwdriver) carefully ease off the pulley.
8   Recover the large diameter belt guide washer.
9   The drivebelt may now be lifted away.

15   Valves and lash adjusters – removal

1   Remove the spring clip from the hydraulic valve lash adjuster end of the cam followers (where applicable).
2   Using special tool T74P-6565-A inserted beneath the camshaft, fully compress the lash adjuster of the valve(s) to be removed, ensuring that the cam peak is facing away from the follower. This will permit the cam followers to be removed. Keep the cam followers in order so that they can be refitted in their original positions. **Note**: *On some valves it may be found necessary to compress the valve spring slightly as well, in order to remove the cam followers.*
3   Using a valve spring compressor, compress the valve springs and lift out the keys.
4   Remove the spring retainer and valve spring, then pry off the valve seal from the valve stem.
5   Push out the valve and keep it with its cam followers. Repeat this for the other valves.
6   Lift out the hydraulic lash adjusters, keeping each one with its respective cam follower and valve.

16 Camshaft – removal

1   It is not necessary to remove the engine from the car to remove the camshaft. However, it will be necessary to remove the cylinder head as described earlier in this Chapter and the cam followers as described in Section 15.

2   Using a metal bar, lock the camshaft drive sprocket. Remove the securing bolt and washer.

3   Draw off the sprocket using a suitable puller (or carefully pry it off using a large screwdriver), then remove the belt guide.

4   Remove the sprocket locating pin from the end of the camshaft.

5   From the rear bearing pedestal, remove the camshaft retaining plate (2 screws).

6   Using a hammer and a brass or aluminum drift, drive out the camshaft towards the front of the engine, taking the front seal with it. Take great care that the camshaft bearings and journals are not damaged as it is pushed out.

17 Thermostat and water pump – removal

1   If the cylinder head and block are being completely dismantled, the thermostat and housing, and water pump should be removed. Further information on these procedures will be found in Chapter 3.

18 Piston pin – removal

1   A press type piston pin is used and it is important that no damage is caused during removal and refitting. Because of this, should it be necessary to fit new pistons, take the parts along to the local Ford dealer or local repair shop who will have the special equipment to do this job.

19 Piston rings – removal

1   To remove the piston rings, slide them carefully over the top of the piston, taking care not to scratch the aluminum alloy; never slide them off the bottom of the piston skirt. It is very easy to break the cast iron piston rings if they are pulled off roughly, so this operation should be done with extreme care. It is helpful to make use of an old 0.020 inch (0.5 mm) feeler gauge.

2   Lift one end of the piston ring to be removed out of its groove and insert under it the end of the feeler gauge.

3   Turn the feeler gauge slowly round the piston and, as the ring comes out of its groove, apply slight upward pressure so that it rests on the land above. It can then be eased off the piston with the feeler gauge stopping it from slipping into an empty groove if it is any but the top piston ring that is being removed.

20 Lubrication and crankcase ventilation systems – description

1   The pressed steel oil pan is attached to the underside of the crankcase and acts as a reservoir for the engine oil. The oil pump draws oil through a strainer located under the oil surface, passes it along a short passage and into the full-flow oil filter. The freshly filtered oil flows from the center of the filter element and enters the main gallery. Five small drillings connect the main gallery to the five main bearings. The connecting rod bearings are supplied with oil by the front and rear main bearings via skew oil bores. When the crankshaft is rotating, oil is thrown from the hole in each connecting rod bearing and splashes the thrust side of the piston.

2   The auxiliary shaft is lubricated directly from the main oil gallery. The distributor shaft is supplied with oil passing along a drilling inside the auxiliary shaft.

3   A further three drillings connect the main oil gallery to the overhead camshaft to provide lubrication for the camshaft bearings and cam followers. Oil then passes back to the oil pan via large drillings in the cylinder head and cylinder block.

4   A semi-enclosed engine ventilation system is used to control crankcase vapor. It is controlled by the amount of air drawn in by the engine when running and the throughput of the regulator valve.

5   The system is known as the PCV (Positive Crankcase Ventilation) system. The advantage of this system is that should the 'blow-by' exceed the capacity of the PCV valve, excess fumes are fed into the engine through the air cleaner. This is effected by the rise in crankcase pressure which creates a reverse flow in the air intake pipe.

6   Periodically pull the valve and hose from the rubber grommet of the oil separator and inspect the valve for free-movement. If it is sticky in action or is clogged with sludge, dismantle it and clean the component parts.

7   Occasionally check the security and condition of the system connecting hoses.

21 Oil pump – inspection

1   The oil pump cannot be dismantled or repaired in any way. If there is any obvious damage, or in the case of major engine overhaul, a replacement item must be fitted.

2   Detach the oil intake pipe and screen (2 screws and spring washers), and clean the parts thoroughly in gasoline.

3   Reinstall the intake pipe and screen, using a new gasket.

22 Oil filter – removal and installation

1   The oil filter is a complete throw away cartridge screwed into the left-hand side of the cylinder block. Simply unscrew the old unit, clean the seating on the block and lubricate with engine oil. Screw the new one into position taking care not to cross the thread. Continue until the sealing ring just touches the block face then tighten one half turn by hand only. Always run the engine and check for signs of leaks after installation.

2A

23 Engine components – examination for wear

1   When the engine has been stripped down and all parts properly cleaned decisions have to be made as to what needs replacement and the following Sections tell the mechanic what to look for. In any border-line case, it is always best to decide in favor of a new part. Even if a part may still be serviceable, its life will have been reduced by wear and the degree of trouble needed to replace it in the future must be taken into consideration. However, these things are relative and it depends on whether a quick 'survival' job is being done or whether the car as a whole is being regarded as having many thousands of miles of useful and economical life remaining.

24 Crankshaft – inspection and overhaul

1   Look at the main bearing journals and the crankpins, and if there are any scratches or score marks then the shaft will need regrinding. Such conditions will nearly always be accompanied by similar deterioration in the matching bearing shells.

2   Each bearing journal should also be round and can be checked with a micrometer or caliper gauge around the periphery at several points. If there is more than 0.001 in of ovality, regrinding is necessary.

3   A Ford service dept, or machine shop will be able to decide to what extent regrinding is necessary and also supply the special undersize shell bearing to match whatever may need grinding off.

4   Before taking the crankshaft for regrinding check also the cylinder bores and pistons as it may be advantageous to have the whole engine done at the same time.

5   During any major engine repair, pry out the roller pilot bearing from the rear end of the crankshaft; this may require the use of a hook-ended tool to get behind the bearing. Fit the replacement bearing with the seal outwards (where applicable) so that it is just below the surface of the crankshaft flange.

25 Crankshaft, main and connecting rod bearings – inspection and overhaul

1   With careful servicing and regular oil and filter changes, bearings will last for a very long time but they can still fail for unforeseen reasons. With connecting rod bearings, the indication is a regular rhythmic loud knocking from the crankcase. The frequency depends on engine speed and is particularly noticeable when the engine is under load. This symptom is accompanied by a fall in oil pressure although this is not normally noticeable unless an oil pressure gauge is fitted. Main bearing failure is usually indicated by serious vibration, particularly at higher engine revolutions, accompanied by a more significant drop in oil pressure and a 'rumbling' noise.

2   Bearing shells in good condition have bearing surfaces with a smooth, even matte silver/grey color all over. Worn bearings will show patches of a different color when the bearing metal has worn away and exposed the underlay. Damaged bearings will be pitted or scored. It is always well worthwhile fitting new shells as their cost is relatively low. If the crankshaft is in good condition it is merely a question of obtaining another set of standard size. A reground crankshaft will need new bearing shells as a matter of course.

3   A good way to check for wear and taper of a crankshaft or connecting rod journal is by using Plastigage. Place a piece of Plastigage across the full width of the bearing surface, about $\frac{1}{4}$ in off center, install the bearing cap and tighten to specification. Remove the cap and measure the width of the Plastigage at its widest point to obtain the minimum clearance and the narrowest point for the maximum clearance using the supplied gauge. The difference between these two measurements equals the taper. Be sure to remove all traces of the Plastigage from the journal after measurement.

26 Cylinder bores – inspection and overhaul

1   A new cylinder bore is perfectly round and the walls parallel throughout its length. The action of the piston, tends to wear the walls at right angles to the piston pin due to side thrust. This wear takes place principally on that section of the cylinder swept by the piston rings.

2   It is possible to get an indication of bore wear by removing the cylinder heads with the engine still in the car. With the piston down in the bore first signs of wear can be seen and felt just below the top of the bore where the top piston ring reaches and there will be a noticeable lip. If there is no lip it is fairly reasonable to expect that bore wear is not severe and any lack of compression or excessive oil consumption is due to worn or broken piston rings or pistons (see Section 27). Unless the engine is to be removed, the lip must be removed with a ridge reaming tool.

3   If it is possible to obtain a bore measuring micrometer measure the bore in the thrust plane below the lip and again at the bottom of the cylinder in the same plane. If the difference is more than 0.003 inch (0.08 mm) then a rebore is necessary. Similarly, a difference of 0.003 inch (0.08 mm) or more across the bore diameter is a sign of ovality calling for rebore.

4   Any bor   which is significantly scratched or scored will need reboring. This symptom usually indicates that the piston or rings are damaged also. In the event of only one cylinder being in need of reboring, it will still be necessary for all four to be bored and fitted with new oversize pistons and rings. Your dealer or local machine shop will be able to rebore and obtain the necessary matched pistons. If the crankshaft is undergoing regrinding also, it is a good idea to let the same firm renovate and reassemble the crankshaft and pistons to the block. A reputable firm normally gives a guarantee for such work. In cases where engines have been rebored already to their maximum, new cylinder liners are available which may be fitted. In such cases the same reboring processes have to be followed and the services of a machine shop are required.

27 Pistons and piston rings – inspection and testing

1   Worn pistons and rings can usually be diagnosed when the

symptoms of excessive oil consumption and lower compression occur and are sometimes, though not always, associated with worn cylinder bores. Compression testers that fit into the spark plug hole are available, and these can indicate where low compression is occurring. Wear usually accelerates the more it is left so when the symptoms occur early action can possibly save the expense of a rebore.

2   Another symptom of piston wear is piston slap – a knocking noise from the crankcase not to be confused with the connecting rod bearing failure. It can be heard clearly at low engine speed when there is no load (idling for example) and is much less audible when the engine speed increases. Piston wear usually occurs in the skirt or lower end of the piston and is indicated by vertical streaks in the worn area which is always on the thrust side. It can also be seen where the skirt thickness is different.

3   Piston ring wear can be checked by first removing the rings from the pistons as described in Section 19. Then place the rings in the cylinder bores from the top, pushing them down about $1\frac{1}{2}$ inches (38 mm) with the head of a piston (from which the rings have been removed), so that they rest square in the cylinder bore. Then measure the gap at the ends of the ring with a feeler gauge. If it exceeds that given in the Specifications, they need replacement.

4   The grooves in which the rings locate in the piston can also become enlarged in use. The clearance between ring and piston, in the groove, should not exceed that given in the Specifications.

5   However, it is rare that a piston is only worn in the ring grooves and the need to replace them for this fault alone is hardly ever encountered. Wherever pistons are replaced the weight of the four piston/connecting rod assemblies should be kept within the limit variations of 8 gms to maintain engine balance.

28 Connecting rods and piston pins – inspection and overhaul

1   Piston pins are a shrink fit into the connecting rods. Neither of these would normally need replacement unless the pistons were being changed, in which case the new pistons would automatically be supplied with new piston pins.

2   Connecting rods are not subject to wear but in extreme circumstances such as engine seizure they could be distorted. Such conditions may be visually apparent but where doubt exists they should be changed. The bearing caps should also be examined for indications of filing down which may have been attempted in the mistaken idea that bearing slackness could be remedied in this way. If there are such signs then the connecting rods should be replaced with new ones.

29 Camshaft and camshaft bearings – inspection and overhaul

1   The camshaft bearings should be examined for signs of scoring and pitting. If they need replacement they will have to be dealt with professionally as, although it may be relatively easy to remove the old ones, the correct fitting of new ones requires special tools. If they are not fitted evenly and square from the very start they can be distorted, thus causing localized wear in a very short time. See your Ford dealer or local machine shop for this work.

2   The camshaft itself may show signs of wear on the bearing journals or cam lobes. The main decision to take is what degree of wear justifies replacement, which is costly. Any signs of scoring or damage to the bearing journals cannot be removed by grinding. Replacement of the whole camshaft is the only solution. **Note:** *Where excessive cam lobe wear is evident, refer to the following Section.*

3   The cam lobes themselves may show signs of ridging or pitting on the high points. If ridging is light then it may be possible to smooth it out with fine emery. The cam lobes, however, are surface hardened and once this is penetrated, wear will be very rapid thereafter.

4   Ensure that the camshaft oilways are unobstructed.

5   To check the thrust plate for wear, position the camshaft into its location in the cylinder head and fit the thrust plate at the rear. Using a dial gauge, check the total shaft endfloat by tapping the camshaft carefully back-and-forth along its length. If the endplay is outside the specified limit, replace the thrust plate.

30 Cam followers – inspection

1   The faces of the cam followers which bear on the camshaft should show no signs of pitting, scoring or other forms of wear. They should not be a loose sloppy fit on the ballheaded bolt.
2   Inspect the face which bears onto the valve stem and if pitted, the cam follower must be replaced with a new one.
3   If excessive cam follower wear is evident (and possibly excessive cam lobe wear), this may be due to a malfunction of the valve drive lubrication tube. If this has occurred, replace the tube and the cam follower. If more than one cam follower is excessively worn, replace the camshaft, all the cam followers and the lubrication tube. This also applies where excessive cam lobe wear is found.
4   During any operation which requires removal of the valve rocker cover ensure that oil is being discharged from the lubrication tube nozzles by cranking the engine on the starter motor. During routine maintenance operations, this can be done after checking the valve clearances.

31 Auxiliary shaft and bearings – inspection and overhaul

1   The procedure for the auxiliary shaft and bearing is similar to that described in Section 29 for the camshaft.
2   Examine the skew gear for wear and damaged teeth. If either is evident, a replacement shaft must be obtained.

32 Valves and valves seats – inspection and overhaul

1   With the valve removed from the cylinder head examine the head for signs of cracking, burning away and pitting of the edge where it sits in the port. The valve seats in the cylinder head should also be examined for the same signs. Usually it is the valve that deteriorates first but if a bad valve is not rectified that seat will suffer and this is more difficult to repair.
2   Provided there are no obvious signs of serious pitting the valve should be ground with its seat. This may be done by placing a smear of carborundum paste on the edge of the valve and, using a suction type valve holder, grinding the valve in place. This is done with a semi-rotary action, rotating the handle of the valve holder between the hands and lifting it occasionally to re-distribute the traces of paste. Use a coarse paste to start with. As soon as a matte grey unbroken line appears on both the valve and seat the valve is 'ground in'. All traces of carbon should also be cleaned from the head and neck of the valve stem. A wire brush mounted in a power drill is a quick and effective way of doing this.
3   If the valve requires replacement it should be ground into the seat in the same way as the old valve.
4   Another form of valve wear can occur on the stem where it runs in the guide in the cylinder head. This can be detected by trying to rock the valve from side to side. If there is any movement at all it is an indication that the valve stem or guide is worn. Check the stem first with a micrometer at points along and around its length and if they are not within the specified size new valves will probably solve the problem. If the guides are worn, however, they will need reboring for oversize valves or for fitting guide inserts. The valve seats will also need recutting to ensure they are concentric with the stems. This work should be entrusted to your Ford dealer or local auto-machine shop works.

5   When valve stems are badly burnt or pitted, requiring replacement, inserts may be fitted – or replaced if already fitted once before – again this is a specialist task to be carried out by a suitable rebuilding firm.
6   When all valve grinding is complete it is essential that every trace of grinding paste is removed from the valves and ports in the cylinder head. This should be done by thorough washing in the proper solvent and blowing out with a jet of air. If particles of carborundum should work their way into the engine they would cause havoc with bearings or cylinder walls.

33 Hydraulic lash adjusters (valve lifters) – inspection and overhaul

1   Examine the outside of each lash adjuster for wear and scoring. If lightly scored, very fine emery cloth can be used to polish out the marks. However, if wear is evident, it is recommended that the complete adjuster is replaced with a new one.
2   Carefully pry off the retaining ring, take out the follower arm fulcrum and dismantle the complete adjuster. The component parts are shown in the accompanying figure.
3   Examine all the parts of each adjuster for damage, wear, corrosion and gum deposits; obtain replacement parts for any which are unserviceable. Do not mix up the parts from the different adjusters.
4   Reassemble the adjusters, lightly lubricating the parts with engine oil. Do not attempt to fill them with oil.
5   Testing of the lifters is not practicable without the use of special equipment. However, this is available at Ford dealers or most machine shops and can be very useful where there is any doubt about serviceability.

34 Timing gears and belt – inspection

1   Any wear which takes place in the timing mechanism will be on the teeth of the drivebelt or due to stretch of the fabric. Whenever the engine is to be stripped for major overhaul a new belt should be fitted.
2   It is very useful for the timing gears (sprockets) to wear at the teeth. If the securing bolt/nuts have been loose it is possible for the keyway or hub bore to wear. Check these two points and if damage or wear is evident a new gear must be obtained.

35 Flywheel – inspection and overhaul

1   If the ring gear is badly worn or has missing teeth it should be replaced. The old ring can be removed from the flywheel by cutting a notch between two teeth with a hacksaw and then splitting it with a cold chisel.
2   To fit a new ring gear requires heating the ring to 400°F (204°C). This can be done by polishing four equally spaced sections of the gear, laying it on a suitable heat resistant surface (such as fire bricks) and heating it evenly with a blow torch until the polished areas turn a light yellow tinge. Do not overheat or the hard wearing properties will be lost. The gear has a chamfered inner edge which should go against the shoulder when put on the flywheel. When hot enough place the gear in position quickly, tapping it home, and let it cool naturally without quenching it.

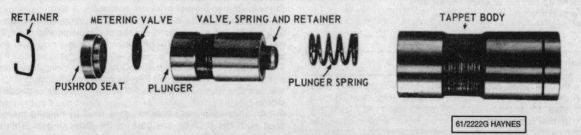

RETAINER   METERING VALVE   VALVE, SPRING AND RETAINER   TAPPET BODY

PUSHROD SEAT   PLUNGER   PLUNGER SPRING

61/2222G HAYNES

Fig. 2.1 Typical lash adjuster (valve lifter) components (Sec 32)

36 Cylinder head and piston crowns – carbon removal

1   When the cylinder head is removed, either in the course of an overhaul or for inspection of bores or valve condition when the engine is in the car, it is normal to remove all carbon deposits from the piston crowns and head.

2   This is best done with a cup shaped wire brush and an electric drill and is fairly straightforward when the engine is dismantled and the pistons removed. Sometimes hard spots of carbon are not easily removed except by a scraper. When cleaning the pistons with a scraper, take care not to damage the surface of the piston in any way.

3   When the engine is in the car, certain precautions must be taken when removing carbon from the piston crowns in order to prevent dislodged pieces of carbon from falling into the interior of the engine which could cause damage to cylinder bores, piston and rings – or if allowed into the water passages – damage to the water pump. Turn the engine so that the piston being worked on is at the top of its stroke and then mask off the adjacent cylinder bores and all surrounding water jacket orifices with paper and adhesive tape. Press grease into the gap all round the piston to keep carbon particles out and then scrape all carbon away by hand carefully. Do not use a power drill and wire brush when the engine is in the car as it will virtually be impossible to keep all the carbon dust clear of the engine. When completed, carefully clear out the grease around the rim of the piston with a matchstick or something similar – bringing any carbon particles with it. Repeat the process on the other piston crown. It is not recommended that a ring of carbon be left round the edge of the piston on the theory that it will aid oil consumption. This was valid in the earlier days of long stroke, low revving engines but modern engines, fuels and lubricants cause fewer carbon deposits anyway and any left behind tend merely to cause hot spots.

37 Valve guides – inspection

1   Examine the valve guides internally for wear. If the valves are a very loose fit in the guides and there is the slightest suspicion of lateral rocking using a new valve, then the guides will have to be reamed and oversize valves fitted. This is a job best left to the local Ford dealer, or machine shop.

38 Oil pan – inspection

1   Wash out the oil pan in solvent and wipe dry. Inspect the exterior for signs of damage or excessive rust. If evident, a new oil pan must be obtained. To ensure an oil tight joint scrape away all traces of the old gasket from the cylinder block mating face.

39 Engine reassembly – general

1   All components of the engine must be cleaned of oil, sludge and old gasket and the working area should also be cleared and clean. In addition to the normal range of good quality socket wrenches and general tools which are essential, the following must be available before reassembling begins:

1   *Complete set of new gaskets*
2   *Supply of clean lint-free cloths*
3   *Clean oil can full of clean engine oil*
4   *Torque wrench*
5   *All new spare parts as necessary*

40 Crankshaft – reinstallation

Ensure that the crankcase is thoroughly clean and that all oilways are clear. A thin twist drill or a piece of wire is useful for cleaning them out. If possible blow them out with compressed air. Treat the crankshaft in the same fashion, and then inject engine oil in the crankshaft oilways. Commence work of rebuilding the engine by refitting the crankshaft and main bearings.

1   Wipe the bearing shell locations in the crankcase with a lint-free cloth.

2   Wipe the crankshaft journals with a soft lint-free cloth.

3   If the old main bearing shells are to be replaced (not to do so is false economy unless they are virtually new) fit the five upper halves of the main bearing shells to their location in the crankcase.

4   Identify each main bearing cap and place in order. The number is cast into the cap and with intermediate caps an arrow indicates that the cap is fitted the correct way round.

5   Lubricate the new crankshaft rear oil seals in engine oil and fit one in the rear crankcase groove and the other in the rear main bearing cap groove making sure the oil seal tabs face towards the rear of the engine.

6   Wipe the cap bearing shell location with a soft lint-free rag.

7   Fit the main bearing lower shells onto each main bearing cap.

8   Apply a little grease to each side of the center bearing so as to retain the thrust washers.

9   Fit the upper halves of the thrust washers into their grooves on either side of the main bearing. The slots must face outwards.

10 Lubricate the crankshaft journals and the upper and lower main bearing shells with engine oil.

11 Carefully lower the crankshaft into the crankcase.

12 Lubricate the crankshaft main bearing journals again and then fit No.1 bearing cap. Fit the two securing bolts but do not tighten yet.

13 Apply a little non-setting gasket sealant to the crankshaft rear main bearing cap location.

14 Next fit No.5 cap. Fit the two securing bolts but as before do not tighten yet.

15 Apply a little grease to either side of the center main bearing cap so as to retain the thrust washers. Fit the thrust washers with the tag located in the groove and the slots facing outwards.

16 Fit the center main bearing cap and the two securing bolts. Then refit the intermediate main bearing caps. Make sure that the arrows always point towards the front of the engine.

17 Lightly tighten all main bearing cap securing bolts and then fully tighten in a progressive manner to the final torque wrench setting as specified.

18 Using a screwdriver, ease the crankshaft fully forward and with feeler gauges check the clearance between the crankshaft journal side and the thrust washers. The clearance must not exceed that given in the Specifications. Oversize thrust washers are available.

19 Test the crankshaft for freedom of rotation. Should it be stiff to turn or possess high spots, a most careful inspection must be made with a micrometer, preferably by a qualified mechanic, to get to the root of the trouble. It is very seldom that any trouble of this nature will be experienced when fitting the crankshaft.

41 Pistons and connecting rods – reassembly

1   As a press type piston pin is used (see Section 18) this operation must be carried out by the local Ford dealers. Do not forget that the notch in the piston crown must face towards the front of the engine.

42 Piston rings – installation

1   Check that the piston ring grooves and oilways are thoroughly clean and unblocked. Piston rings must always be fitted over the head of the piston and never from the bottom.

2   The easiest method to use when fitting rings is to wrap a 0.20 in (0.5 mm) feeler gauge round the top of the piston and place the rings one at a time, starting with the bottom oil control ring, over the feeler gauge.

3   The feeler gauge, complete with ring, can then be slid down the piston over the other piston ring grooves until the correct groove is reached. The piston ring is then slid gently off the feeler gauge into the groove.

4   An alternative method is to fit the rings by holding them slightly open with the thumbs and both of the index fingers. This method requires a steady hand and great care, as it is easy to open the ring too much and break it.

43 Pistons – installation

The pistons, complete with connecting rods, can be fitted to the cylinder bores in the following sequence:
1   With a wad of clean rag wipe the cylinder bores clean.
2   The pistons, complete with connecting rods, are fitted to their bores from the top of the block.
3   Locate the piston ring gaps as shown.

The oil control ring segment gaps are to be approximately 80° away from the expander gap and not in the area of the skirt.
The piston should be installed in the block so that the expander gap is towards the front and the segment gap is towards the rear.

4   Well lubricate the piston and rings with engine oil.
5   Fit a universal piston ring compressor and prepare to install the first piston into the bore. Make sure it is the correct piston connecting rod assembly for that particular bore, that the connecting rod is the correct way round and that the front of the piston is towards the front of the bore, ie, towards the front of the engine.
6   Again lubricate the piston skirt and insert into the bore up to the bottom of the piston ring compressor.
7   Gently but firmly tap the piston through the piston ring compressor and into the cylinder bore with a wooden, or plastic faced, hammer.

44 Connecting rods to crankshaft – installation

1   Wipe clean the connecting rod upper shell bearing location and the underside of the shell bearing, and fit the shell bearing in position with its locating tongue engaged with the corresponding cut-out in the rod.
2   If the old shell bearings are nearly new and are being refitted then ensure they are refitted in their correct locations on the correct rods.
3   Generously lubricate the crankpin journals with engine oil and turn the crankshaft so that the crankpin is in the most advantageous position for the connecting rods to be drawn onto it.
4   Wipe clean the connecting rod cap and back of the shell bearing, and fit the shell bearing in position ensuring that the locating tongue at the back of the bearing engages with the locating groove in the connecting rod cap.
5   Generously lubricate the shell bearing and fit the connecting rod cap to the connecting rod.
6   Reinstall the connecting rod nuts and pinch them tight.
7   Tighten the nuts with a torque wrench to the specified torque.
8   When all the connecting rods have been fitted, rotate the crankshaft to check that everything is free, and that there are no high spots causing binding. The bottom half of the engine is now near completion.

45 Oil pump and strainer – installation

1   Wipe the mating faces of the oil pump and underside of the cylinder block.
2   Insert the hexagonal driveshaft into the end of the oil pump.
3   Install the oil pump and refit the two special bolts. Using special tool '21-020' and a torque wrench tighten the two bolts to the specified torque.
4   Reinstall the one bolt and spring washer that secures the oil pump pick-up pipe support bracket to the crankcase.

46 Auxiliary shaft – installation

1   Lubricate the auxiliary shaft bearing surfaces with engine oil, then insert the shaft into the block. Tap it gently with a soft-faced hammer to ensure that it is fully home.
2   Fit the retaining plate and secure it with the two screws.

47 Auxiliary shaft and cylinder front covers – installation

Note: *If only one of the covers has been removed, the existing gasket may be cut away and a new gasket suitably cut.*
1   Lubricate a new auxiliary shaft seal with engine oil and fit it into the auxiliary shaft cover so that the seal lips are towards the cylinder block face.
2   Position a new gasket on the cylinder block endface; position the auxiliary shaft cover over the spigot of the shaft.
3   Fit the cover retaining bolts but do not tighten them until the cylinder front cover has been fitted or the gasket may distort.
4   Fit the cylinder front cover in a similar manner to that described for the auxiliary shaft cover.
5   Position the front cover over the crankshaft spigot and loosely fit the retaining bolts.
6   Using the crankshaft sprocket as a centralizing tool, tighten the front cover bolts to the specified torque.
7   Tighten the auxiliary shaft cover bolts to the specified torque.

48 Oil pan – installation

1   Wipe the mating faces of the underside of the crankcase and the oil pan.
2   Smear some non-setting gasket sealant on the underside of the crankcase.
3   Fit the oil pan gasket and end seals making sure that the bolt holes line up.
4   Install the oil pan to the gaskets taking care not to dislodge, and secure in position with the bolts.
5   Tighten the oil pan bolts in a clockwise direction starting at hole 'A', to a final torque wrench setting as specified, in the order shown in the accompanying figure.

49 Water pump – installation

Install the water pump to the cylinder block (if removed) referring to Chapter 3 as necessary.

50 Rear cover plate, flywheel and clutch – installation

1   Wipe the mating faces of the rear cover plate and cylinder block and carefully fit the rear cover plate to the two dowels.
2   Wipe the mating faces of the flywheel and crankshaft and install the flywheel to the crankshaft, aligning the previously made marks unless new parts have been fitted. A reinforcing plate is fitted to the flywheel on automatic models.
3   Fit the 6 crankshaft securing bolts and lightly tighten.
4   Lock the flywheel using a screwdriver engaged in the starter ring gear and tighten the securing bolts in a diagonal and progressive manner to a final torque wrench setting as specified.
5   Refit the clutch disc and pressure plate assembly to the flywheel making sure the disc is the right way round.
6   Secure the pressure plate assembly with the 6 retaining bolts and spring washers.
7   Center the clutch disc using an old input shaft or piece of wooden dowel, and fully tighten the retaining bolts.

51 Valves – installation

1   With the valves suitably ground in (see Section 32) and kept in their correct order, start with No.1 cylinder and insert the valve into its guide.
2   Lubricate the valve stem with engine oil and slide on a new oil seal. The spring must be uppermost.
3   Fit the valve spring and retainer.

2A

4   Using a universal valve spring compressor, compress the valve spring, until the keys can be slid into position. Note these keys have serrations which engage in slots in the valve stem. Release the valve spring compressor.
5   Repeat this procedure until all eight valves and valve springs are fitted.

52 Camshaft – installation

1   Lubricate liberally the camshaft journals and bearings with engine oil, then carefully install the shaft in the cylinder head.
2   Fit the retainer plate and screws at the rear end.
3   Lubricate a new camshaft seal with engine oil and carefully tap it into position at the front of the cylinder head.
4   Fit the belt guide and pin to the front end of the camshaft, and carefully tap on the sprocket.
5   Fit a new sprocket bolt and tighten it to the specified torque.

53 Hydraulic lash adjusters (valve lifters) and cam followers – installation

1   Smear the hydraulic lash adjusters with engine oil and then install each one into its respective position.
2   Smear the rubbing surface of the camshaft lobes and cam followers with engine oil.
3   Using special tool T74P-6565-B to compress each lash adjuster, position each cam follower on its respective valve end and adjuster, ensuring that the camshaft is rotated as necessary. Fit the retaining spring clips (where applicable). **Note**: *On some valves it may be found necessary to compress the valve spring slightly when fitting the cam followers.*

54 Cylinder head – installation

1   Wipe the mating surfaces of the cylinder head and cylinder block.
2   Carefully place a new gasket on the cylinder block, ensuring that it is the correct way up (each gasket is marked 'FRONT UP').
3   Rotate the camshaft so that the sprocket retaining pin is in the position shown, then position the head on the block. If the crankshaft needs to be rotated for any reason, ensure that the pistons are approximately halfway down the bores or they may contact the valves.
4   Fit and tighten the cylinder head bolts progressively to the specified torque, in the order shown.

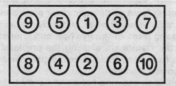

Fig. 2.2 Cylinder head bolt tightening sequence

55 Thermostat housing and thermostat – refitting

Refit the thermostat housing and thermostat to the cylinder head (if removed), referring to Chapter 3, if necessary.

56 Inner belt cover, auxiliary shaft sprocket and crankshaft sprocket – installation

1   Install the inner belt cover to the cylinder block (two bolts).
2   Ensure that the crankshaft sprocket key is in position, then carefully tap on the sprocket.
3   Ensure that the auxiliary shaft sprocket locking pin is in position, then carefully tap on the sprocket.
4   Fit the auxiliary shaft washer and bolt, and tighten to the specified torque.

57 Timing belt tensioner and timing belt – installation

1   Rotate the camshaft until the index mark on the sprocket aligns with the timing pointer on the belt inner cover.
2   Rotate the crankshaft until No.1 piston is at top-dead-center (TDC). This position can be checked either by rotating the crankshaft while carefully inserting a thin screwdriver through a spark plug hole, or by positioning the belt outer cover and pulley on the engine to align the pulley 'O' mark with the timing pointer.
3   Without disturbing the crankshaft and camshaft positions, install the belt tensioner but do not tighten the bolts yet.
4   Install the timing belt over the crankshaft sprocket, then counter-clockwise over the auxiliary shaft and camshaft sprockets, then behind the tensioner jockey wheel. If difficulty is experienced, use a lever to pull the tensioner jockey wheel away from the belt.
5   Rotate the crankshaft two full turns in a clockwise direction to remove all slack from the belt.
6   Ensure that the timing marks are correctly aligned, then tighten the adjuster/bolts to the specified torque.

58 Belt outer cover and crankshaft pulley – installation

1   Position the belt guide on the end of the crankshaft.
2   Install the belt outer cover, noting that spacers are used on two of the bolts.
3   Fit the crankshaft pulley, washer and retaining bolt. Tighten the bolt to the specified torque.

59 Valve lash – adjustment

1   With the engine rocker cover removed, rotate the crankshaft so that the base circle of the camshaft lobe of the first valve to be checked is facing the cam follower.
2   Using special tool T74P-6565-A, compress the valve lash adjuster fully and hold it in this position.
3   Using a suitable feeler gauge, check that the gap is as given in the Specifications for the hydraulic lash adjuster.
4   If outside the allowable limit, either the cam follower is worn, the valve spring assembled height is incorrect, the camshaft is worn, or the lash adjuster is unserviceable.

60 Rocker cover – installation

1   Clean the mating surfaces of the rocker cover and cylinder head, then lightly smear on a little non-setting gasket sealant.
2   Position a new gasket in the rocker cover, ensuring that the locating tabs are correctly positioned in the slots.
3   Fit the rocker cover. Fit and tighten the eight screws around the base to the specified torque.
4   Fit and tighten the two screws at the front end of the cover to the specified torque.

61 Engine – preparation for installation

1   Having completed the engine rebuilding, it is now necessary to refit the items which were taken off prior to the commencement of major dismantling. These will differ according to the extent of the work done and the original equipment fitted, but will typically be:

a)   *Oil pressure sender:* Coat threads with a non-setting gasket sealant and screw into the cylinder head.
b)   *Water temperature sender:* Coat threads with a non-setting gasket sealant and screw into cylinder block.
c)   *Fan:* Refer to Chapter 3, if necessary.
d)   *Exhaust manifold:* Ensure that the mating surfaces are clean then apply a light even film of graphite grease. Install the manifold and tighten the bolts in two steps to the specified torque in the order shown. Do not forget the lifting eye at No. 7 bolt.

e) *Spark plugs:* Fit new spark plugs of the type stated on the engine emission control decal.

f) *Intake manifold:* Ensure that the mating surfaces of the manifold and cylinder head are clean then install the manifold using a new gasket. Tighten the bolts in two steps to the specified torque in the order shown. Do not forget the lifting eye at No. 7 bolt.

g) *Manifold ancillaries:* Refit the manifold ancillaries. These will vary according to the particular vehicle, but will typically be as shown in the accompanying figures.

h) *Carburetor:* Install the carburetor, EGR valve and spacer assembly using new gaskets. The layout of the components is shown. Do not forget the choke hose; do not fit the air cleaner at this stage.

j) *Fan:* Refer to Chapter 3, if necessary.

k) *Distributor:* Align the index marks and refer to Chapter 5, to ensure that the ignition timing is correct.

l) *Oil filter:* If not already fitted, refer to Section 22.

m) *Fuel pump:* Refer to Chapter 4, if necessary.

n) *Alternator:* Reinstall loosely; do not fit the drivebelt.

p) *Thermactor pump, compressor, PVC system, oil level dipstick, miscellaneous emission control items and associated interconnecting hoses etc.*

62 Engine – installation (without transmission)

1   Raise the engine on the hoist and position it over the car engine compartment so that the rear end is sloping downward.

2   Lower the engine so that exhaust manifold lines up approximately with the exhaust muffler inlet pipe.

3   *Automatic transmission:* Start the converter pilot into the crankshaft.

4   *Manual transmission:* Start the transmission main drive gear (input shaft) into the clutch hub. If necessary rotate the engine slightly *clockwise* to align the splines.

5   Ensure that the engine is settled on its mounts, then detach the hoist chains.

6   From beneath the car install the flywheel housing or converter upper attaching bolts.

7   *Automatic transmission:* Attach the converter to the flywheel and tighten the nuts to the specified torque. Refer to Chapter 7 for further information, if necessary. Install the converter bolt access plug.

8   Fit the front engine mount nuts.

9   Connect the exhaust pipe to the manifold, using a new gasket (if applicable).

10 Reinstall the starter motor and electrical cables.

11 Remove the plugs from the fuel lines and reconnect them to the fuel pump. If not already done, reconnect the fuel line to the carburetor.

12 Position the power steering pump on its brackets and install the upper bolts.

13 Fit the engine shield.

14 From inside the engine compartment fit the power steering pump pulley.

15 Reconnect the engine ground lead.

16 Fit the alternator adjusting arm bolt and the electrical connector(s).

17 Connect the wire to the electrically assisted choke.

18 Connect the coil wire and vacuum hose to the distributor.

19 Connect the vacuum amplifier.

20 Connect the wire to the water temperature sender in the cylinder block.

21 Connect the idle solenoid wires.

22 Position the accelerator cable on the ball stud and install the ball stud on the clip. Snap the bracket clip into position on the bracket. Where applicable, install the kick-down cable.

23 Reinstall the line to the oil pressure sender.

24 Reinstall the brake vacuum unit hose.

25 Reconnect the engine heater and vacuum hoses.

26 Reinstall the drivebelts to the engine driven accessories. Refer to Chapter 3 for the correct tension.

27 Reinstall the radiator. Refer to Chapter 3 if necessary.

28 Reinstall the oil cooler lines (where applicable).

29 Reinstall the radiator hoses.

30 Where applicable, refit the fan shroud.

31 Refill the cooling system with the correct amount of water/antifreeze (or inhibitor) mixture. Refer to Chapter 3 as necessary.

32 Fill the crankcase with the specified amount and type of oil.

33 Reinstall the air cleaner and the vacuum hoses. Refer to Chapter 4 if necessary.

34 Connect the battery leads.

35 Have a last look round the engine compartment to ensure that no hoses or electrical connections have been left off.

63 Engine – installation (with manual transmission)

1   The procedure for reinstalling the engine and manual transmission is basically as described in the previous Section. However, the following differences should be noted:

a) Support the weight of the transmission with a hydraulic jack prior to fitting the rear mounting.

b) Do not forget to reconnect the speedometer cable and transmission electrical connections. Refer to Chapter 7 for further information, if necessary.

c) Check the clutch adjustment after the cable has been reconnected. Refer to Chapter 8 for further information.

d) When reconnecting the propeller shaft, ensure that the index marks are correctly aligned. Refer to Chapter 8 for further information if necessary.

64 Engine – initial start-up after overhaul or major repair

1   Make sure that the battery is fully charged and that all lubricants, coolant and fuel are replenished.

2   If the fuel system has been dismantled it will require several revolutions of the engine on the starter motor to pump the gasoline up to the carburetor.

3   As soon as the engine fires and runs, keep it going at a fast idle only (no faster) and bring it up to normal working temperature. When the thermostat opens the coolant level will fall and must therefore be topped-up again as necessary.

4   As the engine warms up there will be odd smells and some smoke from parts getting hot and burning off oil deposits. The signs to look for are leaks of water or oil, which will be obvious, if serious. Check also the exhaust pipe and manifold connections as these do not always find their exact gastight position until the warmth and vibration have acted on them and it is almost certain that they will need tightening further. This should be done, of course, with the engine stopped.

5   When normal running temperature has been reached, adjust the engine idle speed, as described in Chapter 4.

6   Stop the engine and wait a few minutes to see if any lubricant or coolant is dripping out when the engine is stationary.

7   After the engine has run for 20 minutes remove the engine rocker cover and recheck the tightness of the cylinder head bolts. Also check the tightness of the oil pan bolts. In both cases use a torque wrench.

8   Refit the hood to the previously drawn alignment marks and check that the hood fits correctly when shut.

9   Road test the car to check that the timing is correct and that the engine is giving the necessary smoothness and power. Do not race the engine; if new bearings and/or pistons have been fitted it should be treated as a new engine and run in at a reduced speed for the first 1000 miles (2000 km).

65 Turbocharger – overview

1   As will be noted in the Contents, the following Sections are not only devoted to those descriptions and tasks necessary to understanding the turbocharged engine, but also includes portions which cover the descriptions, testing, and replacement of all components unique to turbocharged models.

2   Although some small bits of information will be also found in the electrical components chapter (Chapter 10), all other references are contained here. Please note that some changes made are the result of ongoing updating and may not be found in earlier cars.

2A

66 Turbocharger – general information

Turbocharging offers a way of raising the horsepower and torque output of an engine without adding the power-robbing drives and gears of a supercharger. The turbocharger which is mounted on the 2.3L engine increases the horsepower output by approximately 35% and a 25% increase in torque. This is not a constant increase, as the turbocharger assembly works on a 'demand' basis, only. This means that additionally compressed gases are not fed into the engine except under load conditions (acceleration and climbing). The rest of the time, the engine is normally aspirated and operates on normal amounts of fuel. In this way, a net fuel saving is realized over the total operation of the car.

The turbocharger unit consists of two turbine wheels mounted to a common shaft and each wheel is enclosed by a shroud which directs air flow. One shroud connects to the exhaust manifold. This is the turbine unit. The other shroud is linked to the carburetor and the intake manifold and is known as the compressor. In practice, these units operate as follows:

Compression in the cylinder of the engine is not just a mechanical action. When the fuel/air mixture is burned it gains heat (superheats) and, therefore pressure. When this pressurized gas is routed through a small exhaust port and along a narrow exhaust pipe, it gains velocity. Directing this stream of gases into the turbine unit provides power to the turbine. The turbine housing is 'snail-shaped', keeping the gases tightly compressed as they enter the housing and allowing them to expand and cool as they leave. The change in heat and velocity provides power to the turbine wheel.

On the opposite end of the shaft, the compressor wheel is driven by the turbine. As the carburetor sits on top of the compressor, the air/fuel mixture is drawn out of the carburetor and compressed. The compressor housing is also 'snail-shaped' but in the opposite direction from that of the turbine housing. The air/fuel charge is drawn through a large orifice and gradually compressed, until a charge of compressed gases exits the compressor. This charge carries a much greater amount of fuel and air and packs it into the same size space (cylinder) as a normally-aspirated engine. With a greater initial charge, each cylinder produces more power.

As the superheated gases escape through the exhaust ports, the process is begun again. Turbine speeds can reach 120 000 rpm during normal operation of the engine. Since the speed of the engine also determines the speed of the turbine and the size of the charge, certain safety measures are provided to prevent damage to the engine and turbocharger.

A wastegate is installed to control turbine speed and pressure build-up. The wastegate is operated by an actuator, which is a canister containing a spring-loaded diaphragm. As the pressure in the compressor housing changes, the actuator diaphragm moves, opening and closing the wastegate by means of an actuating lever.

The opening of the wastegate allows exhaust gases to bypass the turbine, slowing turbine and compressor wheel speeds. This prevents two conditions which would occur without the wastegate. On acceleration, exhaust gases are driving the turbine at a speed higher than new compressed air/fuel is being demanded. The packing of pressurized gases slows the compressor blades such that if acceleration occurred at that moment, there would be a 'throttle lag' while the turbocharger worked back up to operating speeds. On acceleration, the closing of the wastegate directs all exhaust gases into the turbine housing, preventing lag and helping maintain turbine speed.

67 Turbocharger – cautions

1   The turbocharger is driven by superheated exhaust gases and routinely operates at extremely high temperatures. The turbocharger castings retain heat for a very long time and must not be touched for a period of at least three hours after the car engine was last run. Even at this time, it is advisable to wear heavy gloves to prevent the possibility of burns.
2   High speeds of rotation in the turbocharger unit mean that the bearing life and operation is dependent upon a constant flow of engine oil. Careful attention should be paid to the condition of the oil lines and the tightness of their fittings. Never overtighten the hollow bolts, as this will deform the unions and cause leakage.

3   Because the turbocharger is so dependent upon clean oil, drain the engine oil and change the oil filter any time the turbocharger is removed. If a bearing fails in the turbocharger or the engine, flush all engine and turbocharger oil passageways completely before re-assembling. When the engine of a turbocharged car is torn down for rebuilding, perform all of the standard passageway routines, as you would for a normally aspirated engine, then flush all oilways once again with fresh oil. When flushing is completed, drain the engine oil and fill once again with fresh oil and install a new oil filter.
4   A turbocharger is a ducted fan, and, like any turbine, its greatest enemy is dirt and foreign objects. A stray nut, metal chip, or rock passing through a turbine rotating at 120 000 rpm can cause untold damage. The best defense against foreign object damage is to work on your engine and turbocharger unit only after the engine has been cleaned. Cover all inlets and pipes. Account for each and every nut, screw, and washer before starting the engine after assembly is complete. Finally, never rush your engine work. Work only as fast as 100% accuracy permits.
5   Turbocharged engines are very simple to understand and most work is a straightforward operation. Observe the cautions above and you will add significantly to the operating life of your engine.

68 Turbocharger – system pressure integrity check

1   Remove the negative lead from the battery.
2   Remove the wastegate actuator pressure hose from the intake manifold and apply 7 psi (48 kPa) of compressed air to this hose. The wastegate actuating rod should move. If the actuating rod does move, move onto Section 5 and perform steps 2, 3, and 4, then reinstall the pressure hose. If the actuating rod does not move, continue with the steps below.
3   Carefully inspect all hoses and fittings for blockage or poor fit. Clean or replace parts as required.
4   Check the distributor diaphragm for leakage (Chapter 5).
5   Check the boost retard switch for leakage and operation (Section 71).
6   Check the boost light switch assembly for leakage and operation.
7   When all of the above tests have been done and satisfactory results received, move on to Section 69 and perform steps 2, 3 and 4. When these tests have been completed, perform steps 1 and 2 from Section 70.

69 Turbocharger wastegate actuator – testing

1   Make sure that the wastegate actuating rod is properly attached to its operating arm and that the clip is in place. If this is not the case, remove the wastegate actuator pressure hose from the intake manifold and apply 6 psi (41 kPa) to the hose. Hold this pressure and install the clip on the actuating rod. Reinstall the hose.
2   Remove the two hoses from the actuator unit.
3   Apply a vacuum of 25 in-Hg (84 kPa) to the vacuum-sided hose. Hold this vacuum for 60 seconds and note the drop in vacuum. If the vacuum drops to 18 in-Hg (61 kPa) or less, replace the actuator unit.
4   Apply a pressure of 5 psi (34 kPa) to the pressure-side hose. Hold this pressure for 60 seconds and note the drop in pressure. If pressure drops to 2 psi (14 kPa) or less, replace the actuator unit.
5   Install a dial indicator on the turbocharger so that the movement of the wastegate operating arm can be measured. Zero the dial indicator.
6   Apply pressure to the pressure-side hose slowly, until 0.015 of linear travel has been measured by the indicator. Read the pressure gauge on the outside pressure source. The pressure read should be 6.8 $\pm$ 0.5 psi (46.89 $\pm$ 3.45 kPa). If the pressure read is not within these specifications, or if the actuating arm does not move, replace the actuator unit.
7   Release all pressure and remove all measuring devices from the car. Install of components removed for these tests.

70 Turbocharger outlet elbow and wastegate assembly – testing

1   Make sure that the wastegate actuating rod is properly attached to its operating arm and that the clip is in place. If this is not the case, remove the wastegate actuator pressure hose from the intake manifold and apply 6 psi (41 kPa) to the hose. Hold this pressure and install the clip on the actuating rod. Reinstall the hose.

2   Remove the clip from the wastegate actuating rod and disconnect the rod from the arm. Check the operating arm for freedom of movement. It must rotate freely through at least 40° of travel without binding. If this is not the case, replace the outlet elbow and wastegate assembly.

3   Remove the turbocharger outlet pipe and check to see if the wastegate poppet valve is free to move on its pintle and that the valve is seating squarely in the bypass hole. If this is not the case, check to see if the sealing problem is caused by build-up around the sealing surface and clean as required. If this does not allow proper operation of the poppet, replace the outlet elbow and wastegate. Be sure not to leave any scrapings or other deposits in the turbocharger housing. Do not start the engin or reassemble the turbocharger assembly until you are sure of absolute cleanliness in the unit.

4   Reinstall the wastegate actuating arm as above.

71 Turbocharger boost pressure activated spark retard – testing

1   Make sure that the engine timing is set according to the directions in Chapter 5 before performing the remaining tasks in this Section.

2   If your engine is equipped with a spark sensing module, disconnect it from the pressure switch before continuing.

3   Remove the pressure supply line to the ignition timing pressure switch and plug the line. Install an adapter, part number T79P-6634-A or its equivalent, so that an external pressure source may be connected.

4   Remove the vacuum advance from the distributor and plug the line.

5   Install a hand-held tachometer to the engine according to the manufacturer's directions.

6   Have an assistant start the engine and accelerate to between 1300 and 1400 rpm.

7   Apply pressure at the adapter. If the engine speed does not retard in the manner described in the chart below, continue with the testing which is described below. If the engine performs as outlined, disconnect all test apparatus and reconnect all fittings.

Spark retard test	
Pressure (psi)	**RPM decrease**
0 to 0.49	none
0.5 to 1.0	greater than 75 rpm
1.0 to 3.74	no additional change
3.75 to 4.25	at least 100 rpm more
release pressure of 0	should return to 1300 to 1400 rpm

8   If the tests above do not give the specified results, substitute, but do not install a new pressure switch assembly and perform the test above. If the rpm decreases as specified, reconnect the original switch and test again. If decrease in rpm is noted, assume the first test was erroneous and reconnect all fittings. If the decrease in rpm does not occur, replace the original switch with the new one. If installation and testing of the new switch does not produce the decrease in rpm expected, continue with the steps below.

9   Substitute, but do not install a new dual mode ignition module (Chapter 5) and retest as above. If the rpm decreases as specified, reconnect the original module and verify its malfunction by retesting, then replace the module.

10   Remove all test equipment and reconnect all fittings.

72 Turbocharger – removal and installation

1   Disconnect the negative lead from the battery.

2   Remove the two nuts which hold the turbocharger heat shield to the turbine housing and remove the shield.

3   Raise the car on a garage hoist or place it on jack stands.

4   Remove the four bolts which attach the crossover pipes to the turbocharger. Remove the crossover pipe at that end.

5   Disconnect the exhaust pipe from the check valve located just above the catalytic converter.

6   Remove the bolts which attach the crossover pipe to the engine manifold. Loosen and lower the crossover pipe. Remove the exhaust pipe retaining bolts at the inlet of the rear catalytic converter.

7   Remove the rear turbocharger brace bolts and the brace.

8   Lower the car. Remove the air cleaner and duct assembly. Place a shop rag over the carburetor mouth to prevent dirt and parts falling in.

9   Disconnect the oil supply line from the turbocharger central housing as shown in the accompanying figure.

10   Disconnect the two hoses from the wastegate actuator diaphragm.

11   Remove the accelerator cable and its two mounting bolts from the intake manifold.

12   Disconnect the turbocharger vacuum line at the intake manifold.

13   In order to provide sufficient room for removal of the turbocharger unit, the bolt which attaches the oil dipstick tube to its mount must be removed as shown.

14   Loosen the flange nuts at both ends of the EGR tube and remove the tube.

15   Remove the three nuts and one bolt which attach the turbocharger to the inlet manifold as shown.

16   If any vacuum tubes remain attached, label and remove them from the turbocharger housing.

17   Lift the turbocharger out of the engine compartment.

18   Installation is the reverse of the removal procedure.

19   There are three O-rings which must be replaced prior to assembly. These are installed at the compressor inlet-to-manifold inlet join; compressor outlet-to-inlet manifold join, and the oil drain line adapter-to-the inlet manifold join as shown. Apply small amounts of multi-purpose grease to the compressor before installing the O-rings to aid assembly.

73 Turbocharger – checking axial play

1   This test must be performed just prior to, and immediately after, stripdown and assembly of the turbocharger.

2   Remove the turbocharger from the car (Section 72).

3   Remove the wastegate actuating rod retaining clip and disconnect the rod from the operating arm.

4   Remove the 4 exterior and one interior bolts from the wastegate and outlet elbow. Remove the wastegate elbow.

5   Attach a dial indicator to the turbine housing so that the plunger rests on the end of the turbine fan shaft as shown.

6   Using hand pressure only, move the turbine fan as far away from the dial indicator as possible and zero the indicator. Push the turbine wheel alternately toward and away from the dial indicator and record the clearance shown.

7   If the thrust bearing clearance indicated is less than 0.001 in or greater than 0.003 in, the turbocharger must be replaced.

8   When installing the outlet elbow, torque the bolts to 164 to 181 in-lb (19 to 20 Nm).

74 Turbocharger – checking radial play

1   This test must be performed just prior to, and immediately after, stripdown and assembly of the turbocharger.

2   Remove the turbocharger from the car (Section 72).

3   Remove the retaining clip from the wastegate actuating rod and disconnect the actuating rod.

4   Remove the four external and one internal bolts which attach the wastegate and outlet elbow to the turbine housing and remove the outlet elbow.

5   Attach a dial indicator to the central housing in such a manner that the indicator with an offset rod installed may pass through the oil outlet port and contact the shaft of the turbine. The extension carries part number T79L-4201-A and may be purchased through an authorized dealer, or a similar part may be fabricated. The accompanying figures show the shape of the extension and the preferred method of mounting the dial indicator.

6   Using hand pressure, push the ends of the compressor and turbine fans equally and simultaneously away from the dial indicator and zero the indicator dial.

2A

7   Apply pressure equally and simultaneously to the ends of the compressor and turbine fans in a direction toward the dial indicator and note the amount of travel indicated by the dial.

8   Apply pressure equally and simultaneously to the ends of the compressor and turbine fans in a direction away from the dial indicator and check that the indicator returns to Zero.

9   Perform the last two steps above as many times as necessary to obtain three readings which agree.

10 If the clearance noted is less than 0.003 in or greater than 0.006 in, replace the turbocharger.

11 When installing the outlet elbow, torque the bolts to 164 to 181 in-lb (19 to 20 Nm).

---

75 Turbocharger – stripdown, inspection, and reassembly

---

1   Remove the turbocharger from the car (Section 72).

2   Pull the retaining clip from the wastegate operating shaft and disconnect the shaft.

3   Scribe a line across the turbine housing, the central housing, and the compressor housing. This is necessary to ensure proper alignment of all components upon reassembly.

4   Remove the six bolts which hold the compressor housing to the central housing and separate the components.

5   Remove the O-ring from the central housing and dispose of it. Remove all other O-rings from the compressor housing and dispose of them as well.

6   Visually check the compressor wheel, backing plate, and the inner surfaces of the compressor housing for oil streaks. If any streaking is noted, replace the turbocharger.

7   Carefully examine the compressor wheel and blades for evidence of rubbing, foreign object damage, blade erosion, bent or cracked blades, or signs of wheel slippage on the shaft. If any of the above conditions exist, replace the turbocharger.

8   Install a new O-ring on the central housing. Coat all sealing surfaces with heat-resistant sealer. Install the compressor housing on the central housing, aligning the scribe marks, and install the six mounting bolts. Tighten the bolts in a cross pattern until the

compressor housing is pulled against the central housing. Do not apply the final torques to these bolts at this time.

9   Remove the six bolts which attach the turbine housing to the central housing and separate the two components. If there is evidence of a silicone sealer being used in assembly, clean the sealing surfaces.

10 Visually check the turbine wheel, backing plate, and the inner surfaces of the turbine housing for oil streaks. If any streaking is noted, replace the turbocharger.

11 Carefully examine the turbine wheel and blades for evidence of rubbing, foreign object damage, blade erosion, blade bending and cracking, burning of the blades, and evidence of excessive combustion by-product build-up. Combustion by-products are normally dirty white in color and excessive build-up occurs whenever the amount of by-product is enough to change the shape of the turbine blades. If any of the above conditions exists, replace the turbocharger.

12 If heat-resistant sealer was used on the sealing surface between the central housing and turbine housing, coat all sealing surfaces with new sealer. Align the scribe marks on the turbine housing and the central housing and install the bolts. Tighten the bolts in a cross pattern until snug.

13 Torque the turbine housing bolts to 164 to 181 in-lb (19 to 20 Nm) in a cross pattern.

14 Ensure that the wastegate actuator mounting bracket is properly installed in the joint between the compressor housing and the central housing. Torque the compressor housing bolts to 145 to 165 in-lb (16 to 19 Nm) in a cross pattern.

15 Install new O-rings on all flanges from which they were previously removed before installing the turbocharger.

16 Carefully re-examine all inlets and outlets of the turbocharger to be sure that no dirt, foreign objects, or other material has been introduced into the turbocharger assembly. If you are not positively sure that these assemblies are clean, strip them down and make sure.

17 Install the wastegate operating shaft by aligning the shaft with its bracket and applying 6 psi (41 kPa) air pressure to the pressurized side of the diaphragm. Hold that pressure and install the clip.

18 Perform a check for radial play (Section 74).

19 Perform a check for axial play (Section 73).

20 When the two checks above have been completed with satisfactory results, the turbocharger may be reinstalled in the car.

Chapter 2B   3.3L 6-cylinder engine

Contents

2B

Specifications

Engine, general

Displacement	3.3L (200 CID)
Number of cylinders	6
Bore and stroke	3.68 in x 3.13 in
Firing order	1 – 5 – 3 – 6 – 2 – 4
Oil pressure (hot at 2000 rpm)	30 to 50 psi

⑥ ⑤ ④ ③ ② ❶

Front ↓

36028-1-specs.b HAYNES

3.3L engine
Firing order 1-5-3-6-2-4
Cylinder location and distributor rotation

Drivebelt tension

All, except ¼ in
    new (A) .... 120 to 160 lb
    used .... 75 to 120 lb (B)
¼ in, only
    new (A) .... 50 to 80 lb
    used .... 40 to 60 lb (C)
Ribbed belt without tensioner
    new (A) .... 140 to 170 lb
    used .... 140 to 160 lb (D)
Ribbed belt with tensioner
    new (A) .... 105 to 155 lb
    used .... 105 to 155 lb (E)

    (A) tension measured after belt is installed and before it stretches or seats.
    (B) if less than 75 lb, adjust to 90 to 120 lb
    (C) if less than 40 lb, adjust to 40 to 60 lb
    (D) if less than 110 lb, adjust to 140 to 160 lb
    (E) if less than 105 lb, replace tensioner

Compression pressure .... To be within specifications, lowest cylinder (psi) must be within 75% of pressure (psi) of highest cylinder.

Cylinder head and valve train

Combustion chamber volume .... 57.25 to 60.25 cc

Valve guide bore diameter .... 0.3115 in to 0.3125 in

Valve seats
Width – Intake .... 0.060 in to 0.080 in
Width – Exhaust .... 0.070 in to 0.090 in
Angle .... 45°

Valve arrangement (front to rear) .... E-I-I-E-I-E-E-I-E-I-I-E

Valve stem-to-guide clearance
Intake .... 0.0008 in to 0.0025 in
Exhaust .... 0.0010 in to 0.0027 in
Service clearance limit .... 0.0055 in

Valve head diameter
Intake .... 1.739 in to 1.763 in
Exhaust .... 1.378 in to 1.402 in

Valve face runout limit .... 0.002 in max.

Valve face angle .... 44°

Valve stem diameter (std)
Intake .... 0.3100 in to 0.3107 in
Exhaust .... 0.3098 in to 0.3105 in
(0.015 in oversize)
    Intake .... 0.3250 in to 0.3257 in
    Exhaust .... 0.3248 in to 0.3255 in
(0.030 in oversize)
    Intake .... 0.3400 in to 0.3407 in
    Exhaust .... 0.3398 in to 0.3405 in

Valve springs
Compression pressure (lb at spec. length)
    Intake .... 51 to 57 at 1.59 in
    Exhaust .... 142 to 158 at 1.222 in
Free length (approximate) .... 1.79 in
Assembled height .... 1 9/16 to 1 39/64 in
Service limit .... 10% pressure loss at spec. length
Out-of-square limit .... 5/64 (0.078) in

Rocker arm
Shaft diameter .... 0.7797 in to 0.7807 in
Bore diameter .... 0.7830 in to 0.7845 in
Ratio .... 1.52 : 1

Pushrod runout .... 0.020 in

Gasket surface flatness .... 0.003 inch in any 6 inches; 0.006 in overall

Valve tappet
Diameter (std) .... 0.8740 in to 0.8745 in
Clearance to bore .... 0.0007 in to 0.0027 in
Service limit .... 0.005 in max.
Hydraulic leakdown rate .... 10 to 50 sec (time required for plunger to leak down 1/8 inch with
50 lb load and leakdown fluid in tappet)
Collapsed tappet gap — allowable .... 0.085 in to 0.209 in
Desired gap .... 0.110 in to 0.184 in

Camshaft

Lobe lift
Intake .... 0.245 in
Exhaust .... 0.245 in
Allowable lobe lift loss .... 0.005 in max.
Theoretical valve lift at zero lash
Intake .... 0.372 in
Exhaust .... 0.372 in

Endplay .... 0.001 in to 0.007 in
Service limit .... 0.009 in

Journal to bearing clearance .... 0.001 in to 0.003 in
Service limit .... 0.006 in

Journal diameter (all) .... 1.8095 in to 1.8105 in

Runout limit .... 0.005 in

Front bearing location .... 0.110 in to 0.130 in. Distance in inches that front edge of bearing is
installed below front face of block

Camshaft bearing inside diameter (all) .... 1.8115 in to 1.8125 in

Cylinder block

Head gasket surface flatness .... 0.003 in in any 6 inches; 0.006 in overall

Cylinder bore
Diameter .... 3.6800 in to 3.6848 in
Out-of-round limit .... 0.0015 in
Out-of-round service limit .... 0.005 in
Taper service limit .... 0.010 in

Tappet bore diameter .... 0.8752 in to 0.8767 in

Main bearing bore diameter .... 2.4012 in to 2.4020 in

Distributor shaft bearing bore diameter .... 0.5155 in to 0.5170 in

Crankshaft and flywheel

Main bearing journal diameter .... 2.2482 in to 2.2490 in
Out-of-round limit .... 0.0006 in max.
Taper limit .... 0.0006 in per inch
Journal runout limit .... 0.002 in max.
Runout service limit .... 0.005 in

Thrust bearing journal
Length .... 1.275 in to 1.277 in

Connecting rod journal
Diameter .... 2.1232 in to 2.1240 in
Out-of-round limit .... 0.0006 in max.
Taper limit .... 0.0006 in per inch

Main bearing thrust face
Runout limit .... 0.001 in max.

2B

Flywheel clutch face
Runout limit .... 0.010 in

Flywheel ring gear lateral runout
Standard transmission .... 0.030 in
Automatic transmission .... 0.060 in

Crankshaft free endplay .... 0.004 in to 0.008 in
Service limit .... 0.012 in

Connecting rod bearings
Clearance to crankshaft
    Desired .... 0.0008 in to 0.0015 in
    Allowable .... 0.0008 in to 0.0024 in
Bearing wall thickness – (std) .... 0.0569 in to 0.0574 in. 0.002 in undersize = add 0.001 in to standard thickness

Main bearings
Clearance to crankshaft
    Desired .... 0.0008 in to 0.0015 in
    Allowable .... 0.0008 in to 0.0024 in
Bearing wall thickness (std) .... 0.0757 in to 0.0760 in. 0.002 in undersize = add 0.001 in to standard thickness

Connecting rod, piston and rings

Connecting rod
Piston pin bore diameter .... 0.9104 in to 0.9112 in
Crankshaft bearing bore diameter .... 2.2390 in to 2.2398 in
    Out-of-round limit .... 0.0004 in max.
    Taper limit .... 0.0004 in max.
Length (center to center) .... 4.7135 in to 4.716 in
    Pin bore and crank bearing bore must be parallel
Alignment (bore-to-bore max. dif.)
    Twist .... 0.024 in
    Bend .... 0.012 in
Side clearance (assembled to crank)
    Standard .... 0.0035 in to 0.0105 in
    Service limit .... 0.014 in

Piston
Diameter
    Coded red .... 3.6784 in to 3.6790 in
    Coded blue .... 3.6796 in to 3.6802 in
    0.003 in oversize .... 3.6808 in to 3.6814 in
Piston-to-bore clearance .... 0.0013 in to 0.0021 in
Pin bore diameter .... 0.9124 in to 0.9127 in
Ring groove width
    Compression (top) .... 0.080 in to 0.081 in
    Compression (bottom) .... 0.080 in to 0.081 in
    Oil .... 0.188 in to 0.189 in

Piston pin
Length .... 3.010 in to 3.040 in
Diameter
    Standard .... 0.9119 in to 0.9124 in
    0.001 in oversize .... 0.9130 in to 0.9133 in
    0.002 in oversize .... 0.9140 in to 0.9143 in
Pin-to-piston clearance .... 0.0003 in to 0.0005 in
Pin-to-rod clearance .... Interference fit

Piston rings
Ring width
    Compression (top) .... 0.077 in to 0.078 in
    Compression (bottom) .... 0.077 in to 0.078 in
Side clearance
    Compression (top) .... 0.002 in to 0.004 in
    Compression (bottom) .... 0.002 in to 0.004 in
    Oil ring .... Snug fit
    Service limit .... 0.006 in
Ring gap
    Compression (top) .... 0.008 in to 0.016 in
    Compression (bottom) .... 0.008 in to 0.016 in
    Oil ring (steel rail) .... 0.015 in to 0.055 in

Lubricating system

Oil pump

Relief valve spring tension (lbs at spec. length)	0.90 to 10.01 at 1.078 in
Driveshaft-to-housing bearing clearance	0.0015 in to 0.0030 in
Relief valve to bore clearance	0.0015 in to 0.0030 in
Rotor assembly end clearance (assembled)	0.004 in max.
Outer race-to-housing clearance	0.001 in to 0.013 in

Oil capacity ....

4 quarts – add one quart with filter change

Fuel pump

Static pressure ....

5.0 to 7.0 psi. On engine at curb idle speed, brakes set, temperature normalized. With pump to tank fuel return line pinched off and a new fuel filter installed in fuel line

Minimum volume flow ....

1 pint in 20 seconds. On engine at curb idle speed, brakes set, temperature normalized. The inside diameter of the smallest passage in the test flow circuit must not be less than 0.220 in

Eccentric total lift ....

0.290 in to 0.310 in

Torque specifications

	ft-lb	Nm
Camshaft sprocket to camshaft	35 to 45	48 to 61
Camshaft thrust plate to block	12 to 18	16 to 24
Connecting rod nut	21 to 26	29 to 35
Cylinder front cover bolts	6 to 9	8 to 12
Cylinder head bolts – In sequence		
Step 1	50 to 55	68 to 75
Step 2	60 to 65	81 to 88
Damper or pulley to crankshaft	85 to 100	115 to 136
Fuel filter to carburetor	80 to 100 in-lbs	9 to 11
EGR valve to carburetor spacer or intake manifold	12 to 18	16 to 24
Fuel pump to cylinder block or front cover	12 to 18	16 to 24
Flywheel to crankshaft	75 to 85	102 to 115
Main bearing cap bolts	60 to 70	81 to 85
Manifold to cylinder head exhaust	18 to 24	24 to 33
Oil filter insert to cylinder block	10 to 15	14 to 20
Oil filter to block or adapter	$\frac{1}{2}$ turn after gasket contacts sealing surface – with oiled gasket	
Oil inlet tube to oil pump	10 to 15	14 to 20
Oil pan drain plug	15 to 25	20 to 34
Oil pan to cylinder block	7 to 9	9 to 12
Oil pump to cylinder block	10 to 15	14 to 20
Pulley to damper (bolt)	35 to 50	47 to 68
Rocker arm support shaft to cylinder head	30 to 35	41 to 47
Spark plug to cylinder head	10 to 15	13 to 20
Valve rocker arm cover	3 to 5	4 to 7
Alternator bracket to cylinder		
block (bolt)	35 to 50	47 to 68
Alternator adjusting arm to cylinder block	15 to 20	20 to 27
Alternator adjusting arm to alternator	24 to 34	33 to 46
Thermactor pump bracket to cylinder block	12 to 18	16 to 24
Thermactor pump pivot bolt	22 to 32	30 to 43
Thermactor pump adjusting arm to pump	24 to 34	33 to 46
Thermactor pump adjusting arm to cylinder block	12 to 18	16 to 24
Thermactor pump pulley to pump hub	130 to 180 in-lbs	15 to 20
Fan to water pump hub (bolt)	12 to 18	16 to 24
Carburetor mounting nuts	12 to 15	16 to 20
Carburetor mounting stud	15 max.	20 max.
Distributor clamp hold-down bolt	17 to 25	23 to 34
Vacuum fitting/plugs to intake manifold (with Teflon tape)	6 to 10	8 to 13

1 General information

The 3.3L, 6-cylinder engine is of in-line design, with overhead valves operated by hydraulic tappets and pushrods. Construction is of lightweight cast iron, which saves weight and improves gas mileage.

The camshaft is located at the right of the crankshaft and is driven by the crankshaft via a multi-link timing chain. The camshaft rides on four bearings, the inner race which is a machined part of the shaft and the outer race which is fitted into the engine block and is replaceable.

One well-known aspect of the 6-cylinder engine is the rigidity of the crankshaft. The crankshaft is held in place by seven main bearings, which means that the crankshaft is supported between every cylinder and cannot flex or 'whip' at speed. Each main bearing is fitted with replaceable bearing sections.

All rubbing and wear surfaces of the engine are lubricated by a pressurized oiling system. Oil is held in the oil pan where it is splashed on lower engine surfaces, as well as being pumped to the top of the engine (to the valve train), then forced downward through the other components of the engine until it arrives, once again in the oil pan.

Because various components rub against one another, a certain amount of wear will take place. The rate of component wear depends on the cleanliness of the oil and filter, and the replacement of all other filters at the specified intervals. Oversize components are available to prolong the operational life of the engine. These are oversize pistons, pushrods, valve guides, and undersized parts, such as connecting rod and main bearings.

2   Methods of engine removal

The engine may be lifted out either on its own or in unit with the transmission. On models which have an automatic transmission, it is recommended that the engine be lifted out separate from the transmission, unless a very substantial engine lift is available. Removing the engine and transmission as a unit means that they must be lifted out at a very steep angle. Be sure sufficient overhead clearance is available before you begin work.

3   Engine – rebuilding alternatives

1   The home mechanic is faced with a number of options for completing an engine overhaul. The decision to replace the cylinder block, piston/rod assemblies and crankshaft depends on a number of factors with the number one consideration being the condition of the cylinder block. Other considerations are: cost, competent machine shop facilities, parts availability, time available to complete the project and experience.

2   Some of the rebuilding alternatives are as follows:

Individual parts – If the inspection procedures prove that the engine block and most engine components are in reusable condition, this may be the most economical alternative. The block, crankshaft and piston/rod assemblies should all be inspected carefully. Even if the block shows little wear, the cylinder bores should receive new camshaft bearings and a finish hone; both jobs for a machine shop.

Master kit (crankshaft kit) – This rebuild package usually consists of a reground crankshaft and a matched set of pistons and connecting rods. The pistons will come already installed with new piston pins to the connecting rods. Piston rings and the necessary bearings may or may not be included in the kit. These kits are commonly available for standard cylinder bores, as well as for engine blocks which have been bored to a regular oversize.

Short block – A short block consists of a cylinder block with a crankshaft and piston/rod assemblies already installed. All new bearings are incorporated and all clearances will be within tolerances. Depending on where the short block is purchased, a guarantee may be included. The existing camshaft, valve mechanism, cylinder heads and ancillary parts can be bolted to this short block with little or no machine shop work necessary for the engine overhaul.

Long block – A long block consists of a short block plus oil pump, oil pan, cylinder heads, valve covers, camshaft and valve mechanism, camshaft gear, timing chain and crankcase front cover. All components are installed with new bearings, seals and gaskets incorporated throughout. The installation of manifolds and ancillary parts is all that is necessary. Some form of guarantee is usually included with purchase.

3   Give careful thought to which method is best for your situation and discuss the alternatives with local machine shop owners, parts dealers or dealership parts men.

4   Engine – work which may be performed without engine removal

1   Before setting about the task of removing the engine from the car, consider quite carefully the work which must be performed. A general rule of thumb in engine work is that the engine need not be removed if the component to be adjusted, repaired, or replaced is mounted ahead of the engine block casting or above the cylinder deck atop the engine block. In these instances, it is a simple matter of removing surrounding components, then removing or adjusting the component in question when sufficient work space has been obtained.

5   Engine – removal (without transmission)

1   Providing a good set of tools and lifting tackle is available, the home mechanic should be able to remove the engine without encountering any major problems. Make sure that a set of metric

sockets and wrenches is available in addition to a hydraulic jack and a pair of axle stands. An assistant will make the task easier.

2   First raise the car hood and disconnect the battery leads.

3   Mark the position of the hood hinges with a pencil. Undo the retaining bolts and remove the hood.

4   Remove the air cleaner and exhaust manifold shroud.

5   If air conditioning is fitted remove the compressor unit from the engine mounting bracket but **do not** disconnect the refrigerant hoses. Position the pump out of the way without straining the hoses. Note: *If it is necessary to remove the pump from the car the hoses should be disconnected by an air conditioning specialist.*

6   Remove the plug and drain the crankcase oil into a suitable container.

7   Remove the bottom radiator hose and drain the coolant.

8   Remove the top hose and transmission oil cooler hoses (if fitted) from the radiator, undo and remove the mounting bolts and remove the radiator.

9   Undo the four bolts and remove the fan.

10 Jack up the front of the car and support it on axle stands.

11 Where applicable, remove the engine shield.

12 Remove the starter motor. Further details will be found in Chapter 5, if required.

13 *On automatic transmission models:* remove the torque converter bolt access plug. Remove the three flywheel-to-converter bolts. Remove the converter housing cover and disconnect the converter from the flywheel.

14 *On manual transmission models:* remove the flywheel cover.

15 Remove the flywheel or converter housing cover, as applicable.

16 Detach the exhaust pipe from the exhaust manifold. Remove the packing washer.

17 Remove the nuts from the engine mountings, and remove the nuts and through bolts retaining the rear engine support crossmember.

18 Detach the fuel lines from the fuel pump, plugging the lines to prevent fuel spillage.

19 Where applicable, remove the power steering pump drivebelt and draw off the pulley. The drivebelt arrangement is shown in Chapter 3; refer to Chapter 3 for further information on the pump.

20 Remove the lower bolt securing the power steering pump to the bracket.

21 Lower the car to the ground.

22 Disconnect the heater and vacuum hoses from the engine. It is recommended that a sketch be made showing the various connections to avoid confusion when refitting.

23 Disconnect the power brake hose.

24 Remove the oil pressure union from the connection on the rear left-hand side of the cylinder head.

25 Detach the carburetor cable(s).

26 Disconnect the wire to the throttle solenoid and choke heater.

27 Detach the wire from the water temperature sender on the rear left-hand side of the cylinder block.

28 Disconnect the lines from the vacuum amplifier.

29 From the distributor, disconnect the coil wire and vacuum line.

30 Pull off the multi-plug from the alternator, followed by the ground wire.

31 Remove the bolt from the alternator adjusting arm.

32 Remove the remaining power steering pump-to-bracket bolts, and remove the pump (if fitted).

33 Support the weight of the transmission on a suitable jack, with a wood block interposed between the jack head and the transmission.

34 Attach the hoist hooks to the engine lifting bracket and lift the engine a little.

35 Draw the engine forward to disengage the transmission, ensuring that the transmission is still satisfactorily supported.

36 Lift the engine out, ensuring that no damage occurs to the hoses etc, in the engine compartment or to the engine mounting equipment. Transfer the engine to a suitable working area and detach the accessories. These will vary according to the engine, but would typically be:

Alternator
Thermactor pump
Air conditioning compressor
Clutch

37 Clean the outside of the engine using a water soluble solvent, then transfer it to where it is to be dismantled. On the assumption that engine overhaul is to be carried out, remove the fuel pump, oil filter

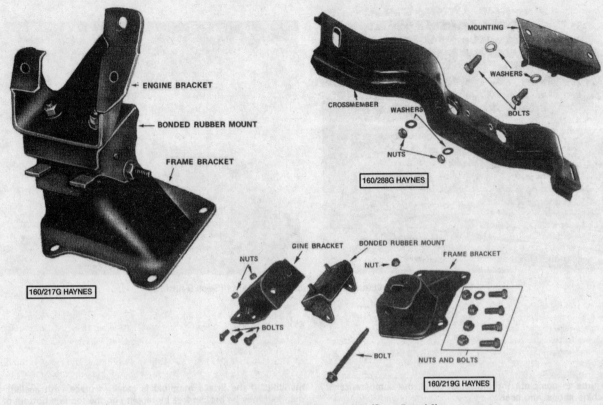

ENGINE BRACKET

BONDED RUBBER MOUNT

FRAME BRACKET

160/217G HAYNES

MOUNTING

WASHERS

BOLTS

CROSSMEMBER

WASHERS

NUTS

160/288G HAYNES

NUTS

GINE BRACKET

BONDED RUBBER MOUNT

NUT

FRAME BRACKET

BOLTS

BOLT

NUTS AND BOLTS

160/219G HAYNES

Fig. 2.2   Six cylinder engine mounts (Secs 5 and 6)

2B

(unscrew), spark plugs, distributor (index mark the distributor body and block to assist with installation), fan, water pump, thermostat, oil pressure and water temperature senders, emission control ancillaries, etc. Refer to the appropriate Sections in this and other Chapters for further information.

6   Engine – removal (with manual transmission)

1   The procedure for removing the engine and transmission together is basically similar to that described in the previous Section. However, the following differences should be noted:

    a)   *Disconnect the gearshift linkage from the transmission, referring to Chapter 7, as necessary.*

    b)   *Detach the driveshaft following the procedure given in Chapter 8.*

    c)   *Disconnect the clutch operating cable from the release arm.*

    d)   *Do not remove the clutch housing bolts. These items are removed after the assembly has been removed from the car. Further information on this will be found in Chapter 8.*

    e)   *Remove the speedometer drive cable, and the transmission electrical connections. If there is any possibility of their being mixed up, suitably label them or make a sketch showing their installed position.*

    f)   *Support the weight of the transmission in a similar manner to that described in the previous Section, paragraph 33, while the rear mounting is being detached.*

    g)   *It is a good idea to do the preliminary cleaning of the engine with the transmission still attached.*

7   Engine – dismantling (general)

1   It is best to mount the engine on a dismantling stand, but if this is not available, stand the engine on a strong bench at a comfortable working height. Failing this, it can be stripped down on the floor.

2   During the dismantling process, the greatest care should be taken to keep the exposed parts free from dirt. As an aid to achieving this, thoroughly clean down the outside of the engine, first removing all traces of oil and dirt.

3   A good grease solvent will make the job much easier, for, after the solvent has been applied and allowed to stand for a time, a vigorous jet of water will wash off the solvent and grease with it. If the dirt is thick and deeply embedded, work the solvent into it with a strong stiff brush.

4   Finally wipe down the exterior of the engine with a rag and only then, when it is quite clean, should the dismantling process begin. As the engine is stripped, clean each part in a bath of solvent. Clean oil passages with a small brush or, preferably, air pressure.

5   Re-use of old gaskets is false economy. To avoid the possibility of trouble after the engine has been reassembled always use new gaskets throughout.

6   Do not throw away the old gaskets, for sometimes it happens that an immediate replacement cannot be found and the old gasket is then very useful as a template. Hang up the gaskets as they are removed.

7   To strip the engine, it is best to work from the top down. When the stage is reached where the crankshaft must be removed, the engine can be turned on its side and all other work carried out with it in this position.

8   Wherever possible, install nuts, bolts and washers finger-tight from wherever they were removed; this helps to avoid loss and confusion. If they cannot be refitted then arrange them in a fashion to make it clear from whence they came.

9   Before dismantling begins it is important that a special tool is obtained for compressing the lash adjusters. This has the Ford number T74P-6585-A.

8   Cylinder head – rebuilding alternatives

1   Just as there are alternatives to engine repair (see Section 3), there are also alternative choices in the repair of the cylinder head of your car. The decision to repair or replace the cylinder head and its components depends, firstly, on the condition of the cylinder head. Other considerations are: your competence as a home mechanic, the

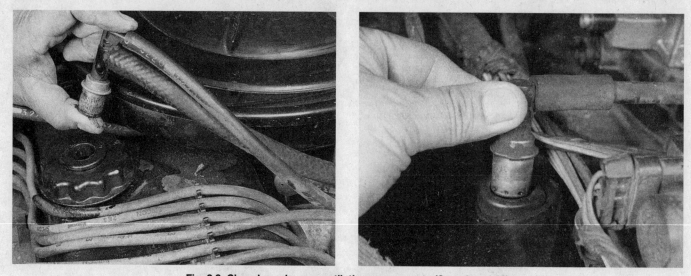

Fig. 2.3 Closed crankcase ventilation components (Secs 9 and 22)

available time to complete the project at hand, the competence of local machine shops, and cost.

2   Some of the rebuilding alternatives are as follows:

Individual parts – If the inspection and measurement procedures prove that the head and most of its components are sound and reuseable, this may be the most economical alternative. Always replace valve springs as a set. It is possible to replace individual valve guides, but due to the cost of this task, we recommend that you replace all valve guides at the same time for long-run economy.

Bare head – If your measurements and inspection prove the valve seats need grinding, the head may be exchanged for a remachined head. The bare head has been stripped, cleaned, valve seats have been recut, new valve guides inserted, and fresh paint applied where necessary. These heads are available on an exchange basis from auto parts stores. Although the valves have to be lapped in, the savings occurs in the time saved in not waiting for a machine shop to complete their work.

Complete head – Like the bare head the complete cylinder head is sold on an exchange basis by auto parts stores. The head is cleaned, stripped, valve seats are recut, new valves are lapped in and new springs and guides are fitted. These heads also also repainted wherever necessary and are ready for the addition of rocker arms, pushrods, and a valve cover to be complete.

Remanufactured heads carry the additional bonus of a guarantee, which is usually included at the time of purchase.

3   Give careful thought and consideration to your circumstances and abilities, then decide which method has the best solution for you. Discuss the alternatives with local shop operators, auto parts dealers, and parts men before you decide.

9   Cylinder head – removal (engine out of car)

1   Remove the carburetor from the intake manifold.

2   Remove the EGR spacer, gaskets, and any other attached items from the carburetor mounting flange on the intake manifold.

3   Remove all other emission control hoses, fittings, and wiring from the intake manifold. We recommend that you sketch the location of the various parts and connections before removing them.

4   Remove the intake manifold mounting bolts and remove the

manifold. If the intake manifold is stuck in place with sealant, the manifold may be broken free by tapping on the top and bottom of the manifold with a large rubber mallet. Never use a hard-faced striking tool for this task as damage to the intake manifold may result. Some models have an intake manifold which is part of the cylinder head casting.

5   Loosen the various drivebelts from the front of the engine and remove them. If they are cracked or worn, replace them when you reassemble the engine (Chapter 3).

6   Remove the Thermactor pump (Chapter 6) and the air conditioning pump, if installed. Remember, do not disconnect any portion of the air conditioning system while it is under pressure.

7   Unbolt the exhaust manifold and remove it. If any difficulty is encountered, rapping on the top and bottom of the manifold with a rubber mallet should help break the seal of any gasket sealer used during assembly.

8   Remove the thermostat housing and thermostat from the front of the cylinder head (Chapter 3).

9   Remove the water temperature sensor housing from the rear of the cylinder head (Chapter 3).

10   The rocker arm cover and cylinder head should now be completely clear of obstructing parts and stripped of all extra parts. If this is not the case, remove any other wires, sensors, fittings, or components which remain, noting their location for ease in assembly.

11   Remove the bolts from the rocker arm cover and remove the cover. If a gasket sealer has been used in previous assembly squeeze the cover tightly and pull upward. Do not insert any object between the rocker arm cover and the cylinder head as damage to the sealing surface may result.

12   Remove the rocker arm shaft support bolts by loosening each in turn, 2 turns until all have been removed. The rocker arm assembly may now be removed by lifting it from the cylinder head.

13   Remove the pushrods, one at a time, labeling each one as you proceed. The Specifications Section will give you the order of the pushrods and valves from front to rear. We recommend you mark each one with a loop of tape and indelible pen, as matching pushrods to their rocker arms is critical to efficient running of your engine.

14   Remove the cylinder head bolts by loosening each one in sequence. Loosen each bolt in turn, going on to the next number in the sequence. Continue until all bolts can be removed.

15 The cylinder head may now be removed. Do not insert any tools between the cylinder head and engine block as damage to the mating surfaces will result. Do not attempt to pry or lever the two components apart in any way. If breaking the seal between the cylinder head and engine block is difficult, rap on either side of the cylinder head with a rubber mallet and rock the cylinder head from side to side while pulling upward. There are locating pins on top of the engine block which will damage the seal surface if the cylinder head is set back down onto them without a proper match.

16 Remove the old gasket from the engine block or cylinder head after the head has been transferred to a workbench for further stripdown.

10 Cylinder head – removal (engine in car)

1 Removal of the cylinder head with the engine in the car is very similar to the procedure given in Section 9. The following additional points should be noted:

   a) *First remove the hood for improved access (Chapter 12).*
   b) *Disconnect the negative lead from the battery.*
   c) *Drain all engine coolant and remove all hoses which are connected to the cylinder head (Chapter 3).*
   d) *Remove the air cleaner, carburetor, and emission controls which are attached to the cylinder head, manifolds, and carburetor. See Chapter 4 for further information, and be sure to make a sketch of all connections before disconnection.*
   e) *Remove whichever drivebelts and accessories are in the way of the removal procedure. In most cases, you will need to remove the thermactor pump and air conditioning pump. If you must evacuate the air conditioning system, have this done by a qualified service specialist before you begin head removal.*
   f) *Detach the spark plug leads and any other connections which are in the way. You may wish to note the location of these components before removal.*

11 Cylinder head – disassembly

1 Before the valves can be removed, the carbon deposits should be removed from the combustion chambers and valve heads. This should be done with a wire brush and a scraper, being very careful not to scratch the head gasket surface.

2 Using a valve spring compressor, compress one of the valve springs and then remove the two-piece retainer at the top of the valve (photo).

3 Release the compressor and lift away the sleeve, spring retainer, spring, stem seal and finally the valve. Carefully identify each of these parts as to the cylinder they were removed from (photo).

4 Follow these same procedures for the remaining valve assemblies.

5 See Section 51 for valve installation procedures.

12 Cylinder front cover and timing chain – removal

1 Although the following steps are presented for performance with the engine removed from the car, the timing chain and front cover may be removed while the engine is installed. It will be necessary to drain and disconnect the cooling system, remove the cooling fan, drivebelts, ancillary driven components, and the crankshaft and water pump drive pulleys before the following steps can be accomplished.

2 If the engine is removed from the car and you have not yet disconnected the cooling fan, the water pump, and crankshaft pulleys, do so now.

3 Remove the cylinder front cover by removing all bolts on the cover at the engine block and oil pan. Carefully pry the cover away from the engine block at the top and insert a thin blade knife. Carefully cut the gasket flush with the engine block. Be sure not to nick or gouge the mating surface of the engine block.

4 Scrape any gasket material left from the above procedure from the engine block.

5 Before removing the timing chain and sprockets, the deflection of the chain must be checked. Turn the crankshaft in a counter-clockwise direction (as seen from the front) and take up the slack on the left side

11.2 Removing valve retainers with compressor tool

11.3 All valve components for each cylinder must be kept separate

12.6 Align the marks on the timing chain sprocket and crankshaft sprocket (arrows) before removal

of the chain. Establish a reference point to the left of the timing chain. Measure the distance from the reference point to the center of the left side of the chain. Turn the crankshaft in a clockwise direction (as seen from the front) and take up the slack on the right side of the timing chain. Press the slack chain on the left side toward the center with your thumb and measure the distance from your reference point to the center of the slack chain on the left side. Subtract the smaller figure from the larger and the difference will be the total deflection. If the deflection of the timing chain is greater than 0.250 in ($\frac{1}{4}$ in) the timing chain and sprockets must be replaced. If you are in doubt on condition at all, replace the timing chain and sprocket. Never replace just the chain or sprockets, replace all at once.

6   Rotate the crankshaft until the two timing marks on the sprockets align. Remove the camshaft sprocket attaching bolt and pull both sprockets evenly from the front of the engine (photo).

7   Clean the chain and sprockets in solvent if you have decided to reuse them. Inspect the teeth of the sprockets for chipping and wear and the chain for any wear pattern showing. If a wear pattern shows on the chain or the sprockets, we recommend that you replace the sprockets and chain.

13 Hydraulic tappets – removal

1   This task may be performed with the engine in or out of the car. Once the cylinder head is removed (Sections 9 and 10), it is a simple matter to perform the following tasks.

2   Using a cylindrical magnet, remove the tappets by inserting it into the tops of the pushrod tubes and contacting the top of the tappet. Work from the front of the engine to the back and keep the tappets in the order of their removal. It is important to match the valve train components for proper performance of the engine (photo).

3   If the tappets are held in place by sludge or gum, it will be necessary to remove the tappets with a plier- or claw-type tool. Your dealer sells one such tool under part number T70L-6500-A. Tool shops and auto parts stores should be able to supply a reasonable alternative.

4   Do not disassemble or mix up the tappets. Disassembly, cleaning, and testing instructions will be found in Section 32.

14 Camshaft – removal

1   Although the camshaft may be removed with the engine installed in the car, we recommend that you perform this task only with the engine removed.

2   Remove the cylinder head (Section 9).

3   Remove the cylinder front cover but not the timing chain (Section 12).

4   Remove the hydraulic tappets (Section 13).

5   Before removing the camshaft, it is necessary to check the camshaft end play. Install a dial indicator on the front of the engine block so the plunger of the indicator rests on the end of the camshaft. Push the camshaft as far to the rear of the engine block as it will go, then 'Zero' the indicator. Press the camshaft to the front of the engine block as far as it will go and record the measurement indicated. Perform this test at least three times to ensure accuracy of measurement. If the end play exceeds the service limit of 0.001 to 0.007 in, the thrust plate must be replaced upon assembly. If the end play measurement is approaching the outside limit, we recommend that you replace the thrust plate.

6   Remove the timing chain and sprockets (Section 12).

7   Remove the camshaft thrust plate.

8   Carefully pull the camshaft squarely out of the block. Be especially careful not to damage the camshaft lobes or bearing surfaces.

15 Flywheel and rear cover plate – removal

1   With the clutch removed, as described in Chapter 8, lock the flywheel using a screwdriver in mesh with the starter ring gear and undo the six bolts that secure the flywheel to the crankshaft in a diagonal and progressive manner. Lift away the bolts.

2   Mark the relative position of the flywheel and crankshaft and then lift away the flywheel.

13.2 Using a magnet to remove the valve tappets

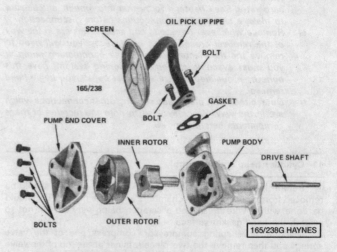

Fig. 2.4 Oil pump and strainer installation (Secs 16 and 4)

3   Undo the remaining engine rear cover plate securing bolts and ease the rear cover plate from the two dowels. Lift away the rear cover plate.

16 Oil pan, oil pump and strainer – removal

1   Undo and remove the bolts that secure the oil pan to the underside of the crankcase.

2   Lift away the oil pan and its gaskets.

3   Undo the two bolts that secure the oil pump to the underside of the crankcase.

4   Lift away the oil pump and strainer assembly.

5   Carefully lift away the oil pump drive making a special note of which way round it is fitted.

17 Pistons, connecting rods and connecting rod bearings – removal

1   Note that the pistons have a notch marked on the crown showing the forward facing side. Inspect the connecting rod bearing caps and connecting rods to make sure identification marks are visible. This is to ensure that the correct caps are fitted to the correct connecting rods and the connecting rods placed in their respective bores.

2 Undo the connecting rod nuts and place to one side in the order in which they were removed.

3 Remove the connecting rod caps, taking care to keep them in the right order and the correct way round. Also ensure that the shell bearings are kept with their correct connecting rods unless the rods are to be replaced.

4 If the connecting rod caps are difficult to remove, they may be gently tapped free with a rubber mallet.

5 To remove the shell bearings, press the bearing opposite the groove in both the connecting rod and its cap, and the bearing will slide out easily.

6 Withdraw the pistons and connecting rods upwards and ensure they are kept in the correct order for replacement in the same bore as they were originally installed.

18 Crankshaft and main bearings – removal

1 Make sure that identification marks are visible on the main bearing caps, so that they may be installed in their original positions and also the correct way round.

2 If the bearing caps are not already marked, mark them as they are removed to ensure correct installation.

3 Undo by one turn at a time the bolts which hold the seven bearing caps.

4 Lift away each main bearing cap and the bottom half of each bearing shell, taking care to keep the bearing shells in the right caps.

5 When removing the rear main bearing cap note that this also retains the crankshaft rear oil seal.

6 When removing the center main bearing cap, note the bottom semi-circular halves of the thrust washers, one half lying on each side of the cap. Lay them with the main bearing cap on the correct side.

7 As the center and rear bearing caps are accurately located by dowels, it may be necessary to gently tap the caps to release them.

8 Slightly rotate the crankshaft to free the upper halves of the bearing shells and thrust washers which can be extracted and placed over the correct bearing caps.

9 Remove the two halves of the rear crankcase oil seal.

10 Remove the crankshaft by lifting it away from the crankcase.

19 Thermostat and water pump – removal

1 If the cylinder head and block are being completely dismantled, the thermostat and housing, and water pump should be removed. Further information on these procedures will be found in Chapter 2.

20 Piston pin – removal

1 A press-type piston pin is used and it is important that no damage is caused during removal and installation. Because of this, should it be necessary to fit new pistons, take the parts along to the local Ford dealer or local repair shop who will have the special equipment to do this job.

21 Pistons rings – removal

1 To remove the piston rings, slide them carefully over the top of the piston, taking care not to scratch the aluminum alloy; never slide them off the bottom of the piston skirt. It is very easy to break the cast iron piston rings if they are pulled off roughly, so this operation should be done with extreme care. It is helpful to make use of an old 0.020 inch (0.5 mm) feeler gauge.

2 Lift one end of the piston ring to be removed out of its groove and insert under it the end of the feeler gauge.

3 Turn the feeler gauge slowly round the piston and, as the ring comes out of its groove, apply slight upward pressure so that it rests on the land above. It can be eased off the piston with the feeler gauge stopping it from slipping into an empty groove if it is any but the top piston ring that is being removed.

22 Lubrication and crankcase ventilation system – description

1 The pressed steel oil pan is attached to the underside of the crankcase and acts as a reservoir for the engine oil. The oil pump draws oil through a strainer located under the oil surface, passes it along a short passage and into the full-flow oil filter. The freshly filtered oil flows from the center of the filter element and enters the main gallery. Seven small drillings connect the main gallery to the seven main bearings. The connecting rod bearings are supplied with oil by the front and rear main bearings via skew oil bores. When the crankshaft is rotating, oil is thrown from the hole in each connecting rod bearing and splashes the thrust side of the piston.

2 The auxiliary shaft is lubricated directly from the main oil gallery. The distributor shaft is supplied with oil passing along a drilling inside the auxiliary shaft.

3 A further three drillings connect the main oil gallery to the overhead camshaft to provide lubrication for the camshaft bearings and cam followers. Oil then passes back to the oil pan via large drillings in the cylinder head and cylinder block.

4 A semi-enclosed engine ventilation system is used to control crankcase vapor. It is controlled by the amount of air drawn in by the engine when running and the throughput of the regulator valve.

5 The system is known as the PCV (Positive Crankcase Ventilation) system. The advantage of this system is that should the 'blow-by' exceed the capacity of the PCV valve, excess fumes are fed into the engine through the air cleaner. This is effected by the rise in crankcase pressure which creates a reverse flow in the air intake pipe.

6 Periodically pull the valve and hose from the rubber grommet of the oil separator and inspect the valve for free-movement. If it is sticky in action or is clogged with sludge, dismantle it and clean the component parts.

7 Occasionally check the security and condition of the system connecting hoses.

23 Oil pump – inspection

1 The oil pump cannot be dismantled or repaired in any way. If there is any obvious damage. or in the case of major engine overhaul, a replacement item mus e installed.

2 Detach the oil intake pipe and screen (2 screws and spring washers), and clean the parts thoroughly in gasoline.

3 Install the intake pipe and screen, using a new solvent.

24 Oil filter – removal and installation

1 The oil filter is a complete throw away cartridge screwed into the left-hand side of the cylinder block. Simply unscrew the old unit, clean the seating on the block and lubricate with engine oil. Screw the new one into position taking care not to cross the thread. Continue until the sealing ring just touches the block face, then tighten one half turn by hand only. Always run the engine and check for signs of leaks after installation.

25 Engine components – examination for wear

1 When the engine has been stripped down and all parts properly cleaned, decisions have to be made as to what needs replacing and the following Sections tell the mechanic what to look for. In any border-line case, it is always best to decide in favor of a new part. Even if a part may still be serviceable, its life will have been reduced by wear and the degree of trouble needed to replace it in the future must be taken into consideration. However, these things are relative and it depends on whether a 'quick' survival job is being done or whether the car as a whole is being regarded as having many thousands of miles of useful and economical life remaining.

26 Crankshaft – inspection and overhaul

1 Look at the main bearing journals and the crankpins, and if there are any scratches or score marks then the shaft will need regrinding. Such conditions will nearly always be accompanied by similar deterioration in the matching bearing shells.

2 Each bearing journal should also be round and can be checked

2B

26.2 Checking the crankshaft with a micrometer

28.2 Removing the lip from the top of the bore with a ridge reamer tool

28.3 Checking the cylinder bore for ovality

with a micrometer or caliper gauge around the periphery at several points. If there is more than 0.001 in of ovality regrinding is necessary (photo).

3   A good way to check for wear and taper of a crankshaft or connecting rod journal is by using Plastigage. Place a piece of Plastigage across the full width of the bearing surface, about $\frac{1}{4}$ in off center, install the bearing cap and tighten to specification. Remove the cap and measure the width of the Plastigage at its widest point to obtain the minimum clearance and the narrowest point for the maximum clearance using the supplied gauge. The difference between these two measurements equals the taper. Be sure to remove all traces of the Plastigage from the journal after measurement.

4   A dealer service department or machine shop will be able to decide to what extent regrinding is necessary and also supply the special undersize shell bearings to match whatever may need grinding off.

5   Before taking the crankshaft for regrinding check also the cylinder bores and pistons as it may be advantageous to have the whole engine done at the same time.

6   During any major engine repair, pry out the roller pilot bearing from the rear end of the crankshaft; this may require the use of a hook-ended tool to get behind the bearing. Fit the replacement bearing with the seal outwards (where applicable) so that it is just below the surface of the crankshaft flange. This procedure is described in Chapter 8.

27 Crankshaft, main and connecting rod bearings – inspection and overhaul

1   With careful servicing and regular oil and filter changes, bearings will last for a very long time but they can still fail for unforeseen reasons. With connecting rod bearings, the indication is a regular rhythmic loud knocking from the crankcase. The frequency depends on engine speed and is particularly noticeable when the engine is under load. This symptom is accompanied by a fall in oil pressure although this is not normally noticeable unless an oil pressure gauge is fitted. Main bearing failure is usually indicated by serious vibration, particularly at higher engine revolutions, accompanied by a more significant drop in oil pressure and a 'rumbling' noise.

2   Bearing shells in good condition have bearing surfaces with a smooth, even matte silver/grey color all over. Worn bearings will show patches of a different color when the bearing metal has worn away and exposed the underlay. Damaged bearings will be pitted or scored. It is always well worthwhile fitting new shells as their cost is relatively low. If the crankshaft is in good condition it is merely a question of obtaining another set of standard size. A reground crankshaft will need new bearing shells as a matter of course.

28 Cylinder bores – inspection and overhaul

1   A new cylinder bore is perfectly round and the walls parallel throughout its length. The action of the piston tends to wear the walls at right angles to the piston pin due to side thrust. This wear takes place principally on that section of the cylinder swept by the piston rings.

2   It is possible to get an indication of bore wear by removing the cylinder heads with the engine still in the car. With the piston down in the bore first signs of wear can be seen and felt just below the top of the bore where the top piston ring reaches and there will be a noticeable lip. The lip should be removed as part of cylinder bore renovation (photo). If there is no lip it is fairly reasonable to expect that bore wear is not severe and any lack of compression or excessive oil consumption is due to worn or broken piston rings or pistons.

3   If it is possible to obtain a bore measuring micrometer measure the bore in the thrust plane below the lip and again at the bottom of the cylinder in the same plane. If the difference is more than 0.003 inch (0.08 mm) then a rebore is necessary. Similarly, a difference of 0.003 inch (0.08 mm) or more across the bore diameter is a sign of ovality calling for rebore (photo).

4   Any bore which is significantly scratched or scored will need reboring. This symptom usually indicates that the piston or rings are damaged also. In the event of only one cylinder being in need of reboring, it will still be necessary for all six to be bored and fitted with new oversize pistons and rings. Your dealer or local machine shop will be able to rebore and obtain the necessary matched pistons. If the crankshaft is undergoing regrinding also, it is a good idea to let the

same firm renovate and reassemble the crankshaft and pistons to the block. A reputable firm normally gives a guarantee for such work. In cases where engines have been rebored already to their maximum, new cylinder liners are available which may be fitted. In such cases the same reboring processes have to be followed and the services of a specialist engineering firm are required.

29 Piston and piston rings – inspection and testing

1   Worn pistons and rings can usually be diagnosed when the symptoms of excessive oil consumption and lower compression occur and are sometimes, though not always, associated with worn cylinder bores. Compression testers that fit into the spark plug hole are available and these can indicate where low compression is occurring. Wear usually accelerates the more it is left so when the symptoms occur early action can possibly save the expense of a rebore.

2   Another symptom of piston wear is piston slap – a knocking noise from the crankcase not to be confused with the connecting rod bearing failure. It can be heard clearly at low engine speed when there is no load (idling for example) and is much less audible when the engine speed increases. Piston wear usually occurs in the skirt or lower end of the piston and is indicated by vertical streaks in the worn area which is always on the thrust side. It can also be seen where the skirt thickness is different.

3   Piston ring wear can be checked by first removing the rings from the piston as described in Section 20. Then place the rings in the cylinder bores from the top, pushing them down about $1\frac{1}{2}$ inches (38 mm) with the head of a piston (from which the rings have been removed), so that they rest square in the cylinder bore. Then measure the gap at the ends of the ring with a feeler gauge. If it exceeds that given in the Specifications, they need replacement (photo).

4   The grooves in which the rings locate in the piston can also become enlarged in use. The clearance between ring and piston, in the groove, should not exceed that given in the Specifications.

5   However, it is rare that a piston is only worn in the ring grooves and the need to replace them for this fault alone is hardly ever encountered. Wherever pistons are replaced the weight of the six piston/connecting rod assemblies should be kept within the limit variations of 8 gms to maintain engine balance.

30 Connecting rod and piston pins – inspection and overhaul

1   Piston pins are a shrink fit into the connecting rods. Neither of these would normally need replacement unless the pistons were being changed, in which case the new pistons would automatically be supplied with new piston pins.

2   Connecting rods are not subject to wear but in extreme circumstances such as engine seizure they could be distorted. Such conditions may be visually apparent but where doubt exists they should be changed. The bearing caps should also be examined for indications of filing down which may have been attempted in the mistaken idea that bearing slackness could be remedied in this way. If there are such signs then the connecting rods should be replaced.

31 Camshaft and camshaft bearings – inspection and overhaul

1   The camshaft bearings should be examined for signs of scoring and pitting. If they need replacement they will have to be dealt with professionally as, although it may be relatively easy to remove the old bearings, the correct fitting of new ones requires special tools. If they are not fitted evenly and square from the very start they can be distorted, thus causing localized wear in a very short time. See your Ford dealer or local engineering specialist for this work.

2   The camshaft itself may show signs of wear on the bearing journals or cam lobes. The main decision to make is what degree of wear justifies replacement, which is costly. Any signs of scoring or damage to the bearing journals cannot be removed by grinding. Replacement of the whole camshaft is the only solution. **Note:** *Where excessive cam lobe wear is evident, refer to the following Section.*

3   The cam lobes themselves may show signs of ridging or pitting on the high points. If ridging is light then it may be possible to smooth it

29.3 Measuring the piston ring end gap inside cylinder bore

32.1 Measuring the valve seat

out with fine emery. The cam lobes, however, are surface hardened and once this is penetrated, wear will be very rapid thereafter.

4   Ensure that the camshaft oilways are unobstructed.

5   To check the thrust plate for wear, position the camshaft into its location in the cylinder head and lift the thrust plate at the rear. Using a dial gauge, check the total shaft endfloat by tapping the camshaft carefully back-and-forth along its length. If the endplay is outside the specified limit, replace the thrust plate.

32 Valves and valve seats – inspection and overhaul

1   With the valves removed from the cylinder head examine the head for signs of cracking, burning away and pitting of the edge where it sits in the port. The valve seats in the cylinder head should also be examined for the same signs (photo). Usually it is the valve that deteriorates first but if a bad valve is not rectified the seat will suffer and this is more difficult to repair.

2   Provided there are no obvious signs of serious pitting the valve should be ground with its seat. This may be done by placing a smear of carborundum paste on the edge of the valve and, using a suction type valve holder, grinding the valve in place. This is done with a semi-rotary action, rotating the handle of the valve holder between the hands and lifting it occasionally to re-distribute the traces of paste. Use a coarse paste to start with. As soon as a matte grey unbroken line

2B

appears on both the valve and seat the valve is 'ground in'. All traces of carbon should also be cleaned from the head and neck of the valve stem. A wire brush mounted in a power drill is a quick and effective way of doing this.

3   If the valve requires replacement it should be ground into the seat in the same way as the old valve.

4   Another form of valve wear can occur on the stem where it runs in the guide in the cylinder head. This can be detected by trying to rock the valve from side to side. If there is any movement at all it is an indication that the valve stem or guide is worn. Check the stem first with a micrometer at points along and around its length and if they are not within the specified size new valves will probably solve the problem (photo). If the guides are worn, however, they will need

32.4 Measuring the valve stem for wear

reboring for oversize valves or for fitting guide inserts. The valve seats will also need recutting to ensure they are concentric with the stems. This work should be entrusted to your dealer or local auto-machine shop.

5   When valve seats are badly burned or pitted, requiring replacement, inserts may be fitted – or replaced if already fitted once before – again this is a specialist task to be carried out by a suitable rebuilding firm.

6   When all valve grinding is complete it is essential that every trace of grinding paste is removed from the valves and ports in the cylinder head. This should be done by thorough washing in parts solvent and blowing out with a jet of air. If particles of carborundum should work their way into the engine they would cause havoc with bearings or cylinder walls.

33 Hydraulic tappets – disassembly, inspection, assembly

1   All tappet assemblies are matched sets of parts. Do not mix parts or mix the order of the tappets. Keep the various components in their proper sequence for ease of reassembly.

2   Carefully clean the outside surfaces of the tappet. Inspect the surface for chips, scratching, or scoring.

3   Grasp the lock ring at the cup end with needle nose pliers and snap it from its groove. It may be necessary to fully depress the plunger so the lock ring may be removed.

4   Remove the pushrod cup, plunger valve disc, and spring from the tappet body and lay them out in their order of removal.

5   Invert the plunger assembly and locate the check valve retainer. Using a flat blade screwdriver, carefully pry the check valve retainer from the plunger.

6   Clean all tappet assembly components and remove all traces of engine oil. Dry the parts with a lint-free cloth or compressed air.

7   Check all parts for tight fit and make sure all moving parts are free of scoring, scratches, or chipping. If any of these conditions is noted, consult your local dealer or mechanic for further advice. Since any of

the conditions above suggests a number of possible engine problems, these people will be able to diagnose the problem most quickly.

8   Reassemble the tappets in the reverse of the reassembly instructions.

9   Tappets may be checked for leakdown rate if they are suspected of being defective. This test requires special equipment and is most economically performed by a dealer or shop.

34 Flywheel – inspection and overhaul

1   If the ring gear is badly worn or has missing teeth it should be replaced. The old ring can be removed from the flywheel by cutting a notch between two teeth with a hacksaw and then splitting it with a cold chisel.

2   To fit a new ring gear requires heating the ring to 400°F (204°C). This can be done by polishing four equally spaced sections of the gear, laying it on a suitable heat resistant surface (such as fire bricks) and heating it evenly with a blow torch until the polished areas turn a light yellow tinge. Do not overheat or the hard wearing properties will be lost. The gear has a chamfered inner edge which should go against the shoulder when put on the flywheel. When hot enough place the gear in position quickly, tapping it home, and let it cool naturally without quenching it.

35 Cylinder head and piston crowns – carbon removal

1   When the cylinder head is removed, either in the course of an overhaul or for inspection of bores or valve condition when the engine is in the car, it is normal to remove all carbon deposits from the piston crowns and head.

2   This is best done with a cup-shaped wire brush and an electric drill and is fairly straightforward when the engine is dismantled and the pistons removed. Sometimes hard spots of carbon are not easily removed except by a scraper. When cleaning the pistons with a scraper, take care not to damage the surface of the piston in any way.

3   When the engine is in the car, certain precautions must be taken when decarbonizing the pistons' crowns in order to prevent dislodged pieces of carbon falling into the interior of the engine which could cause damage to cylinder bores, piston and rings – or if allowed into the water passages – damage to the water pump. Turn the engine so that the piston being worked on is at the top of its stroke and then mask off the adjacent cylinder bores and all surrounding water jacket orifices with paper and adhesive tape. Press grease into the gap all round the piston to keep carbon particles out and then scrape all carbon away by hand carefully. Do not use a power drill and wire brush when the engine is in the car as it will virtually be impossible to keep all the carbon dust clear of the engine. When completed, carefully clear out the grease around the rim of the piston with a matchstick or something similar – bringing any carbon particles with it. Repeat the process on the other piston crown. It is not recommended that a ring of carbon is left around the edge of the piston on the theory that it will aid oil consumption. This was valid in the earlier days of long stroke low revving engines but modern engines, fuels and lubricants cause less carbon deposits anyway and any left behind tend merely to cause hot spots.

36 Valve guides – inspection

1   Examine the valve guides internally for wear. If the valves are a very loose fit in the guides and there is the slightest suspicion of lateral rocking using a new valve, then the guides will have to be reamed and oversize valves fitted. This is a job best left to the local Ford dealer, or machine shop.

37 Oil pan – inspection

1   Wash out the oil pan in solvent and wipe dry. Inspect the exterior for signs of damage or excessive rust. If evident, a new oil pan must be obtained. To ensure an oil tight joint scrape away all traces of the old gasket from the cylinder block mating face.

38 Engine reassembly (general)

1   All components of the engine must be cleaned of oil, sludge and old gasket and the working area should also be cleared and clean. In addition to the normal range of good quality socket wrenches and general tools which are essential, the following must be available before reassembling begins:

1   Complete set of new gaskets
2   Supply of clean lint-free cloths
3   Clean oil can full of clean engine oil
4   Torque wrench
5   All new spare parts as necessary

39 Crankshaft – installation

1   Ensure that the crankcase is thoroughly clean and that all oilways are clear. A thin twist drill or a piece of wire is useful for cleaning them out. If possible blow them out with compressed air.
2   Treat the crankshaft in the same fashion, and then inject engine oil in the crankshaft oilways.
3   Begin the work of rebuilding the engine by installing the crankshaft and main bearings.
4   Wipe the bearing shell locations in the crankcase with a lint-free cloth.
5   Wipe the crankshaft journals with a soft lint-free cloth.
6   If the old main bearing shells are to be reused (to do so is false economy unless they are virtually new) fit the seven upper halves of the main bearing shells to their location in the crankcase.
7   Identify each main bearing cap and place in order. The number is cast into the cap and with intermediate caps an arrow indicates that the cap is fitted the correct way round.
8   Lubricate the new crankshaft rear oil seals in engine oil and fit one in the rear crankcase groove and the other in the rear main bearing cap groove making sure the oil seal tabs face towards the rear of the engine.
9   Wipe the cap bearing shell location with a soft lint-free rag.
10 Fit the main bearing lower shells onto each main bearing cap.
11 Apply a little grease to each side of the center bearing so as to retain the thrust washers.
12 Fit the upper halves of the thrust washers into their grooves on either side of the main bearing. The slots must face outwards.
13 Lubricate the crankshaft journals and the upper and lower main bearing shells with engine oil or assembly lube (photo).
14 Carefully lower the crankshaft into the crankcase.
15 Lubricate the crankshaft main bearing journals again and then fit No. 1 bearing cap. Fit the two securing bolts but do not tighten yet.

16 Apply a little non-setting gasket sealant to the crankshaft rear main bearing cap location.
17 Next fit No. 7 cap. Fit the two securing bolts but as before do not tighten yet.
18 Apply a little grease to either side of the center main bearing cap so as to retain the thrust washers. Fit the thrust washers with the tag located in the groove and the slots facing outwards.
19 Fit the center main bearing cap and the two securing bolts. Then install the intermediate main bearing caps. Make sure that the arrows always point towards the front of the engine.
20 Lightly tighten all main bearing cap securing bolts and then fully tighten in a progressive manner to the final torque wrench setting as specified.
21 Using a screwdriver, ease the crankshaft fully forward and with a dial indicator or feeler gauges check the clearance between the crankshaft journal side and thrust washers. The clearance must not exceed that given in the Specifications. Oversize thgrust washers are available.
22 Test the crankshaft for freedom of rotation. Should it be stiff to turn or possess high spots, a most careful inspection must be made with a micrometer, preferably by a qualified mechanic, to get to the root of the trouble. It is very seldom that any trouble of this nature will be experienced when fitting the crankshaft.

40 Pistons and connecting rods – reassembly

1   As a press-type piston pin is used (see Section 19) this operation must be carried out by the local dealer. Do not forget that the notch in the piston crown must face toward the front of the engine.

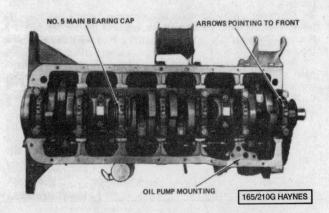

Fig. 2.5a Make sure the main bearing caps are installed in their correct positions, with the arrows pointing towards the front of the engine

Fig. 2.5b Checking crankshaft endplay with dial indicator

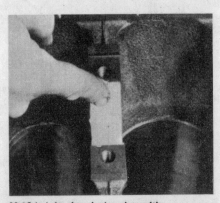

39.13 Lubricating the bearing with assembly lube

41.1A Cleaning the piston ring grooves with tool

41.1B Installing the piston rings with tool

41 Piston rings – installation

1   Check that the piston ring grooves and oilways are thoroughly clean and unblocked. Piston rings must always be fitted over the head of the piston and never from the bottom (photos).

2   The easiest method to use when fitting rings is to wrap a 0.20 in (0.5 mm) feeler gauge round the top of the piston and place the rings one at a time, starting with the bottom oil control ring, over the feeler gauge.

3   The feeler gauge, complete with ring, can then be slid down the piston over the other piston ring grooves until the correct groove is reached. The piston ring is then slid gently off the feeler gauge into the groove.

4   An alternative method is to fit the rings by holding them slightly open with the thumbs and both of the index fingers. This method requires a steady hand and great care, as it is easy to open the ring too much and break it.

42 Pistons – installation

1   The pistons, complete with connecting rods, can be fitted to the cylinder bores in the following sequence:

2   With a wad of clean rag wipe the cylinder bores clean.

3   The pistons, complete with connecting rods, are fitted to their bores from the top of the block.

4   Locate the piston ring gaps as shown in the accompanying figure. **Note**: *The oil control ring segment gaps are to be approximately 80° away from the expander gap and not in the area of the skirt. The piston should be installed in the block so that the expander gap is towards the front and the segment gap is towards the rear.*

5   Well lubricate the piston and rings with engine oil and push lengths of rubber hose over the rod bolts. This will protect the cylinder and crankshaft from damage (photo).

6   Fit a universal piston ring compressor and prepare to install the first piston into the bore. Make sure it is the correct piston connecting rod assembly for that particular bore, that the connecting rod is the correct way round and that the front of the piston is towards the front of the bore, ie, towards the front of the engine.

7   Again lubricate the piston skirt and insert into the bore up to the bottom of the piston ring compressor.

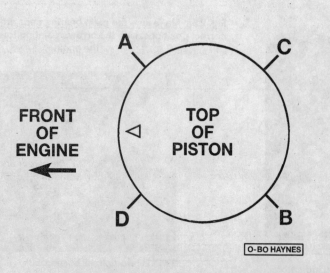

Fig. 2.6 **Piston ring gap spacing (Sec 42)**

A   *Oil ring side rail gap - lower*
B   *Oil ring side rail gap - upper*
C   *Top compression ring gap*
D   *Second compression ring gap and oil ring spacer gap*

O-BO HAYNES

42.8 Tapping the piston into the bore through the compressor

43.5 Drawing the connecting rod snugly up to the crankshaft

8   Gently but firmly tap the piston through the piston ring compressor and into the cylinder bore with a wooden, or plastic faced, hammer (photo).
9   Remove the hose pieces.

43 Connecting rods – installation

1   Wipe clean the connecting rod upper shell bearing location and the underside of the shell bearing, and fit the shell bearing in position with its locating tongue engaged with the corresponding cut-out in the rod.
2   If the old shell bearings are nearly new and are being refitted then ensure they are installed in their correct locations on the correct rods.
3   Generously lubricate the crankpin journals with engine oil and turn the crankshaft so that the crankpin is in the most advantageous position for the connecting rods to be drawn onto it.
4   Wipe clean the connecting rod cap and back of the shell bearing, and fit the shell bearing in position ensuring that the locating tongue at the back of the bearing engages with the locating groove in the connecting rod cap.
5   Generously lubricate the shell bearing and install the connecting rod cap to the connecting rod (photo).
6   Install the connecting rod nuts and tighten finger-tight.
7   Tighten the nuts with a torque wrench to the specified torque.
8   When all the connecting rods have been installed, rotate the crankshaft to check that everything is free, and that there are no high spots causing binding. The bottom half of the engine is now near completion.

44 Oil pump and strainer – installation

1   Wipe the mating faces of the oil pump and underside of the cylinder block.
2   Insert the hexagonal driveshaft into the end of the oil pump.
3   Install the oil pump and the two bolts. Tighten the two bolts to the specified torque.

45 Oil pan – installation

1   Wipe the mating faces of the underside of the crankcase and the oil pan.
2   Smear some non-setting gasket sealant on the underside of the crankcase.
3   Fit the oil pan gasket and end seals making sure that the bolt holes line up.
4   Install the oil pan taking care not to dislodge the gaskets and secure in position with the bolts.
5   Tighten the oil pan bolts in a progressive manner, to a final torque wrench setting as specified.

46 Camshaft – installation

1   Coat the bearing and cam lobe surfaces with thick coatings of multipurpose grease. Spread the grease evenly on all surfaces.

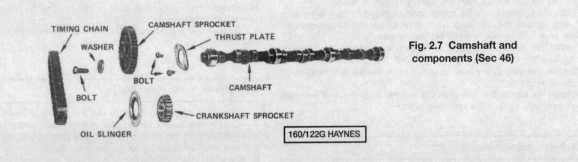

Fig. 2.7 Camshaft and components (Sec 46)

TIMING CHAIN
WASHER
CAMSHAFT SPROCKET
THRUST PLATE
BOLT
CAMSHAFT
BOLT
OIL SLINGER
CRANKSHAFT SPROCKET

160/122G HAYNES

2B

2   Carefully insert the camshaft into its hole. Do not allow the cam lobes or the bearing surfaces to contact the outer bearing races or the sides of the hole (photo).

3   When the camshaft contacts the rear bearing plug, install the thrust plate on the front and tighten the thrust plate bolts evenly. Torque the bolts to their specified torque (Specifications).

47 Cylinder front cover and timing chain – installation

1   Place the camshaft sprocket and the crankshaft sprocket in place and turn them until the timing marks on the sprockets face one another.

2   Remove the sprockets and place them inside the timing chain. Make sure the timing marks still face each other.

3   Slide the two sprockets, complete with the timing chain on the ends of the crankshaft and camshaft.

4   Install the camshaft sprocket bolt and torque to specification.

5   Before installing the cylinder front cover, check the condition of the oil seal which fits over the crankshaft. If the seal is dried or has shown signs of leaking, it must be replaced. Carefully pry the seal from its groove. Install the new seal with a seal pusher or a socket which has the same outside diameter as the seal.

6   Smear oil resistant sealer on a new front cover gasket and position the gasket on the front cover. Coat all exposed portions of the gasket with sealer. Cut and locate the sections of the gasket which fit the oil pan on the oil pan. Apply sealer to all exposed surfaces of the gasket.

7   Install the cylinder front cover. To prevent damage to the seal as it contacts with the Woodruff key on the crankshaft, place a thin wall socket over the crankshaft end. Make sure the outside diameter of the socket is less than or equal to the inside diameter of the seal.

8   Torque all mounting bolts to their specified torque.

48 Hydraulic tappets – installation

1   If your tappets were disassembled, but not tested, they must be filled with test fluid before installation. Tested and new tappets will already be filled.

2   Lubricate the outside surfaces of the tappets with engine oil.

3   Place a magnet on the cup end of the tappet and slide it into place in the appropriate pushrod tube. Remember to install each tappet in its proper hole.

49 Water pump – installation

1   Install the water pump to the cylinder block (if removed), referring to Chapter 2 as necessary.

50 Rear cover plate (flywheel) and clutch – installation

1   Wipe the mating faces of the rear cover plate and cylinder block and carefully fit the rear cover plate to the two dowels.

2   Wipe the mating faces of the flywheel and crankshaft and install the flywheel to the crankshaft, aligning the previously made marks unless new parts are being used. A reinforcing plate is fitted to the flywheel on automatic models.

3   Fit the six crankshaft securing bolts and lightly tighten.

4   Lock the flywheel using a screwdriver engaged in the starter ring gear and tighten the securing bolts in a diagonal and progressive manner to a final torque wrench setting as specified.

5   Install the clutch disc and pressure plate assembly to the flywheel making sure the disc is the right way round.

6   Secure the pressure plate assembly with the six retaining bolts and spring washers.

7   Center the clutch disc using an old input shaft or piece of wooden dowel, and fully tighten the retaining bolts.

51 Valves – installation

1   With the valves suitably ground in (see Secion 32) and kept in

46.2 When inserting the camshaft, be careful not to contact the sides of the bores with the lobes

51.4 Compressing the valve springs with a tool so that the valve retainers can be installed

their correct order, start with No. 1 cylinder and insert the valve into its guide.

2   Lubricate the valve stem with engine oil and slide on a new oil seal. The spring must be uppermost.

3   Fit the valve spring and retainer.

4   Using a universal valve spring compressor, compress the valve spring, until the keys can be slid into position. Note these keys have serrations which engage in slots in the valve stem. Release the valve spring compressor (photo).

5   Repeat this procedure until all twelve valves and valve springs are installed.

52 Cylinder head – installation

1   Wipe the mating surfaces of the engine block and cylinder head.

2   Coat a new cylinder head gasket with sealer and place it over the locating pegs on the engine block. The gasket is usually marked with a 'front' and 'up' marking for proper installation.

3   Carefully place the cylinder head over the locating pins and set into place.

52.4 Installing the pushrods. Note the assembly lube where the rod will contact the rocker

52.7A Pushrod properly seated in the rocker arm

52.7B Tightening the rocker arm shaft bolts

4   Install the twelve pushrods in their proper order (photo).
5   Install the cylinder head bolts and tighten them evenly in the order shown.
6   When all cylinder head bolts are snug, torque them in order to 50 to 55 ft-lb (68 to 75 Nm), then torque them once again to 60 to 65 ft-lb (81 to 88 Nm).
7   Install the rocker arm support shaft in its proper location and tighten the bolts two turns each from the innermost bolts outward until snug. Torque the bolts, from the inside outward, to 30 to 35 ft-lb (41 to 47 Nm) (photos).

53 Valves – adjusting

1   Turn the engine until the No. 1 cylinder is at TDC of the compression stroke. With the spark plug removed and your finger over the hole, you can feel the compression.
2   Using tool number 6513-K, or a similar tool, compress each rocker arm in the following order so the hydraulic lifter's plunger will bottom. Do not press too hard, or the pushrod may be bent. Compress the rocker arms in the following order while checking for clearance:

Cyl. No. 1 Intake
Cyl. No. 1 Exhaust
Cyl. No. 2 Intake
Cyl. No. 3 Exhaust
Cyl. No. 4 Intake
Cyl. No. 5 Exhaust

While you compress each hydraulic lifter in turn, insert a feeler gauge between the pad of the rocker arm and the top of the valve on that particular rocker arm. The allowable clearance is 0.085 to 0.209 in and the desired clearances are 0.110 to 0.184 in. If the clearance measured is greater or less than the amounts above, the pushrod must be replaced with a shorter or longer pushrod, whichever will bring the clearances back within specifications. To replace a pushrod, do not do so until you are sure the piston is hot at TDC.
3   When all the above clearances have been measured and corrected, turn the crankshaft until the No. 6 cylinder is at TDC of the compression stroke. Perform the same tests on the following rocker arms:

Cyl. No. 2 Exhaust
Cyl. No. 3 Intake
Cyl. No. 4 Exhaust
Cyl. No. 5 Intake
Cyl. No. 6 Intake
Cyl. No. 6 Exhaust

Make corrections as required in the manner outlined above.

54 Rocker arm cover – installation

1   Clean the mating surfaces of the cylinder head and the rocker arm cover.
2   Coat each of the gasket halves with a light coating of non-hardening gasket sealer and locate the gaskets in their proper spots.

← FRONT

⑭ ⑩ ⑥ ② ③ ⑦ ⑪

⑬ ⑨ ⑤ ① ④ ⑧ ⑫

24064-2b-10.21

Fig. 2.8 Cylinder head bolt tightening sequence (Sec 52)

① ④ ⑤ ⑥ ⑧ ⑪

② ③ ⑦ ⑨ ⑩

36028-2b-2.9 HAYNES

Fig. 2.9 Exhaust manifold bolt tightening sequence (Sec 55)

3   Set the rocker arm cover in place and install the bolts. Torque the bolts in a 'bow tie' pattern beginning at the middle and working outward. The specified torque is 3 to 5 ft-lb (4 to 7 Nm).

55 Engine – preparation for installation

1   Having completed the engine rebuilding, it is now necessary to install the items which were taken off prior to the commencement of major dismantling. These will differ according to the extent of the work done and the original equipment fitted, but will typically be:

a)   *Oil pressure sender:* Coat threads with a non-setting gasket sealant and screw into the cylinder head.
b)   *Water temperature sender:* Coat threads with a non-setting gasket sealant and screw into cylinder block.
c)   *Fan:* Refer to Chapter 3, if necessary.
d)   *Exhaust manifold:* Ensure that the mating surfaces are clean then apply a light even film of graphite grease. Install the manifold and then the bolts in two steps to the specified torque.
e)   *Spark plugs:* Fit new spark plugs of the type stated on the engine emission control decal.
f)   *Intake manifold:* Since the intake manifold is integral with the cylinder head, the carburetor must be kept covered to avoid the ingestion of debris during reinstallation.
g)   *Manifold ancillaries:* Install the manifold ancillaries. These will vary according to the particular vehicle.
h)   *Carburetor:* Install the carburetor, EGR valve and spacer assembly using new gaskets. Do not forget the choke hose; do not fit the air cleaner at this stage.
i)   *Distributor:* Align the index marks and refer to Chapter 5, to ensure that the ignition timing is correct.
j)   *Oil filter:* If not already installed, refer to Section 23.
k)   *Fuel pump:* Refer to Chapter 4, if necessary.

2B

l) *Alternator: Reinstall loosely; do not fit the drivebelt.*
m) *Thermactor pump, compressor, PVC system, oil level dipstick, miscellaneous emission control items and associated interconnecting hoses etc.*

56 Engine – installation (without transmission)

1 Raise the engine on the hoist and position it over the car engine compartment so that the rear end is sloping downward,
2 Lower the engine so that the exhaust manifold lines up approximately with the exhaust muffler inlet pipe.
3 *Automatic transmission:* Start the converter pilot into the crankshaft.
4 *Manual transmission:* Start the transmission main drive gear (input shaft) into the clutch hub. If necessary rotate the engine slightly *clockwise* to align the splines.
5 Ensure that the engine is settled on its mounts, then detach the hoist chains.
6 From beneath the car install the flywheel housing or converter upper attaching bolts.
7 *Automatic transmission:* Attach the converter to the flywheel and tighten the nuts to the specified torque. Refer to Chapter 7 for further information, if necessary. Install the converter bolt access plug.
8 Fit the front engine mount nuts.
9 Connect the exhaust pipe to the manifold, using a new gasket (if applicable).
10 Install the starter motor and electrical cables.
11 Remove the plugs from the fuel lines and reconnect them to the fuel pump. If not already done, reconnect the fuel line to the carburetor.
12 Position the power steering pump on its brackets and install the upper bolts.
13 Fit the engine shield.
14 From inside the engine compartment fit the power steering pump pulley.
15 Reconnect the engine ground lead.
16 Fit the alternator adjusting arm bolt and the electrical connector(s).
17 Connect the wire to the electrically assisted choke.
18 Connect the coil wire and vacuum hose to the distributor.
19 Connect the vacuum amplifier.
20 Connect the wire to the water temperature sender in the cylinder block.
21 Connect the idle solenoid wires.
22 Position the accelerator cable on the ball stud and install the ball stud on the clip. Snap the bracket clip into position on the bracket. Where applicable, install the kick-down cable.
23 Install the line to the oil pressure sender.
24 Install the brake vacuum unit hose.
25 Reconnect the engine heater and vacuum hoses.
26 Install the drivebelts to the engine-driven accessories. Refer to Chapter 3 for the correct tension.

27 Install the radiator. Refer to Chapter 3 if necessary.
28 Install the oil cooler lines (where applicable).
29 Install the radiator hoses.
30 Where applicable, install the fan shroud.
31 Refill the cooling system with the correct amount of water/antifreeze (or inhibitor) mixture. Refer to Chapter 3 as necessary.
32 Fill the crankcase with the specified amount and type of oil.
33 Install the air cleaner and the vacuum hoses. Refer to Chapter 4 if necessary.
34 Connect the battery leads.
35 Have a last look round the engine compartment to ensure that no hoses or electrical connections have been left off.

57 Engine – installation (with manual transmission)

1 The procedure for installing the engine and manual transmission is basically as described in the previous Section. However, the following differences should be noted:

a) *Support the weight of the transmission with a hydraulic jack prior to installing the rear mountings.*
b) *Do not forget to reconnect the speedometer cable and transmission electrical connections. Refer to Chapter 7 for further information, if necessary.*
c) *Check the clutch adjustment after the cable has been reconnected. Refer to Chapter 8 for further information.*
d) *When reconnecting the driveshaft, ensure that the index marks are correctly aligned. Refer to Chapter 8 for further information if necessary.*

58 Engine – initial start-up after overhaul or major repair

1 Make sure that the battery is fully charged and that all lubricants, coolant and fuel are replenished.
2 If the fuel system has been dismantled it will require several revolutions of the engine on the starter motor to pump the gas up to the carburetor.
3 As soon as the engine fires and runs, keep it going at a fast idle only (no faster) and bring it up to normal working temperature. When the thermostat opens the coolant level will fall and must therefore be topped-up again as necessary.
4 As the engine warms up there will be odd smells and some smoke from parts getting hot and burning off deposits. The signs to look for are leaks of water or oil, which will be obvious, if serious. Check also the exhaust pipe and manifold connections as these do not always find their exact gastight position until the warmth and vibration have acted on them and it is almost certain that they will need tightening further. This should be done, of course, with the engine stopped.
5 When normal running temperature has been reached, adjust the engine idle speed, as described in Chapter 4.
6 Stop the engine and wait a few minutes to see if any lubricant or coolant is dripping.

Chapter 2C 4.2L and 5.0L V8 engines

Refer to Chapter 13 for specifications and information on later models

Contents

Specifications

Engine, general

Engine type	90° V8 pushrod operated OHV
Compression ratio	
4.2L	8.8 : 1
5.0L	8.4 : 1
Displacement	4.2L (255 cu in) or 5.0L (302 cu in)
Bore and stroke	
4.2L	3.68 x 3.00 in
5.0L	4.0 x 3.00 in
Firing order	1-5-4-2-6-3-7-8

Cylinder head and valve train

Valve guide bore diameter	0.3433 to 0.3443 in
Valve seats	
Width – Intake	0.060 to 0.080 in
Width – Exhaust	0.060 to 0.080 in
Angle	45°
Runout limit	0.002 in
Valve arrangement (front to rear)	L.H. E-I-E-I-E-I-E-I
	R.H. I-E-I-E-I-E-I-E
Valve stem-to-guide clearance	
Intake	
4.2L	0.0010 in
5.0L	0.0027 in

4.2L and 5.0L engines
Firing order 1-5-4-2-6-3-7-8
Cylinder location and
distributor rotation

Exhaust
   4.2L .... 0.0015 in
   5.0L .... 0.0032 in
   Service clearance limit .... 0.0055 in
Valve head diameter
   4.2L .... 1.770 in
   5.0L .... 1.794 in
   Exhaust
      4.2L .... 1.439 in
      5.0L .... 1.463 in
Valve face runout limit .... 0.002 in
Valve face angle .... 44°
Valve stem diameter (standard)
   Intake .... 0.3416 to 0.3423 in
   Exhaust .... 0.3411 to 0.3418 in
Valve stem diameter (0.015 in oversize)
   Intake .... 0.3566 to 0.3568 in
   Exhaust .... 0.3561 to 0.3568 in
Valve stem diameter (0.030 in oversize)
   Intake .... 0.3716 to 0.3723 in
   Exhaust .... 0.3711 to 0.3718 in
Valve springs
   Free length (approximate)
      Intake .... 2.04 in
      Exhaust .... 1.85 in
   Assembled height
      Intake .... 1.6719 to 1.7031 in
      Exhaust .... 1.5781 to 1.6094 in
   Out-of-square limit .... 0.0781 in
Rocker arm ratio .... 1.58 : 1
Pushrod runout .... 0.015 in
Valve tappet, lifter or adjuster
   Diameter (standard) .... 0.8740 to 0.8745 in
   Clearance to bore .... 0.0007 to 0.0027 in
   Service limit .... 0.005 in
   Out-of-service limit .... $\frac{5}{64}$ in
Hydraulic tappet clearance (collapsed)
   Allowable
      4.2L .... 0.098 to 0.198 in
      5.0L .... 0.071 to 0.193 in
   Desirable
      4.2L .... 0.123 to 0.173 in
      5.0L .... 0.096 to 0.163 in
Camshaft end play .... 0.001 to 0.007 in
   Service limit .... 0.009 in
Journal to bearing clearance .... 0.001 to 0.003 in
   Service limit .... 0.006 in
Camshaft gear backlash .... 0.006 to 0.101 in
Journal diameter
   Number 1 .... 2.0805 to 2.0815 in
   Number 2 .... 2.0655 to 2.0665 in
   Number 3 .... 2.0505 to 2.0515 in
   Number 4 .... 2.0355 to 2.0365 in
   Number 5 .... 2.0205 to 2.0215 in
   Runout limit .... 0.005 max.
   Out-of-round limit .... 0.005 max.
Bearing inside diameter
   Number 1 .... 2.0825 to 2.0835 in
   Number 2 .... 2.0675 to 2.0685 in
   Number 3 .... 2.0525 to 2.0535 in
   Number 4 .... 2.0375 to 2.0385 in
   Number 5 .... 2.0225 to 2.0235 in
Front bearing location .... 0.005 to 0.020 in – Distance front edge of bearing is below front face of cylinder block

Cylinder block

Head gasket surface flatness .... 0.003 inches in any 6 inches – 0.006 in overall
Cylinder bore
   Diameter
      4.2L .... 3.6800 to 3.6835 in
      5.0L .... 4.004 to 4.0052 in
   Out-of-round limit .... 0.0015 in
   Out-of-round service limit .... 0.005 in
   Taper service limit .... 0.010 in
Tappet bore diameter .... 0.8752 to 0.8767 in
Main bearing bore diameter .... 2.4412 to 2.4420 in

Crankshaft and flywheel

Main bearing journal diameter	2.2490 to 2.2482 in
Out-of-round limit	0.0006 in max.
Taper limit	0.006 in max.
Journal runout limit	0.002 in
Runout service limit	0.005 in
Thrust bearing journal	
Length	1.137 to 1.139 in
Connecting rod journal	
Diameter	2.1328 to 2.1236 in
Out-of-round limit	0.0006 in
Taper limit	0.0006 per in max.
Main bearing thrust face	
Runout limit	0.001 in max.
Flywheel clutch face	
Runout limit	0.010 in
Flywheel ring-gear lateral runout limit	
Standard transmission	0.030 in
Automatic transmission	0.060 in
Crankshaft free endplay	0.004 to 0.008 in
Service limit	0.012 in max.
Crankshaft runout to rear face of block	0.005 in max.

Connecting rod bearings

Clearance to crankshaft	
Desired	0.0008 to 0.0015 in
Allowable	
4.2L	0.0008 to 0.0024 in
5.0L	0.0007 to 0.0025 in
Bearing wall thickness (standard)	0.0572 to 0.0577 in (for 0.002 in under size, add 0.001 in to standard thickness)

Main bearings

Clearance to crankshaft	
Desired	Number 1, 0.0001 to 0.0015 in – Others, 0.0004 – 0.0015 in
Allowable	Number 1, 0.0001 to 0.0017 in – Others, 0.0004 – 0.0021 in

Connecting rod

Piston pin bore diameter	0.9096 to 0.9127 in
Crankshaft bearing bore diameter	2.2390 to 2.2398 in
Out-of-round limit	0.0004 in max.
Taper limit	0.0004 in max.
Length (center to center)	5.0885 to 5.0915 in
Alignment (bore to bore maximum difference)	
Twist	0.024 in
Bend	0.012 in
Side clearance (assembled to crankshaft)	
Standard	0.010 to 0.020 in
Service limit	0.023 in

Piston

Diameter	
Coded red	
4.2L	3.6784 to 3.6790 in
5.0L	3.9978 to 3.9984 in
Coded blue	
4.2L	3.6798 to 3.6804 in
5.0L	3.9990 to 3.9996 in
0.0003 in oversize	
4.2L	3.6812 to 3.6818 in
5.0L	4.0002 to 4.0008 in
Piston-to-bore clearance	0.0018 to 0.0026 in
Pin bore diameter	0.9127 to 0.9127 in
Ring groove width	
Compression (top)	0.080 to 0.081 in
Compression (bottom)	0.080 to 0.081 in
Oil	0.199 to 0.189 in

Piston pin

Length	3.010 to 3.040 in
Diameter	
Standard	0.9119 to 0.9124 in
0.001 in oversize	0.9130 to 0.9124 in
0.002 in oversize	0.9140 to 0.9143 in
Piston-to-pin clearance	0.0002 to 0.0004 in
Pin-to-rod clearance	Interference fit

2C

Piston rings

Ring width	
Compression (top)	0.077 to 0.078 in
Compression (bottom)	0.077 to 0.078 in
Oil ring	Snug fit
Service limit	0.006 in max
Ring gap	
Compression (top)	0.010 to 0.020 in
Compression (bottom)	0.010 to 0.020 in
Oil ring (steel rail)	0.015 to 0.055 in

Lubrication system

Oil pump	
Relief valve spring tension (lbs at specified length)	10.6 to 12.2 @ 1.704 in
Drive shaft-to-housing bearing clearance	0.0015 to 0.0030 in
Relief valve-to-bore clearance	0.0015 to 0.0030 in
Rotor assembly end clearance (assembled)	0.004 in max
Outer race-to-housing clearance	0.001 to 0.013
Oil capacity (U.S. qts)	4

Torque specifications

	Ft-lb	N-m
Alternator adjustment arm-to-alternator bolt	24 to 40	32 to 54
Alternator adjustment arm-to-engine block	12 to 18	16 to 24
Alternator bracket-to-engine block	12 to 18	16 to 24
Camshaft sprocket-to-camshaft bolt	40 to 45	54 to 61
Camshaft thrust plate-to-engine block bolts	9 to 12	12 to 16
Carburetor mounting nuts	12 to 15	16 to 20
Connecting rod nuts	19 to 24	26 to 32
Cylinder head bolts		
Step 1	55 to 65	75 to 88
Step 2	65 to 72	88 to 97
Damper-to-crankshaft bolt	70 to 90	95 to 122
Distributor hold-down bolt	18 to 26	24 to 35
EGR valve-to-carburetor spacer	12 to 18	16 to 24
Engine block front cover bolts	12 to 18	16 to 24
Exhaust manifold-to-cylinder head	18 to 24	24 to 32
Fan-to-water pump hub	12 to 18	16 to 24
Flywheel-to-crankshaft bolts	75 to 85	102 to 115
Fuel pump-to-engine block	19 to 27	26 to 37
Intake manifold-to-cylinder head	20 to 22	28 to 30
Main bearing cap bolts	60 to 70	81 to 95
Oil inlet tube-to-main bearing cap nut	22 to 32	32 to 43
Oil inlet tube-to-oil pump bolt	10 to 15	14 to 20
Oil pan drain plug	15 to 25	20 to 34
Oil pan-to-engine block bolts	9 to 11	12 to 15
Oil pump-to-engine block bolts	22 to 32	30 to 43
Pulley-to-damper bolts	35 to 50	47 to 68
Rocker arm stud bolts	18 to 25	24 to 34
Spark plugs	10 to 15	14 to 22
Thermactor pump adjustment arm-to-pump	22 to 32	30 to 43
Thermactor pump bracket-to-engine block	30 to 45	41 to 61
Thermactor pump pivot bolt	22 to 32	30 to 43
Thermactor pump pulley-to-hub bolts	13 to 18	15 to 20
Valve cover bolts	3 to 5	4 to 7
Water outlet housing bolts	9 to 12	12 to 16
Water pump-to-front cover bolts	12 to 18	16 to 24

All fasteners not listed use the following torque wrench setting:

Metric thread sizes

M-6	6 to 9	9 to 12
M-8	14 to 21	19 to 28
M-10	28 to 40	38 to 54
M-12	50 to 71	68 to 96
M-14	80 to 140	109 to 154

Pipe thread sizes		
1/8	5 to 8	7 to 10
1/4	12 to 18	17 to 24
3/8	22 to 33	30 to 44
1/2	25 to 35	34 to 47

U.S. thread sizes		
1/4 by 20	6 to 9	8 to 12
5/16 by 18	12 to 18	17 to 24
5/16 by 24	14 to 20	19 to 27
3/8 by 16	22 to 32	30 to 43
3/8 by 24	27 to 38	37 to 52
7/16 by 14	40 to 55	55 to 75
7/16 by 20	40 to 60	55 to 81
1/2 by 13	55 to 80	75 to 108

1 General information

The V8 engines covered in this Chapter are of 5.0 liter (302 CID) (1979 models) and 4.2 liter (255 CID) (1980 models) displacement. Both engines are very similar in design, varying mainly in some detail and dimensions (see Specifications).

The cylinder bores are machined directly into the cast cylinder block which is integral with the crankcase. The one-piece crankshaft is supported within the crankcase on five replaceable shell-type bearings.

The valve gear is actuated by a five bearing camshaft located in the 'V' section of the two cylinder banks, and is chain driven from a sprocket on the front of the crankshaft. A gear on the front of the camshaft drives the distributor which in turn drives the oil pump via an intermediate shaft.

The intake manifold is bolted between the cylinder heads and has internal water passages and exhaust gas crossover to help in vaporizing the fuel. The fuel is fed into each bank through two separate passages.

All engines have hydraulically-operated valve lifters which are quiet in operation and do not require frequent adjustment.

All models use a replaceable spin-on oil filter. Some models use a dual sump oil pan with two drain plugs and both plugs must be removed when draining the pan to avoid an incorrect oil level reading after filling.

A positive type crankcase ventilation (PCV) system is used to direct crankcase fumes back into the engine via the intake manifold. Various additional emissions systems are used depending on model and year to meet emissions laws (refer to Chap. 6).

2 Engine removal – general

1 The engine can be lifted out by itself or with the transmission attached. If the engine and transmission are removed as a unit they have to be lifted out at an extreme angle so make sure that there is sufficient vertical clearance and lifting capacity available.

2 You will need a good lifting hoist, a set of tools, a hydraulic jack and pair of jack stands to do the job. Also, the help of an assistant will make the operation easier, faster and safer.

3 It is a good idea to plan ahead and have the proper containers for catching fluids and for the orderly collection of parts as they are removed.

3 Engine removal – without transmission

1 Scribe around the hood hinges with a pencil to mark their position for ease of re-installation and remove the hood.

2 Drain the cooling system and crankcase into suitable containers.

3 Place fender protectors or old blankets over the fenders and cowl.

4 Disconnect the battery and alternator ground cables from the engine block. Remove the ground strap from the block and position it out of the way.

5 Referring to Chapter 3, remove the air cleaner and duct assembly.

6 Disconnect the upper and lower radiator hoses and remove them. On automatic transmission-equipped vehicles, disconnect the transmission oil cooler lines from the radiator.

7 Remove the radiator, fan, spacer, pulley and shroud.

8 Disconnect all of the Thermactor belts, hoses and lines and unbolt and remove the Thermactor.

9 Unplug the connector at the rear of the alternator, unbolt and remove the alternator.

10 Disconnect the oil pressure sending unit wire and the flexible fuel line, making sure to plug the line.

11 Remove the power steering drive belt, unbolt the power steering pump and position it out of the way so that the fluid will not drain out.

12 Disconnect the accelerator cable from the carburetor. Remove the speed control cable, if equipped.

13 Disconnect the throttle valve vacuum line at the intake manifold and unbolt the automatic transmission filler tube from the cylinder block.

14 If the vehicle is equipped with air conditioning, unbolt the compressor and secure it out of the way. **Note** *Do not attempt to remove any of the hoses as the system is pressurized.*

15 Disconnect the brake booster vacuum line if so equipped, at the intake manifold.

16 Disconnect the heater hoses from the water pump and intake manifold and remove the coolant temperature sending unit wire from the unit.

17 Remove the bolts securing the flywheel or converter housing to the engine. Disconnect the downshift rod.

18 Unplug the primary wiring connector from the ignition coil and remove the wiring harness from the left valve cover.

19 Disconnect any remaining emissions or electrical connectings still attached to the engine which may interfere with removal.

2C

20 After chocking the rear wheels, jack up the front of the vehicle and support it on jack stands. For better access, remove the front wheels.
21 Disconnect the starter cable and remove the starter.
22 Unbolt the muffler inlet pipes at the exhaust manifolds and move the pipes out of the way.
23 On manual-transmission-equipped vehicles, remove the clutch release cable from the release lever.
24 On automatic-transmission-equipped vehicles, disconnect the transmission cooler lines from the converter inspection cover and remove the cover.
25 Remove the bolts securing the torque converter to the flywheel, using a larger wrench to turn the crankshaft pulley bolt to rotate the engine. After all the bolts are removed, secure the converter assembly to the housing as it will be lifted out with the engine.
26 On manual transmission-equipped vehicles, remove the bolts securing the bellhousing to the engine block.
27 Replace the front wheels and lower the vehicle to the ground.
28 Support the transmission with a jack and attach lifting chains to the exhaust manifolds.
29 Raise the engine slightly with the lifting hoist and remove the engine mount through-bolts and insulators.
30 Lift the engine and pull it forward from the transmission. Make sure that the converter remains attached to the engine on automatic transmission equipped vehicles.
31 Lift the engine carefully, making sure that the rear cover plate does not contact the body.
32 Once the engine is clear of the engine compartment, lower it onto a workbench or the floor and support it with blocks of wood so that it doesn't fall over.

4   Engine removal – transmission attached

1   It is not recommended that the engine be removed with the automatic transmission attached, due to the weight involved. Should it be necessary to remove both units, refer to Chapter 7 and remove the transmission first. The engine can then be removed as described in Section 3.
2   To remove the engine with manual transmission attached, follow the procedure described in Section 3, paragraphs 1 through 23, except for those having to do with the automatic transmission.
3   Remove the gearshift lever, referring to Chapter 7.
4   From beneath the car, remove the transmission drain plug and allow the oil to drain for five minutes. Replace the plug.
5   After marking its position, remove the driveshaft (refer to Chapter 8).
6   Support the weight of the transmission with a small jack.
7   Remove the bolts attaching the crossmember to the transmission extension and the body and remove the crossmember.
8   Check that all cables and controls have been detached and are out of the way.
9   With the jack still in position under the transmission, start lifting and moving the engine forward.

10 Because the transmission is attached, the engine will have to be lifted out at an extreme angle. As the weight is toward the rear, it will be fairly easy to achieve this angle.
11 Continue to raise the engine and move it forward at the necessary angle. At this stage the forward edge of the bellhousing is likely to catch against the front crossmember and the tail of the gearbox will need raising until the whole unit is forward and clear of it.
12 As the maximum height of the lifting tackle is reached, it will be necessary to switch the entire engine/transmission unit so that the tail can be lifted clear while the hoist is moved away or the vehicle is lowered from the jack stands and rolled rearward.
13 The whole unit should be lowered to the ground or workbench as soon as possible and the transmission separated from the engine.

5   Engine dismantling – general

1   Ideally, the engine should be mounted on a proper stand for overhaul but it is anticipated that most owners will have a strong bench on which to place it instead. If a sufficiently large strong bench is not available, then the work can be done at ground level. It is essential, however, that some form of substantial wooden surface is available. Timber should be at least $\frac{3}{4}$ inch thick, otherwise the weight of the engine will cause projections to punch holes straight through it.
2   It will save a great deal of time later if the exterior of the engine is thoroughly cleaned down before any dismantling begins. This can be done by using a proprietary solvent which can be brushed on and then the dirt sprayed off with a water jet. This will dispose of all the heavy muck and grit once and for all so that later cleaning of individual components will be a relatively clean process.
3   As the engine is stripped down, clean each part as it comes off. Try to avoid immersing parts with oilways in solvent as pockets of liquid could remain and cause oil dilution in the critical first few revolutions after reassembly. Clean oilways with pipe cleaners, or, preferably, an air jet.
4   Where possible avoid damaging gaskets on removal, especially if new ones have not been obtained. They can be used as patterns if new ones have to be specially cut.
5   It is helpful to obtain a few blocks of wood to support the engine while it is in the process of being dismantled. Start dismantling at the top of the engine and then turn the block over and deal with the oil pan and crankshaft etc., afterwards.
6   Nuts and bolts should be refitted in their locations where possible to avoid confusion later. As an alternative keep each group of nuts and bolts (all the timing gear cover bolts for example) together in a jar or can.
7   Many items when dismantled must be refitted in the same position, if they are not being replaced. These include valves, rocker arms, valve lifters, pistons, pushrods, bearings and connecting rods. Some of these are marked on assembly to avoid any possibility of mixing them up during overhaul. Others are not, and it is a great help if adequate preparation is made in advance to classify these parts.

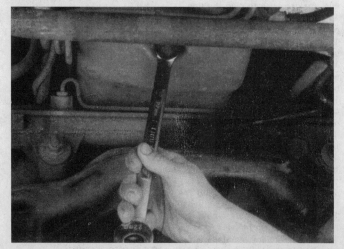
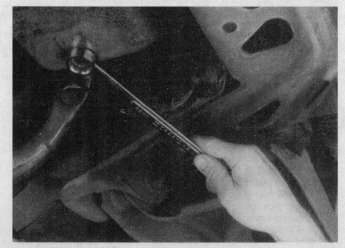

Fig. 2.10 Dual drain plug oil pan (Secs 1 and 13)

Suitably labelled cardboard boxes or trays should be used. The time spent in this preparation will be amply repaid later.

6   Engine accessories – removal

1   Before beginning a complete overhaul, or if the engine is being exchanged for a rebuilt unit, the following items should be removed:

Fuel system components:
Carburetor
Intake and exhaust manifolds
Fuel pump
Fuel lines
Ignition system components:
Spark plugs
Distributor
Coil
Electrical system components (if not removed already):
Alternator and mounting brackets
Starter motor
Cooling system components:
Fan and fan pulley
Water pump thermostat housing and thermostat
Engine:
Crankcase ventilation tube
Oil filter element
Oil pressure sender unit (if fitted)
Oil level dipstick
Oil filler cap
Engine mounting brackets
Clutch:
Clutch pressure plate and total assembly
Clutch friction plate and total assembly
Optional equipment:
Air conditioning compressor
Power steering pump
Thermactor pump

7   Cylinder heads – removal with engine in vehicle

1   Open the hood.
2   For safety reasons disconenct the battery.
3   Remove the air cleaner from the carburetor installation, as described in Chapter 4.
4   Disconnect the accelerator linkage from the carburetor.
5   Refer to Chapter 3 and drain the cooling system.
6   Detach the HT leads from the spark plugs, release the distributor cap securing clips and remove the distributor cap.
7   Loosen the clips and disconnect the hose from the water pump to the water outlet.
8   Detach the vacuum pipe from the distributor body and carburetor installation.
9   Refer to Chapter 4, and remove the carburetor and inlet manifold assembly.This will necessitate removal of the distributor.
10   Remove the two rocker covers by undoing and removing the securing screws and lifting away together with their respective gaskets.
11   Loosen the alternator adjusting arm bolt and remove the alternator mounting bracket bolt and spacer. Push the alternator down out of the way.
12   Remove the accelerator shaft bracket from the left-hand cylinder head and position it out of the way.
13   Loosen the rocker arm studs nuts just enough to enable the rocker arms to be rotated to one side.
14   Lift out the pushrods and keep them in the correct order of removal by pushing them through a piece of cardboard with the valve numbers marked on it (1 to 16).
15   Detach the exhaust downpipes from the exhaust manifold and move the downpipes to the sides of the engine compartment. Leave the manifolds in place as they will act as a lever to assist removal of the heads.
16   Taking each cylinder head in turn, loosen the eight holding down bolts in the order shown. When all are free of tension remove all the bolts.

17   On occasions the heads may have stuck to the head gasket and cylinder block, in which case if pulling up on the exhaust manifolds does not free them they should be struck smartly with a soft faced hammer in order to break the joints. **Do not** try to pry them off with a blade of any description or damage will be caused to the faces of the head or block, or both.
18   With the help of an assistant, lift off the cylinder heads, remove them from the vehicle and place them on the workbench. Remove the exhaust manifolds.
19   Remove the cylinder head gaskets. New ones will be required for reassembly.

8   Cylinder heads – removal with engine out

Follow the sequence given in Section 7, paragraphs 6 to 19 inclusive, disregarding information on parts mentioned that have been previously removed.

9   Cylinder heads – dismantling of valves and springs

1   Remove the rocker arm retaining nuts and lift off the fulcrum seats and rocker arms.

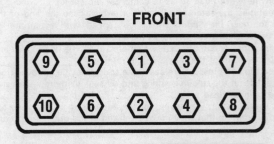

Fig. 2.11 Cylinder head bolt loosening and tightening sequence (Secs 7 and 44)

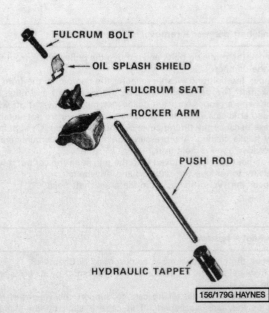

Fig. 2.12 Rocker arm components (Sec 9)

Fig 2.13 Removing valve locks (Sec 9)

2   Lay the cylinder head on its side and using a proper valve spring compressor place the 'U' shaped end over the spring retainer and screw on the valve head so as to compress the spring.
3   Sometimes the retainer will stick, in which case the end of the compressor over the spring should be tapped with a hammer to release the retainer from the locks (collets).
4   As the spring is compressed two tapered locks will be exposed and should be taken from the recess in the retainer.
5   When the compressor is released the spring may be removed from the valve. Lift off the retainer, spring and oil seal. Withdraw the valve from the cylinder head.
6   It is essential that the valves, springs, retainer, locks and seals are all kept in order so that they may be refitted in the original positions

10 Valve lifters – removal

1   Remove the valve lifters and lay them out in the correct order of removal so that they may be refitted in their original bores.
2   Use a magnet to remove the tappets from the bores.

11 Crankshaft damper – removal

1   Remove the retaining bolts and remove the pulley wheel from the front of the damper.
2   Remove the bolt and washer locating the damper to the front of the crankshaft. The damper is keyed to the crankshaft and must be drawn off with a proper sprocket puller. Attempts to lever it off with long bladed articles such as screwdrivers or tire levers are not suitable in this case because the timing cover behind the damper is a light and relatively fragile casting. Any pressure against it could certainly crack it and possibly break a hole in it.
3   The damper may be removed with the engine in the car but it will be necessary to remove the radiator, and drivebelts.
4   Recover the Woodruff key from the crankshaft nose.

12 Flywheel – removal

1   Remove the clutch assembly, as described in Chapter 8.
2   The flywheel is held in position to the crankshaft by six bolts and a locating dowel.
3   Remove the six bolts, taking care to support the weight of the flywheel as they are slackened off in case it slips off the flange. Remove it carefully, taking care not to damage the mating surfaces on the crankshaft and flywheel.

13 Oil pan – removal

1   With the engine out of the car, first invert the engine and then remove the bolts which hold the pan in place.
2   The pan may be stuck quite firmly to the engine if sealing compound has been used on the gasket. It is in order to lever it off in this case. The gasket should be removed and discarded in any case.
3   The oil pan can be removed with the engine still fitted in the vehicle but it is first necessary to raise the engine within the engine compartment approximately 4 inches to provide the necessary clearance.
4   Open the hood and drain the cooling system as described in Chapter 3.
5   Jack up the front of the the vehicle, support it on jack stands and drain the engine oil into a suitable container. If vehicle is equipped with a dual sump oil pan, both drain plugs must be removed to thoroughly drain the crankcase.
6   Refer to Section 3 and disconnect all controls and components that will impede the upward movement of the engine; this will include the radiator shroud and hoses, the two front exhaust pipes, the air cleaner and carburetor linkage, alternator and transmission linkage etc. Disconnect the steering flex coupling and remove the 2 bolts attaching the steering gear to the frame crossmember. Rest the steering gear on the frame away from the oil pan.
7   Remove the converter inspection cover and the front engine mounting securing nuts. Place a jack and wooden block under the oil pan and slowly raise the engine at least 4 inches. Place wooden blocks between the engine and crossmember to hold it in the raised position. Remove the jack.
8   Remove all the retaining bolts and lower the oil pan as far as possible, unbolt the oil pump assembly from inside the crankcase. Allow it to drop into the oil pan and withdraw the oil pan complete with pump.
9   Remove the oil pan gasket. A new one must be obtained for reassembly.

14 Front cover – removal

1   With the engine out of the car, remove the oil pan, crankshaft pulley wheel and damper. Disconnect the fuel pump outlet line, unbolt the fuel pump and move it to one side with the fuel line still attached.
2   Remove the water pump retaining bolts and lift the water pump from the front cover. It may be necessary to tap it with a soft-faced mallet if a jointing compound has been used.
3   Remove the front cover securing nuts and lift it away. If it is stuck, cary out the instructions in paragraph 2. Remove the front cover gasket.
4   If the engine is still in the vehicle it will be necessary to remove the front oil pan bolts which run through the timing cover. It will also be necessary to remove the fan belt, crankshaft pulley wheel and fuel pump.

15 Timing chain and sprockets – removal

1   Remove the front timing chain cover as described in th previous Section and withdraw the oil slinger from the front of the crankshaft.
2   Remove the camshaft sprocket securing bolt and remove the fuel pump eccentric from the sprocket. Replace the front damper bolt and use a wrench to rotate the engine until the sprocket timing marks are aligned.
3   Using a suitable puller, withdraw the crankshaft sprocket and, if necessary the camshaft sprocket; remove both sprockets and chain as a complete assembly.
4   Recover the Woodruff key from the groove in the crankshaft.
5   To test the chain for wear, refer to Section 34 of this Chapter.

16 Camshaft – removal

1   The camshaft can be removed with the engine in the vehicle. (Should camshaft replacement be necessary it will probably be necessary to overhaul other parts of the engine too. If this is the case engine removal should be considered).

2   Refer to Chapter 3 and remove the radiator.

3   Detach the spark plug leads from the spark plugs, release the cap securing clips and place the cap to one side.

4   Detach the distributor vacuum line and then remove the distributor as described in Chapter 5.

5   Remove the alternator as described in Chapter 10.

6   Remove the screws that secure each rocker cover to the cylinder heads. Lift away the rocker covers and gaskets.

7   Refer to Chapter 4 and remove the intake manifold and carburettor installation.

8   Loosen the rocker arm retaining nuts just enough to enable the rocker arms to be rotated to one side.

9   Remove the pushrods and note each rod's original location, and also which way up they are fitted. Keep them in order and the right way up by pushing them through a piece of stiff card with valve numbers marked.

10 Refer to Section 14 and remove the front cover.

11 Refer to Section 15 and remove the camshaft timing sprocket and chain.

12 Remove the 2 screws which secure the camshaft thrust plate to the cylinder block face. Lift away the plate and spacer.

13 Using a magnet, recover the valve lifters from the 'Vee' in the cylinder block. Keep in order as they must be replaced in their original positions.

14 If any valve lifters cannot be removed, retain in their maximum height positions with clips.

15 The camshaft may now be drawn forwards through the cylinder block. Take care that the sharp edges of the cams do not damage the bearings.

17 Oil pump – removal

1   Refer to Section 13 and remove the oil pan.

2   Remove the 2 bolts that secure the pump to the crankcase. Lift away the pump and recover the gasket.

3   The long hexagonal section driveshaft will come out with the pump. This is driven by the distributor shaft.

18 Pistons, connecting rods and bearings – removal

1   Pistons and connecting rods may be removed with the engine in the vehicle, provided the oil pan and cylinder heads are first removed. The bearing shells may be removed with the heads on.

2   Loosen the 2 nuts holding each bearing cap to the connecting rod. Use a good quality socket wrench for this work. A box wrench may be used for removal only – not replacement which calls for a special torque wrench. Having slackened the nuts 2 or 3 turns tap the caps to dislodge them from the connecting rods. Completely remove the nuts and lift away the end caps.

3   Each bearing cap normally has the cylinder number etched on one end as does the connecting rod. However, this must be verified and if in doubt the cap should be marked with a dab of paint or punch mark to ensure that its relationship with the connecting rod and its numerical position in the cylinder block is not altered.

4   The piston and connecting rod may then be pushed out of the top of each cylinder.

5   The connecting rod bearing shells can be removed from the connecting rod and cap by sliding them round in the direction of the notch at the end of the shell and lifting them out. If they are not being replaced it is vital they are not interchanged – either between pistons or between cap and connecting rod.

19 Piston rings – removal

1   Remove the pistons from the egine.

2   The rings come off over the top of the pistons. Starting with the top one, lift one end of the ring out of the groove and gradually ease it out all the way round. With the second and third rings an old feeler blade is useful for sliding them over the other grooves. However, as rings are only normally removed if they are going to be replaced it should not matter if breakages occur.

20 Piston pin – removal

The piston pins need removing if the pistons are being replaced. New pistons are supplied with new pins for fitting to the existing connecting rods. The piston pin is semi-floating, that is, it is a tight shrink fit with the connecting rod and a moving fit in the piston. To press it out requires considerable force and under usual circumstances a proper press and special tools are essential, otherwise piston damage will occur. If damage to the pistons does not matter, then the pins may be pressed out using suitable diameter pieces of rod and tube between the jaws of a vise. However, this is not recommended as the connecting rod might be damaged also. It is recommended that piston pins and pistons are removed from, and refitted to, connecting rods, by Ford dealers with the necessary facilities.

21 Crankshaft rear oil seal – removal and installation

1   It is possible to remove the crankshaft rear oil seal with the engine in or out of the vehicle. Where the engine is being completely removed, refer to Section 22 and remove the crankshaft. Remove the two halves of the seal from the upper rear main bearing and cap.

2   With the engine in the vehicle, drain the engine oil and remove the oil pan and pump as described in Section 13.

3   Undo the two bolts and carefully pry the rear main bearing cap from the crankshaft. Remove the oil seal from the cap and if a locating pin is fitted in the bottom of the groove in the cap, drive it out using a pin punch.

4   Loosen all the main bearing cap bolts to enable the crankshaft to drop down slightly, but **not** more than $\frac{1}{32}$ in (0.79 mm).

5   Using a piece of brass rod, push one end of the upper half of the oil seal upwards to rotate it around the crankshaft. When the other end of the seal is protruding sufficiently, grip it with a pair of pliers and carefully pull it out while continuing to push on the other end with the piece of wire. Great care must be taken not to scratch the crankshaft oil seal surface.

6   Clean out the oil seal grooves in the cylinder block and cap using a suitable solvent.

7   Soak the new rubber seals in clean engine oil prior to fitting.

8   Fit the upper half of the seal in the cylinder block with the inner lip facing towards the front of the engine. Slide the seal around the crankshaft until $\frac{3}{8}$ in (9 mm) protrudes from the base of the block.

9   Repeat the procedure for the lower half of the seal, allowing an equal amount of the seal to protrude beyond the opposite end of the bearing cap.

10 Fit the rear bearing cap and seal ensuring the protruding ends of the seals correctly enter the respective grooves. Apply a bead of sealer to the rear corners of the block and sides of the cap.

11 Tighten all the main bearing cap bolts to the specified torque wrench setting.

12 Fit the new coil pan seals and gaksets and refit the oil pump and oil pan as described in Sections 41 and 43 respectively.

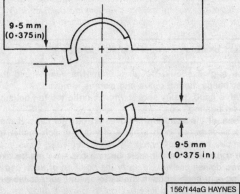

9·5 mm
(0·375 in)

9·5 mm
(0·375 in)

156/144aG HAYNES

Fig. 2.14 Crankshaft rear oil seal installation (Sec 21)

Fig. 2.15 Crankshaft, bearings and components (Sec 22)

22 Main bearings and crankshaft – removal

1   The engine should be taken from the vehicle and the oil pan, cylinder heads, timing gears and pistons removed.
2   With a good quality socket wrench undo the ten bolts holding the five main bearing caps.
3   When all the bolts are removed lift out the caps. If the are tight, tap the sides gently with a piece of wood or soft mallet to dislodge them.
4   On some engines the main bearing caps are marked from 1 – 5. However, if they are not, identify the position of each cap with paint marks or light center punch marks to ensure correct reassembly.

5   Lift out the crankshaft from the cylinder block taking care not to damage the journals.
6   Slide out the bearing shells from the cylinder block and bearing caps noting that the center shells also function as thrust bearings.

23 Lubrication and crankcase ventilation systems – description

1   The oil pump is located in the crankcase and is driven from the distributor by a hexagonal driveshaft. An oil pressure relief valve is incorporated in the pump body. Oil under pressure is directed via a full flow filter to the main, connecting rod and camshaft bearings and to the hydraulic valve lifters pushrods and rocker arms.

2   A drilling in the front cylinder block face enables oil to pass through to the timing chain and sprocket.

3   Oil from the valve gear drains down over the camshaft lobes and distributor drive gear before passing back into the oil pan.

4   The cylinder bores are lubricated by a squirt of oil from a drilling in each connecting rod. The piston pins are lubricated continuously by the oil mist thrown up inside the crankcase.

5   The crankcase has a positive ventilation system (PCV). Instead of allowing engine fumes to escape into the atmosphere they are drawn back into the engine via a hose and non-return valve connected between the oil filler cap on the rocker cover and the intake manifold.

24 Oil filter – removal and installation

1   The oil filter is a complete throw-away cartridge screwed into the left-hand side of the engine block. Simply unscrew the old unit, clean the seating on the block and screw the new one in, taking care not to cross the thread. Continue until the sealing ring just touches the block face. Then tighten one half turn. Always run the engine and check for signs of leaks after installation.

25 Engine components – examination for wear

1   When the engine has been stripped down and all parts properly cleaned, decisions have to be made as to what needs replacement and the following Sections tell the examiner what to look for. In any border-line case it is always best to decide in favor of a new part. Even if a part may still be serviceable its life will have been reduced by wear and the degree of trouble needed to replace it in the future must be taken into consideration. However, these things are relative and it depends on whether a quick 'survival' job is being done or whether the car as a while is being regarded as having many thousands of miles of useful and economical life remaining.

26 Crankshaft – inspection and overhaul

1   Look at the 5 main bearing journals and the 8 crankpins and if there are any scratches or score marks then the shaft will need grinding. Such conditions will nearly always be accompanied by similar deterioration in the matching bearing shells.

2   Each bearing journal should also be round and can be checked with a micrometer or caliper gauge around the periphery at several points. If there is more than 0.006 in (0.0152 mm) of ovality, regrinding is necessary.

3   A dealer or engine rebuilder will be able to decide to what extent regrinding is necessary and also supply the special under-size shell bearings to match whatever may need grinding off the journals.

4   Before taking the crankshaft for regrinding, check also the cylinder bores and pistons as it may be more convenient to have the machining operations performed at the same time by the same rebuilder.

27 Crankshaft (main) bearings and connecting rod bearings – inspection and overhaul

1   With careful servicing and regular oil and filter changes bearings will last for a very long time but they can still fail for unforeseen reasons. With connecting rod bearings the indications are a regular rhythmic loud knocking from the crankcase, the frequency depending on engine speed. It is particularly noticeable when the engine in under load. This symptom is accompanied by a fall in oil pressure although this is not normally noticeable unless an oil pressure gauge is fitted. Main bearing failure is usually indicated by serious vibration, particularly at higher engine revolutions, accompanied by a more significant drop in oil pressure and a 'rumbling' noise.

2   Bearing shells in good condition have bearing surfaces with a smooth, even, matt silver/grey color all over. Worn bearings will show patches of a different color where the bearing metal has worn away and exposed the underlay. Damaged bearings will be pitted or scored. It is nearly always well worthwhile fitting new shells as their cost is relatively low. If the crankshaft is in good condition it is merely a question of obtaining another set of standard size. A reground crankshaft will need new bearing shells as a matter of course.

3   A good way to check for wear and taper of a crankshaft or connecting rod journal is by using Plastigage. Place a piece of Plastigage across the full width of the bearing surface, about ⅓ in off center, install the bearing cap and tighten to specification. Remove the cap and measure the width of the Plastigage at its widest point to obtain the minimum clearance and the narrowest point for the maximum clearance using the supplied gauge. The difference between these two measurements equals the taper. Be sure to remove all traces of the Plastigage from the journal after measurement.

28 Cylinder bores – inspection and overhaul

1   A new cylinder is perfectly round and the walls parallel throughout its length. The action of the pistons tends to wear the walls at right angles to the wrist pin due to side thrust. This wear takes place principally on that section of the cylinder swept by the piston rings.

2   It is possible to get an indication of bore wear by removing the cylinder heads with the engine still in the car. With the piston down in the bore fist signs of wear can be seen and felt just below the top of the bore where the top piston ring reaches and there will be a noticeable lip. If there is no lip it is fairly reasonable to expect that bore wear is low and any lack of compression or excessive oil consumption is due to worn or broken piston rings or pistons (see next Section).

3   If it is possible to obtain a bore measuring micrometer, measure the bore in the thrust plane below the lip and again at the bottom of the cylinder in the same plane. If the difference is more than 0.010 inch (0.254 mm) then a rebore is necessary. Similarly, a difference of 0.005 inch (0.127 mm) or more across the bore diameter is a sign of ovality calling for a rebore.

4   Any bore which is significantly scratched or scored will need reboring. This symptom usually indicates that the piston or rings are damaged in that cylinder. In the event of only one cylinder being in need of reboring it will still be necesary for all eight to be bored and fitted with new oversize pistons and rings. Your dealer or local machine shop will be able to rebore and obtain the necessary matched pistons. If the crankshaft is undergoing regrinding it is a good idea to let the same firm renovate and reassemble the crankshaft and pistons to the block. A reputable firm normally gives a guarantee for such work. In cases where engines have been rebored already to their maximum, new cylinder liners are available which may be installed. In such cases the same reboring processes have to be followed and the services of a machine shop are required.

29 Pistons and piston rings – inspection and overhaul

1   Worn pistons and rings can usually be diagnosed when the symptons of excessive oil consumption and low compression occur and are sometimes, though not always, associated with worn cylinder bores. Compression testers that fit into the spark plug holes are available and these can indicate where low compresson is occurring.

Fig. 2.16 Measure ring end gap at bottom of ring travel to determine wear (Sec 29)

2C

Wear usually accelerates the more it is left so when the symptoms occur, early action can possibly save the expense of a rebore.

2   Another symptom of piston wear is piston slap – a knocking noise from the crankcase not to be confused with connecting rod bearing failure. It can be heard clearly at low engine speed when there is no load (idling for example) and the engine is cold, and is much less audible when the engine speed increases. Piston wear usually occurs in the skirt or lower end of the piston and is indicated by vertical streaks in the worn area which is always on the thrust side. It can also be seen where the skirt thickness is different.

3   Piston ring wear can be checked by first removing the rings from the pistons, as described in Section 19. Then place the rings in the cylinder bores from the top, pushing them down about 1.5 inches (38 mm) with the head of a piston (from which the rings have been removed) so that they rest square in the cylinder. Then measure the gap at the ends of the ring with a feeler gauge. If it exceeds 0.020 in (0.508 mm) for the 2 top compression rings, or 0.055 in for the oil control ring then they need replacement.

4   The groove in which the rings locate in the piston can also become enlarged due to wear. The clearance between the ring and piston should not exceed 0.004 in (0.1016 mm) for the top and second ring. The bottom oil control ring should be a snug fit in the groove with no visible clearance.

5   However, it is rare that a piston is only worn in the ring grooves and the need to replace them for this fault alone is hardly ever encountered.

30 Connecting rods and piston pins – inspection

1   Piston pins are a shrink fit into the connecting rods. Neither of these components would normally need replacement unless the pistons were being changed, in which case the new pistons would automatically be supplied with new pins.

2   Connecting rods are not subject to wear but in extreme circumstances such as engine seizure, they could be distorted. Such conditions may be visually apparent but where doubt exists they should be changed. The bearing caps should also be examined for indications of filing down which may have been attempted in the mistaken idea that bearing looseness could be remedied in this way. If there are such signs then the connecting rods should be replaced.

31 Camshaft and camshaft bearings – inspection

The camshaft bearings should be examined for signs of scoring and pitting. If they need replacement they will have to be dealt with professionally as, although it may be relatively easy to remove the old ones, the correct fitting of new ones requires special tools. If they are not fitted evenly and square from the very start they can be distorted, thus causing localized wear in a very short time. See your dealer or local machine shop for this work.

2   The camshaft itself may show signs of wear on the bearing journals, cam lobes or the skew gear. The main decision to take is what degree of wear justifies replacement which is costly. Any signs of scoring or damage to the bearing journals must be rectified and as under-size bearing brushes are not supplied the journals cannot be reground. Replacement of the whole camshaft is the only solution. Similarly. excessive wear on the skew gear which can be seen where the distributor driveshaft teeth mesh, will mean replacement of the whole camshaft.

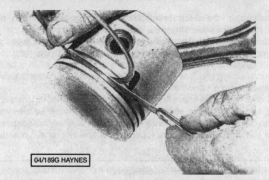

04/189G HAYNES

Fig. 2.17 Measuring piston ring side gap (Sec 29)

3   The cam lobes themselves may show signs of ridging or pitting on the high points. If the ridging is light then it may be possible to smooth it out with fine emery cloth. The cam lobes, however, are surface hardened and once this penetrated wear will be very rapid thereafter. The cams are also offset and tapered to cause the valve lifters to rotate – thus ensuring that wear is even – so do not mistake this condition for wear.

32 Valve lifters – inspection

1   The faces of the valve lifters which bear on the camshaft should show no signs of pitting, scoring or other forms of wear. They should also not be a loose fit in their housing. Wear is only normally encountered at very high mileages or in cases of neglected engine lubrication.

2   Although it is possible to dismantle the valve lifters by removing the spring clip and tapping out the valve assembly, it is not worthwhile fitting new components to an old valve body and the best policy is to replace all the valve lifters whenever a major engine overhaul is carried out.

33 Valves and valve seats – inspection and overhaul

1   With the valve removed from the cylinder heads examine the heads for signs of cracking, burning away and pitting of the edge where it seats in the port. The seats of the valves in the cylinder head should also be examined for the same signs. Usually it is the valve that deteriorates first but if bad valve is not rectified the seat will suffer and this is more difficult to repair.

2   Providing the valve heads and seats are not cracked or badly pitted, minor burn marks and blemishes can be removed by using carborundum paste.

3   This may be done by placing a smear of carborundum paste on the edge of the valve and, using a suction type valve holder, lapping the valve in place. This is done with a semi-rotary action, twisting the handle of the valve holder between the hands and lifting it occasionally to redistribute the paste. Use a coarse paste to start with and finish with a fine paste. As soon as a matt grey unbroken line appears on both the valve and the seat the valve is 'lapped-in'. All traces of carbon should also be cleaned from the head and the neck of the valve stem; A wire brush mounted in a power drill is a quick and effective way of doing this.

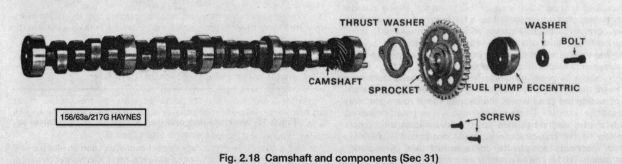

156/63a/217G HAYNES

Fig. 2.18 Camshaft and components (Sec 31)

4   If an exhaust valve requires replacement it should be lapped into the seat in the same way as an old valve.

5   Another form of valve wear can occur on the stem where it runs in the guide in the cylinder head. This can be detected by trying to rock the valve from side to side. If there is any movement at all it is an indication that the valve stem or guide is worn. Check the stem first with a micrometer at points all along and around its length and if they are not within the specified size new valves will probably solve the problem. If the guides are worn, however, they will need reboring for oversize valves or for fitting guide inserts. The valve seats will also need recutting to ensure they are concentric with the stems. This work should be given to your dealer or local machine shop.

6   When all valve lapping is completed it is essential that every trace of paste is removed from the valves and ports in the cylinder head. This should be done by a thorough washing in gasoline or kerosene and blowing out with a jet of air. If particles of carborundum paste should work their way into the engine they would cause havoc with bearings or cylinder walls.

34   Timing chain and sprockets – inspection and overhaul

1   Examine the sprocket teeth for excessive wear and replace if necessary.

2   Check the timing chain for wear and slackness in the pins and links. As a guide, temporarily refit the chain and sprockets and rotate the crankshaft so that one side of the chain is under tension. Now check that the maximum possible sideways movement of the slack side of the chain does not exceed ½ in (12.5 mm).

3   If any doubt exists regarding the condition of the chain the most sensible policy is to replace it.

35   Flywheel ring gear – inspection and overhaul

1   If the ring gear is badly worn or has missing teeth it should be replaced. The old ring can be removed from the flywheel by cutting a notch between two teeth with a hacksaw and then splitting it with a cold chisel.

2   To fit a new ring gear requires heating the ring to 400°F (204°C). This can be done by polishing four equally spaced sections of the gear, laying it on a suitable heat resistant surface (such as fire bricks) and heating it evenly with a torch until the polished areas turn a light yellow tint. Do not overheat or the hard wearing properties will be lost. The gear has a chamfered inner edge which should go against the shoulder when put on the flywheel. When hot enough place the gear in position quickly, tapping it home if necessary and let it cool naturally without quenching in any way.

36   Oil pump – inspection

1   The oil pump maintains a pressure of around 40 to 60 psi. An oil pressure gauge is fitted to give earlier warning of falling oil pressures due either to overheating, pump failure or bearing wear.

2   At a major engine overhaul it is as well to check the pump and exchange it for a reconditioned unit if necessary. The efficient operation of the oil pump depends on the finely machined tolerances between the moving parts of the rotor and the body and reconditioning of these is generally not within the competence of the non-specialist owner.

3   To dismantle the pump, first remove it from the engine, as described in Section 17.

4   Remove the two bolts holding the end cover to the body and remove the cover and relief valve parts which will be released.

5   Remove the four bolts securing the rotor end plate.

6   The necessary clearances may now be checked using a machined straight edge (a good steel rule) and a feeler gauge.

7   On bi-rotor type pumps the critical clearances are between the lobes of the center rotor and convex faces of the outer rotor, between the outer rotor and the pump body, and between both rotors and the end cover plate.

8   The rotor lobe clearances may be checked as shown in the accompanying figure. The clearances should not exceed 0.006 in (0.152 mm). The clearance between the outer rotor and pump body should not exceed 0.013 in (0.33 mm).

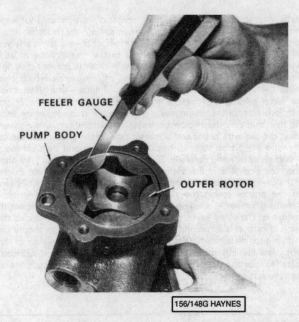

Fig. 2.19 Checking oil pump rotor side clearances (Sec 36)

Fig. 2.20 Checking oil pump rotor endfloat (Sec 36)

9   The endfloat clearance can be measured by placing a straight edge across the end of the pump and measuring the gap between the rotors and the straight edge. The gap on either rotor should not exceed 0.005 in (0.127 mm).

10   If any clearances are out of specification, the oil pump must be replaced with a new one.

11   When reassembling the pump and replacing the end cover make sure that the interior is scrupulously clean and that the pressure relief valve parts are assembled in the correct positions.

37   Cylinder heads and piston crowns – cleaning

1   When cylinder heads are removed either in the course of an overhaul or for inspection of bores or valve condition when the engine is in the vehicle, it is normal to remove all carbon deposits from the piston crowns and heads.

2   This is best done with a cup-shaped wire brush and an electric drill and is fairly straightforward when the engine is dismantled and the

pistons removed. Sometimes hard spots of carbon are not easily removed except by a scraper. When cleaning the pistons with a scraper take care not to damage the surface of the piston in any way.
3   When the engine is in the vehicle certain precautions must be taken when removing the piston crowns, in order to prevent dislodged pieces of carbon falling into the interior of the engine which could cause damage to cylinder bores, pistons and rings — or if allowed into the water passages — damage to the water pump. Turn the engine, therefore, so that the piston being worked on is at the top of its stroke and then mask off the adjacent cylinder bore and all surrounding water jacket orifices with paper and adhesive tape. Press grease into the gap all round the piston to keep carbon particles out and then scrape all carbon away by hand carefully. Do not use a power drill and wire brush when the engine is in the car as it will be virtually impossible to keep all the carbon dust clear of the engine. When completed carefully clear out the grease round the rim of the piston with a matchstick or something similar — bringing any carbon particles with it. Repeat the process on the other seven piston crowns. It is not recommended that a ring of carbon is left round the edge of the piston on the theory that it will reduce oil consumption. This was valid in the earlier days of long stroke low revving engines but modern engines, fuels and lubricants cause less carbon deposits anyway and any left behind tends merely to cause hot spots.

38 Oil pan – inspection

1   Wash out the oil pan with the proper solvent and wipe dry. Inspect the exterior for signs of damage or excessive rust. If evident, a new oil pan must be obtained. To ensure an oil tight joint scrape away all traces of the old gasket from the cylinder block mating face.

39 Engine reassembly – general

All components of the engine must be cleaned of oil, sludge and old gasket and the working area should also be cleared and clean. In addition to the normal range of good quality socket wrenches and general tools which are essential, the following must be available before reassembling begins:

   a) *Complete set of new gaskets*
   b) *Supply of clean lint-free cloths*
   c) *Clean oil can full of new engine oil*
   d) *Torque wrench*
   e) *All new spare parts as necessary*

40 Engine reassembly – camshaft and crankshaft

1   Insert the camshaft carefully into the block, taking care not to let any of the cam lobes damage the bearings.
2   Replace the camshaft thrust plate and secure it with the two screws. These screws must be tightened firmly.
3   Ensure that the crankcase is thoroughly clean and that all oilways are clear. A thin twist drill is useful for cleaning the oilways, or if possible they may be blown out with compressed air. Treat the crankshaft in the same fashion, and then inject engine oil into the oilways.
4   Select the halves of the five main bearing shells that have the oil slots and grooves and fit them into the crankcase bearing housings (photo). Ensure that the notches in the ends of the shells are correctly located in the cut-outs in the housings.
5   Note that the center main bearing shells have flanges, which act as thrust washers. These are available in various thicknesses in order to be able to set the crankshaft endfloat.
6   Push the upper half of the crankshaft oil seal into the recess at the rear of the crankcase. For further information on fitting the rear crankshaft oil seal refer to Section 21.
7   Lubricate the crankshaft journals with engine oil and carefully lower the crankshaft into position.

Fig. 2.21 Crankshaft thrust bearing alignment procedure (Sec 40)

8   Fit the lower (plain) shells into the main bearing caps
9   Push the lower half of the crankshaft oil seal into the recess in the rear main bearing cap.
10 Fit the rear and main bearing caps over the crankshaft and temporarily tighten the retaining bolts.
11 Check the crankshaft endfloat using feeler gauges. If the endfloat is not within 0.004 – 0.008 in (0.101 – 0.202 mm) the crankshaft should be removed and the center thrust bearings replaced with ones of the necessary thickness to achieve this tolerance.
12 When the crankshaft endfloat is correct, fit all the main bearing caps and retaining bolts. Note that the bearing caps should be marked with a number from 1 to 5 and an arrow to ensure they are installed in the correct position.
13 Finally, tighten the main bearing cap bolts to the specified torque wrench setting.

41 Engine reassembly – pistons, connecting rods and oil pump

1   The subsequent paragraphs on assembly assume that all the checks described in Sections 29 to 30 have been carried out. Also the engine has been partially assembled as described in Section 40.
2   The assembly of new pistons to connecting rods should have been carried out as detailed in Section 20. The new pistons should be supplied with rings already fitted.
3   If new rings are being fitted to existing pistons the following procedure should be followed. Having removed the old rings make sure that each ring groove in the piston is completely cleaned of carbon deposits. This is done most easily by using a special groove cleaner tool or by breaking one of the old rings and using the sharp end as a scraper. Be careful not to remove any metal from the groove by mistake.
4   The end-gap of the new piston rings – three for each piston – must be checked in the cylinder bores as described in Section 29.
5   Check Specifications for the minimum end gap for all three rings. If the gap is too small, one end of the ring must be filed to increase the gap. To do this the ring should be gripped in a vise between two thin pieces of soft metal in such a way that only the end to be filed is gripped and so that it only protrudes above the jaws of the vise a very small distance. This will eliminate the possibility of bending and breaking the ring while filing the end. Use a thin, fine file and proceed in easy stages – checking the gap by refitting the ring in the bore until the necessary minimum gap is obtained. This must be done with every ring, checking each one in the bore to which it will eventually be fitted. To avoid mistakes it is best to complete one set of rings at a time and refit the piston in the cylinder bore before proceeding to the next.

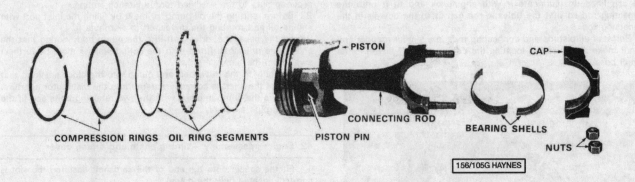

Fig. 2.22 Correct piston and connecting rod positioning (Sec 41)

6   To fit the rings onto the pistons calls for patience and care if breakages are to be avoided. The three rings for each piston must all be fitted over the crown, so obviously the first one to go on is the slotted oil control ring. Hold the ring over the top of the piston and spread the ends just enough to get it around the circumference. Then, with the fingers, ease it down, keeping it parallel to the ring grooves by 'walking' the ring ends alternately down the piston. Being wider than the compression rings no difficulty should be encountered in getting it over the first two grooves in the piston.

7   The lower compression ring, which goes on next, must only be fitted one way up. It is marked 'TOP' to indicate its upper face.

8   Start fitting this ring by spreading the ends to get it located over the top of the piston.

9   The lower compression ring has to be guided over the top ring groove and this can be done by using a suitable cut piece of tin which can be placed so as to cover the top groove under the ends of the ring.

10 Alternatively, a feeler blade may be slid around under the ring to guide it into its groove.

11 The top ring may be fitted either way up as it is barrel faced.

12 With the rings fitted, the piston/connecting rod assembly is ready for refitment in the cylinder.

13 Each connecting rod and bearing cap should have been marked on removal but in any case the cylinder number is etched lightly on the end of the cap and connecting rod alongside.

14 The connecting rod and bearing caps are numbered from 1 to 4 in the right bank of the cylinder block and from 5 to 8 in the left bank with the lower number commencing at the front of the block. The numbered side of the rod and cap must face toward the outside of the cylinder block and the notch in the top of the piston must face toward the front of the engine.

IMPORTANT: One side of the bearing cap and connecting rod is chamfered and this must be positioned toward the crankpin thrust face of the crankshaft to allow for the small radius between the journal and web (photo).

15 Before refitting the pistons, position the three rings around each piston so that the gaps are spaced from each other as shown in Fig. 2.70.

16 Clean the cylinder bores using a clean piece of lint-free cloth and lubricate the bores with some engine oil.

17 Fit a new shell bearing half into the first connecting rod ensuring the oil feed hole in the shell lines up with the hole in the connecting rod (Fig. 2.71).

18 Push the piston into the cylinder bore (the correct way round) until the oil control ring touches the face of the block. Then, using a piston ring compressor contract the rings and tap the piston into the cylinder (photo). Take great care to be sure that a ring is not trapped on the top edge of the cylinder bore and when tapping the piston in do not use any force. If this is not done the rings could easily be broken.

19 When the piston has been fully located in the bore push it down so that the end of the connecting rod seats on the journal on the crankshaft. Make sure the journal is well lubricated with engine oil.

20 Maintaining absolute cleanliness all the time, fit the other shell

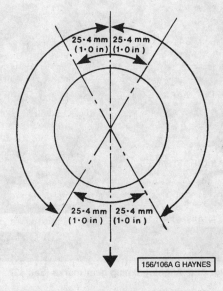

Fig. 2.23 Piston ring end gap positioning (Sec 41)

2C

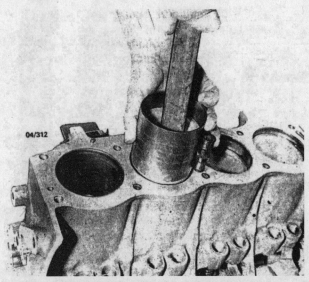

Fig. 2.24 Installing piston (Sec 41)

bearing half into the cap, once again with the notches in the bearing and cap lined up. Lubricate it with engine oil and fit it onto the connecting rod so that the holes in the cap fit to the dowels in the connecting rod.

21 Reinstall all pistons and connecting rods in a similar manner and do not make any mistakes locating the correct number piston in the correct bore.

22 When all the connecting rod caps are correctly fitted tighten the securing nuts to the specified torque wrench setting.

23 Before refitting the oil pump, prime it by filling the inlet port with engine oil and rotating the driveshaft to distribute it.

24 Fit the hexagonal driveshaft into the pump body noting that the end of the driveshaft fitted with the spring washer must be furthest away from the pump.

25 Carefully fit the driveshaft and pump into the block ensuring that the end of the shaft is correctly entered into the distributor aperture.

26 Secure the pump in place with the two retaining bolts and fit the filter and pipe assembly.

42 Engine reassembly – timing chain and timing cover

1   Fit the spacer onto the end of the camshaft ensuring the slot is correctly located over the dowel.

2   Rotate the camshaft so that the dowel is facing downward and then rotate the crankshaft so that the keyway in the front end of the crankshaft is facing upward in line with the camshaft dowel.

Note: *If the task is being carried out with the engine in the vehicle and the distributor has not been removed, lift off the distributor cap and check that the rotor is pointing toward the No. 1 cylinder spark plug lead position. If it is not, rotate the camshaft a full 360° until it is.*

3   Lay the camshaft and crankshaft sprockets on the bench so that the single dot on the camshaft sprocket perimeter is directly opposite the mark on the crankshaft sprocket. Maintain them in this position and fit the timing chain around both sprockets.

4   Carefully fit both sprockets and the chain onto the camshaft and crankshaft and tap them onto the dowel and keyway respectively.

5   Now make a careful check to ensure the timing marks are still correctly aligned.

6   Position the fuel pump eccentric on the camshaft dowel and secure it with the washer and bolt. Tighten the bolt to the specified torque wrench setting.

7   Place the oil thrower in position on the end of the crankshaft

8   Fit a new seal in the timing cover aperture ensuring it is the correct way round. Tap it fully home using a flat block of wood.

9   Select the front cover gasket and using a suitable sealing compound position it on the engine front plate and install the cover.

10 Place the front cover bolts in position and screw them up loosely. Fit the crankshaft damper onto the keyway of the crankshaft (photo). See that the boss of the damper is lubricated where the oil seal runs.

11 Reinstalling the crankshaft damper before tightening the cover bolts, centralises the seal to the damper. The bolts holding the cover may then be tightened to the specified torque wrench settings.

Fig. 2.25 Aligning timing gear marks (Sec 42)

Fig. 2.26 Fuel pump eccentric and oil slinger installation (Sec 42)

Fig. 2.27 Timing cover seal installation (Sec 42)

43 Engine reassembly – rear plate, crankshaft damper, oil pan and flywheel

1   If the engine rear plate has been removed it should now be refitted. Make sure that both metal faces are quite clean before reinstalling. No gasket is used.

2   Install the bolt and washer which locates the crankshaft damper, block the crankshaft with a piece of wood against the side of the crankcase and tighten the bolt to the specified torque wrench setting.

3   Clean all traces of old gasket which may remain from the oil pan joint faces and cover the faces of both the crankcase and pan with sealing compound. The oil pan gasket is in four sections which dovetail together and these should be carefully positioned and the joints interlocked.

4   The engine is then ready for the oil pan to be re-installed.

5   Clean the interior of the pan thoroughly, apply sealer to the joint edge and place it in position.

6   Install all the oil pan bolts and tighten them evenly to the specified torque wrench setting.

Fig. 2.28 Oil pan and gasket seals (Sec 43)

7   The flywheel may now be re-installed. Make sure that the mating flanges are clean and free from burrs and that the bolt holes line up correctly.

8   Screw in six retaining bolts and tighten them evenly to the specified torque wrench setting.

44 Engine reassembly – valve gear, cylinder heads and intake manifolds

1   When the cylinder heads have been cleaned and the valves lapped in as described in Sections 37 and 33, the cylinder heads may be reassembled. If the valves have been removed as described in Section 9, there will no confusion as to which valve belongs in which position.

2   Make sure all traces of carbon and paste have been removed, lubricate the valve stem with engine oil and place it in the appropriate guide.

3   It will then protrude through the top of the cylinder head.

4   Fit a new seal cup over the valve stem.

5   Place the valve spring over the valve stem.

6   Fit the circular retainer over the spring with the protruding center boss retainer downwards.

7   Using a proper valve spring compressor tool, compress the spring down the valve stem sufficiently enough to enable the two halves of the locks (collets) to be fitted into the groove in the valve stem. If necessary the locks should be smeared with grease to keep them in psition. The spring compressor may then be released. Watch to ensure that the locks stay together in position as the retainer comes past them. If the retainer is a little off center it may force one lock out of its groove in which case the spring must be recompressed and the lock repositioned. When the compressor is finally released, tap the head of the valve with a soft mallet to make sure the valve assembly is securely held in position.

8   Stand the engine the right way up on the bench and refit the valve lifters if they have been removed from the block. If these have been kept in order on removal, as suggested, it will be a simple matter to refit them.

9   Make sure that the cylinder head faces are clean and free from grease or oil and place the new head gaskets in position. To ensure correct location 'FRONT' is usually marked on the upper side of the gasket.

2C

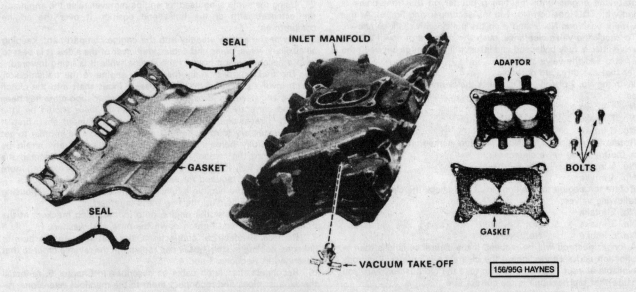

Fig. 2.29 Intake manifold and components (Sec 44)

10 Carefully place the cylinder heads in position on the block

11 Make sure the cylinder head bolts are clean and lightly oiled and refit them. Nip them all down lightly and then tighten them in the sequence shown in Fig. 2.56. The bolts should be tightened down to progressive torque loadings – (see Specifications) and finally to the specified torque wrench setting.

12 Now fit the pushrods into position, makings sure that they are reinstalled the same way up as they came out and according to the original valve position. This will not be difficult if they have been kept in order.

13 Position the rocker arms over the pushrods and valve stems and carefully tighten the remaining nuts just enough to retain the pushrods in their correct position. The valve clearances must be adjusted either now or at a later stage as described in the following Section.

14 To reinstall the inlet manifold first ensure that the cylinder head faces are clean and then lightly coat them with a suitable jointing compound.

15 Carefully stick the gaskets in place ensuring that the small front and rear pieces are interlocked with the two main gaskets.

16 Lower the intake manifold into place and check that none of the gaskets have been pushed out of position.

17 Insert the intake manifold securing bolts. Note that some of the bolts are longer than others and care must be taken to ensure that they are reinstalled in the correct hole.

18 Tighten the inlet manifold bolts progressively in the sequence shown in the accompanying figure and then finally tighten them to the specified torque wrench setting.

45 Valve lash – adjustment

1 The engines on all models use hydraulic valve lifters which automatically compensate for valve gear wear once the initial clearance has been correctly set. With the hydraulic lifter collapsed, the valve stem to lifter clearance must be periodically checked to make sure that it is within specification.

2 Repeated valve reconditioning such as valve or seat refacing can decrease the clearances to the point where the lifter cannot compensate and the valve could actually be left open. In this case, a shorter or longer pushrod will be required to bring the valve gear back into proper relationship.

3 To determine whether a shorter or longer pushrod may be required, rotate the engine with the ignition off until No. 1 piston is at TDC. This can be checked by removing the spark plug and placing your finger over the hole and rotating the engine until pressure is felt. This indicates that the piston is rising on the compression stroke. Continue to rotate the engine until the timing pointer on the front cover is aligned with TDC (position No. 1 in the accompanying figure). At this time, mark positions No. 2 and 3 on the pulley with chalk as shown.

4 To check the valve clearance, push the rocker arm down so that the valve lifter is fully collapsed and insert a feeler gauge between the rocker arm and the valve stem tip.
ameter that the threaded portion.

5 With the No. 1 piston at TDC, check the clerances on the following valves:

No. 1 intake	No. 1 exhaust
No. 7 intake	No. 5 exhaust
No. 8 intake	No. 4 exhaust

6 Rotate the engine to the No. 2 position marked on the pulley and check the following valve clearances:

| No. 5 intake | No. 2 exhaust |
| No. 4 intake | No. 6 exhaust |

7 Rotate the engine to position No. 3 and check the clerances on the following valves:

No. 2 intake	No. 7 exhaust
No. 3 intake	No. 3 exhaust
No. 6 intake	No. 8 exhaust

8 A longer pushrod will be required if the clearance is less than in Specification and a shorter one if the clearance is greater. Pushrods are available at your dealer, be sure to take the old pushrod with you to ensure that the new one is the correct size.

Position 1: No 1 at TDC at end of compression stroke
Position 2: Rotate crankshaft 180° clockwise from position 1 ($\frac{1}{2}$ turn)
Position 3: Rotate crankshaft 270° clockwise from position 2 ($\frac{3}{4}$ turn)

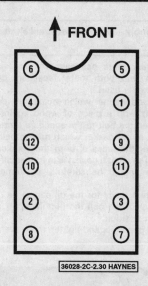

↑ FRONT

36028-2C-2.30 HAYNES

Fig 2.30 Intake manifold bolt tightening sequence (Sec 44)

46 Engine reassembly – installing auxiliary components

1 The exhaust manifolds are best reinstalled before putting the engine back into the car as they provide very useful holds if the engine has been manhandled at all. Note that no gaskets are used on the exhaust manifolds.

2 Reinstall each manifold, tighten the bolts evenly and bend over the locking tabs.

3 The auxiliary engine components must be re-installed and the method of doing this is detailed in the appropriate Chapters. Section 9 of this Chapter gives a full list of the items involved. When this has been done the engine is ready to put back into the car.

4 For details on how to re-install the distributor and ignition timing refer to Chapter 5.

47 Engine – installation

1 The procedure for installing the engine into the vehicle is basically the reversal of the removal procedure described in Sections 3 and 4.

2 Using the same sling used for engine removal, raise the engine on the extended arm of the hoist and position it over the engine compartment.

3 Lower the engine steadily into the engine compartment, keeping all auxiliary wires, pipes and cables well clear of the sides. It is best to have a second person guiding the engine while it is being lowered.

4 The tricky part is finally mating the engine to the transmission, which involves locating the transmission input shaft into the clutch housing and flywheel. Provided that the clutch friction plate has been centered correctly as described in Chapter 8, there should be little difficulty. Grease the splines of the transmission input shaft first. It may be necessary to rock the engine from side to side in order to get the engine fully home. Under no circumstances let any strain be imparted onto the transmission input shaft. This could occur if the shaft was not fully located and the engine was raised or lowered more than the amount required for very slight adjustment of position.

5 As soon as the engine is fully up to the transmission bellhousing replace the bolts holding the two parts together.

6 Now, finally lower the engine onto its mounting brackets at the front and replace and tighten down the nuts, and washers.

7 Replace all electrical connections, the fuel lines and carburetor linkages, cooling system hoses and radiator in the reverse order to that described in Sections 3 and 4.

8 Reconnect the clutch cable as described in Chapter 5, re-install the exhaust pipes and reconnect them to the manifold extensions, re-install the plate covering the lower half of the bellhousing and remove the supporting jack.

9 Fill the engine with fresh oil and refill with coolant.

48 Engine – initial start-up after overhaul or major repair

1   Make sure that the battery is fully charged and that all lubricants, coolants and fuel are replenished.

2   If the fuel system has been dismantled, it will require several revolutions of the engine on the starter motor to get the gas up to the carburetor. It will help if the plugs are removed and the engine turned over on the starter motor. This will ensure that gas is delivered to the carburetor and also that oil is being circulated around the engine prior to starting.

3   As soon as the engine fires and runs keep it going at a fast idle only (no faster) and bring it up to normal working temperature.

4   As the engine warms up there will be odd smells and some smoke from parts getting hot and burning off oil deposits. The signs to look for are leaks of oil or water which will be obvious if serious. Check also the clamp connections of the exhaust pipes to the manifolds as these do not always 'find' their exact gas-tight position until warmth and vibration have acted on them and it is almost certain that they need tightening further. This should be done, of course, with the engine stopped.

5   When the running temperature has been reached adjust the idling speed as described in Chapter 4.

6   Stop the engine and wait a few minutes to see if any lubricant or coolant is dripping out when the engine is stationary.

7   Road test the vehicle to check that the timing is correct and giving the necessary smoothness and power. Do not race the engine – if new bearings and/or pistons and rings have been installed it should be treated as a new engine and run in at reduced revolutions for 500 miles (800 km).

2C

Notes

Chapter 3 Cooling, heating and air conditioning systems

Refer to Chapter 13 for specifications and information on later models

Contents

Specifications

System type
Standard engine .... Pressurized, assisted by belt-driven water pump and fan
Turbo engine .... Pressurized, assisted by belt-driven water pump and electric fan
Thermostat type .... Wax pellet
Opening temperature
2.3L engine .... 188° to 195°F
3.3L, 4.2L and 5.0L engine .... 193° to 200°F
Fully open (all models) .... 212°F
Radiator type .... Corrugated fin, light metal construction of cross- or down-flow type
Pressure cap operating pressure
Specified .... 13 psi
Lower limit .... 11 psi
Upper limit .... 17 psi
Water pump type .... Belt-driven impeller
Cooling system capacities*
1978 thru 1979
2.3L engine (standard) .... 8.6 US qts
2.3L (air conditioning) .... 10.2 US qts
3.3L engine (all models) .... 9.0 US qts
5.0L engine (all models) .... 14.0 US qts
1980
2.3L engine (all models) .... 10.2 US qts
3.3L engine (all models) .... 9.0 US qts
4.2L engine (all models) .... 14.3 US qts
1981
2.3L engine (standard) .... 8.6 US qts
2.3L engine (air conditioning) .... 9.2 US qts
3.3L engine (all models) .... 9.0 US qts
4.2L engine (standard) .... 14.8 US qts
4.2L engine (air conditioning) .... 15.2 US qts
Coolant type .... 50/50 mix of Ford ESE-M97B18-C coolant or equivalent non-phosphate ethylene glycol anti-freeze

Approximate figures. Consult your owner's manual for actual capacity.

3

Drivebelt tension

$\frac{1}{4}$ in V-belt	
new (A)	50 to 80 lb
used	40 to 60 lb (B)
All other V- and cogged belts	
new (A)	120 to 160 lb
used	75 to 120 lb (C)
V-ribbed	
new (A)	140 to 170 lb
used	110 to 130 lb (D)

(A)   a new belt has been installed for less than one revolution of the pulley, a used belt for ten minutes of operation, or more
(B)   if less than 40 lb, readjust to 40 to 60 lb
(C)   if less than 75 lb, readjust to 90 to 120 lb
(D)   if less than 100 lb, readjust to 90 to 120 lb

Torque specifications

	Ft-lb	Nm
Fan shroud-to-radiator	2 to 4	3 to 5
Fan pulley-to-hub	12 to 18	16 to 24
Automatic transmission oil cooler fittings	9 to 12	12 to 24
Radiator hose clamps	1 to 2	2 to 3
Water pump-to-engine		
2.3L	14 to 21	19 to 28
3.3L	15 to 20	20 to 27
4.2L/5.0L	12 to 18	16 to 24

1 Cooling system – general information

The basic components of the cooling system consists of a radiator, which is connected to the engine by top and bottom hoses, a fan and a belt-driven water pump. Small bore hoses transfer coolant to the heater and automatic choke control unit.

Radiators are of either the crossflow or downflow type, depending on application.

Vehicles equipped with automatic transmissions use radiators with transmission oil coolers incorporated in their tanks.

The cooling system is pressurized so that higher coolant temperature may be maintained without boiling the coolant. Pressure is controlled by a spring-loaded radiator cap. If coolant pressure exceeds

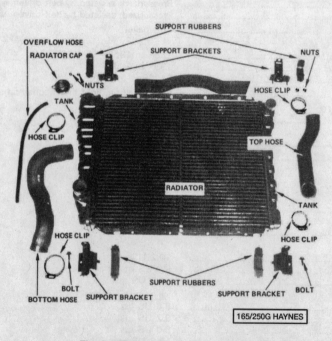

Fig. 3.1 Typical crosssflow radiator (Sec 1)

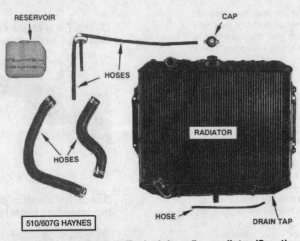

Fig. 3.2 Typical downflow radiator (Sec 1)

the preset limit of the spring, it releases and the pressure is bled from the system.

Constant coolant temperature is controlled by the thermostat. The thermostat remains closed during initial startup, restricting coolant flow and allowing fast warmup to operating temperature. Once operating temperature is reached, the thermostat opens and allow a free flow of coolant throughout the system.

All models use a coolant recovery system consisting of a plastic reservoir connected to the radiator inlet by a hose. When the coolant in the radiator expands, it is released by the radiator pressure cap into the reservoir. When the coolant in the radiator cools, it contracts and pulls the coolant in the reservoir back into the radiator through a vacuum relief valve in the pressure cap.

Proper operation of the cooling system can be maintained by ensuring that the coolant passages are free of restriction and hoses kept in good condition and the drive belts are frequently checked and properly adjusted.

---

2 Cooling system – draining, flushing, coolant mixing and filling

Note: *If equipped with turbocharger read the caution in Section 14.*
1   Do not perform the following tasks if the engine has been run to operating temperature. Hot steam and coolant can scald, and the pressures present in the system can force scalding liquid out causing widespread burning. If you wish to perform these tasks after operating

your car, leave it in a shady spot for at least one hour, or until the temperature gauge registers a nearly-cold engine when the ignition is switched on, but the engine is not started.
2   The car must be parked on a level, flat spot. Run the engine only long enough to move the vehicle, then shut it off immediately.
3   Place the heater controls on their hottest setting.
4   Raise the hood of the car and remove the radiator cap. If the engine and radiator are warm enough to give off noticeable heat, do not remove the cap. Once heat cannot be felt or when the engine becomes cool enough to touch comfortably with the palm of your hand, the radiator cap may be removed. Place a towel or heavy rag over the cap and turn the cap to its first detent position and allow any remaining pressure to dissipate, then twist it to the second position and remove.
5   Place a pan beneath the radiator to catch draining coolant. Coolant is poisonous and should not be poured into gutters or dumped into storm drains.
6   Open the drain petcock. On crossflow radiators this is located at the bottom of the right side reservoir tank and faces the rear of the vehicle. Vertical-flow radiators have their drain petcocks located on the right side of the lower reservoir tank.
7   When the system has been drained, close the petcock and tighten it until it is snug. Before disposing of the used coolant, check to see if it is rusty in color. If it is, and the coolant is very cloudy, it is advisable to flush the radiator and engine coolant passages.
8   Flushing may be performed in a number of ways. The easiest method is to flush the system with a brand-name flushing fluid

Fig. 3.3 Typical coolant recovery system (Sec 1)

Fig. 3.4 Typical radiator draincock location (Sec 2)

according to the manufacturer's directions. To remove the greatest amounts of scale and deposits, it is further recommended that you reverse-flush the system prior to filling. At least one manufacturer in the U.S. produces and markets a special fixture for this purpose. These are available through many auto parts stores.

9   If the reverse-flushing fixture is not available, or if you do not wish to undertake the expense, the most common method of flushing the engine block and radiator is with a garden hose adapter which can be installed in the lower spigot of the radiator and the lower hose adapter at the engine. This adapter provides a female garden hose coupling so that a garden hose may be hooked directly to the engine and radiator.

10 Begin reverse flushing by removing the thermostat (Section 12), then installing the hose. Turn the water on to a high pressure, then off several times to loosen the scale and all larger deposits. After this has been done several times, allow a steady stream of water to flow through the engine or radiator to flush out all loosened deposits.

11 If scale build-up is very severe due to the minerals in local water, consider using distilled water in place of tap water when refilling the cooling system.

12 When you are satisfied that the engine block water passages and the radiator are clean, fill the system with a mixture of ethylene glycol-based antifreeze mixed in the proper proportions (see manufacturer's specifications) with water, or with a 50/50 mixture of water and Ford Long Life Coolant, which is available from all authorized dealers. Before filling the system, make sure that the hoses are tightly clamped (Section 3), the drain plug has been tightened, and that the thermostat has been replaced (if it was removed for flushing the engine). The system is filled by pouring coolant into the radiator filler neck opening, which is covered by the radiator cap when the car is in use.

13 When the system has been filled, start the engine and allow it to run until the thermostat opens. Fill the radiator again until the proper levels of coolant are reached. On crossflow radiators, fill with coolant until it is within $2\frac{1}{2}$ to 4 in below the radiator cap seal. Vertical-flow radiators should be filled to a level $\frac{3}{4}$ to $1\frac{1}{2}$ in below the radiator cap seal.

14 When proper fill levels have been reached, and brief acceleration of the engine does not cause the coolant level to drop, the system is properly filled. Replace the radiator cap and tighten it fully. Continue to run the engine until proper pressure is built up. Inspect all joints and connections for water-tightness.

---

3   Hoses — removal, inspection, and installation

---

1   A key ingredient in the proper operation of the cooling system is the routine inspection of hoses and their connectors for condition. Another ingredient to long hose life is the proper removal and installation procedure, as incorrect methods will shorten the useful life of the hose and may also lead to the damaging of other engine components.

2   Routine inspection of hoses involves checking of all connections for watertight fit and all hoses for cracking. Squeeze each hose at several points along its length and closely inspect the surface for cracking, splitting, or breaks. If cracking is severe, replace the hose.

3   To remove the hoses, first park the car on a flat, level surface.

4   Disconnect the negative lead from the battery.

5   It is necessary to drain only enough coolant from the system to allow removal of the hose. Upper hoses will require far less draining than lower. Use the instructions in Section 2 for draining.

6   Loosen the hose clamps at each end of the hose.

7   Grasp the hose firmly, at the flange, twist and pull simultaneously. Discretion is required for this job. Do not 'muscle' the connectors on the radiator, for instance, as they are of soft, thin, alloy sheet and will deform or break very easily.

8   If the above procedure doesn't work, the hose will have to be cut from the flange to avoid the possibility of damaging flanges and other related parts.

9   Using a razor blade or art knife, carefully slit the hose in several shallow cuts. These cutting tools are manufactured of metal harder than the flanges and will gouge the flanges. These gouges will be the primary site of fatigue cracking later in the life of the engine, so take the time to cut the hose, only.

10 When the hose has been cut, carefully peel it away from the flange. Do not insert any tools or levers between the hose and the

Check for a chafed area that could fail prematurely.

Check for a soft area indicating the hose has deteriorated inside.

Overtightening the clamp on a hardened hose will damage the hose and cause a leak.

Check each hose for swelling and oil-soaked ends. Cracks and breaks can be located by squeezing the hose.

Fig. 3.5 Conditions to look for when inspecting hoses (Sec 2)

flange as these will also gouge or deform the flange, making sealing of the new hose difficult.

11 Inspect the inside surfaces of all removed hoses for evidence of mineral build-up and rust in the cooling system. If there is evidence of build-up, flush the system (Section 2).

12 Installation of the hoses is the reverse of removal.

13 Coat the flange surface with waterproof sealer.

14 Slide the hose over the flange and position the clamp as shown in the accompanying figure.

15 Tighten the clamp until the hose is snug on the flange.

16 Fill the cooling system with fresh coolant mixed according to the directions in Section 2.

17 Start the engine and allow it to reach operating temperature. Check all connections for leakage.

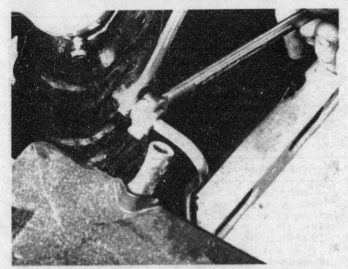

4.5 Hold the fitting closest to the radiator with a wrench when removing the transmission cooler lines to avoid damage to the radiator

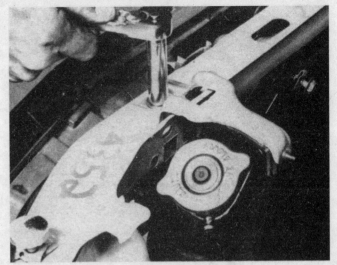

4.6A Removing crossflow radiator mounting bolts

4 Radiator – removal and installation

1   Park the car on a flat, level surface.
2   Disconnect the negative lead from the battery.
3   Drain the cooling system (Section 2).
4   Remove the cooling fan and shroud (Sections 7 or 10).
5   Remove the upper and lower hoses from the radiator. If your car is equipped with an automatic transmission, disconnect the hoses from the transmission oil cooler and plug the lines with rubber plugs. Place a pan beneath the radiator to catch any transmission fluid which may escape during the removal of the radiator (photo).
6   On cars with crossflow radiators, remove the two bolts which hold the radiator to its upper mounts. Remove the upper mounts. Lift the radiator from the car (photos).
7   On cars with vertical-flow radiators, remove the four mounting bolts, two on each side of the radiator, and lift the radiator from the car.
8   Installation is the reverse of the removal procedure.
9   If a new radiator is to be installed, the draincock from the old radiator must be installed. On automatic transmission models, the oil line adapters must also be installed, using an oil resistant sealer.

4.6B Lift the radiator out carefully to avoid damaging the cooling fins

5 Radiator – pressure testing, repair, and service

1   Aside from the tasks outlined in this Chapter, we recommend that you seek the services of a competent radiator repair shop for the performance of the above, and any other unlisted tasks. These shops are set up to perform this type of work on an efficient and low cost basis.

6 Radiator cap – pressure test

1   This task requires the use of several specialized tools which may be purchased from an authorized dealer. If you do not wish to undertake the expense of such equipment, have your dealer or a garage perform the following test.
2   Remove the radiator cap from the radiator filler neck. The engine must be cool at this time.
3   Wash the cap with water, paying careful attention to the cleaning of the rubber seal and the vacuum relief valve (Fig. 3.9).
4   Immerse the cap in water and install it on the end of special tool 21-0012 (Radiator Cap Pressure Test Adapter) or an equivalent. Leave this assembly immersed in your container of water.

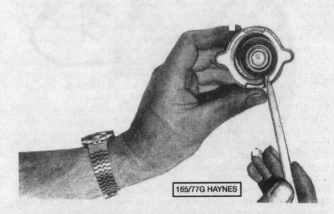

165/77G HAYNES

Fig. 3.6 Areas to check when inspecting the radiator cap (Sec 6)

3

5   Immerse the filler neck seal from the testing kit and install it in the other end of the filler neck adapter.

6   Remove the assembly from the water and install it on the radiator filler neck adapter, pressure tester.

7   Connect the special pressure test pump (an air pump with pressure gauge installed) according to the directions in the testing kit.

8   Depress the plunger of the pressure test pump slowly and note the highest pressure obtained. Do not depress the plunger quickly or false readings will result.

9   Release the pressure by turning the pressure relief screw counter-clockwise. Perform this test at least twice more to be sure of the reading, then check your results with the pressure test specification at the beginning of this Chapter. If the readings are not within the acceptable limits given, replace the radiator cap. If they are within the limits, have an authorized garage perform a pressure test on your cooling system.

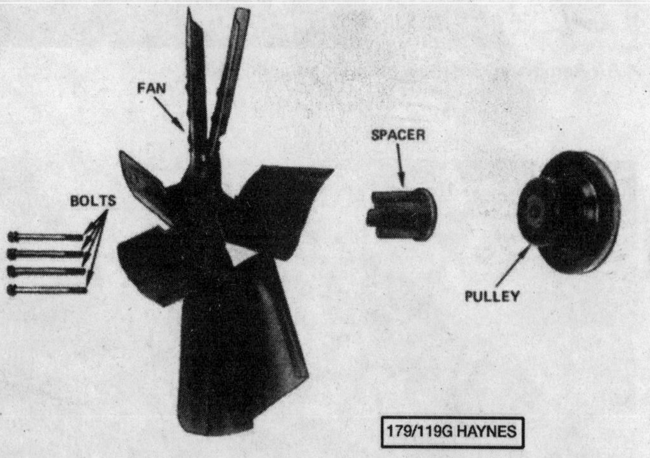

Fig. 3.7 Typical fan installation (non-Turbo) (Secs 7 and 8)

7 Cooling fan (except Turbo) – removal and installation

1   Disconnect the negative lead from the battery.

2   Remove the bolts which hold the fan shroud in place and remove the shroud.

3   Remove the bolts which hold the fan to the pulley and remove the fan.

4   Installation is the reverse of the removal procedure.

5   Tighten the fan bolts in a cross pattern.

6   Tighten the fan shroud mounting bolts in a cross pattern.

8 Cooling fan (all models) – inspection

1   Carefully check each of the fan blades for signs of cracking, material separations, and breakage. Be especially watchful when checking around the root of each blade, particularly on molded nylon blades, as this is an area of great stress and is most likely to show signs of stress first.

2   If any breaks, cracks, bends, or other damage is noted, do not reinstall the same fan. If it is necessary to use the car you are working on to go to a dealer and purchase another fan, do not, under any circumstances, start the engine while the hood is open, nor should you open the hood while the engine is running. Replace the fan immediately.

9 Thermostat – removal and installation

1   All engines in this line share a common variation from normal automotive practice in that the thermostat is designed to allow accurate placement of the thermostat by locking it into the housing.

2   Park the car on a flat, level surface.

3   Disconnect the negative lead from the battery.

4   Following the procedures in Section 2, drain about 2 quarts of coolant from the radiator.

5   Remove the two bolts which hold the thermostat housing to the engine block.

6   Carefully pull the housing from the block. There is a coating of gasket sealer whose grip must be broken. Do not insert any tools or other objects into the join between the housing and the block as damage to the sealing surfaces may result.

7   Remove the thermostat housing from the coolant hose by loosening the hose clamp and then twisting and pulling the housing from the hose at the same time. If removal is not possible in this way, follow the additional instructions provided in Section 3.

8   To remove the thermostat from the housing, hold the housing with

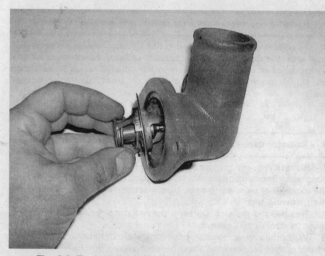

Fig. 3.8 Electric cooling fan (turbo) (Secs 8 and 15)

Fig. 3.9 Typical 6 and V8 thermostat installation (Sec 9)

the thermostat facing you. Turn the thermostat about $\frac{1}{4}$-turn or until the slots in the thermostat align with the tabs on the housing. Pull the thermostat toward you.

9 Check the thermostat to see if it is in the open position (piston is extended beyond the seat). If it is open dispose of it. If it is closed, perform the thermostat check outlined in Section 13, if you intend to reuse it.

10 Installation is the reverse of the removal procedure.

11 Clean all sealing surfaces with a gasket scraper or putty knife before assembling the thermostat and housing. Carefully clean all scraped material from the sealing surfaces.

12 Coat both sides of the gasket with a light coating of waterproof gasket sealer (photo).

13 Tighten both bolts evenly and allow the sealer to be squeezed flat, fill the cooling system with fresh coolant and water mixed according to the directions in Section 2.

10 Thermostat – testing

1 Remove the thermostat from its housing (Section 9).

2 Fill a pan with water and bring it to a boil.

3 Immerse the thermostat in the boiling water. The piston must raise at least $\frac{1}{8}$ in from the seat within one minute of immersion at 212°F (100°C). A greater extension is not cause for disposal, although a lesser extension will result in the thermostat needing replacement.

11 Water pump – description, removal, and installation

1 The water pump is of the impeller type and is driven by an accessory drivebelt off the oil pump. Operation of the pump is dependent upon proper drivebelt adjustment (Section 16) and proper condition of the pump.

2 The water pump need never be removed unless the engine block is being stripped down for rebuilding, or if the pump itself proves defective. Signs of water pump failure include coolant leakage, noisy operation, and excess vibration of the cooling fan and driveshaft (upon which the fan is mounted and from which the impeller is driven [except Electrodrive models]). Do not confuse an out-of-balance fan with a defective water pump. Always remove the fan (Section 7) and check the radial play of the water pump shaft. This is accomplished by grasping the water pump pulley and attempting to rock the mounting shaft up and down and from side to side. If rocking is felt the problem is most likely with the water pump. Removal of the water pump is as follows:

3 Disconnect the negative lead from the battery.

4 Remove the fan and shroud (Section 7).

5 Drain the cooling system (Section 2).

6 Loosen and remove all drivebelts (Section 16).

7 On some models, one of the water pump mounting bolts is also a bracket for the alternator. Remove the nut which holds the bracket in place and move it out of your work area.

8 Remove the four bolts which hold the fan pulley to the water pump flange and remove the pulley.

9 Remove the hoses which are connected to the water pump.

10 Remove the four bolts which hold the water pump to the engine block.

11 The water pump is located by three locating pins which match up to holes in the engine block. In order to break the seal between the engine and the pump, it is necessary to rap on the water pump flange with a rubber mallet or a hammer and block of wood. Do not insert any tools or other levering devices between the engine block and the water pump in an attempt to pry them apart as damage to the sealing surfaces may result (photo).

12 Clean all sealing surfaces with a gasket removal tool or a putty knife. Do not use a razor blade as this may damage the sealing surfaces.

13 Installation is the reverse of the removal procedure.

14 Coat the water pump gasket with a thin coating of waterproof sealant before installing it on the seal surface of the water pump (photo).

15 Tighten the four water pump bolts evenly, wait about five minutes for the sealer to be pushed down, then retighten the bolts.

16 Fill the cooling system with fresh coolant when parts installation and belt adjustment is complete.

9.12 The thermostat ready for installation with the gasket retained in place with grease or sealer

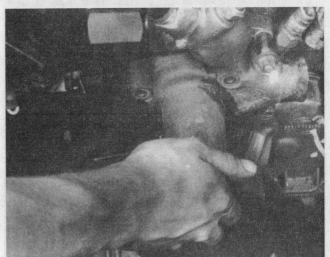

11.11 Rock the water pump up and down to break the gasket seal. Do not pry on the gasket surfaces

3

11.14 The water pump ready for installation, gasket retained with sealer

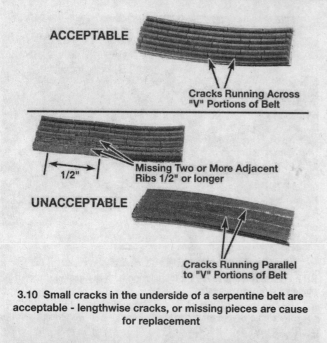

ACCEPTABLE

Cracks Running Across "V" Portions of Belt

1/2"

Missing Two or More Adjacent Ribs 1/2" or longer

UNACCEPTABLE

Cracks Running Parallel to "V" Portions of Belt

3.10 Small cracks in the underside of a serpentine belt are acceptable - lengthwise cracks, or missing pieces are cause for replacement

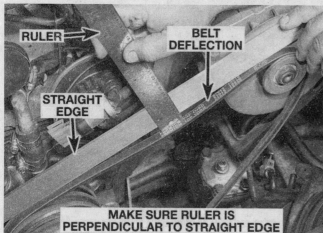

RULER

BELT DEFLECTION

STRAIGHT EDGE

MAKE SURE RULER IS PERPENDICULAR TO STRAIGHT EDGE

Fig. 3.11 Measuring belt deflection (Sec 13)

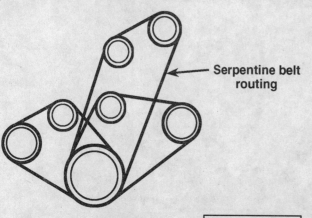

Serpentine belt routing

36028-03-3.12 HAYNES

Fig. 3.12 Typical ribbed belt installation (Sec 13)

12 Water pump – rebuilding

1   Water pumps are not an item which can be rebuilt economically by the home mechanic. We suggest that you purchase a new unit or investigate the purchase of a rebuilt exchange unit from an auto parts store.

13 Drivebelts – description, removal and installation

Note: *If equipped with turbocharger, see Caution in Section 14.*

1   Drivebelts are used to drive all ancillaries including the cooling fan, alternator, Thermactor pump, air conditioning pump and power steering pump. The belts vary in size and design, according to function.

2   Belts are considered stretched after ten minutes of use and must be adjusted. Ford Motor Company and its subsidiaries do not use 'inches of belt deflection' as a means of determining belt adjustment, but refer to 'pounds of adjustment'. This is determined by use of a tensionometer, available from an authorized Ford dealer. The 'pounds of tension' is based on the design of the belt being tested.

3   Belts are of three types; V-belts, cogged belts and V-ribbed belts. The V-ribbed belt is differentiated by the appearance of its inner surface which appears to be made up of several V-belts placed side by side (Fig. 3.14).

4   Drivebelt adjustment should be performed in the following manner. Locate each of the belts and measure the width. Using the tensionometer, adjust the belt to the tensions given in the Specifications Section at the beginning of the Chapter.

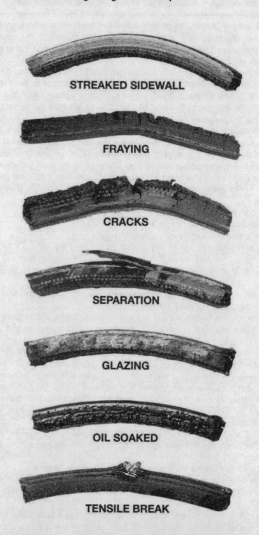

STREAKED SIDEWALL

FRAYING

CRACKS

SEPARATION

GLAZING

OIL SOAKED

TENSILE BREAK

Fig. 3.13 Typical drivebelt wear and damage

13.8 Using a pry bar to maintain tension when adjusting the drivebelt

5   If no tensionometer tool is available, belts can be adjusted using a straightedge and a ruler as shown in Fig. 3.15. Belts with a free span of less than twelve inches should have a deflection of between $\frac{1}{8}$ and $\frac{1}{4}$ inch (3 to 6 mm). The deflection of a belt with a span greater than twelve inches should be between $\frac{1}{8}$ and $\frac{3}{8}$ in (3 to 9 mm).

6   Vehicles equipped with ribbed belts must only be checked with the tensionometer because of the higher tension used with this type of belt. The deflection testing method described in Section 5 is not valid on these belts.

7   Drive belts should be inspected periodically for fraying, glazed or burned appearance (Fig. 3.17).

8   To adjust a drivebelt, loosen the bolt(s) on the component the belt is driving and, using a suitable pry bar, hold tension on the belt while the bolt is tightened (photo). Check the belt tension after tightening.

9   To remove a drivebelt, loosen the adjusting bolt and push the component inward toward the engine until the belt can be removed. Installation is the reverse of removal and the belt should be re-tensioned after ten minutes of running.

14 Electrodrive cooling fan (Turbo) – general information

Caution: Since the electric cooling fan is activated by temperature it may start at any time, even when the ignition is off. Always disconnect the battery negative cable when working in the vicinity of the fan.

The electric cooling fan is installed on 1980 turbocharged engines. The electrically-driven fan motor is activated by temperature switches in the radiator and the carburetor.

The fan operates whenever engine coolant temperatures reach 233 ° F (112 ° C) during normal driving. When the engine is shut off, the carburetor sensor activates the fan when the carburetor temperature reaches 155°F (68°C). A timer keeps the fan running for 20 minutes so that the fuel will not be vaporized, causing hard starting.

The fan motor is centrally mounted in the fan shroud and the fan is attached to the motor shaft by a retaining clip.

15 Electrodrive cooling fan (Turbo) – removal and installation

1   Disconnect the negative lead from the battery.

2   Unclip the fan motor wires from the shroud and unplug the connector at the motor pigtail connector.

3   Remove the four screws which mount the shroud to the radiator support and lift the shroud, complete with fan motor and fan from the car.

4   Set the shroud on a flat, clean area so that no dirt is transferred back into the engine compartment.

5   Remove the U-shaped retainer clip from the shaft and slide the fan from the motor shaft as shown in the accompanying figure.

6   Remove the three nuts which hold the fan motor to the shroud and lift the motor straight off the mounting studs.

7   Before assembling the motor, fan, and shroud for installation, make sure that the inspection of the fan has been carried out (Section 8).

8   Assembly and installation is the reverse of the stripdown procedure.

9   The fan motor mounting studs are pressed into the shroud and will break out or strip if overtightened. Tighten the nuts evenly until all are snug. Use thread sealer to prevent the nuts backing off.

10 Install the fan and retainer clip on the motor shaft. There is a key on the shaft to locate the fan.

11 Position the shroud on the radiator support brackets and install the four screws. Tighten the screws evenly.

12 Clip the wiring into position and reconnect the electrical plug.

13 Connect the battery cable.

16 Electrodrive cooling fan (Turbo) – testing the fan motor

1   There are three major components whose failure or improper operation will lead to overheating and hard hot starting. These components are the fan motor, fan relay, and the timer relay. To save time, the following test is divided into three sections. Perform the first test, then choose the symptom which best describes the remaining problem and complete that task. If problems persist, perform the entire test sequence, then seek the help of an authorized dealer if the problem is not solved.

Engine overheats and is hard to start

2   Unplug the motor connector. Using a jumper wire, connect the negative terminal to ground and the positive terminal to the positive terminal of the battery. If the motor does not run, replace it. If the motor does run, isolate the problem you are experiencing from the list below and perform the appropriate tests.

Engine overheats

3   Disconnect the timer relay plug. Turn the ignition ON and connect the coolant temperature switch to ground. If the fan does not run, replace the coolant temperature switch. If the fan does run, continue the steps below.

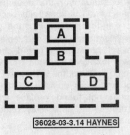

36028-03-3.14 HAYNES

Fig. 3.14 Electric fan coolant timer relay plug (Turbo) (Sec 16)

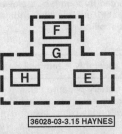

36028-03-3.15 HAYNES

Fig. 3.15 Electric fan timer relay connector (Turbo) (Sec 16)

Fig. 3.16 Typical heater core (Sec 17)

3.17 Remove the blower motor retaining screws and
remove the blower motor

4   Disconnect the coolant relay plug at the relay and check for power
at point A from the battery and point B from the ignition. See the
accompanying figure for the location of testing points. If power from
these sources is not found, check the fusible link and the fuse and
replace as necessary. Perform this test again. If power is found,
continue. If power is not found, check the wires for continuity and the
connectors for tight fit. If power is found, continue.
5   Turn the ignition OFF. Check the wire from point D to the motor
connector for continuity. Check the wire from point C to the coolant
temperature switch connector. If continuity is not found, service the
wiring and connectors as necessary. If continuity is found, replace the
coolant relay, remove the testing equipment, restore all connections.

Hard hot starting
6   Unplug the coolant relay plug. Turn the ignition ON and disconnect the carburetor temperature switch connector. Using a jumper
wire, connect the temperature switch connector to ground. If the fan
motor runs, replace the carburetor temperature switch. If the fan
motor does not run, continue with the steps below.
7   Unplug the connector at the timer relay and check for current from
point E to the battery and from point F to the ignition. If power is not
found, check fusible link H and fuse 6 and replace parts as necessary.
Repeat the test above. If power is not found, check and replace wiring
as necessary. If power is found, continue the tasks below.
8   Turn the ignition OFF. Check the wiring and connectors from point
G to the fan motor and from point H to the coolant temperature
switch. If continuity is not found, replace wiring as necessary. If
continuity is found, replace the timer relay, remove all test equipment,
and restore all connections.

17 Heating system – general information

The heating system operates by circulating engine coolant through
a heater core in the dash panel. The heater core is basically a small
radiator and air is forced through it by a blower to heat the interior of
the vehicle. This heated air is mixed with air from the ventilation
system to regulate temperature.

18 Heater blower assembly – removal and installation

1   Disconnect the battery negative cable.
2   Remove the screws securing the right ventilator assembly duct
and cable to the lower edge of the instrument panel and remove the
assemblies.
3   Remove the glove box liner and the 2 plastic rivets securing the
grille to the ventilator floor outlet and remove the grille from the
bottom of the ventilator.

3.18 Remove the clip from the blower motor and
slide the fan off of the shaft

4   Remove the right register duct and register assembly to give
access to the upper right ventilator retaining screw. The screw can
then be removed using a long extension through the register opening.
5   Remove the screws retaining the ventilator assembly to the
blower assembly and slide the ventilator assembly to the blower
assembly and slide the ventilator assembly to the right and then down
to remove it.
6   Disconnect the control cable from the door crank arm and remove
the cable assembly.
7   Disconnect the orange and black striped wire from the heater
blower resistor assembly and push it back into the case.
8   Remove the right side cowl trim panel and disconnect the black
blower ground terminal plug.
9   Remove the 3 screws retaining the blower motor flange to the
housing. For better access to the screws, it may be necessary to
remove the blower wheel. This is accomplished by removing the motor
hub clamp spring with hose clamp pliers and sliding the wheel from
the shaft.
10 Installation is the reverse of removal with attention paid to the
following paragraph.
11 The plastic rivets removed in paragraph 3 can be replaced with
two 10 x 12 in metal screws. Use a new push nut when re-connecting
the cable removed in Paragraph 6. When reinstalling the blower motor
wheel, refer to the accompanying figure and use a new hub clamp
spring.

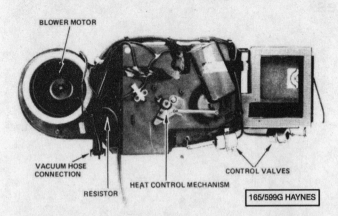

BLOWER MOTOR

VACUUM HOSE
CONNECTION

RESISTOR

HEAT CONTROL MECHANISM

CONTROL VALVES

165/599G HAYNES

Fig. 3.19 Heater case and components (Secs 19 and 20)

19 Heater core – removal and installation

1   Loosen the radiator cap, open the radiator draincock and partially drain the cooling system which will also drain the heater core.
2   Disconnect the heater core inlet and outlet hoses where they enter the back of the core (see the accompanying figure). Plug the heater core tubes to prevent spillage when the core is removed inside the vehicle.
3   Remove the glove box inner liner to give access to the heater core cover. Note: *Some vehicles may not have a removable cover for access to the heater core. To replace the core on such vehicles, the entire heater case must be removed and disassembled.*
4   Remove the instrument panel cowl brace.
5   Move the temperature control lever to the 'Warm' position.
6   Through the glove box opening, remove the 4 screws retaining the heater core cover and remove the cover (see the accompanying figure).
7   Loosen the 3 heater case mounting studs from the engine compartment side.
8   Push the heater core tubes and seal toward the inside of the vehicle to separate the core assembly from the heater case.
9   Withdraw the heater core assembly through the glove box and remove it.
10 Installation is the reverse of removal. Refill the cooling system and check the heater for proper operation.

20 Heater case – removal and installation

1   Disconnect the battery negative cable.
2   Remove the right ventilator and register duct assembly as described in Section 18.
3   Remove the screw retaining the right half of the floor heat distribution duct to the temperature control cable housing bracket (see

the accompanying figure). Remove the duct assembly by sliding it toward the passenger side of the vehicle.
4   Remove the 2 retaining screws securing the left half of the floor distribution duct to the heater core assembly. If the vehicle has any but the standard AM radio, the radio must be removed to give sufficient room for the left half of the duct to be removed.
5   Remove the left half of the duct by sliding it toward the driver side of the vehicle.
6   Remove the glove box and door and the instrument panel brace.
7   Remove the heater case-to-cowl bracket.
8   Disconnect the heater controls.
9   Disconnect the wiring harness at the resistor assembly.
10 Remove the right side cowl trim panel and disconnect the heater blower motor ground wire.
11 Partially drain the cooling system and disconnect the heater hoses from the heater core as described in Section 19.
12 Remove the 3 stud nuts securing the heater case to the dash and remove the heater case assembly as shown in the accompanying figure.
13 To install, place the heater case in position so that the 3 mounting studs fit through the dash panel mounting holes and install the mounting nuts finger-tight.
14 Install the heater case mounting bracket over the stud on the heater case-to-cowl bracket.
15 Install the glove box and instrument panel-to-cowl brace. Fully tighten the heater case stud nuts.
16 Install the heater core inlet and outlet hoses and refill the cooling system to the proper level.
17 Connect the wiring harness to the resistor assembly.
18 Install the heater blower ground terminal.
19 Install the right side cowl trim panel and re-connect the heater controls.
20 Place the left half of the floor heat distribution duct onto the left end opening of the heater case assembly and engage the retaining clip. Install the 2 retaining screws.
21 Install the right half of the heat distribution duct to the end opening of the left half of the floor heat distribution duct.
22 Install the distribution duct bracket to the temperature control housing mounting bracket. Install the radio.
23 Install the right ventilator assembly as shown.
24 Run the engine, check for leaks and test the heater for proper operation.

21 Air conditioner – general information

The air conditioner cools the vehicle interior by transferring heat to a refrigerant which is pumped through the condenser mounted in front of the radiator. The refrigerant is then circulated back to the interior of the vehicle through a compressor and back to the condenser.

The volume and circulation of the cooled air is controlled by a four-position blower and a system of outlets and doors in the ventilation system.

Other than keeping the condenser fins free of obstuctions, checking the hose condition and drivebelt tension, maintenance or repairs of the air conditioner should be left to your dealer or a qualified repair shop.

3

Notes

Chapter 4 Fuel and exhaust systems

Refer to Chapter 13 for specifications and information on later models

Contents

4

Specifications

Fuel pump
Type .... Mechanical, operated by the camshaft, diaphragm in pump provides
vacuum (Electric in Turbo)

Static pressure
2.3L and 3.3L .... 5.0 to 7.0 psi
4.2L and 5.0L .... 6.0 to 8.0 psi

Minimum volume flow
2.3L .... 1 US pt in 25 seconds
3.3L .... 1 US pt in 30 seconds
4.2L and 5.0L .... 1 US pt in 20 seconds

Carburetor
2.3L
49-state .... Holley 5200 2-V
California .... Holley 6500 2-V
3.3L
49-state .... Holley 1946 1-V
California .... Holley 1946C 1-V
4.2L, all .... Motorcraft 7200VV 2-V
1979 5.0L
49-state .... Motorcraft 2150 2-V
California .... Motorcraft 2700VV 2-V
Engine speed setting, all .... Refer to emission decal
Fuel tank capacity (approximate) .... 16.0 US gallons

Filters
Fuel filter .... Disposable in-line filter with paper element
Air filter .... Replaceable paper element

Torque specifications

	ft-lb	Nm
Fuel pump-to-block		
2.3L	19 to 28	26 to 35
3.3L	16 to 24	21 to 32
4.2L and 5.0L	19 to 27	26 to 37
Carburettor-to-intake manifold		
2.3L	10 to 15	14 to 19
3.3L, 4.2L and 5.0L	12 to 15	16 to 19

1   General description

All vehicles use a rear-mounted fuel tank and the fuel is drawn from the tank to the carburetor by a fuel pump.

On Turbocharged models the fuel pump is electric while on all others it is mechanically actuated by the engine camshaft.

The exhaust systems of all vehicles incorporate a catalytic converter which requires that unleaded fuel be used.

2   U.S. Federal regulations – emission controls

The fuel system is designed so that the car will comply with all US Federal regulations covering emission hydrocarbons and carbon monoxide. To achieve this, the ignition system must be accurately set using the proper equipment. Proper ignition timing is a must before attempting any other emission-related adjustments. The information in this Chapter is given to assist the reader to clean and/or replace certain components before taking the vehicle to the local Ford dealer or repair shop for final adjustments. Failure to do this could mean that the car will not comply with the regulations.

3   Thermostatic air cleaner and duct system – general description

1   The air cleaner on all models is retained by studs projecting from the top of the carburetor with wing nuts.
2   An additional feature is the control system for intake air to ensure that fuel atomization within the carburetor takes place using air at the correct temperature. This is effected by a duct system which draws in fresh air or pre-heated air from a heat shroud around the engine exhaust manifold.
3   Operation of the system can be summarized as follows:
4   When the engine is cold, heated air is directed from the exhaust manifold into the air cleaner, but as the engine warms up, cold air is progressively mixed with this warm air to maintain a carburetor air temperature of 105° to 130°F (40.5 to 76.8°C). At high ambient temperatures the hot air intake is closed off completely.
5   The mixing of air is regulated by a vacuum-operated motor on the air cleaner duct, which is controlled by a bi-metal temperature sensor and cold weather modulator valve.
6   An additional feature on cars with catalytic converters or Cold Temperature Actuated Vacuum (CTAV) systems is an ambient temperature sensor mounted within the air cleaner. This switch is operated by ambient temperature changes and under certain conditions will override the cold weather modulator system.

4   Thermostatic air cleaner – testing

Vacuum motor and valve assembly
1   Check that the valve is open when the engine is switched off. Start the engine, and check that the valve closes when idling (except where the engine is hot). If this fails to happen, check for disconnected or leaking vacuum lines, and for correct operation of the bi-metal sensor (see below).
2   If the valve closes, open and close the throttle rapidly. The valve should open at temperatures above 55°F (12.7°C) during the throttle operation. If this does not happen, check the valve for binding.

Bi-metal switch
3   The bi-metal switch can be checked by subjecting it to heated air, either from the engine or from an external source (eg, a hair dryer). Do not immerse it in water or damage may occur.

Cold weather modulator valve
4   Without the use of a supply of refrigerant R-12 and a vacuum source, testing is impractical. If the modulator valve is suspected of being faulty it should be tested by your Ford dealer.

5   Air cleaner element – removal and installation

1   Remove the wing nut(s) attaching the air cleaner top plate to the air cleaner housing.
2   Remove the air cleaner top and take out the air filter element.
3   Installation is the reverse of removal. On 2.3L air cleaners, recheck the torque on the first wing nut after tightening the second one.

Fig. 4.1 Typical thermostatic air cleaner and components (Secs 3, 4 and 5)

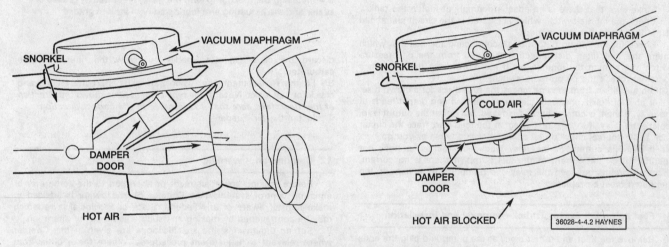

Fig. 4.2 Vacuum-operated duct operation (Secs 3 and 4)

36028-4-4.2 HAYNES

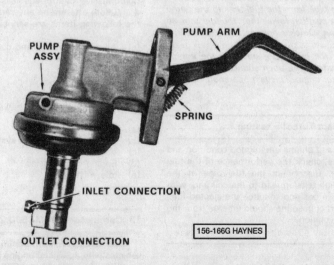

156-166G HAYNES

Fig. 4.3 Typical mechanical fuel pump

4

6   Fuel pump (except Turbo) – general description

The fuel pump is bolted to the left side of the engine front cover. The fuel pump actuator arm is operated by the camshaft or, on V8 models, an eccentric bolted to the end of the camshaft.

The pump is a sealed unit and must be discarded and replaced by a new one if a fault develops.

7   Electric fuel pump (Turbo) – general description

1   Electric fuel pumps are installed in all Turbo models with automatic transmissions. This pump is of the submersible type and is located in the fuel tank.
2   The testing section which follows will enable you to determine whether or not the fuel pump in your car is working. We recommend that you leave all removal and installation of the pump assembly itself to the mechanics in an authorized dealership.

8   Electric fuel pump (Turbo) – testing

1   Make sure that there is an adequate supply of fuel in the tank.
2   Check the inertia switch, which is located in the circuit just ahead of the fuel pump has not tripped.
3   Check for fuel pump output by disconnecting the fuel line which enters the fuel filter, disconnecting the lead from the oil pressure switch and turning the ignition on. If fuel flows from the line into a container, check the oil pressure switch.
4   If no fuel flows from the line, check the fuse block for a blown fuse.
5   If no fuel flows, check the power at the feed and output leads of the relay. If there is current at the feed lead, but not at the output lead, replace the relay. If there is no current at the feed lead, trace the circuit back to its source, checking all connectors and wires as you go.
6   If there is current at the relay leads and the pump does not operate, check the current at the fuel pump. If there is no current, check all circuits between the relay and pump. If ther is current, the fuel pump must be replaced.

9   Fuel pump (all except Turbo) – removal and installation

1   Remove the inlet and outlet pipes at the pump and plug the ends to stop fuel loss or dirt finding its way into the fuel system (photo).
2   Undo and remove the two bolts and spring washers that secure the pump to the cylinder block.
3   Lift away the fuel pump and gasket.
4   Installing the fuel pump is the reverse sequence to removal but there are several additional points that should be noted: (photo)
   (a) *Tighten the pump securing bolts to the specified torque*
   (b) *Before reconnecting the pipe from the fuel tank to the pump inlet, move the end to a position lower than the fuel tank so that fuel can syphon out. Quickly connect the pipe to the pump inlet*
   (c) *Disconnect the pipe at the carburetor and turn the engine over until gasoline flows from the open end. Quickly connect the pipe to the carburetor union. This last operation will help to prime the pump*

10   Fuel pump (all models except Turbo) – testing

1   Assuming that the fuel lines and unions are in good condition and that there are no leaks anywhere, check the performance of the fuel pump in the following manner. Disconnect the fuel pipe at the carburetor inlet union, and the high tension lead to the coil and, with a suitable container or large rag in position to catch the ejected fuel, turn the engine over. A good spurt of gasoline should emerge from the end of the pipe every second revolution.

11   Fuel filter – replacement

1   Initially remove the carburetor air cleaner.
2   Loosen the fuel line clips at the filter, pull off the fuel lines and

9.4 Installing the fuel pump with the gasket retained by grease or sealer and the actuating arm lubricated with lithium grease

discard the clips. On later models, unscrew the filter from the carburetor.
3   Fit the replacement filter using new clips, start the engine and check for fuel leaks. **Note:** *If the replacement filter shows the direction of fuel flow, take care that it is installed in the correct direction.*
4   Install the air cleaner.

12   Carburetion – warning

1   Before making any adjustment or alteration to the carburetor or emission control systems (see Chapter 6), the owner is advised to make himself aware of any Federal, State or Provincial laws which may be contravened by making any such adjustment or alteration.
2   Setting dimensions and specifications are given in this Chapter where relevant to adjustment procedures. Where these differ from those given on the engine tune-up decal, the decal information should be assumed to be correct.
3   Where the use of special test equipment is called for (eg, exhaust gas CO analyzer, etc), and this equipment is not available, any setting or calibration should be regarded as a temporary measure only and should be rechecked by a suitably equipped dealer or carburetion/emission control specialist at the earliest opportunity.
4   Before attempting any carburetor adjustments, first ascertain that the following items are serviceable or correctly set:

(a)   All vacuum hoses and connections
(b)   Ignition system
(c)   Spark plugs
(d)   Ignition initial advance

5   If satisfactory adjustment cannot be obtained check the following:

(a)   Carburetor fuel level
(b)   Crankcase ventilation system
(c)   Valve clearance
(d)   Engine compression
(e)   Idle mixture

13   Carburetor (5200/6500 2-V) – general information, 2.3L

The Holley/Weber Model 6500 Feedback carburetor is fitted to all vehicles with a 2.3 liter engine in California. The Model 6500 carburetor differs from the Model 2500 in design by the addition of a more elaborate fuel metering system in order to comply with California emission standards. All of the adjustments are otherwise identical.

Vehicles designed for sale outside California are equipped with the Holley/Motorcraft 5200 2-V carburetor.

Both carburetors are of a two stage, double venturi design. The second venturi is larger than the primary and is linkage operated. The primary stage comprises a curb idle system, idle transfer system, accelerator pump system, main metering and power enrichment systems.

The secondary venturi includes a secondary idle system, main metering system, transfer system and power enrichment.

Both stages draw fuel from a common bowl.

On both carburetors the choke is electrically operated.

Due to changes during production, the carburetor on your specific vehicle may differ from those in this manual. Refer to your local dealer for updates or specific information.

14 Fast idle cam clearance (5200/6500) – adjustment

1 Insert the unmarked shank of a twist drill 0.1 in (2.5 mm) diameter between the lower edge of the choke plate and the air horn wall. **Note:** *a No. 38 drill is 0.1015 in; No. 39 drill is 0.0995 in.*
2 With the fast idle screw held on the bottom step of the fast idle cam, against the top step, the choke lever tang and the fast idle cam arm should *just* be in contact. Bend the choke lever tang up or down as necessary.

15 Carburetor curb idle (5200/6500), TSP-off and fast idle speed adjustments

Note: *Read Section 2 before beginning.*
1 Remove the air cleaner and plug all vacuum lines at the vacuum source end.
2 Apply the parking brake and block the roadwheels.
3 Check, and adjust if necessary, the choke and throttle linkage for freedom of movement.
4 Start the engine and run it up to normal operating temperature.
5 Disconnect the EGR vacuum line at the valve, and plug the line.
6 Where applicable, set the air conditioning to OFF.
7 Where applicable, remove the spark delay valve and route the primary advance vacuum signal directly to the distributor vacuum diaphragm unit (advance side).
8 Set the automatic transmission to 'Park', or manual transmission to 'Neutral', then run the engine at normal operating temperature. Check that the choke plates are closed, then set the throttle so that the fast idle adjustment screw contacts the kick-down step of the choke cam; adjust the fast idle adjusting screw to obtain the specified rpm as shown in the accompanying figure.
9 Set the throttle to the high step of the choke cam and allow the engine to run for 5 seconds (approximately).
10 Rotate the choke cam until the fast idle adjustment screw contacts the choke cam kick-down step. Allow the engine speed to stabilize, then recheck the fast idle rpm, as described in paragraphs 8 and 9; readjust if necessary, then repeat the procedure given in the first sentence of this paragraph to ensure the same, consistent result.
11 Allow the engine to return to the normal idle, then for automatic transmission models select 'Drive'.
12 Where no TSP assembly is fitted, adjust the curb idle screw in or out to obtain the specified curb idle speed, then proceed to paragraph 16.
13 Where a TSP assembly is fitted, adjust the curb idle screw which contacts the solenoid plunger to obtain the specified curb idle speed (the solenoid is energized and the plunger extended when the ignition is ON) as shown in the accompanying figure.
14 Now collapse the solenoid plunger by forcing the throttle linkage against the plunger, grasping the throttle lever and solenoid housing between the thumb and index finger to alleviate movement of the solenoid assembly position.
15 Adjust the TSP-off adjusting screw to obtain the specified TSP-off idle speed.
16 Open the throttle slightly to allow the solenoid plunger to extend.
17 Provided that all adjustments are now satisfactory, stop the engine, then install the air cleaner and its associated vacuum lines.

18 Restart the engine and if necessary run it up to normal operating temperature. With the engine running at 2000 rpm (approximately) select 'Park' (automatic transmission) or 'Neutral' (manual transmission). Allow 5 seconds (approximately) for the speed to stabilize, then let the engine return to idle; set automatic transmission models to 'Drive'. Recheck the curb idle speed, and if necessary readjust as described in paragraph 12 onwards.
19 Install all vacuum lines.

16 Carburetor (5200/6500) – idle mixture adjustment

Note: *Idle mixture adjustment can only be satisfactorily carried out by using special test equipment. Refer to your local dealer or repair shop for proper adjustment.*

17 Carburetor (5200/6500) – choke plate vacuum pull-down

1 Remove the air cleaner if the carburetor is installed on the engine.
2 Remove the three screws and the ring retaining the choke thermostatic spring cover. Do not remove the screw retaining the water cover.
3 Pull the cover assembly away and remove the electric assist assembly.
4 Set the fast idle cam on the second step, then use a screwdriver to push the diaphragm stem back against its stop.
5 Insert the unmarked shank of a twist drill 0.20 in (5 mm) between the lower edge of the choke plate and the air horn wall. **Note:** *No. 7 drill is 0.201 in; No. 8 drill is 0.199 in.*
6 Adjust the choke plate-to-air horn wall clearance by turning the vacuum diaphragm adjusting screw, as necessary, with a hexagonal wrench.

18 Carburetor (5200/6500) – dry float setting

1 The dry float setting can only be checked at the appropriate stage of carburetor disassembly.
2 With the bowl cover inverted, and the float tang resting lightly on the spring loaded fuel inlet needle, measure the clearance between the edge of the float and the bowl cover using the unmarked shank of a twist drill of 0.44.0.48 in (11.2/12.2 mm) diameter. **Note:** $\frac{7}{16}$ *in (0.4375 mm) drill plus feeler gauges can be used.*
3 To adjust the clearance, bend the float tang as necessary so that both floats are equally adjusted. Do not scratch or otherwise damage the float tang.

19 Carburetor (5200/6500) – secondary throttle stop screw

1 The secondary throttle stop screw can only be set at the appropriate stage of carburetor disassembly.
2 Back off the screw until the secondary throttle plate seats in its bore as shown in the accompanying figure.
3 Turn the screw until it touches the tab on the secondary throttle lever, then turn it an additional $\frac{1}{4}$ turn.

20 Carburetor (5200/6500) – removal and installation (2.3L)

1 Remove the air cleaner as described in Section 5.
2 Disconnect the fuel feed line from the carburetor.
3 Disconnect the electrical leads and vacuum lines from the carburetor.
4 Disconnect the throttle cable/kick-down cable from the carburetor.
5 Partially drain the cooling system and disconnect the water hoses from the choke housing.
6 Using suitably cranked ring/socket wrenches, remove the carburetor mounting nuts. Lift off the carburetor and gasket.
7 Installing the carburetor is basically the reverse of the removal procedure, but ensure that a new flange gasket is used.

4

21 Carburetor (5200/6500) – dismantling and reassembly

1   Before dismantling wash the exterior of the carburetor and wipe off using a lint-free rag. Select a clean area of the workbench and lay several layers of newspaper on the top. Obtain several small containers for putting some of the small parts in, which could be easily lost. Whenever a part is to be removed look at it first so that it may be installed in its original position. As each part is removed place it in order along one edge of the newspaper so that by using this method reassembly is made easier.

Carburetor bowl cover

2   Unscrew and remove the fuel filter retainer from the upper body. Recover the filter.
3   Disconnect the choke plate operating rod at its upper end.
4   Undo and remove the screws and spring washers that retain the upper body to the lower body. Lift away the upper body and the gasket.
5   Carefully extract the float pivot pin and lift out the float assembly followed by the needle valve.
6   Unscrew the needle valve seat and remove the gasket.
7   Remove the three enrichment valve vacuum diaphragm screws. Remove the washers and diaphragm.

Automatic choke

8   Remove the single screw and washer from the choke housing. Remove the cover and gasket.
9   Remove the thermostatic spring housing retaining ring screws. Remove the retaining ring, housing and electric choke heater.
10 Remove the choke housing assembly screws; note the long screw on the long leg of the assembly. Move the housing away from the main body, disengaging the fast idle rod. Remove the O-ring from the vacuum port.
11 Remove the choke shaft nut, lock washer, lever and fast idle cam.
12 Remove the fast idle lever retaining screw, the fast idle lever and the spacer. Take off the screw and spring from the lever.
13 Remove the choke diaphragm cover screws. Remove the cover, spring and diaphragm/shaft.

Accelerator pump

14 Remove the four pump screws and the pump cover. Remove the pump diaphragm and spring.
15 Remove the pump discharge screw assembly, the discharge nozzle and the two gaskets. Remove the two discharge check balls.

Main body

16 Remove the primary high speed plug and the main well tube.
17 Remove the secondary high speed bleed plug and the main well tube. Note the size of the primary and secondary plugs and tubes to ensure correct assembly.
18 Remove the primary and secondary main jets, noting their sizes to ensure correct assembly.
19 Remove the enrichment valve and gasket.
20 From the side of the carburetor body, remove the idle jet retainers and idle jets.
21 Turn the idle limiter cap counter-clockwise to the rich stop. Remove the cap, then count the exact number of turns to *just* seat the idle mixture needle. Remove the needle and spring.
22 Detach the secondary operating lever return spring.
23 Remove the primary throttle lever nut and locking tab. Remove the lever and flat washer followed by the secondary lever assembly and lever bushing.
24 Remove the idle adjustment lever spring and shaft washer. Note how the primary throttle return spring is hooked over the idle adjustment lever and the carburetor body.
25 Remove the idle speed screw and spring from the idle adjustment lever.
26 Remove the secondary throttle lever nut, lock washer, flat washer and the lever itself.
27 Remove the secondary idle adjustment screw.
28 Remove the solenoid throttle positioner (TSP) from the carburetor body if considered necessary.

29 Dismantling is now complete and all parts should be thoroughly washed and cleaned in a suitable solvent. Remove any sediment in the float chamber and drillings but take care not to scratch the fine drillings while doing so. Remove all traces of old gaskets using a sharp knife. When all parts are clean reassembly can begin.

a)   Main body: Ensure that the idle mixture screws are installed in exactly the same position as determined at paragraph 21, then install a new limiter cap with the stop tab against the rich side of the stop on the carburetor body. Now ensure that the main jets, primary and secondary main well tubes, and high speed bleeds are correctly fitted in their respective positions.
b)   Accelerator pump: When installing the return spring and pump diaphragm assembly, start the four cover screws, then hold the pump lever partly open to align the gasket; then tighten the screws.
c)   Automatic choke: When installing the diaphragm adjusting screw, initially adjust it so that the threads are flush with the inside of the cover. Fit the fast idle rod with the end which has one tab in the fast idle adjustment lever, and the end which has two tabs in the primary throttle lever. Adjust the choke plate pull-down as described in Section 17. Before installing the electric choke heater ensure that the choke plate is either fully open or fully closed.
d)   Bowl cover: When installing the enrichment valve vacuum diaphragm, depress the spring and fit the screws and washers fingertight. Hold the stem so that the diaphragm is horizontal, then tighten the screws evenly. Adjust the dry float setting as described in Section 18.

22 Carburetor (1946 1-V) – general description. 3.3L

1   The Holley Model 1946 1-V is used on 3.3 liter six-cylinder engines. It uses seven systems to provide for the proper air/fuel mixture for fuel economy, emissions and driveability. The systems are as follows: fuel inlet system, idle system, main metering system, power enrichment system, accelerator pump system, external fuel bowl vent system and the automatic choke system.
2   Three main assemblies comprise the carburetor, the air horn, main body and throttle body.

23 Carburetor (1946 1-V) – adjustments, notes and precautions

1   When making any adjustments to the carburetor, make sure that all hoses and lines are connected to the air cleaner assembly even when the assembly is moved to clear the carburetor. The air cleaner assembly, including the filter, should be fitted for any adjustment governing engine speed.
2   Due to the interaction of emission controls and temperature changes, the engine speed may oscillate. If this is encountered, use the average engine speed.
3   Do not allow the vehicle to idle for long periods of time as overheating of the catalytic converter may result in excessive underbody temperatures.
4   Always apply the parking brake and block the wheels before making any underhood carburetor adjustments.
5   Except where otherwise noted, turn all accessories to OFF.
6   The fuel evaporative purge valve MUST be disconnected. Disconnect as follows: Trace the purge valve vacuum hose from the purge valve to the first place the vacuum hose can be disconnected from the underhood routing, eg: vacuum tee connection. Disconnect the hose and plug both the hose and the open connection.

24 Fast idle rpm (1946 1-V) – adjustment and check

1   Connect a tachometer to the engine.
2   Disconnect the EGR hose from the valve and plug the hose.
3   With the choke off and the engine running at normal operating temperature, raise the speed of the engine to 2500 rpm for 15 seconds. Place the fast idle lever on the specified step of the fast idle cam (Refer to the mission decal in the engine compartment).
4   Allow the engine speed to stabilize and measure the engine speed

(rpm). Depending upon the engine and the state of tune, it may require anywhere from 15 seconds to 2 minutes for the engine speed (number of rpm) to stabilize.
5   Repeat the above step three times to ensure accuracy.
6   Adjust the fast idle screw as necessary.
7   Repeat the rpm check if an adjustment has been made.
8   Turn the engine off the reconnect the EGR hose.

25 Curb idle speed (1946 1-V) – adjustment and check

1   Connect a tachometer to the engine.
2   Turn the air conditioner to OFF (where installed).
3   Check for the engine to be at normal operating temperature (approximately 5 minutes running) and that the choke is completely open.
4   Measure each engine speed as defined on the engine emission decal in the engine compartment.
5   Recheck each rpm range by raising the rpm to 2500 for 15 seconds to 2 minutes and measure within two minutes of returning to idle.

26 Anti-diesel throttle speed positioner (1946 1-V) – adjustment

1   To adjust curb idle speed with the TSP on, turn the adjusting screw until the curb idle speed is attained.
2   With the TSP in the off position, collapse the TSP plunger by forcing the throttle lever pad against the plunger.
3   Turn the adjusting screw until the specified rpm is attained as noted on the mission decal.

27 Air conditioning TSP (1946 1-V) – adjustment

1   With the air conditioning off, adjust the curb idle speed as shown on the emission decal.
2   To adjust the TSP with the air conditioning on, move the selector on the climate control to A/C ON.
3   Manually open the throttle to allow the TSP plunger to extend fully. Release the throttle.
4   Disconnect the air conditioner clutch wire at the compressor.
5   Adjust the TSP adjusting screw to the rpm noted on the emission decal.
6   After adjusting, move the selector to OFF and reconnect the compressor wire.
7   Reconnect the fuel evaporative purge valve hose.
8   Turn the engine to OFF and remove any test equipment.
9   Check for loose hoses and all lines for proper installation.
10   Check air cleaner installation.

28 Carburetor (1946 1-V) – removal and installation (3.3L)

1   Before undertaking any removal of hoses or connections, mark the junctions with tape to ensure that the proper connections will be made upon installation. There are many hoses that look identical but perform very different functions.
2   Remove the air cleaner wing nut and remove the air cleaner element and housing. The housing can be relocated without removing all of the hoses.
3   Disconnect the throttle cable from the throttle lever.
4   Label and disconnect the distributor vacuum line. EGR vacuum line, venturi vacuum line and the fuel line from the carburetor.
5   Disconnect the TSP electrical connection at the wire/connector junction.
6   Disconnect the choke connector.
7   Remove the choke clean air hose at the air horn.
8   Remove the carburetor mounting nuts and lift the carburetor, mounting gasket, spacer (if equipped) and lower gasket off the manifold.
9   Cover the open manifold with a clean shop cloth.
10   The carburetor is installed in the reverse order of removal with the following precautions.

11   Tighten the mounting bolts alternately to avoid warping the carburetor base or manifold.
12   Readjust the curb idle speed and fast idle speed as necessary.

29 Carburetor (1946 1-V) – disassembly (3.3L)

1   Remove the carburetor from the vehicle.
2   **Note**: *Use the EGR spacer for a holding fixture for the carburetor. Do not immerse the cover in carburetor cleaner. Do not use wire or metal scraper to remove old gasket material, use a hard plastic scraper like those used for paint mixing.*
3   Remove the choke cover retaining screws, retainer, gasket and bi-metal cover.
4   The parts may be cleaned by wiping with a clean shop towel and/or compressed air. If any parts are corroded or damaged, replace them.
5   Remove the two diaphragm pull-down bracket screws and disconnect the vacuum hose from the main carburetor body.
6   Remove the pull-down diaphragm and linkage as an assembly.
7   Make a drawing of the position of the spring on the vent bowl cover to ensure the proper positioning upon assembly. Remove the three screws securing the fuel bowl cover from the top of the air horn.
8   Remove the bowl vent attaching clamp and remove the bowl vent assembly.
9   Remove the fast idle cam retainer and cam.
10   Remove the choke control lever screw.
11   Remove the throttle return spring bracket, nut and lock washer.
12   Note the slot the accelerator pump link is located in for proper reassembly.
13   Remove the return spring and bracket.
14   Remove the accelerator pump link.
15   Remove the seven screws securing the air horn (top casting) to the main carburetor body.
16   Lift the air horn from the main body. If the air horn sticks, tap the side of the casting with a plastic mallet.
17   Turn the air horn upside-down and remove the air horn gasket.
18   Remove the accelerator pump operating rod, attaching screw and retainer clamp.
19   Remove the spring plate and screw.
20   Remove the pump operating rod and grommet from the bowl cover by rotating the rod assembly.
21   The main well tube should not be removed but should be blown clean with compressed air.
22   Remove the three screws securing the choke thermostat housing, retainer, and gasket.
23   This completes the removal of the air horn from the main carburetor body and full disassembly. The choke plate and shaft should only be removed in the case of corrosion or damage. The air horn should be left upside-down to avoid damaging the gasket surface, main well assembly, or any other components.
24   Turn the carburetor main body upside-down and catch the accelerator pump discharge weight and ball. Place the weight and ball aside for reassembly.
25   Remove the fuel inlet valve, fitting and gasket.
26   Remove the float shaft retainer, float shaft and float.
27   Carefully remove the main metering jet with a jet wrench. If a wrench is not available, use a $\frac{3}{8}$ inch wide screwdriver to remove the jet. If the jet is even slightly damaged it should be replaced.
28   Remove the enrichment valve assembly. If the proper special wrench is not available, file a slot in the center of a flat screwdriver blade $\frac{1}{16}$ inch wide to clear the enrichment valve stem.
29   Remove the two hot idle compensator cover screws, cover, valve and gaskets.
30   Remove the three screws securing the main body to the throttle body. Tap the casting if they stick, do not pry apart.
31   Remove the low idle speed adjusting screw and spring.
32   Remove the solenoid.
33   This completes the main carburetor body removal and disassembly.
34   The idle mixture adjustment screw is behind a metal cap and should only be removed if problems exist. Refer to your local repair shop or authorized dealer for this work.
35   Remove the curb idle speed adjusting screw, spring, fast idle speed adjusting screw and spring.

4

30 Carburetor (1946 1-V) – assembly and primary adjustment (3.3L)

1 Work on a clean area with clean parts and tools.
2 Reassemble the fast idle speed adjusting screw (round head), the curb idle speed adjusting screw (hex head) and springs on the throttle shaft and lever assembly on the throttle body.
3 On the main body, install the low idle speed adjusting screw and spring.
4 Turn the main body and install the throttle body gasket, throttle body and three retaining screws. Tighten them securely.
5 Place the hot idle compensator valve gasket and valve into the main body. Install the cover and gasket and secure with 2 screws.
6 Assemble the enrichment valve assembly. Snap the small end of the enrichment valve spring over the shoulder of the large end of the pin, insert the pin from the threaded end and install the assembly into the carburetor. Tighten with the modified screwdriver as removed earlier.
7 Install the main metering jet.
8 Install the float hinge pin into the float arm and place it into position in the main body. Secure with the hinge retainer.
9 Install the fuel inlet valve assembly and gasket. Check the float level as follows.
10 California vehicles and 49-state vehicles are adjusted differently. Refer to the accompanying figure for the proper adjustment. Adjust only where noted.
11 Repeat the step to ensure accuracy and check for free operation of the float.
12 Install the accelerator pump cup over the retaining tap on the end of the pump piston rod. Install the pump spring and retainer plate on the piston rod. The larger diameter end of the pump spring should contact the retainer plate and seat over the shoulder.
13 Hold the assembly together, connect the pump rod through the slotted hole in the piston rod and rotate the rod so that the plate can be secured in position with the retaining screw.
14 Install the pump operating clamp and screw.
15 Place the air horn gasket over the alignment pin and set the air horn into place. Do not force the assembly. Check for proper alignment of the enrichment valve piston stem and valve pin.
16 Install the seven air horn securing screws.
17 Attach the accelerator pump link into the pump operating rod and into the slot from which it was removed during disassembly.
18 Install the throttle return spring bracket, washer and spring.
19 Install the attaching nut and tighten.
20 Install the return spring to the throttle body stop.
21 Install the fast idle cam link into position. Install the cam and retainer.
22 Install the choke control lever and screw
23 Position the bowl vent assembly and hinge pin in the housing and install the pin attaching screw.
24 Place the small end of the bowl vent spring over the shoulder of the vent arm. Position the cover and gasket and secure with the three cover retaining screws.
25 Connect the choke pull-down diaphragm linkage and install the two bracket attaching screws.
26 Install the manifold vacuum tube to diaphragm assembly hose.
27 Place the bi-metal choke gasket, choke and cap onto the carburetor casting. Check for proper engagement of the spring tab to the slotted choke shaft lever. Install the cap retaining screws.
28 Install the carburetor to the vehicle, attach all lines, connections and hoses.
29 Complete the adjustments shown for the carburetor. Refer to your local authorized dealer or repair shop for final adjustment and emission compliance.

31 Carburetor (2150 - 2-V) – general description

The Motorcraft 2150-2V carburetor is used on the 4.2L and 5.0L V8 49-state engines.

The 2150 -2V carburetor is composed of two main assemblies; the main body and the air horn. The air horn assembly serves as the main body cover and contains the choke plate and fuel bowl vent valve. Also in this assembly is the pullover enrichment system which provides additional fuel flow when there is high air flow through the air horn.

Fuel is drawn from the fuel bowl into the air flow through bleeds in the metered orifice.

In the main body are the throttle plate, accelerator pump assembly, fuel bowl and mechanical high-speed bleed cam.

Some models are equipped with high altitude compensators which consist of a choke in the bypass air intake for improved high altitude cold starts.

On most vehicles the choke is electronically operated.

32 Choke plate vacuum pulldown (2150-2V) – adjustment

1 Run the engine until it is up to operating temperature (about 5 minutes) and then shut it off.
2 Remove the carburetor air cleaner to provide access to the carburetor.
3 Rotate the choke housing to the rich setting which will lightly close the choke plate. Rotate the housing an additional 90° as shown.
4 Push the choke pulldown diaphragm to the closed position.
5 Use a ½ in drill bit shank to measure the clearance between the air horn wall and lower edge of the choke plate.
6 To decrease the choke pulldown, turn the adjusting screw clockwise and to increase it, turn the screw counterclockwise (Fig. 4.32).
7 The fast idle cam must be adjusted after choke vacuum pulldown has been adjusted.

33 Fast idle cam (2150-2V) – adjustment

1 With the choke housing rotated to the rich position as described in Section 11, push the throttle open to set the fast idle cam.
2 Close the choke as described in step 4 of Section 11.
3 Open the throttle while watching the fast idle cam and idle speed screw. The cam should drop to the kickdown step and idle speed screw should be opposite the 'V' notch on the cam.
4 To align the fast idle speed screw with the 'V' notch, turn the hex headed screw in the plastic fast idle cam lever as shown.
5 To de-choke after adjusting the choke plate lower edge and the air horn wall as described in step 5, Section 11. To adjust the clearance, bend the metal tang on the fast idle speed lever as shown.
6 After all adjustments are made, reset the choke thermostat housing to the specifications on the emissions decal.

34 Carburetor (2150-2V) – fast idle, curb idle and TSP off adjustment

1 Start the engine and run it up to operating temperature. Shut the engine off and remove the air cleaner. The air cleaner assembly must be in position when engine speeds are measured.
2 Apply the parking brake and block the rear wheels.
3 Check, and adjust if necessary, the choke and throttle linkage for freedom of movement.
4 Where applicable, turn the air conditioner OFF.
5 Disconnect the evaporative purge line from the carburetor and plug it.
6 Connect a tachometer to the engine.
7 Disconnect the EGR vacuum hose and plug it. If the vehicle is equipped with a ported vacuum switch (PVS), do not disconnect the EGR line.
8 Disconnect the distributor vacuum hose from the advance side of the distributor and plug it.
9 Follow the vacuum hose from the thermactor dump valve to the carburetor and disconnect the dump valve vacuum hose nearest the carburetor. Plug the original vacuum source and connect the dump valve directly to the manifold vacuum.
10 With the transmission in Park (automatic) or Neutral (manual) and the choke plate fully open, run the engine at 2500 rpm for 15 seconds. Place the fast idle lever on the step of the fast idle cam specified on the emissions decal. Allow the engine speed to stabilize (10 to 15 seconds) and measure the fast idle rpm.

11 Repeat this procedure three times and adjust the fast idle rpm if not as specified.

12 Before adjusting the curb idle, it is necessary to determine which of the various throttle positioners and engine speed control devices the carburetor is equipped with. Refer to Chapter 6 for a description of these devices.

13 Make all adjustments after determining the curb idle speed by following the procedure described in steps 1 through 11.

14 On vehicles without air conditioning or other solenoid devices, the curb idle is adjusted by turning the throttle screw.

15 If the carburetor is equipped with a dashpot to control the throttle closing, the dashpot plunger must be collapsed with the engine off. Check the clearance between the plunger and the throttle lever pad and adjust, if necessary, to the specifications on the emissions label. Each time the curb idle is adjusted, the dashpot clearance must also be adjusted.

16 On anti-diesel TSP-equipped vehicles, the curb idle is adjusted by collapsing the TSP plunger by forcing the throttle lever pad against the plunger. The curb idle is then adjusted by turning the throttle stop adjusting screw.

17 If equipped with air conditioning, dashpot and TSP, turn the air conditioning off and determine the curb idle rpm. Adjust to the specified air conditioning off curb idle by turning the throttle stop screw. Turn the engine off, collapse the TSP plunger and check the clearance between the plunger and check the clearance between the plunger and throttle lever pad. To adjust, turn the long screw which is part of the assembly mounting bracket.

18 Reconnect all vacuum lines and Thermactor hoses to their proper locations and re-install the air cleaner.

35 Carburetor (2150-2V) – dry float setting

1 The dry float setting can only be checked at the appropriate stage of carburetor disassembly.

2 Remove the carburetor air horn, raise the float and seat the fuel inlet needle.

3 Remove the gasket and depress the float tab to assure seating of the fuel inlet needle while being careful not to damage the needles Viton tip.

4 Measure from a point near the center, $\frac{1}{8}$ in (3.2 mm) from the free end of the float to the top surface of the carburetor body. This measurement must be $\frac{7}{16}$ in. Bend the tab on the float to adjust the level. Alternatively, the float level can be checked using a cardboard gauge available at your dealer.

36 Carburetor – idle mixture adjustment

Note: *Idle mixture adjustment can only be satisfactorily carried out by using special test equipment. Refer to your local dealer or repair shop for proper adjustment.*

37 Carburetor (2150, 2700VV and 7200VV) – removal and installation

1 Remove the air cleaner as described in Section 5.1.

2 Disconnect the fuel feed line from the carburetor.

3 Disconnect the electrical leads and vacuum lines from the carburetor.

4 Disconnect the throttle cable/kick-down cable from the carburetor.

5 Using suitable cranked wrenches, remove the carburetor mounting nuts and lift the carburetor, gasket and spacer (if equipped) from the manifold.

6 Installation is basically a reverse of the removal procedure, but ensure that a new flange gasket is used.

38 Carburetor (2150-2V) – dismantling and reassembly

1 Before dismantling, wash the exterior of the carburetor in the proper solvent and wipe off using a lint-free rag. Select a clean area of the workbench and lay several layers of newspaper on the top. Obtain several small containers to segregate the many small parts which will be removed from the carburetor.

2 Remove the air cleaner anchor screw and automatic choke control rod retainer.

3 Remove the air horn attaching screws, lockwashers, carburetor identification tag, air horn and gasket.

4 Loosen the screw securing the choke control rod to the choke shaft lever. Remove the choke control rod and slide out the plastic dust seal.

5 Remove the choke plate screws after removing the staking marks on their ends and remove the choke plate by sliding it out of the top of the air horn.

6 Remove the bypass air choke plate and screws and slide the choke shaft out of the air horn.

7 From the automatic choke, remove the fast idle cam retainer, the thermostatic choke spring housing, clamp and retainer.

8 Remove the choke housing assembly, gasket and the fast idle cam and rod from the fast idle cam lever.

9 On the main body, use a screwdriver to pry the float shaft retainer from the fuel inlet seat as shown in the accompanying figure. Remove the float, float shaft and fuel inlet needle assembly.

10 Remove the retainer and float shaft from the float lever and remove the fuel filler bowl.

11 Remove the fuel inlet needle, seat filter screen and main jets.

12 Remove the booster venturi, metering rod assembly and gasket. Turn the main body upside down and let the accelerator pump, discharge weight and ball fall into your hand.

13 Disassemble the lift rod from the booster by removing the lift rod spring retaining clip and spring and separating the lift rod assembly from the booster. Do not remove the metering rod hanger from the lift rod.

14 Remove the roll pin from the accelerator pump cover, using a suitable punch. Retain the roll pin and remove the accelerator pump link and rod assembly, pump cover, diaphragm assembly and spring as shown.

15 To remove the Elastomer valve from the accelerator pump assembly, grasp it firmly and pull it out. Examine the valve, and if the tip is broken off, be sure to remove it from the fuel bowl. Discard the valve.

16 Turn the main body upside down and remove the enrichment valve cover and gasket. Using an 8-point socket, remove the enrichment valve and gasket.

17 Remove the idle fuel mixture adjusting screws and springs. Remove the idle screw limiter caps.

18 Remove the fast idle adjusting lever assembly and then remove the idle screw and spring from the lever.

19 Before removing the throttle plates, lightly scribe along the throttle shaft and mark each plate for re-installation in the proper bore as shown. File off the staked portion of the throttle plate screws before removing them. Remove any burrs from the shaft after removal so that the shaft can be withdrawn without damage to the throttle shaft bores. Be ready to catch the mechanical high-speed cam located between the throttle plates when the shaft is removed.

20 If an altitude compensator is installed, remove the 4 screws attaching the assembly to the main body and remove the compensator assembly. Remove the 3 screws holding the aneroid valve and separate the aneroid, gasket and valve.

21 Dismantling is now complete and all parts should be thoroughly cleaned in a suitable solvent. Remove any sediment from the fuel bowl and passages, taking care not to scratch any of the passages. Remove all traces of gaskets with a suitable scraper.

22 Reassembly is basically a reversal of dismantling with attention paid to the following:

(a) *Check that all holes in new gaskets are properly punched and that they are clean of foreign material.*

(b) *When installing a new elastomer valve in the accelerator pump assembly, lubricate its tip before inserting it into the accelerator pump cavity hole. Reach into the fuel bowl with needle nosed pliers and pull the valve tip into the fuel bowl. Cut off the tip forward of the retainer shoulder*

(c) *Install the idle mixture adjusting screw needles by turning them with your fingers until they just contact the seat and then backing them off 1½ turns. Do not install the limiter caps at this time. The enrichment valve cover and gasket must be installed next as the limiter stops on the cover provide a positive stop for the limiter caps.*

(d) After installing the throttle plates in the main body, hold the assembly up to the light. Little or no light should be seen between the throttle plates and bores. Fully tighten and stake the throttle plate screws at this time.

(e) When checking the float setting, make sure that the elastomer valve in the accelerator pump does not interfere with the float.

39 Carburetor (2700VV-2V and 7200VV-2V) – general description

The Motorcraft 2700VV and 7200VV carburetors are unusual in that they don't have a fixed venturi area, the area instead carying according to load and speed.

The carburetor features dual venturi valves connect to two tapered main metering rods which ride in the main metering jets. The dual venturi valves are controlled by engine vacuum and the throttle position and when the venturi valve position is changed, the metering rods move along with them. This varies the fuel flow by changing the main metering jets.

The speed of the air passing through the carburetor remains fairly constant with this design and maintains even fuel/air mixtures throughout the engine operating range.

Supplementary systems to adjust to varying air which are used in a fixed venturi carburetor are not necessary on the variable venturi design.

The Motorcraft 7200VV variable venturi carburetor is basically the same design as the 2700VV, the major difference being the addition of feedback control system designed to work in conjunction with an onboard electronic control system (EEC). The EEC system is described in Chapter 5.

The feedback system inproves drivability, fuel economy and exhaust emissions by more precisely controlling the fuel/air ratio because of the continuous response to the flow of commands from the EEC system.

The 7200VV carburetor has no provision for vacuum adjustment as vacuum control is set at the factory.

40 Carburetor – adjustments, notes and precautions

1 When making any adjustments to the carburetor, make sure that all hoses and lines are connected to the air cleaner assembly even when the assembly is moved to clear the carburetor. The air cleaner assembly, including the filter, should be fitted for any adjustment governing engine speed.

2 Due to the interaction of emission controls and temperature changes, the engine speed may oscillate. If this is encountered, use the average engine speed.

3 Do not allow the vehicle to idle for long periods of time as overheating of the catalytic converter may result in excessive under body temperatures.

4 Always apply the parking brake and block the wheels before making any underhood carburetor adjustments.

5 Except where otherwise noted, turn all the accessories to OFF.

6 The fuel evaporative purge valve MUST be disconnected. Disconnect as follows: Trace the purge valve vacuum hose from the purge valve to the first place the vacuum hose can be disconnected from the underhood routing, eg vacuum tee connection. Disconnect the hose and plug both the hose and the open connection.

41 Fast idle rpm (2700/7200VV) – adjustment and check

1 Connect a tachometer to the engine.

2 Disconnect the EGR hose from the valve and plug the hose.

3 With the choke off and the engine running at normal operating temperature, raise the speed of the engine to 2500 rpm for 15 seconds. Place the fast idle lever on the specified step of the fast idle cam (Refer to the emission decal in the engine compartment).

4 Allow the engine speed to stabilize and measure the engine speed (rpm). Depending upon the engine and the state of tune, it may require anywhere from 15 seconds to 2 minutes for the engine speed (number of rpm) to stabilize.

5 Repeat the above step three times to ensure accuracy.

6 Adjust the fast idle screw as necessary.

7 Repeat the rpm check if an adjustment has been made.

8 Turn the engine off the reconnect the EGR hose.

42 Curb idle speed (2700/7200VV) – adjustment and check

1 Connect a tachometer to the engine.

2 Disconnect the EGR hose from the valve and plug the hose.

3 Disconnect the fuel evaporative purge hose as described in Step 6, Section 40.

4 Check the engine curb idle as described in steps 1 through 5 of Section 41.

5 The method of adjustment of curb idle is determined by the type of throttle positioning device installed on the carburetor. The adjusting procedures are as follows:

(a) 2700VV carburetors with solenoid positioners must be in Drive when the curb idle rpm is checked. The curb idle is adjusted by turning the adjustment screw in the bracket.

(b) On vehicles with no solenoids or positioners, turn the throttle adjustment screw to obtain the specified curb idle rpm.

(c) On dashpot equipped carburetors, adjust the curb idle with the throttle stop adjustment screw. Turn the engine off, collapse the dashpot plunger and measure the distance between the throttle lever pad and adjust to specifications if necessary. Start the engine and check the curb idle, repeating the procedure until the proper curb idle is obtained

(d) On 7200VV carburetors equipped with vacuum-operated throttle modulator (VOTM), turn the throttle stop screw counterclockwise and recheck. If the curb idle rpm is below specifications, shut off the engine and turn the throttle stop screw a full turn clockwise. Start the engine and recheck the curb idle, repeating the procedure until the idle is within specifications.

43 Accelerator pump lever lash (2700VV and 7200VV)– checking and adjustment

1 Each time the curb idle is adjusted, the accelerator pump lever lash must be checked and if necessary, adjusted.

2 After setting curb idle adjustment as described in Section 42, take up the accelerator pump clearance by pushing down on the nylon nut on the top of the pump.

3 Use a feeler guage to check the clearance between the accelerator pump stem and lever.

4 Turn the nylon nut on the accelerator pump clockwise until the clearance is between 0.010 and 0.020 in.

5 To set the accelerator lever lash preload, turn the accelerator pump rod counterclockwise one turn.

44 Choke cap (2700/7200VV) – removal and installation

1 The choke cap on 2700/7200VV carburetors is held in place by 3 screws or in the case of California vehicles, 3 rivets.

2 To remove the choke cap, remove the 3 screws and lift the cap and gasket away from the carburetor. On California vehicles, the 2 top rivets are removed by drilling them out. The bottom rivet is located in a blind hole and must be tapped out, using a suitable punch and hammer. The choke cap, gasket and retainer can then be removed from the carburetor.

3 Reinstallation is a revrse of removal on choke caps retained with screws. California vehicles require the use of a suitable rivet gun and three $\frac{1}{4}$ in by $\frac{1}{2}$ in rivets. It may be necessary to remove the carburetor when installing the rivets.

45 Cold enrichment rod, control vacuum regulator (CVR) and choke control diaphragm (2799/7200VV) – adjustment

1 Remove the choke cap as described in Section 23.

2 Remove the choke pulldown diaphragm and spring.

3   Install a choke weight on the choke bi-metal lever, Ford part T77L-9848-A or equivalent. Place the fast idle pick-up lever on the first highest step of the fast idle cam.

4   Install a dial indicator (Ford tool 4201-C or equivalent) on the carburetor so that the indicator tip contacts the top surface of the enrichment rod and adjust the dial to zero. Slightly raise the choke weight and then release it, making sure that the zero reading repeats.

5   Remove the choke weight.

6   After installing the stator cap at the index position, the dial indicator should read to specification. If it doesn't, adjust the rod height by turning the adjusting nut clockwise to increase height and counterclockwise to decrease it.

7   To check the setting, repeat steps 3 through 6.

8   To adjust the control vacuum regulator (CVR), remove the stator cap and leave the dial indicator installed but not reset to zero.

9   Set the fast idle on the highest step.

10 Press the CCVR rod down until it bottoms in its seat and read the travel on the dial indicator.

11 If adjustment is necessary, place a $\frac{1}{2}$ in box wrench on the CVR adjusting nut to prevent it from turning as shown in the accompanying figure.

12 Using a $\frac{3}{32}$ in allen wrench, turn the CVR rod counterclockwise to increase its travel or clockwise to decrease it.

13 With the stator cap removed and dial indicator still installed but not reset to zero, seat the choke diaphragm assembly in the direction of the fast idle cam.

14 If the dial indicator reading is not within specification, turn the choke diaphragm clockwise to decrease or counterclockwise to increase the height as shown.

15 The cold idle enrichment rod height must be checked after each adjustment of the CVR and choke control diaphragm.

46 Fast idle cam (2700/7200VV) – adjustment

1   Remove the choke cap as described in Section 44.

2   Counting the highest step as the first, install the fast idle lever in the corner of the step specified on the emissions label.

3   Install the stator cap and rotate it clockwise until the lever contacts the adjusting screw.

4   Line up the index mark on the stator cap with the specified mark on the choke casing by turning the fast idle cam adjusting screw. This screw may be hard to turn as it was coated with Loc-Tite at the time of manufacture.

5   Remove the stator cap and re-install the choke cap to the setting specified on the emissions label.

47 Venturi valve limiter (2700/7200VV) – adjustment

1   Remove the carburetor.

2   Remove the venturi valve cover, gasket and roller bearings.

3   Using a suitable punch, remove the expansion plug at the rear of the main body on the throttle side.

4   Remove the venturi valve limiter screw assembly, using a $\frac{5}{32}$ in allen wrench as shown and block the throttle plates open.

5   Lightly close the venturi valve and check the gap between the valve and the air horn wall. Adjust if necessary.

6   Move the venturi valve to the wide open position and insert an allen wrench into the stop screw hole. To adjust the flap, turn the limiter adjusting screw counterclockwise to decrease the clearance and clockwise to increase it.

7   Remove the allen wrench, lightly close the valve and re-check the gap.

8   Re-install the venturi valve limiter stop screw and turn it clockwise until it contacts the valve.

9   Open the venturi valve all the way and check the gap between the valve and the air horn. Adjust the stop screw to specification if necessary.

10 After installing a new expansion plug, re-install the venturi valve cover, gasket and bearing and re-install the carburetor.

48 Carburetor (2700/7200VV) - disassembly

1   Remove the carburetor as described in Section 37.

2   Place the carburetor on a clean working surface and obtain a variety of small containers for collecting and separating parts as they are removed.

Upper body

3   Remove the fuel inlet fitting, filter, gasket and spring. Remove the E-rings on the accelerator pump rod and remove the rods.

4   Remove the air cleaner stud (not shown) from the carburetor body.

5   Remove the seven screws holding the upper body in place and remove the upper body. Mark the two long screws for re-installation in their original location. Place the upper body upside down in a clean work area.

6   Remove the float hinge pin, float assembly and gasket.

7   Remove the accelerator pump link retaining screw and nut, adjusting nut and pump link. Remove the accelerator pump overtravel spring, E-clip and washer.

9   Remove the accelerator pump rod and dust seal.

10 Remove the choke control rod and carefully lift the retainer and slide the dust seal out.

11 Remove the choke hinge pin E-ring and slide the pin out of the casting.

12 Remove the cold enrichment rod adjusting nut, lever, adjusting swivel control vacuum regulator and adjusting nut as an assembly as shown. Slide the cold enrichment rod out of the upper body.

13 Remove the two screws securing the venturi valve cover. Hold the cover in place as you turn the carburetor over and remove the cover, gasket and bearings.

14 Press out the tapered plugs from the venturi valve pivotal pins using Ford tool T770-9928-A or equivalent.

15 Push the venturi plugs out as you slide the venturi valve to the rear and clear of the casting. Remove the venturi valve pivot pin bushings.

16 Remove the metering rod pins from the outboard sides of the venturi valve, the metering rods and the springs. Mark the rods "throttle" and "choke" for ease of proper reassembly. Make sure to always block the venturi valve wide open whenever working on the jets.

17 Remove the cap plugs recessed into the upper body casting using Ford tool T77L-9533-B or equivalent as shown.

18 The main jet setting is crucial to the carburetors overall calibration so the following sequence must be strictly adhered to:

    a) *Using Ford tool T77L-9533-A, turn each main jet clockwise, counting the turns as you go. Write down the number of turns to the nearest quarter turn.*

    b) *Unscrew the jet assembly and then remove the O-ring. For ease of proper assembly, identify the jets as to "throttle" or "choke" side.*

    c) *Remove the accelerator pump plunger assembly and then remove the pump return spring, pump cup and plunger.*

    d) *If necessary for cleaning, remove the 1/8 inch pipe plug from the fuel inlet boss.*

    e) *From the throttle side of the venturi valve, remove the venturi valve limiting screw.*

Main body

19 Remove the venturi valve diaphragm screws, cover, spring guide and spring. Loosen the cover by tapping it lightly. Do not pry. Carefully loosen the venturi diaphragm and slide it from the main body.

20 Turn the carburetor upside down, holding your hand under it to catch the accelerator pump check ball and weight.

21 Remove the five throttle body retaining screws and remove the throttle body and gasket.

22 On the 7200VV only, use a 5/8 inch socket to remove the feedback stepper motor, gasket, pintle valve and spring.

23 On the 2700VV only, remove the choke heat seal screw and shield.

4

Throttle body

24   Remove the throttle return control device assembly.

25   Remove the choke thermostatic spring and housing assembly. On California vehicles, this housing is retained by rivets, refer to Section 44 for removal procedure.

26   Remove the choke thermostatic lever and screw and slide the choke shaft lever assembly out of the casting. Remove the fast idle cam and E-clip and the adjusting screw. Remove the fast idle intermediate lever.

27   Remove the chock control diaphragm lever assembly. Remove the choke control diaphragm assembly and rod.

28   Should the chock housing bushing have to be removed, it will have to be pressed out, while the casting is being supported, so that it is not damaged. The bushing is staked in place and the staked areas will have to be ground off before pressing.

29   Remove the TSP off idle speed screw, throttle shaft nut, nylon bushing, fast idle lever, fast idle adjusting lever and screw.

30   On the 7200VV only, remove the large E-clip, throttle positioning sensor and roll pin.

31   If the throttle plates are to be removed, lightly scribe along the shaft and mark the plate "T" and "C" to ensure proper reassembly. The throttle plate screws are staked in place so their staked areas must be filed or ground off. Remove the throttle plate screws and discard them and remove the plates.

32   When removing the throttle shaft assembly, the limiter lever stop pin will have to be driven down until it is flush with the shaft.

33   Remove the E-clip adjacent to the venturi valve limiter and slide the throttle shaft assembly from the casting and remove the adjusting screw.

34   Remove the venturi valve limiter and bushing assembly.

35   Disassembly is now complete and all components should be cleaned in the proper solvent and inspected for wear. All traces of gasket should be removed from the carburetor body and all passages cleaned of dirt and gum deposits.

---

49   Carburetor (2700/7200VV) - reassembly and adjustment

Throttle body

1   After supporting the throttle shaft assembly, carefully drive out the venturi valve limiter stop pin and roll pin (if equipped). Place the venturi valve limiter assembly in the throttle body and insert the throttle shaft and install the E-clips.

2   Install the throttle plates, according to the scribed marks made during disassembly. Close the throttle, tap the plates to center them and tighten the screws. Stake the ends of the screws so that they won't come loose.

3   Drive the new venturi valve limiter stop pin into the shaft, leaving about 1/8 inch exposed. Install the roll pin and on the 7200VV install the throttle positioner sensor and E-clip.

4   Install the fast idle adjusting lever, nylon bushing, fast idle lever and throttle shaft retaining nut. Install the TSP Off idle speed adjusting screw.

5   The choke housing bushing must be pressed into position with the housing supported and the bushing then staked in place.

6   Install the fast idle intermediate diaphragm rod into position and engage the rod and E-clip. After sliding the choke shaft pin and lever assembly into the casting, install the choke thermostatic lever and screw. Install the choke control diaphragm spring, cover and screws.

7   Install the choke thermostat gasket, housing and retaining ring. On California vehicles, follow the procedure in Section 44. Adjust the cap to the specified setting.

8   Install the throttle return control devices, if equipped.

Main body

9   Place the throttle body gasket on the main body and install the main body to the throttle body.

10   Drop the accelerator pump check ball and weight into the pump discharge channel.

11   The venturi valve limiter stop screw, torque retention spring and plug are not to be installed at this time, but as one of the final steps of the upper body assembly.

12   Slide the venturi valve diaphragm into the main body and install the venturi valve spring, spring guide, cover and screws.

13   On the 7200VV only, install the feedback motor, gasket, pintle valve and pintle spring.

14   On the 2700VV only, install the choke heat shield.

Upper body

15   Install the 1/8 inch pipe plug into the fuel inlet box.

16   Install the venturi valve limiter screw into the venturi valve.

17   Install the O-rings on the main metering jets. Lubricate the O-rings with mild soapy solution prior to installation.

18   Install each main metering jet by turning it clockwise with Ford tool T77L-9533-A or equivalent, until seated in the casting. At this point, turn each jet counterclockwise the same number of turns recorded in Step 18a of Section 48.

19   Install the jet plugs, using the Ford jet plug driver tool T77L-9533-C or equivalent. Tap lightly on the end of the tool until it bottoms against the face of the casting.

20   Install the metering rods, springs and pivot pins on the venturi valve. Install the venturi valve and carefully guide the metering rods into the main metering jets. Press downward on the metering rods and if the springs are properly assembled, they will spring back.

21   Install the venturi valve pivot pin bushings and pivot pins. Use Ford tool T77P-9928-A or equivalent to press the tapered plugs into the venturi valve pivot pins.

22   Install the venturi valve cover plate, roller bearings, gasket and attaching screws.

23   Install the accelerator pump operating rod and dust seal. Attach the E-clip and washer. Slide the overtravel spring over the accelerator pump operating rod.

24   Insert the accelerator pump lever and swivel assembly into the pump link. Install the accelerator pump link screw, two nuts, and the accelerator pump adjustment nut.

25   Install the fuel inlet valve seat gasket, the seat and valve. Install the float gasket, float assembly and hinge pin.

26   Assembly the accelerator pump return spring, cup and plunger. Place the pump piston assembly in the hold in the upper body.

27   Assembly the upper body to the main body. Holding the pump piston with your finger, guide it into the main body pump cavity, making sure the venturi valve limiter diaphragm stem engages the venturi valve. Install screws.

28   Install the fuel filter spring, filter, inlet filter gasket and fitting.

29   Install the air cleaner stud.

30   Install the choke control rod dust seal. Tap it gently to straighten the retainer.

31   Slide the cold enrichment rod into the upper body. Assembly the cold enrichment assembly consisting of lever, adjusting rod nut, swivel, control vacuum regulator and adjusting nut and install it.

32   Install the choke control rod. See Section 45 for the final adjustment procedure.

33   Engage the accelerator pump operating rod to the choke control rod and install the E-ring retainers.

34   At this point, install the venturi valve limiter stop screw and torque retention spring. Follow the adjustment procedure in Section 47, installing the plug after the adjustment is made.

35   Adjust the carburetor to the operating specifications on the emissions label.

50 Fuel tank – removal and installation

1 Disconnect the battery terminals.
2 Using a suitable length of pipe siphon out as much gas from the tank as possible. Do not use your mouth to start the flow.
3 Remove the four screws securing the filler pipe to the bodywork aperture and carefully ease the bottom end of the pipe out of the sealing ring in the side of the tank.
4 Jack up the rear of the car and suitably support it for access beneath.
5 Disconnect the fuel feed and vapor pipes at the tank and detach them from the clips along the tank front edge.
6 Disconnect the electrical leads from the sender unit.
7 Undo and remove the two support strap retaining nuts at the rear of the tank while supporting the weight of the tank.
8 Push the straps downwards and lift the tank out toward the rear of the car.
9 If it is necessary to remove the sender unit, this can be unscrewed from the tank using the appropriate special tool. Alternatively a suitable C-wrench or drift can probably be used, but great care should be taken that the flange is not damaged and that there is no danger from sparks if a hammer has to be used.
10 Taking care not to damage the sealing washer, pry out the tank-to-filler pipe seal.
13 Refit the sender unit using a new seal, as the original one will almost certainly be damaged.
14 The remainder of the installation procedure is the reverse of removal. A smear of engine oil on the tank filler pipe exterior will aid its fitting.
15 Do not overtighten the tank retaining strap nuts.

51 Fuel tank – cleaning and repair

1 With time it is likely that sediment will collect in the bottom of the fuel tank. Condensation, resulting in rust and other impurities, will usually be found in the fuel tank of any car more than three or four years old.
2 When the tank is removed it should be vigorously flushed out with hot water and detergent and, if facilities are avaiable, steam cleaned.
3 **Note:** *Never weld, solder or bring a naked light close to an empty fuel tank. All repairs should be done by a professional due to the extremely hazardous conditions.*

52 Throttle cable and kick-down rod – removal and installation

1 Pry the throttle cable retainer bushing from the top end of the accelerator pedal and remove the inner cable from the pedal assembly **Note:** *On later model cars the cable is retained by a Tinnerman type fastener which must be pried off the end of the cable.*
2 Remove the circular retaining clip holding the inner cable to the underside of the dash panel.
3 Remove the two screws retaining the outer cable to the dash panel.
4 Disconnect the control rod from the carburetor linkage.
5 Remove the screw or spring clip retaining the outer cable to the engine bracket.
6 The complete cable assembly can now be removed.
7 To remove the kick-down rod (automatic transmission only)., remove the 'C' type spring clips and pins at each end of the rod and remove the rod.
8 Install the throttle cable and kick-down rod using the reverse procedure to removal.

53 Accelerator pedal – removal and installation

1 Remove the inner throttle cable from the pedal assembly as described in the previous Section.
2 Undo the two nuts retaining the pedal to the floor bracket and remove the pedal assembly. **Note:** *If a pedal extension pad is installed this will have to be uncrimped from the pedal prior to pedal removal.*
3 Install the accelerator pedal using the reverse procedure to removal.

54 Exhaust system – general information

Note: *Because of manufacturing changes, the exhaust system on your car may differ from those shown in this manual. If problems arise, consult your dealer or qualified repair shop.*
    All models use a single exhaust system consisting of an inlet pipe, catalytic converter and muffler. Some models also use a resonator.
    The exhaust system is serviced in four pieces: the rear section of the inlet pipe, catalytic converter, muffler inlet pipe and muffler.
    Due to the high quality temperatures of the exhaust system, do not work on the exhaust system until at least one hour after the car has been run or driven.

55 Inlet pipe – removal and installation

1 Raise and support the vehicle.
2 Support the muffler assembly with a length of. wire.
3 Remove the converter-to-inlet pipe mounting bots.
4 Remove the front hanger mounting screws from the inlet pipe.
5 Remove the nuts securing the inlet pipe to the exhaust manifold.
6 Installation is the reverse of removal with the following precautions.
7 Clean all flange and gasket surfaces.
8 Use new gaskets.
9 Install the entire system loosely, aligning all components, then tighten.
10 Check for absence of leaks and noise.

56 Muffler assembly – removal and installation

1 Raise and support the vehicle. Support the vehicle allowing the rear axle to hang at full extension without the wheel assemblies touching the ground.
2 Remove the nuts securing the converter to the muffler pipe flange.
3 Remove the rear hanger to muffler support screws.
4 Pull the muffler assembly toward the rear and disconnect the catalytic converter.
5 Remove the screws securing the hanger assembly to the muffler support.
6 Installation is the reverse of removal.

57 Catalytic converter – removal and installation

1 Raise and support the vehicle.
2 Remove the screws securing the heat shields to the converter and carefully remove the shield. Be careful of sharp edges.
3 Remove the fasteners securing both ends of the catalytic converter and lower the converter from the car.
4 Installation is the reverse of removal.

4

Notes

Chapter 5 Engine electrical system

Contents

Specifications

Distributor

Type	Solid state, breakerless
Automatic advance	Vacuum and centrifugal
Direction of rotation	
2.3L and 3.3L	Clockwise
4.2L and 5.0L	Counterclockwise
Static advance	Refer to emission control decal

Coil
Motorcraft 8 volt. Oil filled

Firing order

2.3L	1–3–4–2
3.3L	1–5–3–6–2–4
4.2L and 5.0L	1–5–4–2–6–3–3–7–8

Spark plugs
Refer to emission control decal

Alternator (rear terminal)

Wire color codes	Orange, black and green
Amp rating at 15 volts	
Orange	40 amp
Black	65 amp
Green	60 amp
Watt rating at 15 volts	
Orange	600 watts
Black	975 watts
Green	900 watts
Brush length	
New	$\frac{1}{2}$ in
Wear limit	$\frac{5}{16}$ in

Alternator (side terminal)

Wire color codes	Red, black
Amp rating at 15 volts	
Red	70 amps
Black	100 amps
Watt rating at 15 volts	
Red	1050 watts
Black	1350 watts
Brush length	
New	$\frac{1}{2}$ in
Wear limit	$\frac{5}{16}$ in

5

Starter

Type	Positive engagement
Diameter	4 in, 4 $\frac{1}{2}$ in
Current draw under normal load	
4 in	
1978 thru 1979	150 to 200 amps
1980 thru 1981	150 to 250 amps
4 $\frac{1}{2}$ in	
1978 thru 1979	150 to 180 amps
1980 thru 1981	150 to 210 amps

Torque specifications

	ft-lbs	Nm
Spark plugs		
2.3L	5 to 10	7 to 13
3.3L, 4.2L and 5.0L	10 to 15	13 to 20
Distributor hold-down clamp		
2.3L	14 to 21	19 to 28
3.3L	17 to 25	23 to 34
4.2L and 5.0L	18 to 26	24 to 35
Alternator through-bolt	3 to 4	4 to 6
Alternator pulley nut	60 to 100	82 to 135
Alternator brush holder screw	1.5 to 2.2	2 to 3
Starter mounting bolt	15 to 20	20 to 27
Starter through-bolt	4 to 6	6 to 8
Starter cable attaching screw	6 to 8	8 to 12

1 General information

All models are equipped with an electronic (breakerless) type distributor. Mechanically, this system is similar to the contact breaker type with the exception that the distributor cam and contact breaker are replaced by an armature and magnetic pick-up. The coil primary circuit is controlled by an amplifier module.

The system is made up of a primary (low voltage) circuit and a secondary (high voltage) circuit.

When the ignition is switched on, the ignition primary circuit is energized. When the distributor armature 'teeth' approach the magnetic coil assembly, a voltage is induced which signals the amplifier to turn off the coil primary circuit. A timing circuit in the amplifier module turns the coil current on after the coil field has collapsed.

When on, current flows from the battery through the ignition switch, through the coil primary winding, through the amplifer module and then to ground. When the current is off, the magnetic field in the ignition coil collapses, inducing a high voltage in the coil secondary winding. This is conducted to the distributor where the rotor directs it to the appropriate spark plug. This process is repeated for each power stroke of the engine.

The distributor is equipped with devices to control the actual point of ignition according to the engine speed and load. As the engine speed increases, two centrifugal weights move outwards and alter the position of the armature in relation to the distributor shaft to advance the spark slightly. As engine load increases (as when climbing hills or accelerating), a reduction in intake manifold vacuum causes the baseplate assembly to move slightly in the opposite direction under the action of the spring in the vacuum unit, retarding the spark slightly and tending to counteract the centrifugal advance. Under light loading conditions (moderate, steady driving) the comparatively high intake manifold vacuum on the vacuum advance diaphragm causes the baseplate assembly to move in the opposite direction of the distributor shaft rotation, giving a larger amount of spark advance.

Some models are equipped with a dual diaphragm vacuum assembly which is operated by two different sources of vacuum. The outer (primary) diaphragm is operated by the carburetor venturi vacuum and provides timing advance. The inner (secondary) diaphragm is operated by intake manifold vacuum and retarded ignition timing.

For most practical do-it-yourself purposes, ignition timing is carried out as on conventional systems. A monolithic timing system is incorporated on some models which can only be used with special electronic equipment, a procedure beyond the scope of this manual.

The Electronic Engine Control (EEC) system is installed on some vehicles to provide improved drivability and emission control. The EEC system works in conjunction with an onboard computer and a feedback carburetor to control virtually every aspect of engine and ignition operation. Checking or adjusting of the EEC system is possible only with special equipment and procedures described in this chapter pertain only to non-EEC-equipped vehicles.

Faults in the breakerless ignition system which cannot be rectified by the substitution of parts or cleaning and tightening connections should be referred to a properly equipped dealer or repair shop.

2 Ignition system servicing and Federal regulations (all models)

1　In order to conform with the Federal regulations which govern the emission of hydrocarbons and carbon monoxide from car exhaust systems, the engine carburetion and ignition systems have been suitably modified.

2　It is critically important that the ignition system is kept in good operational order and to achieve this, accurate analytical equipment is needed to check and reset the distributor function. This will be found at a local repair shop or dealer.

3　Information contained in this chapter is supplied to enable the home mechanic to set the ignition system roughly to enable you to start the engine. Thereafter the car must be taken to the local dealer or repair shop for final tuning.

3 Spark plugs – removal, checking and installation

Note: *During this operation, the end of your wrench may be near the battery. To avoid an electrical shock, either cover the top of the battery with a heavy cloth or disconnect the negative cable.*

1　Before removing any spark plug wires, check that they are properly numbered as to their original location. Mark the wires with tape if necessary or remove only one plug at a time so that the wires are always in order.

2　Remove each spark plug wire by grasping the molded boot, twisting it slightly and then pulling it away from the end of the spark plug. Do not pull on the wire itself because it could separate the connector inside the boot. If this happens, the wire must be replaced with a new one.

3　Using an insulated spark plug socket, loosen each spark plug about two turns and carefully clean around the plug hole so that no dirt can enter when the plug is removed.

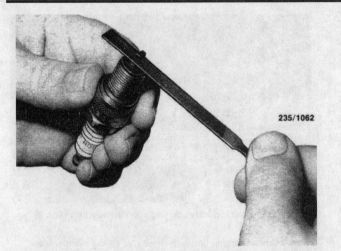

Fig.5.1 Cleaning spark plug electrode with a file (Sec 3)

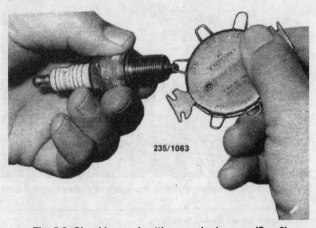

Fig. 5.2 Checking and setting spark plug gap (Sec 3)

4   Fully remove each of the spark plugs by hand.
5   Inspect the firing ends of the plugs for deposits and electrode condition. Inspect the insulators for cracks and discoloration.
6   If the plug appears usable, clean it with a wire brush to remove carbon deposits from the electrodes and threads.
7   Use a small file to clean the electrode surfaces.
8   Set the spark plug electrode gap to the setting on the emission control decal by bending the outer electrode, never the center one.
9   Position each plug into its cylinder head port and thread into the hole by hand.
10   Fully tighten each of the plugs to the proper torque specifications.
11   Using a clean standard screwdriver, apply a thin film of silicone grease on the entire interior surface of the spark plug wire boot.
12   Push each of the spark plug wires into position on the ends of the plugs, again using a twisting motion to fully seat the boots. Make sure that the wires are re-installed in their original positions.
13   Uncover or re-connect the battery.

4 Spark plug wires – inspection and replacement

1   The wires leading from the distributor cap to the spark plugs and the single wires from the center of the cap to the ignition coil are called the secondary or high-tension wires. These wires play an important role in the overall operation of the ignition system and should be periodically inspected and replaced if necessary.
2   These wires are of the radio resistance type designed to filter out electrical impulses which are the source of ignition noise interference. Replacement wires should always be of this type.
3   Any time a high-tension wire is disconnected, silicone grease should be applied in a thin coat to the inside boot surface, distributor cap, ignition coil junction or wherever the connection is made to maintain conductivity.
4   Use a clean rag to wipe each wire clean over its entire length and inspect for cracks, burns or damage.
5   Suspect wires can be checked for short circuits, using an ohmmeter.
6   Disconnect the distributor cap from the top of the distributor.
7   Disconnect one of the spark plug leads from its spark plug by grasping the molded boot, twisting and then pulling the wire from the plug.
8   If the spark plug wire boot is faulty, it should be cut off and replaced with a new one. Apply a thin coat of silicone lubricant to the area on the old wire where it will contact the new boot. Guide the boot onto the wire as shown in the accompanying figure.
9   To check the wire with an ohmmeter, place one probe inside the plug boot with the other touching the appropriate terminal inside the distributor cap.
10   If the resistance of the wire exceeds 5000 ohms per inch, the wire should be completely removed from the distributor cap and the resistance measured directly from the wire ends.
11   If the resistance still exceeds 5000 ohms per inch, the wire should be replaced with a new one.

12   All wires should be checked in the same manner.
13   If the wires are in good condition, apply a thin coat of silicone grease to the inside of each disconnected boot and reinstall.
14   When replacing plug wires, remove one at a time to avoid mixing them up. It is a good idea for the home mechanic to purchase replacement plug wire sets which are pre-cut to the proper length and ready to install.

5 Ignition timing – preparation

1   Before you begin the task of timing the engine or checking the timing, a few special tools must be gathered and some preparatory steps taken.
2   Engine timing requires the following tools:

a)   Induction strobe light or Sun meter pickup probe
b)   Hand held dwell-tachometer
c)   Proper box end wrench to fit the distributor hold-down bolt
d)   White paint and thin brush
e)   Shop cloths and cleaning solvent

With the items above readily at hand, perform the following:
3   Clean the surface of the front damper and the pointer with the solvent and cloths.
4   Turn the engine over until the proper timing mark, indicated on the engine decal, is aligned with the pointer. With the white paint and thin brush, carefully paint in the proper timing mark. (On some engines it may be necessary to mark both the proper degree line on the damper and the damper notch).
5   When the brush is cleaned and the paint put away, you can begin the timing checks and adjustments.

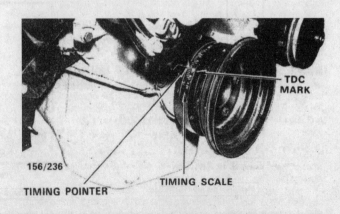

Fig. 5.3 Typical timing marks (Secs 5 and 6)

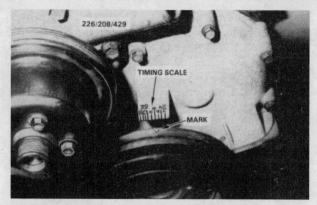

Fig. 5.4 Timing pointer marks on the damper pulley (Secs 5 and 6)

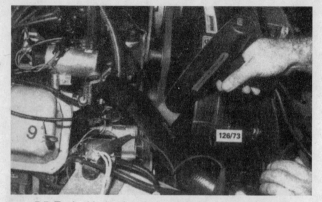

5.5 Typical inductive timing light installation (Sec 6)

6 Engine initial timing – setting

1   Place the transmission in Park (automatic transmission) or Neutral (manual).
2   Start the engine and allow it to reach normal operating temperature.
3   Shut off the engine and connect a hand-held tachometer and inductive timing light to the engine, following the manufacturer's instructions.
4   Remove the vacuum hose from the distributor advance connection and plug the hose.
5   With the engine at normal idle (consult emission decal), shine the beam of the timing light against the timing marks on the front marker and note whether timing mark (marked with paint as described in Section 3) is aligned with the pointer. If the timing mark is not aligned, loosen the hold-down bolt on the distributor and turn the distributor until the marks are in alignment. Tighten the bolt.
6   Shut off the engine and remove the plug from the distributor advance hose and reconnect the hose. Remove all of the timing check equipment.

7 Distributor – removal and installation

1   Remove the air cleaner.
2   Disconnect the distributor harness and vacuum advance line.
3   Remove the distributor cap from the top of the distributor. Position the cap (with the wires attached) to one side. Use a length of wire or tape to hold the cap out of the way.
4   Remove the rotor and adaptor section from the top of the distributor. Reinstall the rotor to the top of the distributor shaft.
5   Scribe or paint a mark on the distributor body in a direct line with the rotor arm. A small dab of paint on the rotor is also a useful aid in alignment.

6   Scribe another mark, in line with these two on the cylinder block. These marks are crucial to the re-installation of the distributor in the exact same direction and position.
7   Disconnect the wiring harness connector.
8   Remove the hold-down bolt at the base of the distributor and carefully withdraw the distributor from the engine.
9   If the engine has not been rotated, installation is basically a reversal of removal. If the oil pump shaft was removed with the distributor, coat one end of this shaft with heavy grease and insert it into the hex hole in the distributor shaft.
10 Perfectly align the rotor with the mark on the distributor body and the armature with the marks on the top of the magnetic pickup. Each $\frac{1}{2}$ tooth error is equal to $7\frac{3}{4}°$ timing error.
11 Position the distributor into the cylinder block, aligning the rotor and distributor body markings with the mark on the cylinder block.
12 Install the distributor hold-down clamp and bolt. Do not tighten the bolt completely until the initial timing is checked later.
13 Connect the vacuum hose(s) and the wiring connector.
14 Install the adaptor, rotor and cap.
15 Install the air cleaner.
16 Check the ignition timing as described in Section 6 and tighten the distributor hold-down bolt to specification.

8 Distributor stator assembly – removal and installation

1   Remove the distributor cap, adaptor and rotor from the top of the distributor.
2   Disconnect the electrical harness plug.
3   Using a small gear puller or two screwdrivers, pry the armature from the sleeve and plate assembly.
4   Remove the roll pin, using caution not to damage the pickup coil wires.

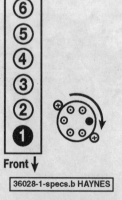

Fig. 5.6 Ignition timing marks, firing order and distributor location (3.3L engine) (Sec 6)

Fig. 5.7 Ignition timing marks, firing order and distributor location for V8 engines (Sec 6)

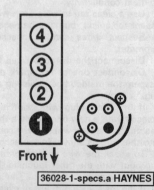

Fig. 5.8 Ignition timing marks, firing order and distributor location for 2.3L engine (Sec 6)

5   Remove the E-clip washer and wave washer which are used to secure the stator assembly to the lower plate.
6   Remove the ground screw and lift the stator assembly off the plate.
7   To install, place the stator assembly into position, inserting the post into diaphragm pull rod hole.
8   Slide the wiring grommet into the slot at the edge of the lower plate and secure the ground screw.
9   Install the washers and E-clip to secure the pickup coil assembly. The wave washer should have the outer edges up.
10 Install the armature on the sleeve and plate assembly making sure the roll pin is engaged in the matching slots.
11 Install the rotor, adaptor and cap. Connect the wiring harness plug.

9 Distributor vacuum advance unit – removal and installation

1   Remove the distributor cap, rotor and adaptor.
2   Disconnect the vacuum line(s).
3   Remove the attaching screws at the diaphragm unit and lift away the diaphragm unit and identification tag. The unit is best removed by tilting downward to disengage the link from the stator assembly.
4   Upon installation, hook the diaphragm link in position and place the unit against the distributor body.
5   Install the identification tag and tighten the attaching screws.
6   Connect the vacuum hose(s).
7   Install the adaptor, rotor and cap.
8   Included with the new diaphragm will be approved method for calibrating the new diaphragm unit. Follow the instructions given.

10 Alternator – general information

The main advantage of the alternator lies in its ability to provide a high charge at low revolutions. Driving slowly in heavy traffic with a generator invariably means no charge is reaching the battery. In similar conditions even with the wiper, heater, lights and perhaps radio switched on the alternator will ensure a charge reaches the battery.

The alternator is of rotating field, ventilated design. It comprises 3-phase output winding; a twelve pole rotor carrying the field windings – each end of the rotor shaft runs in ball race bearings which are lubricated for lift; natural finish aluminum die case end brackets, incorporating the mounting lugs; a rectifier pack for converting AC output of the machine to DC for battery charging, and an output control regulator.

The rotor is belt driven from the engine through a pulley keyed to the rotor shaft. A pressed steel fan adjacent to the pulley draws cooling air through the unit. This fan forms an integral part of the alternator specification. It has been designed to provide adequate air flow with minimum noise, and to withstand the high stresses associated with maximum speed. Rotation is clockwise viewed on the drive end. Maximum continuous rotor speed is 12 500 rpm.

Rectification of the alternator output is achieved by six silicone diodes housed in a rectifier pack and connected as a 3-phase full wave bridge. The rectifier pack is attached to the outer face of the slip ring end bracket and contains also three 'field' diodes. At normal operating speeds, rectified current from the stator output windings flows through these diodes to provide the self excitation of the rotor field, via brushes bearing on face type slip rings.

The slip rings are carried on a small diameter molded form attached to the rotor shaft outboard of the slip ring end bearing. The inner ring is centered on the rotor shaft axle, while the outer ring has a mean diameter of $\frac{3}{4}$ inch approximately. By keeping the mean diameter of the slip rings to a minimum, relative speeds between brushes and rings, and hence wear, are also minimal. The slip rings are connected to the rotor field windings by wires carried in grooves in the rotor shaft.

The brush gear is housed in a molding fitted to the inside of the rear casing. This molding thus encloses the slip ring and brush gear assembly, and together with the shield bearing, protects the assembly against the entry of dust and moisture.

Vehicles are equipped with either a side or rear terminal alternator (refer to accompanying figures). Both types operate in the same manner and differ only in internal wiring.

Ammeter-equipped vehicles use a different type of regulator than those with alternator warning indicator lamps. The regulators are similar in appearance but are not interchangeable. The units are solid state and are calibrated at the factory and are not adjustable.

11 Alternator – maintenance

1   The equipment has been designed for the minimum amount of maintenance in service, the only items subject to wear being the brushes and bearings.
2   Brushes should be examined after about 75 000 miles (120 000 km) and replaced with new ones if necessary. The bearings are pre-packed with grease for life, and should not require further attention.
3   Check the fan belt at the specified service intervals for correct adjustment which should be 0.5 inch (13 mm) total movement at the center of the run between the alternator and water pump pulleys.

12 Alternator – special procedures

Note: *Whenever the electrical system of the car is being attended to, and external means of starting the engine is used, there are certain precautions that must be taken, otherwise serious and expensive damage to the alternator can result.*
1   Always make sure that the negative terminal of the battery is grounded. If the terminal connections are accidentally reversed or if the battery has been reverse charged the alternator diodes will be damaged.
2   The output terminal on the alternator marked 'BAT' or 'B+' must never be grounded but should always be connected directly to the positive terminal of the battery.
3   Whenever the alternator is to be removed or when disconnecting the terminals of the alternator circuit, always disconnect the battery ground terminal first.
4   The alternator must never be operated without the battery to alternator cable connected.
5   If the battery is to be charged by external means always disconnect both the battery cables before the external charger is connected.
6   Should it be necessary to use a booster charger or booster battery to start the engine always double check that the negative cable is connected to negative terminal and the positive cable to positive terminal.

13 Alternator – removal and installation

1   Disconnect the battery negative cable.
2   Loosen the alternator adjusting bolt.
3   Loosen the alternator pivot bolt.
4   Disconnect the electrical connections.
5   Support the alternator while removing the drivebelt adjusting and pivot bolts.
6   Lift the alternator away from the vehicle.
7   Installation is the reverse of removal. Tighten the bolts to specifications.
8   Adjust the drivebelts to specification.

14 Alternator – fault diagnosis and repair

1   Due to the special training and equipment necessary to test or service the alternator it is recommended that if a fault is suspected the vehicle should be taken to a dealer or a shop with the proper equipment. Because of this the home mechanic should limit maintenance to checking connections and the inspection and replacement of the brushes.
2   The ammeter (ALT) gauge or alternator warning lamp on the instrument panel indicates the charge or discharge (D) current passing into or out of the battery. With the electrical equipment switched on and the engine idling the gauge needle may show a discharge condition. At fast idle or at normal driving speeds the needle should stay on the 'charge' side of the gauge, with the charged state of the battery determining just how far over.

5

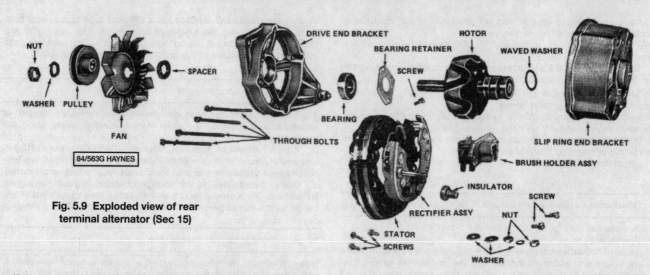

Fig. 5.9 Exploded view of rear terminal alternator (Sec 15)

3   If the gauge does not show a charge or (if equipped) the alternator lamp is on, there is a fault in the system. Before inspecting the brushes or replacing the alternator the battery condition, belt tension and electrical cable connections should be checked.

15 Alternator brushes (rear terminal type) – removal, inspection and installation

1   Remove the alternator as described in Section 13.
2   Scribe a line across the length of the alternator housing to ensure correct reassembly.
3   Remove the 3 housing through-bolts and the nuts and insulators from the rear housing. Make a careful note of all insulator locations.
4   Withdraw the rear housing section from the stator, rotor and front housing assembly.
5   Remove the brushes and springs from the brush holder assembly which is located inside the rear housing.
6   Check the length of the brushes against the wear dimension given in specifications at the beginning of the Chapter and replace with new ones if necessary.

7   Install the springs and brushes into the holder assembly and retain them in place by inserting a piece of stiff wire through the rear housing and brush terminal insulator. Make sure that enough wire protrudes through the rear of the housing so that it may be withdrawn at a later stage.
8   Install the rear housing rotor and front housing assembly to the stator, making sure that the scribed marks are aligned.
9   Install the 3 housing through-bolts and rear end insulators and nuts but do not tighten at this time.
10 Carefully extract the piece of wire from the rear housing and check that the brushes are seated on the slip ring. Tighten the through-bolts and rear housing nuts.
11 Install the alternator as described in Section 13.

16 Alternator brushes (side terminal type) – removal, inspection and installation

1   Remove the alternator as described in Section 13 and scribe a mark on both end housings and the stator for ease of reassembly.

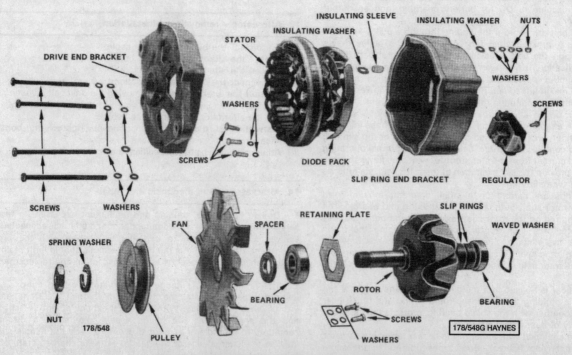

Fig. 5.10 Exploded view of side terminal alternator (Sec 16)

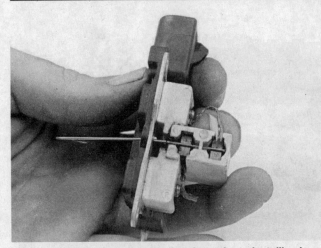

Fig. 5.11 Method of retracting brushes prior to installing brush holder on side terminal alternator (Sec 16)

2 Remove the 4 through-bolts and separate the front housing and rotor from the rear housing and stator. Be careful that you do not separate the rear housing and stator.

3 Use a soldering iron to unsolder and disengage the brush holder from the rear housing. Remove the brushes and springs from the brush holders.

4 Remove the 2 brush holder attaching screws and lift the brush holder from the rear housing.

5 Remove any sealing compound from the brush holder and rear housing.

6 Inspect the brushes for damage and check their dimensions against specifications. If they are out of specification, replace them with new ones.

7 To reassemble, install the springs and brushes in the brush holders, inserting a piece of stiff wire to hold them in place.

8 Place the brush holder in position to the rear housing, using the wire to retract the brushes through the hole in the rear housing.

9 Install the brush holder attaching screws and push the holder toward the shaft opening as you tighten the screws.

10 Press the brush holder lead onto the rectifier lead and solder in place. **Note**: *The rectifier can be overheated and damaged if the soldering is not done quickly.*

11 Place the rotor and front housing in position in the stator and rear housing. After aligning the scribe marks, install the 4 through-bolts.

12 Turn the fan and pulley to check for binding in the alternator.

13 Withdraw the wire which is retracting the brushes and seal the hole with waterproof cement.

17 Starter motor system – general description

The starter motor system consists of a motor with an integral positive engagement drive, the battery, a remote control starter switch, a neutral start switch on some models, the starter relay and the necessary wiring.

When the ignition switch is turned to the start position the starter relay is energized through the starter control circuit. The relay then connects the battery to the starter motor.

Cars equipped with an *automatic transmission and floor shift* have a neutral start switch in the starter control circuit which prevents operation of the starter if the selector lever is not in the 'N' or 'P' positions. Vehicles with *column shift automatic transmission* have an ignition switch mechanism which performs the same function.

With the starter in its rest position one of the field coils is connected directly to ground through a set of contacts. When the starter is first connected to the battery, a large current flows through the grounded field coil and operates a movable pole shoe. The poleshoe is attached to the starter drive plunger lever and so the drive is engaged with the ring gear on the flywheel.

When the movable pole shoe is fully seated, it opens the field coil grounding contacts and the starter is in a normal operational condition.

A special holding coil is used to maintain the movable pole shoe in the fully seated position while the starter is turning the engine.

18 Starter motor – testing on engine

1 If the starter motor fails to operate, then check the condition of the battery by turning on the headlights. If they glow brightly for several seconds and then gradually dim, the battery is in a discharged condition.

2 If the headlights continue to glow brightly and it is obvious that the battery is in good condition, check the tightness of the battery leads and all cables relative to the starting system. If possible, check the wiring with a voltmeter or test light for breaks or short circuits.

3 Check that there is current at the relay when the ignition switch is operated. If there is, then the relay should be suspect.

4 If there is no current at the relay, then suspect the ignition switch. On models with automatic transmission check the neutral start switch.

5 Should the above checks prove negative then the starter motor brushes probably need replacement or at the worst there is an internal fault in the motor.

19 Starter motor – removal and installation

1 On all models, disconnect the battery negative cable.

2.3L engine

2 Disconnect the starter cable from the motor.

3 Raise the vehicle and support it securely on jack stands.

4 From underneath the vehicle, remove the attaching bolts and withdraw the starter.

3.3L engine

5 Remove the top starter bolt (photo).

20 Starter motor – dismantling, overhaul and reassembly

1 Loosen the brush cover band retaining screw and remove the brush cover band and starter drive plunger lever cover.

2 Note the positions of the leads to ensure correct reassembly and then remove the commutator brushes from the brush holder.

3 Undo and remove the long through-bolts and lift off the drive end housing.

4 Remove the starter drive plunger lever return spring.

5 Remove the pivot pin that retains the starter gear plunger lever, using a suitable diameter pin punch.

6 Lift away the lever and withdraw the armature.

7 Remove the stop ring retainer followed by the stop ring that retains the starter drive gear onto the end of the armature shaft. The stop ring must be discarded and a new one obtained ready for reassembly.

8 Slide the starter drive assembly from the end of the armature.

9 Remove the brush endplate.

10 Unscrew the two screws that secure the ground brushes to the frame.

11 Dismantling should now be considered to be complete as removal of the field coils requires special equipment.

12 Clean the field coils, armature, commutator, armature shaft, brush endplate and drive end housing using a lint-free cloth and brush. Other parts may be washed in a suitable solvent.

13 Carefully inspect the armature windings for broken or burned insulation and unsoldered connections.

14 Test the four field coils for an open circuit. Connect a 12 volt battery and 12 volt bulb to one of the leads between the field terminal post and the tapping point of the field coils to which the brushes are connected. An open circuit is proved by the bulb not lighting.

15 If the bulb lights it does not necessarily mean that the field coils are in order, as there is a possibility that one of the coils will be grounded to the starter yoke or pole shoes. To check this remove the lead from the brush connector and place it against a clean portion of the starter yoke. If the bulb lights, the field coils are grounding.

16 Replacement of the field coils calls for the use of a wheel operated screwdriver, a soldering iron, caulking and riveting operations, and is beyond the scope of the majority of owners. The starter yoke should be taken to a reputable automotive electrical shop for new field coils to be fitted. Alternatively purchase an exchange starter motor.

5

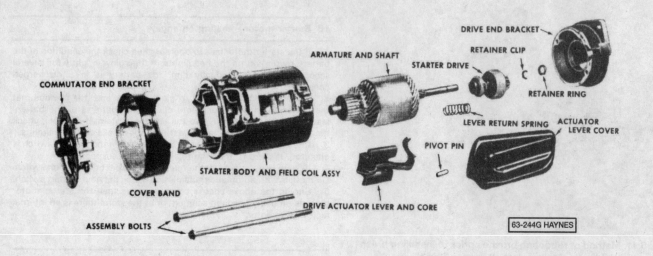

Fig. 5.12 Exploded view of starter motor (Secs 17 and 20)

17 If the armature is damaged this will be evident on inspection. Look for signs of burning, discoloration and for conductors that have lifted away from the commutator. Reassembly is a straightforward reversal of the dismantling procedure.

18 If a bearing is worn so allowing excessive side play of the armature shaft, the bearing bush must be replaced with a new one. Drift out the old bush with a piece of suitable diameter rod, preferably with a shoulder on it to stop the bush collapsing.

19 Soak a new bush in engine oil for 24 hours or, if time does not permit, heat in an oil bath at 100°C (212°F) for two hours prior to fitting.

20 As a new bush must not be reamed after fitting, it must be pressed into position using a small mandrel of the same internal diameter as the bush and with a shoulder on it. Place the bush on the mandrel and press into position using a bench vise.

21 If the bushes are replaced, their flexible connectors must be unsoldered and the connectors of new brushes soldered in their place. Check that the new brushes move freely in their holders as detailed above. If cleaning the commutator with gasoline fails to remove all the burnt areas and spots, then wrap a piece of glass paper around the commutator and rotate the armature.

22 If the commutator is very badly worn, remove the drive gear. Then mount the armature in a lathe and, with the lathe turning at high speed, take a very fine cut off the commutator. Do not undercut the mica insulators between the commutator segments.

23 Make sure that the drive moves freely on the armature shaft splines without binding or sticking.

24 To reassemble the starter motor is the reverse sequence to dismantling. The following additional points should be noted:

19.5 Location of starter bolts on 3.3L engine

a) Fill the drive end housing approximately $\frac{1}{4}$ full with grease.
b) Always use a new stop ring.
c) Lightly lubricate the armature shaft splines with a Lubriplate 777 or thin oil.

Chapter 6 Emissions systems

Contents

Specifications

Torque specifications

	Ft-lb	Nm
EGR valve-to-carburetor spacer or intake manifold	12 to 18	16 to 24
Thermactor pump bracket-to-cylinder block	12 to 18	16 to 24
Thermactor pump pivot bolt	22 to 32	30 to 43
Thermactor pump adjusting arm-to-pump		
1978 thru 1979	12 to 18	16 to 24
1980 thru 1981	24 to 34	33 to 46
Thermactor pump adjusting arm-to-cylinder block		
1978 thru 1979	20 to 28	27 to 38
1980 thru 1981	12 to 18	16 to 24
Thermactor pump pulley-to-shaft		
1978 thru 1979	10 to 11	13 to 15
1980 thru 1981	11 to 15	15 to 20

1 General information

1 In order to meet federal anti-pollution laws, each car is equipped with a variety of emission control systems, depending on the model and the state in which it was sold.

2 Since the emissions systems control so many engine functions, drivability, fuel consumption as well as conformance to the law can be affected should any faults develop. Consequently, keeping the emissions system operating at peak efficiency is very important.

3 This Chapter will describe all of the systems which may be installed in order to cover all models.

4 The emissions label located under the hood contains information important to properly maintaining the emission control systems as well as for keeping the vehicle properly tuned.

5 Before beginning any work on the emision control systems, read Section 2, Chapter 4 to avoid going contrary to any of the emission control regulations.

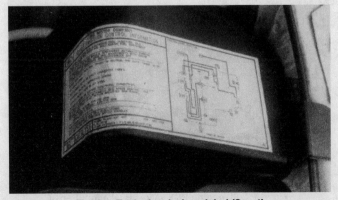

Fig. 6.1 Typical emissions label (Sec 1)

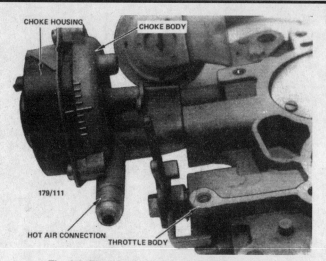

Fig. 6.2 Electrically assisted choke (Sec 2)

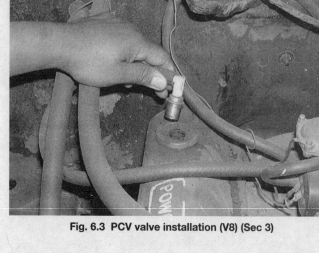

Fig. 6.3 PCV valve installation (V8) (Sec 3)

2   Electrically assisted choke heater – description and testing

1   Some carburetors have an electrically operated heater to aid in fast choke release and help reduce emissions during warm up.
2   The choke assist system consists of a choke cap, thermostatic spring, bi-metal temperature sensing switch and positive temperature coefficient (PTC) heater. The system is grounded to the carburetor and receives current from the center tap of the alternator.
3   At temperatures below 60°F (16°C), the sensing switch remains open and normal thermostatic spring action takes place. Above 60°F the sensing switch allows current from the alternator to activate the heater, warming the thermostatic spring so it opens faster. The thermostatic spring then pulls down the choke.
4   A fast idle cam latch works in conjunction with the choke to hold the cam in the high position until the choke backs off, allowing the latch to rotate to the normal run position.
5   Fast idle cam and choke pulldown adjustment are described in Chapter 4.
6   The only test that can be carried out on this assembly, without special test equipment, is a continuity check of the heater coil. If an ohmmeter is available, check for the specified resistance. If no ohmmeter is available, disconnect the stator lead from the choke cap terminal and connect it to one terminal of a 12 volt low wattage bulb (such as an instrument panel bulb). Ground the other terminal of the bulb and check that it illuminates when the engine is running. If it fails to illuminate, check the alternator output and the choke lead for continuity. If the bulb illuminates, disconnect the bulb ground terminal and reconnect it to the choke lead. If the bulb does not illuminate when the engine is warm, a faulty choke is indicated.

3   Positive crankcase ventilation (PCV) system – description and maintenance

1   The PCV system consists of the PCV valve, oil filler cap and associated hoses.
2   The system operates by drawing vapors that escape past the piston rings back into the intake manifold, allowing fresh air to flow through the oil filler cap into the crankcase.
3   Maintenance of the PCV system consists of periodically removing the hoses, valve and filler cap and cleaning them and checking for obstructions.
4   If a fault is suspected in the PCV valve, it is easily removed by grasping it at the elbow and pulling it from the engine (Figs. 6.3 and 6.4). Replacement involves assembling the new valve to the elbow and installing it. The new PCV valve and plastic fitting are supplied unassembled and it is a good idea to soak the fitting in hot water prior to installation to the valve.

4   Evaporative emission control (EEC) – description and maintenance

1   This system is designed to limit the emission of fuel vapors to the atmosphere. It is composed of the fuel tank, pressure and vacuum sensitive fuel filler cap, a restrictor bleed orifice, charcoal canister and the associated connecting lines.

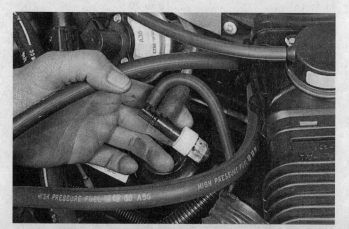

Fig. 6.4 3.3L engine PCV valve installation (Sec 3)

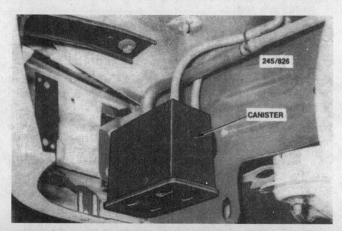

Fig 6.5 Evaporative emissions system and charcoal canister layout (Sec 4)

Fig. 6.6 A typical electronic type EGR valve (3.8L V6 shown) - to replace it, unplug the electrical connector from the position sensor and remove the two mounting nuts (arrows) (Sec 5)

5.6 Removing the EGR valve (3.3L engine)

Fig. 6.7 Cold weather modulator (CWM)

2   When the fuel tank is filled, vapors are discharged to the atmosphere through the filler tube, and a space between the inner fuel filler tube and the outer neck. When fuel covers the filler control tube, vapors can no longer escape and a vapor lock is created by the orifice; therefore, there can be no flow to the vapor charcoal canister.

3   When thermal expansion occurs in the fuel tank, vapor is forced through the orifice and is drawn into the carburetor intake system as soon as the engine is started.

4   Some models incorporate a fuel bowl vent valve to direct vapors which collect in the carburetor back into the canister when the engine is off.

5   Maintenance consists of checking for leaks in the system and for proper operation of the purge valve on the canister.

5   Exhaust gas recirculation (EGR) system – description and maintenance

Note: *Testing procedures can be found in Chapter 1.*

1   This system is designed to re-introduce small amounts of exhaust gas into the combustion cycle to reduce the generation of oxides of nitrogen (NOx). The amount of gas re-introduced is governed by engine vacuum and temperature.

2   The EGR valve is a vacuum-operated unit installed between the carburetor and intake manifold which, when open, allows exhaust gases to enter the manifold.

3   Three types of valves are used, depending on emission requirements. There are the poppet, tapered stem and integral transducer backpressure type.

4   Some models use a wide-open throttle valve (WOT) which closes the EGR valve when the engine is at or near wide-open throttle.

5   Electronic ignition equipped engines use a vacuum-operated EGR valve which incorporates a cooler assembly and position sensor.

6   The EGR valve can be removed for cleaning, but where it is damaged, corroded or extremely dirty it is preferable to replace it with a new valve (photo). If the valve is to be cleaned, check that the orifice in the body is clear and take care not to enlarge it. The internal deposits can be removed with a small power-driven rotary wire brush. Deposits around the valve stem and disc can be removed using a steel blade approximately 0.029 in (0.7 mm) thick in a sawing motion around the stem shoulder at both sides of the disc. Clean the cavity and passages in the main body, ensuring that the poppet wobbles and moves axially before reassembly.

6   Inlet air temperature regulation – description

Control of engine inlet air temperature is accomplished by the use of a thermostatic air cleaner and duct system. The operation of this system is described in Section 3, Chapter 4.

Some models incorporate a cold weather modulator (CWM) in the air cleaner assembly. At temperatures below 55°F (13°C) the CWM prevents the air cleaner duct door from opening to non-heated intake air. At temperatures below 55°, the CWM does not operate. Under acceleration in cold conditions the CWM will hold the duct door open.

7   Thermactor exhaust control system – description and maintenance

1   This system is designed to reduce the hydrocarbon (HC) and carbon monoxide (CO) content of the exhaust gases by continuing the oxidation of the unburned gases after they leave the combustion chamber. This air mixes with the hot exhaust gases and promotes further oxidation, thus reducing their concentration and converting some of them into carbon dioxide and water. Some models also inject Thermactor air directly into the catalytic converter.

2   The air pump draws in air through an impeller-type, centrifugal fan and exhausts it from the exhaust manifold through a vacuum controlled air bypass valve and check valve. Under normal conditions Thermactor air passes straight through the bypass valve, but during deceleration, when there is a high level of intake manifold vacuum, the diaphragm check valve operates to shut off the Thermactor air to the air supply valve check valve and exhausts it to the atmosphere. The air supply check valve is a non-return valve which will allow Thermactor air to pass to the exhaust manifold but will not allow exhaust gases to flow in the reverse direction.

3   Some models are equipped with an air injector system called Thermactor II which does not use an air pump. This system uses the natural pulses of the exhaust system to pull the air into the exhaust system. The Thermactor inlet valve incorporates a reed valve connected to the exhaust manifold and air cleaner by hoses (see accompanying figure).

6

Fig. 6.8 To replace the combination air bypass/air control valve (V6 unit shown, others similar), label, then detach, the following (Sec 7):

1 *Vacuum line to control solenoid*
2 *Air pump-to-combination valve hose*
3 *Vacuum line to control solenoid*
4 *Combination valve-to-right exhaust manifold hose*
5 *Combination valve-to-left exhaust manifold hose*

Fig. 6.9 Typical thermactor pump (Sec 7)

4 Several models of air bypass valves are used on the normal Thermactor system, but all are of two main types: normally open or normally closed.
5 Normally open bypass valves remain open because the vacuum is equal on both sides of the diaphragm. Under conditions of suddenly high intake manifold vacuum the diaphragm overcomes its return spring pressure, closing the valve and diverting the Thermactor air to the atmosphere momentarily.
6 A normally closed bypass valve is held in the upward or closed position by manifold pressure and Thermactor air flows to the cylinder heads, blocking the vent port. When the intake manifold fluctuates under acceleration or deceleration, the integral vacuum differential valve cuts off the vacuum, allowing the spring to pull the stem down. This cuts off Thermactor air to the exhaust manifold and diverts the air to the atmosphere.
7 Apart from checking the condition of the drivebelt and hose connections, and checking the drivebelt tension, there is little that can be done without the use of special test equipment. Drivebelt tension should be checked by an authorized dealer with a special tensioning tool. The tensioning procedure is described in Chapter 3.
8 Special equipment is required to carry out a complete test on the bypass valve function and it is recommended that the car be taken to an authorized dealer if a fault is suspected.

8 Catalytic converter – description

1 The catalytic converter is incorporated upstream of the exhaust front muffler. The converter is composed of a ceramic honeycomb-like core housed in a stainless steel pipe. This core is coated with a platinum and paladium catalyst which converts unburned carbon monoxide and hydrocarbons into carbon dioxide and water by a chemical reaction. Converters of this type are called Conventional Oxidation Catalysts (COC) or "two-way" catalysts because they control two of the three exhaust emissions.
2 "Three-Way Catalysts"(TWC) control hydrocarbons (HC), carbon monoxide (CO) and oxides of nitrogen (NOx). Three-way catalysts consists of two converters in one shell, with a mixing chamber in between them. The front chamber is coated with rhodium and platinum for controlling NOx while the rear chamber is a two-way type.
3 Air is injected from the Thermactor system into the mixing chamber to aid in oxidation.
4 No special maintenance of the converter is required, but it can be damaged by the use of leaded fuels, engine misfire, excessive richness

of the carburetor mixture, incorrect operation of the Thermactor system or running out of gasoline.

9 Spark control switches – description

1 Various vacuum switches are used in the emission system for modifying spark timing and engine idle. These vacuum switches have anywhere from from two to four ports, depending on their function.

Ported vacuum switches (PVS)
2 A typical ported vacuum switch is situated in the cooling system to increase idle rpm when the engine overheats. When the coolant is at normal temperature, the vacuum goes through the top and center ports of the PVS, providing the distributor with vacuum advance suitable for normal driving. When hot, the PVS center and bottom ports and connected so that the engine manifold vacuum allows the distributor to advance and increase idle.

Distributor vacuum vent valve
3 Some engines use a distributor vacuum vent valve to both prevent fuel from migrating into the distributor advance diaphragm and to act as a spark advance delay valve. During light acceleration, deceleration and idle, the vent valve dumps vacuum through a check valve (Figs. 6.28 and 6.29). This keeps the distributor from advancing excessively for the load and evacuates the fuel in the spark port line.

Cold start spark advance (CSSA)
4 The CSSA system is located in the distributor spark control system. When coolant temperature is below 128°F (53°C), it momentarily traps the spark port vacuum at the distributor advance diaphragm. The vacuum follows a path through the carburetor vacuum tap, the distributor retard control valve (DRCV), the CSSA ported vacuum switch and then the cooling vacuum switch to the distributor. At coolant temperatures above 128°F, the CSSA PVS operates and the vacuum follows a path from the carburetor spark port through the cooling PVS to the distributor. In an overheating condition (above 225°F, 103°C), the cooling PVS operates as described in paragraph 2.

Cold start spark hold (CSSH)
5 When the engine is cold, the CSSH momentarily provides spark advance for improved cold engine acceleration. Below 128°F, the CSSH ported vacuum switch is closed and the distributor vacuum is routed through a restrictor. Under cold starting conditions, the high vacuum present advances the distributor. During cold acceleration, the vacuum is slowly bled off through the restrictor, slowing the vacuum advance during initial acceleration.

Spark delay valve (SDV)
6 Spark delay valves are designed to slow the air flow in one direction while a check valve allows free flow in the opposite direction. This allows closer control of vacuum operated emission devices.

Chapter 7A Manual transmission

Contents

Specifications

Transmission type .... 3- or 4-speed (all forward gears synchromesh), floor-mounted shift
Application
1978
3-speed .... RAN-type
4-speed .... ET-type
1979 thru 1981
4-speed overdrive .... RUG-type
4-speed .... ET-type
Oil capacities
RAN-type .... 3.5 US qts
ET-type .... 2.8 US qts
RUG-type .... 4.5 US qts
Oil type ESP-M2C83-C
Component endplay
RAN-type 3-speed
Cluster gear-to-case .... 0.004 to 0.018 in
Reverse idler-to-case .... 0.004 to 0.018 in
ET-type 4-speed
Cluster gear-to-case .... 0.006 to 0.018 in
4-speed overdrive
Countershaft gear .... 0.004 to 0.018 in
1st gear .... 0.005 to 0.024 in
2nd gear .... 0.003 to 0.021 in
4th gear .... 0.009 to 0.023 in

Torque specifications

	ft-lb	Nm
RAN-type 3-speed		
Input shaft bearing retainer-to-case	30 to 36	41 to 48
Extension housing-to-case	40 to 42	54 to 56
Access cover-to-case screw	20 to 25	27 to 34
Outer gearshift lever-to-cam and shaft nut	18 to 23	23 to 29
Shift fork-to-shift rail screw	10 to 18	14 to 23
Filler plug	10 to 20	14 to 27
Transmission-to-bellhousing	37 to 42	50 to 56
ET-type 4-speed		
Input shaft bearing retainer-to-case bolt	8 to 10	11 to 13
Extension housing-to-case bolt	33 to 36	45 to 48
Access cover-to-case screw	8 to 10	11 to 13
Filler plug	24 to 27	33 to 27
Detent plug	12 to 14	16 to 18
RUG-type 4-speed overdrive		
Input shaft bearing retainer-to-case	11 to 25	15 to 33
Extension housing-to-case	42 to 50	54 to 67
Top cover-to-case	20 to 25	28 to 33
Filler plug	20 to 25	28 to 33
Detent bolt	10 to 15	14 to 20
Turret assembly bolts	8 to 12	11 to 16
Reverse gear pivot bolt	15 to 25	21 to 33
Back-up lamp switch	8 to 12	11 to 16

1   Transmission (RAN-type) – general information

The RAN-type transmission is equipped with three forward speeds and one reverse.

All forward gears are engaged through synchro-hubs and rings to obtain smooth, silent gear changes. All forward gears on the mainshaft and input shafts are in constant mesh with their corresponding gears on the countershaft gear cluster and are helically cut to achieve quiet running.

The reverse gear has straight-cut gear teeth and drives the first gear through an interposed sliding idler gear.

The gears are engaged by means of two sliding forks. The gears are selected by a floor-mounted shift linkage. Where close tolerances and limits are required during assembly of the transmission, selective thrustwashers and snap-rings are used to eliminate excessive endfloat. This eliminates the need for matched assemblies.

2   Transmission (RAN-type) – removal and installation

1   If it is necessary to remove the transmission by itself it can be taken out from below, leaving the engine in position. A considerable amount of working room below the vehicle will be required and, ideally, ramps or a hoist should be used. With the proper jacks and suitable jackstands available the job can be accomplished without the need for sophisticated equipment.

2   Disconnect the battery ground lead.

3   Remove the lower extension-to-transmission securing bolt and drain the transmission oil into a suitable container.

4   Disconnect the front of the driveshaft from the rear of the transmission, (see Chapter 8) and fasten the shaft out of the way.

5   Disconnect the speedometer drive cable from the transmission extension housing.

6   Remove the spring retaining rings and disconnect the rods from the gearshift levers on the side of the tranmission.

7   Disconnect the lead from the back-up lamp switch.

8   Place jack under the transmission. Raise the transmission slightly and remove the 2 nuts securing the rear support crossmember to the chassis. Remove the bolt securing the extension housing to the crossrnember as shown in the accompanying figure. Unbolt and remove the crossmember and insulators.

9   Lower the transmission assembly just enough to enable the four transmission-to-clutch housing bolts to be removed.

10   Carefully pull the transmission and supporting jack rearwards until the input shaft is clear of the clutch housing. Lower the assembly to the ground.

11   When reinstalling the transmission, ensure that the clutch release lever and bearing are properly located in the clutch housing.

12   Apply a smear of light grease on the transmission input shaft splines and then install the transmission using the reverse procedure to removal. It may be necessary to rotate the engine to align the clutch disc and input shaft splines.

3   Transmission (RAN-type) – dismantling

1   Place the complete unit on a firm bench or table to ensure that you have the following tools available, in addition to the normal range of wrenches etc.

     a)   *Good quality snap-ring pliers, 2 pairs – 1 expanding and 1 contracting.*
     b)   *Copper-headed hammer, at least 2 lb.*
     c)   *Selection of steel and brass drifts*
     d)   *Small containers*
     e)   *Engineer's vise mounted on firm bench.*
     f)   *Selection of steel tubing.*

2   Any attempt to dismantle the transmission without the foregoing is not impossible, but will certainly be very difficult and inconvenient.

3   Read the whole of this Section before starting work.

4   Undo the securing screws and remove the cover plate and gasket from the top of the casing. Drain out any oil remaining in the casing.

5   Remove the spring and detent plug from the aperture in the top left-hand side of the casing (see the accompanying figure).

6   Undo the retaining bolts and withdraw the extension housing from the rear of the casing. Remove the gasket.

7   Undo the retaining bolts and remove the bearing retainer and gasket from the front of the casing.

8   Remove the oil filler plug from the side of the casing. Using a suitably sized drift through the plug aperture, drive out the roll pin that secures the countershaft to the casing.

9   Using a soft alloy drift, carefully tap the countershaft out of the rear of the casing, while supporting the countershaft gear cluster with one hand.

10   When the shaft is removed, lower the countershaft gear cluster and thrustwashers to the bottom of the casing.

11   Remove the snap-ring securing the speedometer drivegear to the output (rear) shaft. Slide the gear off the end of the shaft and remove the gear locking ball from he shaft.

12   Remove the snap-ring securing the rear bearing to the output bearing and, using two screwdrivers, placed between the outer snap-ring and casing, carefully lever the bearing out of the casing and slide it off the end of the output shaft.

Note: *If difficulty is experienced in removing the bearing special tools are available from your dealer.*

13   Place the two shift levers on the side of the casing in the neutral (center) position.

14   Remove the set screw securing the 1st/reverse shift fork to the shift rail. Slide the rail out the rear of the casing.

15   Slide the 1st/reverse synchro-hub forward as far as possible, rotate the shift fork upward and lift it out of the casing.

16   Push the 2nd/3rd gear shift fork rearwards to the 2nd gear position to gain access to the retaining screw and remove it. Using a suitable pair of pliers or grips, rotate the shift rail 90° (as shown in the accompanying figure).

17   Lift the interlock plug out of the casing using a magnet.

18   Carefully tap the rear end of the 2nd/3rd gear shift rail to drive out the expansion plug from the front of the casing. Withdraw the shift rail.

19   Remove the remaining detent plug and spring from the bore in the casing.

20   Pull the input shaft and bearing from the front of the casing.

21   Rotate the 2nd/3rd gear shift fork upward and lift it from the case.

22   Carefully lift the output shaft and gears out through the top of the casing.

23   Slide the reverse gear shaft out of the casing and lift out the reverse idler gear assembly and thrust washers.

24   Lift out the countershaft gear cluster and retrieve the thrust washers and any of the needle bearings that may have fallen out. Note that there are 25 needle bearings in each end of the shaft.

25   If required the shift lever can be removed from the side of the casing by undoing the securing nuts and removing the levers and washers from the shafts. Slide the shafts out of the casing as shown and discard the O-ring seals.

26   The gearbox is now completely disassembled and must be thoroughly cleaned. If there is any quantity of metal chips and fragments in the bottom of the casing it is obvious that several items will be found to be badly worn. The component parts of the gearbox and countershaft should be examined for wear. The input and output shaft assemblies should be broken down further as described in the following Sections.

4   Transmission (RAN-type) – inspection and overhaul

1   Carefully clean and then examine all the component parts for general wear, distortion, slackness of fit and damage to machined faces and threads.

2   Examine the gearwheels for excessive wear and chipping of the teeth. Renew them as necessary.

3   Examine the countershaft for signs of wear, where the countershaft gear cluster roller bearings ride on the shaft. If a small ridge can be felt at either end of the shaft it will be necessary to replace it.

4   The three synchro blocking rings are bound to be badly worn and it is false economy not to replace them. New rings will improve the smoothness and speed of the shift considerably.

5 The needle roller bearings located between the nose of the output shaft and the annulus in the rear of the input shaft are also liable to wear, and should be replaced as a matter of course.

6 Examine the condition of the two ball bearings assemblies, one on the input shaft and one on the output. Check them for noisy operation, looseness between the inner and outer races, and for general wear. Normally they should be replaced on a transmission that is being rebuilt.

7 If either of the synchro-hubs are worn it will be necessary to buy a complete assembly as the parts are not sold individually.

8 If the bush bearing in the extension is badly worn it is best to take the extension to your local Ford dealer or repair shop to have the bearing pulled out and a new one fitted.

9 The oil seals in the extension housing, input shaft bearing retainer and selector levers should be replaced as a matter of course. Drive out the old seals with the aid of a drift or broad screwdriver. It will be found that the seals come out quite easily.

10 With a piece of wood to spread the load evenly, carefully tap new seals into place ensuring that they enter their housings squarely.

11 The only point on the output shaft that is likely to be worn is the nose where it enters the input shaft. However, examine it thoroughly for any signs of scoring, picking up, or flats, and if damage is apparent, replace the shaft with a new one.

5 Input shaft (RAN-type) – dismantling and reassembly

1 The only reason for dismantling the input shaft is to fit a new ball bearing assembly, or, if the input shaft is being replaced and the old bearing is in excellent condition, the fitting of a new shaft to an old bearing.

2 With a pair of expanding snap-ring pliers remove the small snap-ring which secures the bearing to the input shaft.

3 With a soft-headed hammer gently tap the bearing forward and then remove it from the shaft.

4 When fitting the new bearing ensure that the groove cut in the outer periphery faces away from the gear. If the bearing is installed backwards it will not be possible to fit the large snap-ring which retains the bearing in the housing.

5 Using the jaws of a vise as a support behind the bearing, tap the bearing squarely into place by hitting the rear of the input shaft with a plastic or hide faced hammer.

6 Install the snap-ring which holds the bearing to the input shaft.

6 Output shaft (RAN-type) – dismantling and reassembly

1 The output shaft has to be dismantled before some of the synchro-rings can be inspected. For dismantling, it is best to mount the plain section of the shaft in a vise.

2 As each component is removed from the shaft make a careful note of its position and then place it on a clean sheet of paper in the order of removal.

3 Referring to the accompanying figure remove the snap-ring from the front of the output shaft and slide the blocker ring (if not already removed), the synchronizer hub and the 2nd gear off the shaft.

4 Remove the next snap-ring and thrust washer and slide the 1st gear and blocking ring off the shaft.

5 Remove the final snap-ring and press the shaft out of the reverse gear and synchronizer sleeve assembly as shown.

Caution: Do not attempt to remove the 1st gear synchronizer hub from the shaft by trying to hammer it or prying it off with levers as damage will probably result.

6 If it is necessary to dismantle the synchro-hubs and sleeves, first refer to the accompanying figures and etch alignment marks on each component.

7 Push the sleeves off the hubs and remove the inserts and insert springs, making a careful note which way round they are fitted.

8 Do not mix the 1st/reverse synchro-hub components with those from the 2nd/3rd synchro-hub assembly.

9 To assemble a synchro-hub, first position the sleeve on the hub making sure the etched marks line up.

10 Install the three inserts and retain in position with the springs. Make sure that the small ends of the inserts face the inside of the hub.

11 In the case of the 1st/reverse gear synchro assembly ensure the inserts are fully retained by the springs as shown in the accompanying figure.

12 To reassemble the gears and synchro-hubs onto the output shaft, first lubricate the shaft and splines with clean transmission oil.

13 Carefully press the reverse gear and synchronizer assembly onto the shaft as shown in. Secure the gear in place with the snap-ring.

14 Place a blocking ring on the tapered surface of the 1st gear.

15 Slide the 1st gear onto the output shaft with the blocking ring facing toward the rear of the shaft. Rotate the gear as necessary to engage the three notches in the blocking ring with synchronizer inserts.

16 Secure the 1st gear in position with the thrustwasher and snap-ring.

17 Fit a blocking ring onto the tapered surface of the 2nd gear. Slide the 2nd gear and ring onto the shaft ensuring that the tapered side of the gear faces toward the front of the shaft.

18 Finally, slide the 2nd/3rd gear synchronizer onto the end of the shaft and secure it in place with the snap-ring.

19 The output shaft is now completely reassembled.

7 Transmission (RAN-type) – reassembly

1 Insert the reverse gear idler shaft into the rear of the transmission case. Hold the spacer and reverse gear in position (helical gear teeth facing the front of the casing) and slide the shaft fully home.

2 Smear some grease into each end of the countershaft gear cluster and carefully insert the roller bearings. Ideally a dummy shaft of the same outside dimensions as the countershaft but shorter, should be placed inside the countershaft gear cluster to hold the bearings in place.

3 Stick the thrustwasher onto each end of the countershaft gear cluster with grease.

4 Carefully place the countergear assembly in the bottom of the casing but do not fit the countershaft at this stage.

5 Install the output shaft and gear cluster into the casing through the top access hole.

6 Install a new snap-ring in the groove around the rear bearing assembly and carefully drive the bearing along the output shaft until it enters the aperture in the rear of the casing. Note that the groove in the bearing must be positioned towards the rear of the casing.

7 Install a new bearing retainer snap-ring on the output shaft.

8 Check that the roller bearings are correctly located in the end of the input shaft with grease.

9 Insert the input shaft, 3rd gear and synchro-ring assembly through the front of the casing, making sure the end of the output shaft is correctly located in the roller bearing recess of the input shaft.

10 Install a new snap-ring in the front bearing groove and tap the bearing along the input shaft until it enters the aperture in the casing. Carefully tap the bearing fully home.

11 Position the 2nd/3rd gear shift fork on the 2nd/3rd gear synchro-hub.

12 Refer back to Fig. 7.3 and install the lower spring and detent plug into the casing.

13 Push the 2nd/3rd gear synchro-hub as far as possible toward the rear of the casing (2nd gear position).

14 Align the hole in the shifter fork with the casing and push the 2nd/3rd gear shift rail in from the front of the casing. It will be necessary to push the detent plug downward to enable the shaft to enter the bore.

15 Push the shaft into the casing until the detent plug engages in the forward notch (2nd gear position).

16 Secure the fork to the shaft with the set screw and then push the synchro unit forward to the neutral position.

17 Fit the interlock plug into the bore in the side of the casing so that it is resting on top of the shift rail.

18 Push the 1st/reverse gear and synchro unit fully forward to the 1st gear position.

19 Fit the 1st/reverse shift fork in the synchro unit groove, rotate the fork into the correct position and slide the 1st/reverse shift rail in from the rear of the casing.

20 Push the rail (shaft) inward until the center notch (neutral) is in line with the detent bore.

21 Secure the fork to the shaft with the set screw.

22 Install a new shift rail expansion plug in the front of the casing.
23 Place the casing in a vertical position and using a screwdriver through the oil filler hole, align the bore of the countershaft gear and the thrust washers with the bores in the casing.
24 Insert the countershaft from the rear of the casing and gently tap it through the gear cluster, driving out the dummy shaft.
25 If a dummy shaft was not used, insert the countershaft in the same way, but take great care not to dislodge any of the needle roller bearings or thrust washers.
26 Position the shaft so that the hole lines up with the hole in the casing and then the shaft is fully home drive in a new roll pin.
27 Check that the countershaft gears rotate smoothly with no harshness that might indicate dislodged needle bearings.
28 Fit a new front bearing snap-ring onto the input shaft.
29 Install the input shaft retainer using a new gasket.
30 Apply gasket sealer to the bearing retainer bolts and torque them up to the figure given in the Specifications.
31 Fit the spedometer drive gear locking ball into the hole in the output shaft, hold the ball in position and slide the drivegear over it. Secure with a snap-ring.
32 Place a new gasket over the rear end of the transmission casing and install the rear extension housing.
33 Apply sealer to the extension housing retaining bolts and tighten to the specified torque wrench setting.
34 Rotate the input shaft by hand and check that all gears can be selected in turn and both shafts rotate smoothly.
35 Fit the remaining detent plug and spring in the bore in the top of the casing.
36 Coat a new cover gasket with sealant, fit the top cover and tighten the retaining bolts.
37 Temporarily refit the oil filler plug.
38 Reinstall the transmission to the engine as described in Section 2. Refill it with the correct grade and quantity of transmission oil and tighten the plug.

8 Manual transmission (ET-type) – general information

The manual gearboxes used on the models covered by this manual are equipped with four forward and one reverse gear.
All forward gears are engaged through blocker ring synchromesh units, to obtain smooth, silent, gearchanges. All forward gears on the mainshaft are in constant mesh with their corresponding gears on the countershaft gear cluster and are helically cut, to achieve quiet running.
The countershaft reverse gear has straight-cut spur teeth and drives the 1st/2nd gear synchronizer hub on the mainshaft through an interposed sliding idler gear.
Gears are engaged either by a single selector rail and forks, or by levers in the gearbox side cover and forks. Control of the gears is from a floor-mounted shift lever which connects either with the single shift rail, or the three selector levers and link rods.
Where close limits are required during assembly of the gearbox, selective shims are used to eliminate excessive endfloat, or backlash, without the need of using matched assemblies.

9 Transmission (ET type) – removal and installation

1 If the gearbox is to be removed from the car without removing the engine, the gearbox is removed from beneath the car and a large ground clearance is required. If an inspection pit or ramps are not available, jack the car as high as possible, support it securely on blocks or stands and check the wheels.
2 Disconnect the battery.
3 Unscrew the gear lever knob and remove the cover and rubber cover. If a package tray or center console is fitted, these must be removed (refer to Chapter 12 if necessary).
4 Remove the three metric bolts attaching the lever assembly to the transmission. Lift out the gear lever.
5 Place a drip tray beneath the gearbox, remove the drain plug and when the oil has drained, refit the plug and tighten it.
6 Put mating marks on the two faces of the rear axle joint flange. Remove the four bolts from the rear axle pinion flange and the two bolts from the driveshaft center bearing support and withdraw the

driveshaft assembly from the extension housing. Tie a polythene bag around the end of the gearbox extension to keep out dirt and to catch any oil which has not drained.
7 Pull back the rubber boot over the clutch release lever and loosen the adjuster, so that the end of the clutch cable can be unhooked from the clutch release lever.
8 Remove the screw and lock plate securing the speedometer drive and disconnect the drive.
9 Remove the cover from the back-up light switch. Note which way the leads are fitted and then remove them.
10 Detach the exhaust pipe from the exhaust manifold and tie the pipe out of the way, so that the engine and transmission can be lowered.
11 Support the gearbox on a jack, or with blocks and remove the bolt securing the transmission to the rear engine mounting and the four bolts securing the gearbox crossmember to the floor. Remove the crossmember.
12 Lower the transmission a little and insert a block of wood between the sump and the front engine mounting so that the engine does not drop too fast when the transmission is removed. It may be necessary to slide the catalytic converter heat shield forward for clearance.
13 Remove the six bolts securing the clutch housing to the engine. Pull the transmission assembly to the rear to disengage the gearbox driveshaft from the clutch pilot bearing and clutch friction plate. It is important that the engine and transmission are kept in line while this is being done, otherwise the gearbox shaft may be strained and damaged.
14 When the gearbox shaft is clear of the clutch, remove the transmission assembly from beneath the car.
15 When installing, ensure that the two clutch housing guide bushes are fitted to the engine and that the clutch pilot bearing in the end of the crankshaft is in place and is serviceable. Tie the clutch lever to the clutch housing, to prevent the release lever from slipping out while the transmission assembly is being fitted.
16 Smear some molybdenum-based grease (Ford chassis lube) onto the end and splines of the gearbox input shaft and refit the gearbox by reversing the removal procedure.
17 It is important when installing the gearbox, that it is exactly in line with the crankshaft, otherwise the gearbox input shaft will not enter the clutch driven plate and the crankshaft. If there is difficulty in mating the splines of the gearbox shaft and the clutch plate, select a gear to restrain the movement of the gearbox shaft and turn the gearbox slightly until the splines enter. Do not attempt to force the transmission onto the engine. This may damage the splines and make fitting impossible.
18 After installation has been completed, check the oil level in the transmission and top up as necessary with gear oil.

10 Transmission (ET type) – dismantling

1 Remove the clutch release bearing and lever. Remove the clutch housing.
2 Drain the transmission and remove the cover and gasket.
3 Remove the threaded plug, spring and shift rail detent plunger located on the front of the transmission case.
4 At the rear of the transmission, drive out the access plug.
5 Drive out the interlock plate retaining pin and remove.
6 Remove the roll pin from the selector lever arm.
7 Remove the plug at the rear of the extension housing by tapping the front end of the shift rail to displace it.
8 Pull the shift rail out of the back of the extension housing and case.
9 Remove the selector arm shift forks from the case.
10 Remove the extension housing attachment bolts and tap the housing with a plastic mallet to loosen it.
11 Rotate the loosened housing so that the countershaft is aligned with the cutaway in the extension housing flange.
12 Drive the countershaft rearward with a brass drift until it just clears the front of the case. Slide a dummy shaft in the case and gear until the countershaft gear can be lowered to the bottom of the case. Remove the countershaft.
13 Lift the extension housing and mainshaft assembly from the case.
14 Remove the four 10 mm bolts securing the input shaft bearing retainer to the front of the case. Remove the input shaft and bearing retainer assembly.

15 Remove the reverse idler shaft screwing a suitable bolt into the end of the shaft and then levering the shaft out using two open-ended wrenches.

16 Remove the countershaft gear, bearing retaining washers, bearings and dummy shaft from the countershaft gear.

11 Output shaft (ET type) – dismantling and reassembly

1 Remove the 4th gear blocker ring from the output shaft.

2 Remove and discard the snap-ring from the forward end of the input shaft.

3 Remove and discard the 3rd/4th gear snap-ring.

4 Ease the hub and 3rd gear assembly forward by levering gently with a pair of needle nosed pliers.

5 Remove the 3rd/4th gear synchronizer assembly and 3rd gear from the output shaft.

6 Remove the snap-ring and discard it and remove the washer and slide the 2nd gear and blocker ring off the output shaft.

7 Scribe or paint alignment marks on the hub and synchronizer before disassembling. Pull the sleeve off the synchronizer before disassembling. Pull the sleeve off the hub and remove the inserts and springs to disassemble.

8 Remove the snap-ring retaining it to the output shaft bearing and press or tap the output shaft assembly out off the extension housing with a plastic hammer or mallet.

9 Remove the output shaft snap-ring and bearing.

10 Remove the speedometer gear with a press.

11 Press off the 1st gear, spacer and bearing from the output shaft.

12 Since the 1st and 2nd speed synchronizer and hub are serviced as a complete assembly with the shaft, do not attempt to separate them. If they are worn or damaged the whole assembly must be replaced.

13 Before starting reassembly, clean all parts thoroughly and check their condition. Lubricate all parts with transmission oil before installing.

14 Reassemble the synchronizer sleeve and hub, making sure that the marks made in step 7 are lined up. Insert the hub inserts and fit the hub insert springs so that their open ends are staggered relative to each other.

15 Place the synchronizer blocker ring onto the cone of the 2nd gear and slide it onto the output shaft together with the 1st/2nd gear synchronizer hub. The gear on the hub should face forward.

16 Install the synchronizer blocker ring and snap-ring which holds the synchronizer hub in place.

17 Slide on 1st gear, so that the synchronizer cone lies just inside the synchronizer ring which has just been installed. Apply multipurpose grease to the cone surface of 1st gear and all shaft gear journals.

18 Install the spacer on the output shaft so that the large diameter is towards the rear.

19 A special Ford tool is required to determine which thickness snap-ring must be installed to eliminate shaft endplay. It is advisable to have your dealer perform this procedure.

20 Once the proper snap-ring is obtained, position it and the bearing on the end of the output shaft. Place the assembly in a press and press the bearing into position. Install the selected snap-ring in the groove in the output shaft.

21 Install the synchronizer blocker ring to the cone of 3rd gear and install this assembly on the front of the output shaft. Install the 3rd/4th gear synchronizer hub with its wide boss toward the rear and retain it with a snap-ring.

22 The speedometer drivegear must also be installed with a press and a special tool, so this is another procedure best left to your dealer.

12 Input shaft (ET type) – dismantling and reassembly

1 It is not necessary to dismantle the input shaft unless a new bearing or a new shaft is being installed.

2 With a pair of circlip pliers, expand and remove the small circlip which secures the bearing to the input shaft.

3 With a soft headed hammer, gently tap the bearing forward until it can be pulled from the shaft.

4 When fitting the bearing, ensure that the groove in the periphery of the outer bearing track is away from the gear, otherwise it will not be possible to fit the large circlip which retains the bearing in place in the housing.

5 Either stand the input shaft upright on a bench and tap the bearing into place using a piece of tube of suitable diameter, or use the jaws of a vise to support the bearing and tap the rear of the input shaft with a soft faced hammer.

6 When the bearing is fully home, fit the circlip which retains the bearing on the shaft.

13 Countershaft (ET type) – dismantling and reassembly

1 Remove a shim from each end of the countershaft, remove 21 needle rollers from each end of the gear.

2 When reassembling, insert a shim into the bottom of the bore. Daub the bore with general purpose grease and insert the 21 needle rollers. When all the rollers are in place, smear grease over them to retain them and then secure the shim over the ends of the rollers with grease.

14 Transmission (ET type) – inspection and overhaul

1 Carefully clean and then examine all the component parts for signs of excessive wear, damage, distortion or damage to mechanical faces and threads.

2 Examine the gears for excessive wear and broken or chipped teeth. It is not satisfactory to fit a new gear unless its mating gear is also replaced and if the condition of gears is bad, an exchange gearbox should be fitted.

3 Examine the countershaft for wear on the ends which are in contact with the needle rollers and if there is a wear step, a new countershaft should be fitted.

4 The four synchronizer rings are certain to be worn and it is a false economy not to replace them. New rings will improve the smoothness of gearchanging considerably.

5 The needle roller bearing between the nose of the mainshaft and the bore of the input shaft should be discarded and a new one fitted.

6 Check the condition of the bearing on the input shaft and the new one on the output. It is worth replacing these having dismantled the gearbox.

7 If there is excessive wear in the synchronizer units they must be replaced as an assembly, because parts are not sold individually. These units are expensive and as the selector forks are also likely to need replacing, an exchange gearbox may be a more satisfactory solution. If possible compare the synchronizer rings and selector forks with new ones, before deciding what to do.

8 If the bush bearing in the gearbox extension is badly worn, it is best to take the extension to a dealer to have the bearing pulled out and a new one fitted. The gearbox needs to be assembled and the output shaft refitted for this to be done.

9 The oil seals in the extension housing and the front bearing retainer should be replaced. Drive out the old seal with a screwdriver and tap in a new seal with a hammer and piece of wood. Make sure that the seal has entered its bore squarely before attempting to tap it in.

7A

15 Transmission (ET type) – reassembly

1 When any bolt screws into a through bore, sealing compound should be applied to the threads of the bolt before it is inserted.

2 Fit the reverse idler gear with the groove on the gear towards the rear. Insert the idler shaft and drive it in with a plastic headed hammer until the bottom of the step on the end of the shaft is flush with the end of the gearbox. The milled flats should protrude slightly from the gearbox face and should be aligned with a countershaft bore.

3 Fit the large thrust washer to the countershaft bore at the front of the gearbox and the small thrust washer to the countershaft bore at the rear of the box. The tabs on the washers should be towards the case and the washers should be greased to retain them in place.

4 Check that the needle rollers and end washers of the countershaft gear are in place, then lower the gear cluster into the case carefully, making sure that the thrust washers are not displaced.

5   Push the input shaft, together with its ball bearing, into the front of the gearbox until the circlip round the bearing bears against the front of the gearbox case.

6   Fit the drive bearing retainer, using a new gasket, making sure that the oil return bore of the gasket and bearing retainer are aligned. Apply sealing compound to the threads of the bolts, insert them and tighten to the torque wrench setting given in the Specifications.

7   Oil the new input shaft needle roller bearing and push it into the bore of the input shaft. Slide the top gear synchronizer blocker ring on to the cone of the input shaft.

8   Fit the extension housing gasket, then insert the assembled output shaft into the rear of the box and drive it in until the nose of the output shaft is fully engaged in the bore of the front driveshaft bearing.

9   Carefully turn the gearbox upside down, so that the countershaft gear cluster drops into engagement with the output shaft. Check that the gear and the two thrust washers are in line and then carefully push in the countershaft from the rear. If necessary tap the shaft in with a plastic headed hammer, but take great care not to dislodge the thrust washers or needle rollers. When fully home, the bottom of the step on the idler shaft should be in line with the face of the box and the milled flats should be in line with the idler shaft bore (as shown in the accompanying figure).

10 Turn the gearbox the right way up and align the hole in the ball bearing support with the dowel on the extension housing. Fit the extension housing. Apply sealing compound to the threads of the bolts, insert them and tighten to the torque wrench setting given in the Specifications.

11 If a new extension housing bush has been fitted, check that the notch or oil groove in it aligns with the oil return groove in the extension housing. If the new extension housing oil seal has not already been fitted, slide it over the extension shaft and carefully tap it in with a hammer and a block of wood.

12 Fit a new O-ring to the speedometer pinion assembly, refit the assembly and fit the circlip to secure it.

13 Insert the reverse gear interlock plunger, threaded plug and spring. Fit the bolt with a lock plate and insert the bolt Tighten the bolt and bend the lock plates to secure it.

14 Insert all three selector forks into their positions in the gearbox.

15 Slide 1st/2nd gear selector rail through the right-hand bore in the case, then thread it through the 1st/2nd gear selector fork. Align the holes in the fork and rail and tap in the roll pin. Insert the plunger into the case.

16 Fit the plunger into the 3rd/top gear selector rail, insert the rail through the center bore in the case and thread the rail through the 3rd/top gear selector fork. Fit the circlip to the groove in the selector rail. Align the holes in the selector fork and rail, insert the roll pin and tap it home.

17 Push reverse gear selector rail through a left-hand bore in the housing, and then thread it through the reverse gear selector fork. Align the holes in the fork and rail, insert a roll pin and tap it home.

18 Fit the interlock plunger, apply sealing compound to the plug and screw in the plug.

19 Insert reverse gear relay lever and secure it with a roll pin.

20 Insert the selector shaft through the selector housing cover and fit the cover using a new gasket. Insert the cover retaining bolts and screw them in fingertight.

21 Fit the selector shaft bracket.

22 Slide the selector finger onto the selector shaft. Engage the screw in the recess in the shaft and tighten the screw.

23 Drop the three detent balls into their bores in the case, grease the three springs and insert them into the recesses of the gearbox cover. Fit a new cover gasket and position the cover onto it, insert the cover bolts and tighten them to the torque wrench setting given in the Specifications.

24 Check the play between the selector finger and 3rd/top gear selector rail.

25 Fit a new gasket to the extension housing cover. Position the cover, insert the fixing bolts and tighten them to the torque wrench setting given in the Specifications. Apply sealer to a new extension housing plug and install a new plug as shown

26 Make sure that the gearbox drain plug is fitted and tightened, then fill the gearbox to the correct level by pouring in 2.8 pints U.S. (1.3 liters) of oil to specification ESW-M2C83-C (SAE 80 EP).

16 Back-up light switch – installation

1   The back-up light switch is mounted below the rear end of the gearbox extension. To remove the switch, disconnect the leads, unscrew the switch and remove the switch, spring and plunger. When refitting the switch, apply a smear of gasket sealant to the screw threads and refit the plunger, spring and switch.

17 Manual Transmission (RUG-type) – general information

The RUG-type single rail overdrive transmission is equipped with four forward and one reverse gear.

All forward gears are engaged through synchro hubs and rings to obtain smooth, silent gearchanges. All forward gears on the mainshaft and input shaft are in constant mesh with their corresponding gears on the countershaft gear cluster and are helically cut to achieve quiet running.

The countershaft reverse gear has straight-cut spur teeth and drives the toothed 1st/2nd gear synchro-hub on the mainshaft through an interposed sliding idler arm.

Gears are engaged by a single selector rail and forks. Control of the gears is from a floor-mounted shift lever which connects with the single selector rail.

Fourth gear is an overdrive ratio for quieter running and better mileage at highway speeds.

18 Transmission (RUG-type) – removal and installation

1   If the transmission alone is to be removed from the car, it can be taken out from below leaving the engine in position. It will mean that a considerable amount of working room is required beneath the car, and ideally ramps or an inspection pit should be used. However, provided that suitable jacks and supports are available, the task can be accomplished without the need for sophisticated equipment.

2   Disconnect the battery ground lead.

3   From inside the car remove the two front screws from each scuff plate and the side trim panel and pull the carpet back over the gear-shift lever.

4   Remove the four bolts holding the shift lever boot retaining plate and lift the plate and boot off the lever. Remove the shift lever knob if necessary.

5   Undo and remove the three shift lever retaining bolts and remove the lever assembly.

6   Drain the transmission oil into a suitable container.

7   Mark the driveshaft so that it can be re-installed in the same relative position. Remove the driveshaft as described in Chapter 8.

8   Remove the front exhaust pipe section from the manifold flange and the front of the resonator box or converter, if fitted.

9   Disconnect the clutch cable from the clutch release lever and the side of the clutch housing (see Chapter 8).

10 Remove the starter motor retaining bolts and move the motor towards the front of the car.

11 Disconnect the back-up lamp switch wires and the seat belt sensing switch wires if fitted.

12 Remove the speedometer cable retaining screw and pull the cable out of the extension housing.

13 Support the rear of the engine with a block of wood placed on top of a jack and remove the rear engine mounting crossmember.

14 Remove the two bolts that retain the extension crossmember and remove the crossmember.

15 Gradually lower the engine by means of the jack until there is sufficient clearance to remove the four bolts retaining the transmission assembly to the clutch housing.

16 Support the weight of the transmission and undo and remove the four bolts.

17 Carefully withdraw the transmission away from the clutch housing and lower it to the ground.

18 When refitting the transmission, ensure that the clutch release lever and bearing are correctly located in the clutch housing.

19 Apply a smear of light grease on the transmission input shaft splines and then install the transmission using the reverse procedure to removal. **Note**: *It may be necessary to rotate the engine to align the clutch disc and input shaft splines.*

19 Transmission (RUG-type) – disassembly

1   Place the transmission on a firm bench or in a holding fixture. In addition to the normal range of wrenches, tools, etc., you will need the following

    a) Good quality snap-ring pliers, 1 expanding and 1 contracting.
    b) Copper-headed hammer, at least 2 lb.
    c) Selection of steel and brass drifts.
    d) Small containers for parts.
    e) Vise mounted on a firm bench.
    f) Selection of steel tubing for use as dummy shafts.

2   Attempting to disassemble a transmission without the foregoing is not impossible, but will certainly be a much more difficult process.
3   Read this entire Section through before starting work.
4   Unbolt and remove the transmission top cover and discard the gasket.
5   Remove the screw, detent spring and detent plug from the transmission case as shown. It may be necessary to use a magnet to extract these parts from the transmission case.
6   Using a suitable drift, drive the shifter shaft roll pin from the case as shown.
7   From the rear of the extension housing, remove the backup lamp switch assembly, snap-ring and dust cover as shown.
8   Withdraw the shifter shaft from the turret assembly as shown.
9   Unbolt and remove the extension housing from the transmission case, discarding the gasket as shown.
10 Remove the snap-ring which secures the speedometer drive gear to the output shaft. Slide the gear off the shaft and remove the speedometer gear drive ball as shown.
11 Remove the snap-ring securing the output shaft bearing to the shaft and slide the output bearing off as shown.
12 From the front of the transmission case, push the countershaft out through the rear of the case, using a similar size dummy shaft. Lower the countershaft into the bottom of the transmission case.
13 Remove the input shaft bearing retainer bolts and slide the retainer and gasket off the shaft as shown.
14 Remove the snap-ring securing the input shaft bearing to the shaft and slide the bearing off.
15 Remove the input shaft, blocking ring and roller bearing from the case.
16 Remove the overdrive shift pawl, gear selector and interlock plate.
17 Remove the 1-2 gearshift selector arm plate.
18 With a suitable drift, drive the roll pin from the 3rd/overdrive shift fork as shown.
19 Working from the rear of the case, drive the 3rd/overdrive shift rail and expansion plug out as shown. Remove the mainshaft assembly.
20 Remove the 1st and 2nd speed shift forks, followed by the 3rd/overdrive shift fork.
21 Lift out the countershaft gear and thrustwashers, being careful not to drop them into the case.
22 Remove the snap-ring from the front of the output shaft and slide the 3rd gear, overdrive synchronizer, blocking ring and gear off the shaft.
23 Remove the securing snap-ring and thrustwashers and remove 2nd gear.
24 Remove the next snap-ring on the shaft and remove the 1-2 synchronizer assembly.
25 From the rear of the shaft, remove the first gear and blocking ring.
26 Remove the reverse gear roll pin and withdraw the reverse shifter rail from the rear of the case. Remove the gearshift fork and reverse fork spacer.
27 Working from the front of the case, drive the reverse gear shaft out of the rear of the transmission.
28 Remove the reverse idler gear and, being careful not to drop them into the case, the thrustwashers and roller bearings.
29 Remove the retaining clip, the reverse gearshift relay lever and reverse selector fork pivot pin.
30 Remove the overdrive shift control link assembly.
31 From the rear of the case, remove the shift shaft seal.
32 Through the shift shaft rail hole, remove the expansion plug from the front of the case.
33 The transmission is now completely disassembled and must be thoroughly cleaned. Any metal flakes or chips in the case are a good sign that the transmission is worn.

20 Transmission (RUG-type) – inspection and overhaul

1   Carefully clean and inspect all component parts for wear, distortion, looseness of fit and damage to machined faces and threads.
2   Inspect the gears for excessive wear and chipping of the teeth. Replace with new gears as necessary.
3   Inspect the countershafts for signs of wear on the roller bearing surfaces. If a small ridge can be felt on either end of the shafts, it will be necessary to replace the shafts with new ones.
4   If the synchro-rings are badly worn it is a good idea to replace them. New rings will improve the smoothness and speed of gear shifting considerably.
5   The roller bearings located between the nose of the output shaft and the rear of the input shaft are likely to wear and should be replaced.
6   Check the endplay of the countershaft, 1st, 2nd and overdrive gears after assembly on the output shaft with a suitable gauge. If the endplay exceeds the limits in the Specifications section they must be replaced with new parts.
7   If the synchro-hubs are worn, they must be replaced as complete assemblies.
8   The nylon inserts on the selector forks should be replaced even if they appear to be in good condition. If any of the inserts have broken up, allowing any wear on the fork assembly itself, the complete fork should be replaced unless wear is minimal.
9   If the bush bearing in the extension is badly worn it should be replaced with a new one.
10 The transmission case welch plug should be replaced with a new one if there is any sign of leaking.

21 Transmission (RUG-type) – reassembly

1   Reassembly is a reversal of the disassembly procedure with the exception of the following details:
2   The transmission mainshaft bearing rollers, extension housing bushing, reverse idler, bearing rollers and the countershaft gear bearing rollers must be lubricated with 0.5 ounces of Ford ESW-M1C109-A lubricant at assembly. Lubricate the 1st, 2nd and overdrive gear bearing journals with Ford ESP-M2C83-C transmission oil or equivalent. Thoroughly flush the rest of the transmission components with $\frac{1}{2}$ US pint of this oil also.
3   The transmission shifter shaft and gearshift damper bushing should also be lubricated with Ford ESA-M1C175-A lubricant or equivalent prior to installation.
4   Seal the transmission gearshift shaft sleeve at both ends as well as the turret cover assembly with 0.05 ounces of Ford ESE-M4G132-A sealant or equivalent. This will prevent contamination of the shifter mechanism by road dust and dirt.
5   When installing the intermediate and high rail welch plug, it must be seated firmly. It must not protrude above or below the front face of the transmission case more than 0.06 in (1.5 mm) .
6   The gearshift selector arm must be firmly seated in the 1st/2nd shift fork plate slot. The shifter shaft must pass freely through the 1st/2nd shift fork bore without binding.
7   The extension housing must be tightened to torque specifications in the sequence shown.

7A

Notes

Chapter 7B Automatic transmission

Refer to Chapter 13 for specifications and information on later models

Contents

Specifications

Transmission type	3-speed fully automatic, shift control either steering column or floor mounted

Application
1978 thru 1981
2.3L and 3.3L engine	C3
3.3L, 4.2L and 5.0L engine	C4

Fluid capacities (refill from dry)
1978
	US qts
C3 (2.3L and 3.3L engine)	8.0
C4 (3.3L engine)	8.25
C4 (5.0L engine)	10.0

1979
C3 (2.3L and 3.3L engine)	8.0
C4 (3.3L engine)	7.6
C4 (5.0L engine)	10.0

1980
C3 (2.3L and 3.3L engine)	8.0
C4 (3.3L engine)	7.7
C4 (4.2L engine)	10.0

1981
C3 (2.3L and 3.3L engine)	6.5
C4 (2.3L engine)	6.75
C4 (3.3L engine)	7.25
C4 (4.2L engine)	9.5

Fluid type	ESW-M2C83-F, Type F

Torque specifications
C3 transmission

	Ft-lb	Nm
Converter housing-to-case	27 to 39	37 to 52
Extension housing-to-case	27 to 39	37 to 52
Oil pump-to-converter housing	7 to 10	10 to 13
Flywheel-to-converter housing	27 to 49	37 to 66
Main control-to-case	7 to 9	10 to 12
Plate-to-valve body	7 to 9	10 to 12
Servo cover-to-case	7 to 9	10 to 12
Inner race-to-case	7 to 9	10 to 12
Oil pan	12 to 17	17 to 23
Governor-to-collector body	7 to 9	10 to 12
Converter housing-to-engine	28 to 38	38 to 51
Outer downshift lever nut	7 to 11	10 to 14
Inner manual lever nut	30 to 40	41 to 54
Neutral switch-to-case	12 to 15	17 to 20
Front band adjusting locknut	35 to 45	48 to 61
Oil cooler line-to-connector	7 to 10	10 to 13
Converter drain plug	20 to 30	28 to 40
Flywheel-to-crankshaft	48 to 53	66 to 71
Filler tube-to-engine clip	28 to 38	38 to 51

C4 transmission

Oil pan-to-case	12 to 16	17 to 21
Stator support-to-pump	12 to 20	17 to 27
Overrunning clutch race-to-case	13 to 20	18 to 27
Converter housing cover	12 to 16	17 to 21
Rear servo cover	12 to 20	17 to 27
Intermediate servo cover	16 to 22	22 to 29
Oil distributor sleeve	12 to 20	17 to 27
Extension housing-to-case	28 to 40	38 to 54
Front pump-to-case	28 to 38	38 to 51
Transmission-to-engine	40 to 50	55 to 67
Engine separator plate-to-converter housing	5 to 9	7 to 12
Downshift lever-to-shaft	12 to 16	17 to 21
Flywheel-to-converter	20 to 30	28 to 40
Band adjusting screws-to-case	35 to 45	48 to 61
Manual valve inner lever-to-shaft	30 to 40	41 to 54
Front pump pipe plug	6 to 12	9 to 16
Cooler line-to-transmission case	12 to 18	17 to 24
Filler tube-to-oil pan	32 to 42	44 to 56
End plates-to-body	2 to 4	3 to 5
Separator plate-to-lower body	3 to 5	5 to 7
Lower-to-upper body	3 to 5	5 to 7
Pump assembly-to-case	2 to 3	3 to 4

1 Automatic transmission – general information

The automatic transmission takes the place of the conventional clutch and transmission and is comprised of the following two main assemblies:

a) A three element hydrokinetic torque converter coupling, capable of infinitely variable torque multiplication.

b) A hydraulically-operated epicyclic gearbox consisting of a planetary gearset providing three forward ratios and a reverse ratio.

Due to the complexity of the automatic transmission unit, it is recommended that any major fault diagnosis or repair be left to your dealer or a transmission shop. This Chapter will cover information useful to the owner in routine maintenance and adjustment.

Models are equipped with either a C3- or C4-type transmission depending on engine and year of manufacture. Both transmissions are basically similar and any differences will be described under separate Section headings.

All models feature a transmission oil cooler with the cooler element incorporated in the radiator.

Smoother and more consistent downshifts are assured by using a vacuum connection between the transmission and the intake manifold.

Ford specifies a different grade transmission fluid than other manufacturers and this must be used whenever refilling or adding fluid to the transmission. Transmission fluid proper for the vehicle is specified on the certification label on the left front door post.

2 Automatic transmission – fluid level checking

1 Before attempting to check the fluid level, the transmission must be at normal operating temperature (approximately 150°F (65°C)). This is best accomplished by driving the vehicle about 5 miles (8 km) under normal conditions.

2 Park the car on level ground, apply the parking brake and depress the brake pedal.

3 Allow the engine to idle, then move the selector through all the positions three times.

4 Place the selector in Park and allow the engine to idle for 2 more minutes.

5 With the engine idling, withdraw the dipstick and wipe it clean with a lint-free cloth. Replace it and withdraw it again and check the fluid level which should be between "ADD" and "DON'T ADD".

6 If the level is below the "ADD" line, add fluid through the dipstick tube, a little at a time. **Note:** *Do not overfill the transmission. Use only Ford specification fluid.*

3 Automatic transmission (C3) – removal and installation

1 If possible, raise the car on a hoist or place it over an inspection pit. Alternatively, it will be necessary to jack-up the car to obtain the maximum possible amount of working room underneath.

2 Place a large drain pan beneath the transmission sump (oil pan) then, working from the rear, loosen the attaching bolts and allow the fluid to drain. Remove all the bolts except the two front ones to drain as much fluid as possible, then temporarily refit two bolts at the rear to hold it in place.

3 Remove the torque converter drain plug access cover and adapter plate bolts from the lower end of the converter housings.

4 Remove the three flywheel-to-converter attaching bolts, cranking the engine as necessary to gain access by means of a wrench on the crankshaft pulley attaching bolt. **Caution:** *Do not rotate the engine backwards on 2.3L engine-equipped vehicles.*

5 Rotate the engine until the converter drain plug is accessible, then remove the plug, catching the fluid in the drain pan. Fit and tighten the drain plug afterwards.

6 Remove the propeller shaft, referring to Chapter 8, as necessary. Place a polythene bag over the end of the transmission to prevent dirt from entering.

7 Detach the speedometer cable fron the extension housing (photo).

8 Disconnect the shift rod at the transmission manual lever, and the downshift rod at the transmission downshift lever.

9 Remove the starter motor retaining bolts and position the motor out of the way.

10 Disconnect the starter inhibitor (neutral start) switch leads.

11 Disconnect the vacuum lines from the vacuum unit.

12 Position a trolley jack beneath the transmission and raise it to just take the transmission weight.

13 Remove the engine rear support-to-crossmember nut and the transmission extension housing crossmember (photo).

14 Remove the filler tube brace from the filler tube and rear engine support. Disconnect the exhaust pipe at the manifold and support it to one side.

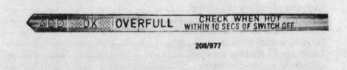

208/977

Fig. 7.1 Automatic dipstick marks showing fill levels (Sec 2)

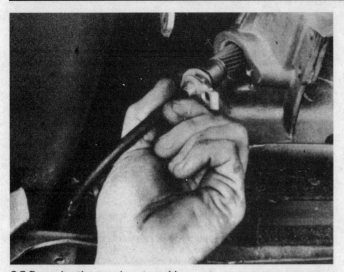

3.7 Removing the speedometer cable

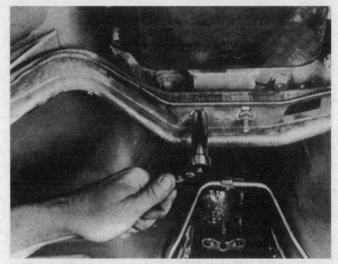

3.13 Removing the transmission crossmember bolts

15 Lower the trolley jack slightly, then place another jack to the front end of the engine. Raise the engine to gain access to the upper converter housing-to-engine attaching bolts.
16 Disconnect the oil cooler lines at the transmission and plug them to prevent dirt from entering.
18 Ensure that the transmission is securely mounted on the trolley jack, then remove the two upper converter housing-to-engine bolts away from the car.
20 Replacing the transmission is essentially the reverse of the removal procedure, but the following points should be noted:

   a) *Rotate the converter to align the bolt drive lugs and drain plug with their holes in the flywheel.*
   b) *Do not allow the transmission to take a 'nose-down' attitude as the converter will move forward and disengage from the pump gear.*
   c) *When installing the three flywheel-to-converter bolts position the flywheel so that the pilot hole is in the six o'clock position (see the accompanying figure). First install one bolt through the pilot hole and torque tighten it, followed by the two remaining bolts. Do not attempt to install it in any other way.*
   d) *Adjust the kick down rod and selector linkage as necessary (see Sections 7, 8 and 9).*
   e) *When the car has been lowered to the ground, add sufficient fluid to bring the level up to the 'MAX' mark on the dipstick with the engine not running. Having done this, check and top-up the fluid level, as described in the previous Section.*

4   Automatic transmission (C4) – removal and installation

Any suspected fault must be referred to the local dealer or transmission shop before unit removal, as with this type of transmission the fault must be confirmed, using specialist equipment, before the unit has been removed from the car.
1 For safety reasons, disconnect the battery ground terminal.
2 Jack up the engine and support on firmly based stands if a lift or pit is not available.
3 Refer to Chapter 8 and remove the propeller shaft.
4 Wrap a polythene bag over the end of the transmission unit to prevent oil seeping out. Alternatively, drain out the unit. If the car has just been driven the oil will be very hot.
5 Undo and remove the two upper converter housing-to-engine securing nuts.
6 Undo and remove the bolt that secures the transmission fluid filler tube to the cylinder block. Lift away the filler tube.
7 Undo and remove the bolts securing the converter cover. This is located at the lower front side of the converter housing. Lift away the cover.
8 Remove the vacuum line hose from the transmission vacuum unit. Detach the vacuum line from the retaining clip.
9 Remove the speedometer cable from the extension housing.

10 Wipe the area around the oil cooler pipe unions on the side of the transmission unit and then detach the pipes. Plug the open ends to stop loss of fluid or dirt ingress.
11 Disconnect the transmission shift rod at the manual selector lever.
12 Disconnect the downshift rod and spring at the transmission downshift lever.
13 Make a note of and then disconnect the neutral start and back-up switch wires from the connectors and retaining clamps.
14 Undo and remove the four nuts securing the torque converter to the flywheel. For this the engine will have to be rotated and the nuts removed working through the aperture left by removal of the converter cover (paragraph 7).
15 Support the weight of the transmission unit using a jack. It will also be necessary to have an assistant to hold the transmission unit.
16 Using an overhead hoist, crane or jack, support the weight of the engine.
17 Undo and remove the bolts securing the transmission unit crossmember to the body.
18 Undo and remove the bolts securing the rear engine support crossmember.
19 Remove the front exhaust pipe section between the manifold and the resonator box (or converter).
20 Undo and remove the bolts securing the starter motor to the torque converter housing and withdraw the starter motor from its location.
21 Undo and remove the remaining bolts securing the torque converter housing to the rear of the engine.
22 Carefully draw the unit rearwards (take care because it is very heavy) and lower to the ground. Support on wooden blocks so that the selector lever is not damaged or bent.
23 To separate the converter housing from the transmission case, first lift off the converter from the transmission unit, taking suitable precautions to catch the fluid upon separation.
24 Undo and remove the bolts and spring washers which secure the converter housing to the transmission case. Lift away the converter housing.
25 Refitting the automatic transmission unit is the reverse sequence to removal, but there are several additional points which will assist you in the completion of this task:

   a) *If the torque converter has been removed, before replacement it will be necessary to align the front pump drive tangs with the slots in the inner gear and then carefully replace the torque converter. Take care not to damage the oil seal.*
   b) *Before mounting the transmission on the engine remove the two dowel pins from the converter housing flange and push them in the engine block. This is only applicable when dowels are fitted.*
   c) *Adjust the manual selector linkage, the throttle downshift cable and the inhibitor switch. Full details of these adjustments will be found in subsequent Sections.*

7B

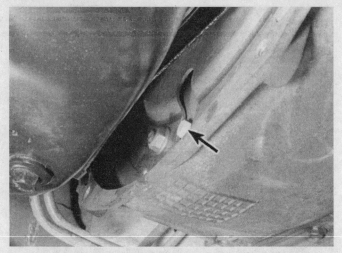

7.2 Converter drain plug and bolts (Sec 4)

5   Selector lever assembly (all models) – removal and installation

1   Chock the front wheels, jack up the vehicle and support it firmly on jack stands.
2   Working under the car, remove the shift lever control rod securing pin. Detach the rod from the stud.
3   Working inside the car, remove the selector lever handle by pulling it abruptly upward with the shifter in neutral.
4   Remove the screws securing the dial indicator to the selector lever assembly and lift away the indicator.
5   Disconnect the indicator illumination lamp electrical connector.
6   Remove the selector housing attachment bolts and lift away the housing.
7   Pull off the housing protective rubber plug and remove the lever attaching nut. Remove the lever from the housing and slide out the illumination lamp.
8   To reinstall, insert the illumination lamp and install the lever to the housing. The attaching nut should be tightened to 20 to 25 ft-lbs (28 to 33 Nm). Check the clearance between the detent pawl and plate.The detent pawl should just clear the highest point on the detent plate when properly adjusted.
9   To adjust pawl height, hold the adjustment screw stationary and turn the lock nut until the correct clearance is obtained.
10 Place the housing and lever assembly in position in the floor pan cutout with the pointer closest to the driver's seat. Install the bolts and tighten to 4 to 6 ft-lbs (6 to 8 Nm).
11 Plug in the illumination lamp connector and install the indicator housing.
12 Push the selector handle firmly into place and check that the handle button works freely.
13 Position the selector lever in 'Drive' against the ''D'' position stop.
14 From under the car, install the shift rod to the selector lever and secure with the washers and pin.
15 Attach the shift rod to the manual lever and check the linkage adjustment.

6   Neutral start switch (all models) – removal and installation

1   Chock the front wheels, jack up the car and support it on firmly based jack stands.
2   From under the car, disconnect the downshift linkage rod from the transmission downshift lever.
3   Apply a little penetrating oil to the downshift lever shaft and nut and allow to soak for a few minutes.
4   Remove the transmission downshift outer lever retaining nut and lift away the lever.
5   Remove the neutral start switch securing bolts.
6   Disconnect the multi-wire connector from the neutral switch and lift away the switch.

7   To reinstall, place the switch on the transmission and secure it finger-tight with the securing bolts.
8   Move the selector lever to the 'N' (Neutral) position. Rotate the switch and fit a No. 43 drill bit into the gauge pin hole. The bit must be inserted a full 0.48 in (12.30 mm) into the 3 holes of the switch (see accompanying figure). Tighten the switch securing bolts fully and remove the drill.
9   Installation is the reverse of the removal procedure. Check that the engine starts only when the selector is in the 'N' and 'P' positions.
Note: *The neutral start switch on the C3 transmission is not adjustable.* Any fault will be due to a malfunctioning switch, wear on the internal actuating cam or faulty wiring. If the switch is suspected of a fault, it should be replaced with a new one. Always use a new O-ring seal and tighten to the specified torque.

7   Floor shift linkage (all models) – adjustment

1   Have an assistant position the shift selector in the 'D' position and hold it in place during adjustment.
2   From under the car, loosen the manual shift lever retaining nut. Move the shift lever to the 'D' position on the transmission itself (second detent position from the rear of the transmission).
3   With both the selector lever and the manual lever in the 'D' position, tighten the attaching nut to 10 to 15 ft-lbs (14 to 20 Nm).
4   After adjustment, check the operation of the selector in all positions.

8   Column shift linkage (all models) – adjustment

1   Place the selector lever in the 'D' position and hang an 8 lb weight on it to ensure that the lever remains in position during adjustment.
2   Loosen the adjusting nut on the shift rod.
3   At the transmission, make sure that the shift lever is in the 'D' position (the second detent position from the full counterclockwise position). Align the flats on the slotted rod with those on the mounting stud.
4   Tighten the adjusting nut on the shift rod to 10 to 12 ft-lbs (14 to 28 Nm).
5   After adjustment, check that the selector operates properly in all positions.

9   Kick-down rod (all models) – adjustment

1   Disconnect the downshift rod return spring and hold the throttle shaft lever in the wide open position.
2   Hold the downshift rod against the through detent stop.
3   Adjust the downshift screw so as to provide a clearance of 0.050 to 0.070 in (1.27 to 1.78 mm) between the screw top and the throttle shaft lever tab.
4   Reconnect the downshift lever spring.

10 Intermediate band (C3 and C4) – adjustment

1   The intermediate or front band should be adjusted if there is noticeable slipping or sluggish shifting.
2   Remove the adjustment screw lock nut located on the left side of the transmission case. Tighten the adjusting screw using a torque wrench set to 10 ft-lbs (13.5 Nm). Then back off the adjustment screw the specified number of turns:
   a) C3 – 1978 thru 1980, $1\frac{1}{2}$ turns. 1981, 2 turns.
   b) C4 – 1978 thru 1981, $1\frac{3}{4}$ turns.
3   A new lock nut should be installed and tightened to 35 to 40 ft-lbs (47 to 54 Nm).

11 Low and reverse band (C4) – adjustment

1   Symptoms of an improperly adjusted low and reverse band are that the transmission won't operate in 'Reverse' and there will be little or no engine braking in 'Low' gear.

12.6 The metal-encased transmission filter ready for removal

2   To adjust, remove the adjusting screw lock nut on the left side of the transmission case. Tighten the screw with a torque wrench to 10 ft-lbs (13.5 Nm) and then back off the adjustment screw 3 full turns.
3   Install a new lock nut and tighten it to between 35 and 45 ft-lbs (47 to 61 Nm).

12 Automatic transmission fluid (all models) – drain and refill

1   Raise the car and support with jack stands.
2   Place a drain pan under the transmission pan.

3   Loosen the bolts securing the transmission pan to the transmission body. As the bolts are removed allow the fluid to drain into the pan.
4   Remove the pan and gasket.
5   Clean the pan with solvent and allow to dry.
6   After allowing the transmission to drain, remove the bolts securing the transmission filter to the transmission (photo).
7   Remove the filter and discard.
8   Clean all mating surfaces with a clean, dry, lint-free cloth.
9   Fit a new transmission filter and reinstall the mounting bolts.
10 Install a new gasket on the pan.
11 Position the pan and gasket on the transmission and install the bolts.
12 Tighten the bolts in a criss-cross pattern to avoid warping the transmission pan.
13 Refill the transmission with approximately 16 pints of automatic transmission fluid (of the correct type).
14 Start the engine, check for leaks.
15 Drive the car for a few minutes to allow the transmission to rise to operating temperature. Recheck the transmission level and fill as required. Check for leaks.

13 Automatic transmission – fault diagnosis

As mentioned earlier in this Chapter, the automatic transmission should be serviced or overhauled only with the proper equipment and knowledge. If a fault is evident after the procedures described in this Chapter are carried out, it is recommended that your local dealer or transmission shop be consulted.

7B

Notes

Chapter 8 Driveline

Contents

Specifications

Clutch

Type	Single dry plate, diaphragm spring
Actuation	Cable

Free play

1978 only	0.030 in

Clutch pedal free travel

1978 all	1½ in
1979	
2.3L, 3.3L engine	5¼ in
5.0L engine	6 ½ in
1980 all	5¼ in
1981 all	Self-adjusting

Driveshaft

Type	One piece, candan-type universal joints

Rear Axle

Type	Hypoid, integral type carrier

Ring gear diameter

2.3L engine	6¾ in (171 mm)
All other engines	7½ in (191 mm)

Ring-and-pinion gear ratios, by ID tag number

1978
7½-in ring gear

WGX-A	2.73:1
WGX-B	3.08:1
WGX-C	2.47:1

1979
6¾-in ring gear

WGF-AM	2.73:1
WGF-AN	3.08:1
WGG-C	2.73:1
WGG-D	3.08:1
WGG-E	3.08:1

7½-in ring gear

WGX-B	3.08:1
WGX-C	2.47:1
WGX-H	3.08:1
WGX-L	2.26:1
WGX-N	2.73:1
WGZ-B	2.26:1
WGZ-C	2.26:1

1980
6¾-in ring gear

WGF-AM	2.73:1
WGF-AN	3.08:1
WGG-C	2.73:1
WGG-D	3.08:1
WGG-E	3.08:1

7½-in ring gear

WGX-R	3.08:1
WGX-S	2.73:1
WGX-T	3.45:1
WGX-U	2.26:1

1981
6¾-in ring gear

WGG-C	2.73:1
WGG-D	3.08:1
WGG-E	3.08:1

7½-in ring gear

WGX-R	3.08:1
WGX-S	2.73:1
WGX-T	3.45:1
WGX-U	2.26:1

Rear axle oil capacity

6¾-in ring gear	2.5 US pints
7½-in ring gear	3.5 US pints
Oil type	Ford ESW-M2C-154-A or equivalent

Axle pinion preload

	in-lb	Nm
6¾-in ring gear		
original bearings	6 to 12	0.68 to 1.36
new bearings	17 to 27	1.9 to 3.0
7½-in ring gear		
original bearings	8 to 14	0.91 to 1.5
new bearings	17 to 27	1.9 to 3.0

Torque specifications
Clutch
Flywheel, housing-to-engine bolt

	ft-lb	Nm
2.3L, 2.3L turbo	12 to 24	16 to 32
All others	38 to 55	52 to 74
Pressure plate-to-flywheel		
2.3L. 2.3L turbo	12 to 24	16 to 32
All others	12 to 20	16 to 27

Driveshaft

Universal joint-to-flange	70 to 95	95 to 130

Rear axle
6¾-in ring gear
  1979 thru 1980

Differential cap bearing bolt	40 to 55	55 to 74
Ring gear attaching bolts	45 to 60	61 to 81
Rear cover screw	25 to 35	34 to 47
Oil filler plug	25 to 45	34 to 67
Rear axleshaft bearing retainer bolt nuts	20 to 40	27 to 54

  1981
    Same as above except:

Differential bearing cap bolt	70 to 85	95 to 115
Oil filler plug	15 to 30	20 to 31

7½-in ring gear
  1980-1981

Differential bearing cap bolt	70 to 85	95 to 115
Differential pinion shaft lock bolt	15 to 22	21 to 29
Ring gear attaching bolts	70 to 85	95 to 115
Rear cover screw	25 to 35	34 to 47
Oil filler plug	25 to 50	34 to 67
Brake backing plate bolt and nuts	20 to 40	28 to 54

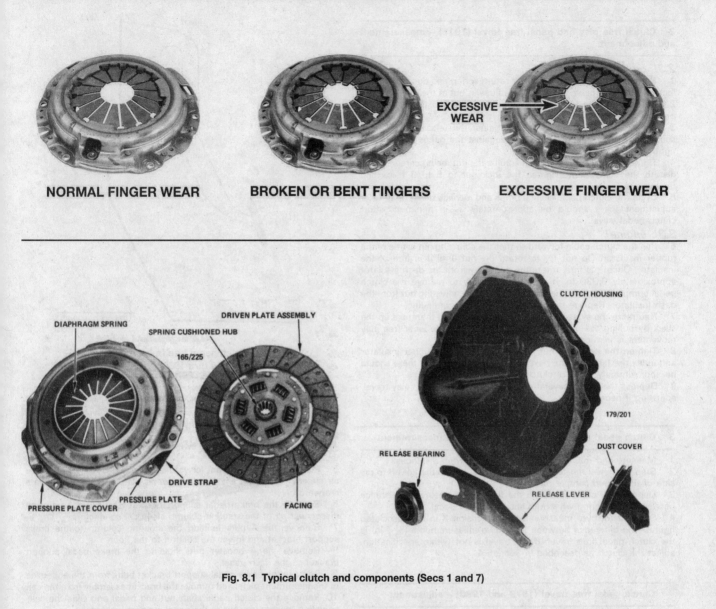

NORMAL FINGER WEAR   **BROKEN OR BENT FINGERS**   **EXCESSIVE FINGER WEAR**

Fig. 8.1 Typical clutch and components (Secs 1 and 7)

1 Clutch – general information

The diaphragm single dry-disc-type clutch, consisting of the clutch disc, pressure plate and clutch release bearing, is actuated by a pedal and cable operated mechanical linkage.

When the clutch pedal is in the up (released) position, the clutch disc is clamped between the friction surface of the engine flywheel and the face of the clutch pressure plate diaphragm, thus transmitting the drive of the engine through the disc which is splined to the transmission. Friction lining material is riveted to the clutch disc and the splined hub is spring-cushioned to absorb transmission shocks.

When the clutch pedal is depressed, the clutch release lever moves the release bearing against the clutch diaphragm, which in turn moves the pressure plate away from the clutch disc, disengaging the clutch and disconnecting the drive to the transmission.

On 1979 and newer models, the release bearing is in constant contact with the clutch fingers so that there is no need for freeplay adjustment on these vehicles. Consequently, adjustment is made to the clutch pedal travel on these models. *1978 models* have provision for both clutch freeplay and pedal free travel adjustment.

Clutch freeplay or pedal free travel should be adjusted after the installation of a new clutch or when the clutch does not engage properly.

On 1981 models, the clutch pedal free play is adjusted automatically by a device mounted in the clutch pedal linkage. The self adjusting mechanism consists of a spring-loaded quadrant, spring-loaded pawl and spring-loaded clutch release cable which preloads the clutch release lever bearing. As the clutch wears, the spring-loaded pawl at the top of the clutch pedal engages the gear quadrant as the pedal is depressed and pulls on the cable to adjust it.

8

2   Clutch free play and pedal free travel (1978) – measurement and adjustment

2.3L engine

1   Remove the clutch release lever return spring and dust shield and loosen the clutch cable lock nut and adjusting nut at the release lever.

2   Pull the release lever forward until it stops and then hold it in place.

3   Place a 0.030 in feeler gauge against the release lever cable spacer and run the adjusting nut up against the gauge until finger-tight.

4   Tighten the lock nut against the adjusting nut, being careful not to disturb the adjustment. Tighten the lock nut to 5 to 8 ft-lbs and remove the feeler gauge.

5   Cycle the clutch pedal several times and recheck the setting. After adjustment there should be approximately $1\frac{1}{2}$-in minimum effort clutch pedal travel.

3.3L engine

6   Pull the clutch cable forward so that the adjusting nut is free of the rubber insulator. Do not try to rotate the nut until it is free of the insulator. Once it is free, rotate the nut away from the dash insulator approximately 0.030 in. It may be necessary to remove the clutch pedal bumper stop from the pedal to loosen the adjusting nut from the dash insulator. Replace the bumper stop before continuing.

7   Neutralize the system by releasing the cable and then take up the slack by pulling the cable slightly so that the release lever free play movement is eliminated.

8   Tighten the adjusting nut lightly up against the rubber insulator and index the tabs into the next notch. After adjustment there should be approximately $1\frac{1}{2}$-in of clutch pedal free travel.

9   Depress the clutch several times and recheck the free play travel, adjusting if necessary.

3   Clutch pedal (1979 and 1980) – free travel measurement

1   Measure and make a notation of the following distances:

2   Steering wheel rim-to-brake pedal, measuring to the flat off to the side of the ribbed contact patch.

3   Depress the clutch pedal to the floor and measure the distance between the steering wheel rim and the clutch pedal.

4   Subtract the two measurements (dimension X in the associated figure). The difference between these two measurements ($\pm \frac{1}{2}$ in) is the clutch pedal free travel. If the travel is not within specification, adjust the clutch as described in Section 4.

4   Clutch pedal free travel (1979 and 1980) – adjustment

2.3L, 2.3L turbo, 4.2L and 5.0L engines

1   Remove the dustshield cover from the clutch cable-to-bellhousing junction.

2   Loosen the cable lock nut.

3   Adjust the cable length by turning the adjusting nut clockwise to raise the pedal or counterclockwise to lower it.

4   Tighten the lock nut to 5 to 8 ft-lb (7 to 11 Nm).

5   Depress the clutch pedal several times and then recheck the pedal travel, readjusting as necessary.

6   Reinstall the dustshield.

3.3L engine

7   From the engine compartment grasp the cable near the cable/firewall junction until the nylon adjusting nut is free from the rubber insulator.

8   Rotate the adjusting nut to obtain the proper pedal travel (see Specifications) with the cable seated back in its operating position.

9   Depress the clutch pedal several times and recheck the ajustment.

5   Self-adjusting clutch mechanism (1981) – removal and installation

1   Disconnect the battery negative cable.

2   Referring to Chapter 11, remove the steering wheel.

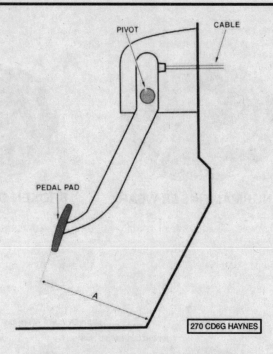

Fig. 8.2 Clutch pedal free travel measurement (1979 thru 1980) (Sec 3)

3   Remove the steering column shrouds and the left lower dash panel.

4   Disconnect the brake lamp switch and master cylinder pushrod at the brake pedal.

5   Push the clutch quadrant forward and disconnect the clutch cable as shown. The quadrant should now be allowed to slowly rotate rearward.

6   Remove the brake pedal support bracket lateral brace bolt and disconnect all of the steering column electrical connectors.

7   Remove the 4 nuts holding the steering column to the brake support bracket and lower the column to the floor.

8   Remove the 4 booster nuts holding the brake pedal support bracket to the dash panel.

9   Remove the brake pedal support bracket bolts from the underside of the instrument panel and remove the bracket assembly from the car.

10   Remove the clutch pedal shaft nut and pedal and slide the self-adjusting mechanism out of the pedal support bracket.

11   Remove the bushings from the self-adjusting mechanism shaft and check them for wear, replacing with new ones if necessary.

12   Installation is the reversal of removal. The self-adjusting mechanism shaft should be lubricated with motor oil prior to installation. After installation the clutch pedal should be depressed several times to adjust the cable.

6   Self-adjusting quadrant pawl (1981) – removal and installation

1   Remove the self-adjusting mechanism as described in Section 5.

2   Remove the 2 hairpin clips holding the quadrant on the shaft assembly.

3   Remove the quadrant and spring and the pawl and spring.

4   Lubricate the pawl and quadrant pivot shafts with lithium grease.

5   Install the pawl, positioning the teeth towards the larger shaft with the spring hole at the end of the arm. The spring hole is not to be positioned beneath the arm (see the accompanying figure)

6   Install the straight portion of the spring into the hole with the coil upwards.

7   Rotate the spring 180 degrees to the left, taking care that the straight portion stays in the hole and then slide the coiled portion over the boss.

8   Hook the bent portion of the spring under the arm and install the retaining clip on the opposite side of the spring.

9   Install the quadrant spring on the shaft with the bent portion inserted into the hole in the arm.

10 Slide the lubricated quadrant onto the shaft and align the projection at the bottom of the quadrant to a position beneath the arm of the shaft assembly. Push the pawl upwards so the bottom tooth of the pawl meshes with the bottom quadrant (as shown) and install the retaining pin.

11 With a pair of pliers, grasp the straight end of the quadrant spring and position it behind the ear of the quadrant.

12 Install the self-adjusting mechanism and the clutch pedal assembly.

7   Clutch cable (1978 thru 1980) – removal and installation

1   Disconnect the battery negative cable.

2   From underneath the vehicle, remove the dust shield from the bellhousing.

2   *On all vehicles except 3.3L* loosen the locknut and disengage the clutch cable from the release lever.

4   On 3.3L vehicles, pull the nylon adjusting nut forward, disengaging the tabs from the insulator in the dash panel and loosening the nut. Do not turn the nut until it is clear of the insulator.

5   Remove the clip retaining the cable to the bellhousing and remove the cable from the vehicle.

6   To reinstall, seat the rubber insulator securely in the dash panel (Fig. 8.4). Route the cable through the insulator into the engine compartment. *On 3.3L engine vehicles*, take care not to seat the plastic nut when routing the cable through the insulator.

8   From inside the vehicle, attach the clutch cable to the relay lever with the retaining clip.

9   From underneath the vehicle, insert the clutch through the hole in the bellhousing and attach it with the retaining clip (see accompanying figure).

10 Check that the cable routing follows a smooth arc with no kinks or bends.

11 Attach the clutch cable to the release lever and adjust the pedal free play (Sec 4). Attach the release lever return spring and install the dust shield.

12 Reconnect the battery negative cable.

8   Self-adjusting clutch cable (1981) – removal and installation

1   Pull the clutch pedal as far back toward the driver's seat as it will go. Push the adjustment quadrant forward and unhook the cable from it. The quadrant will now slowly rotate rearward.

2   From the engine compartment, remove the screw holding the cable assembly insulator to the dash panel (Fig.8.9). Pull the cable through the dash panel into the engine compartment.

3   From underneath the vehicle, remove the dust cover from the bellhousing and remove the rubber plug in the clutch release lever (Fig. 8.10).

5   Slide the ball on the end of the cable assembly through the clutch release lever hole and remove the cable.

6   Remove the dash panel insulator and transfer it to the new clutch cable.

7   Insert the cable through the bellhousing hole into the clutch release lever hole. Slide the ball on the end of the cable assembly away from the hole in the clutch release lever and install the rubber plug as shown.

8   Attach the cable assembly to the bellhousing with the clip retainer and install the dustshield on the housing.

9   Push the cable assembly up into the engine compartment and then through the dash panel. Install the screw in the insulator.

10 Lift the clutch pedal to disengage the pawl and quadrant. Push the quadrant forward and hook the end of the cable over the rear of the quadrant.

11 Depress the clutch several times which will adjust the cable.

9   Clutch pedal (all models) – removal and installation

1   Disconnect the negative battery cable.

2   Remove the clip holding the clutch cable to the pedal relay lever, referring to Section 7 for 1978 thru 1980 models and Section 8 for the self-adjusting 1981 model.

3   Note the position of the pre-load spring, then remove it.

4   Remove the relay lever nut and lever.

5   Slide the pedal assembly from the pedal support bracket, then remove the entire assembly as shown.

6   Inspect the pedal assembly, paying particular attention to the pedal pivot bushings. If they are cracked or galled, replace them.

7   Prior to installation, lightly coat the clutch pedal pivot with 10W oil.

8   Slide the clutch pedal shaft through the pedal support bracket.

9   Install the clutch pedal relay lever over the corresponding 4-sided flats on the clutch pedal flats. Install the nut and tighten to 32 to 50 ft-lbs (43 to 68 Nm).

10 Install the pre-load spring.

11 Hold the pedal against the stop, and install the clutch cable to the relay lever.

12 Attach the retaining clip.

13 Recheck the pedal free travel (Section 3) and adjust if necessary (Section 4).

14 Reconnect the negative battery cable.

10   Clutch (all models) – removal and installation

1   Remove the transmission as described in Chapter 7.

2   Disconnect the clutch release lever retaining spring from the release lever.

3   Disconnect the starter motor cable, then remove the starter motor attaching bolts and lift away the starter motor.

4   Remove the bolts securing the engine rear plate to the front lower part of the flywheel housing. Remove the flywheel housing lower cover (if so equipped).

5   Remove the flywheel housing securing bolts and move the housing back just far enough to clear the pressure plate, then move it to the right to free the pivot from the clutch equalizer bar. Take care not to disturb the linkage and assist spring.

6   Unscrew the six pressure plate cover securing bolts one turn at a time, to prevent distortion of the cover assembly, when releasing the spring tension.

7   If the same pressure plate and cover assembly is to be reinstalled, mark the cover and flywheel so that the assembly can be installed in its original position.

8   Remove the clutch cover assembly and the clutch disc from the flywheel. Make a note of which way round the clutch disc is installed.

9   It is important that no oil or grease gets on the clutch disc friction linings, or the pressure plate and flywheel faces. It is advisable to handle the parts with clean hands and to wipe down the pressure plate and flywheel faces with a clean dry rag before installing the clutch cover assembly.

10 Place the clutch disc and pressure plate assembly in position on the flywheel. If the same assembly is being reinstalled, align the matching marks made at removal, and install the securing bolts. Tighten the bolts alternatively a few turns at a time until the clutch disc is gripped lightly but can still be moved.

11 The clutch disc must now be centered so that when the transmission is installed, the input shaft splines will pass through the splines in the clutch disc hub.

12 Centering can be carried out by inserting a screwdriver through the clutch assembly and moving the clutch disc as necessary to obtain correct centering. Alternatively, if an old input shaft is available, this can be used as an arbor to center the disc; this will eliminate all guesswork and achieve more accurate centering of the clutch disc.

13 After the clutch disc has been located correctly, tighten the securing bolts in an even and diagonal sequence to ensure the cover assembly is secured without distortion. Tighten the bolts to the specified torque wrench setting.

14 Using a lithium base grease, lightly lubricate the outside diameter of the transmission front bearing retainer, both sides of the release lever fork where it contacts the release bearing spring clips, and the

8

Fig. 8.3 The pilot bearing (arrow) should turn smoothly and quietly if it does not replace it (Sec 12)

Fig. 8.4 Remove the old pilot bearing with a small slide-hammer, as shown (Sec 12)

release bearing surface that contacts the pressure plate release fingers. Fill the grease groove in the release bearing hub, then clean all excess grease from inside the bore, otherwise grease will be forced onto the splines by the transmission input shaft bearing retainer and will contaminate the clutch disc.

15 Install the release bearing and hub on the release lever.

16 Install the felt washer on the pivot in the flywheel housing and slip the pivot into the clutch equalizer shaft, taking care not to disturb the linkage; at the same time locate the housing on the dowels in the cylinder block. Install the securing bolts and tighten them to the specified torque.

17 Install the starter motor and connect the cable.

18 Install the transmission as described in Chapter 7.

19 Check and, if necessary, adjust the clutch pedal free play as described in Section 4.

11 Clutch (all models) – inspection and overhaul

1 Inspect the machined surfaces of the flywheel and pressure plate for scoring, ridges and burned marks. Minor defects can be removed by machining, but if any components are badly scored or burned they should be replaced with new ones.

2 Check the wear on the clutch fingers. If there is considerable difference in wear between the fingers, the excessively worn finger is binding which means that the pressure plate assembly must be replaced with a new one. Check the pressure plate for warpage using a steel rule.

3 Lubricate the pressure plate opening with lithium-based grease. Depress the pressure plate fingers fully, apply the grease and then move the fingers up and down until the grease is worked in.

4 Examine the clutch disc for worn or loose lining, distortion, loose nuts at the hub and for broken springs. If any of these defects are found, replace the disc with a new or rebuilt unit.

5 Wipe all oil and dirt off the release bearing but do not clean it in solvent, as it is pre-lubricated. Inspect the bearing retainer for loose spring clips and rivets. Hold the bearing inner race and rotate the outer race and if it is noisy or rough, replace the bearing with a new one. Because of the nominal cost involved it is a good practice to install a new release bearing every time the clutch is replaced.

12 Pilot bearing (all models) – removal and installation

1 A needle roller bearing is used as a clutch pilot bearing on all vehicles. On 2.3L models this is inserted directly into the crankshaft and must be installed with the seal end toward the transmission (Fig. 8.11). The bearings on all other models can be installed only in the proper position.

Fig. 8.5 Use a large socket and hammer, or a soft-faced hammer, to install the new pilot bearing; make sure the bearing is fully seated (Sec 12)

2 Remove the transmission (Chapter 7), clutch, pressure plate and disc (Section 11).

3 Pull the bearing from the crankshaft using a slide hammer or Ford tool T50T-100A or T59L-100B with a puller attachment T58L-101-A.

4 To install the new bearing, coat the opening on the crankshaft with lithium grease. Apply only a small amount of grease as the excess could find its way to the clutch, causing slippage.

5 With the bearing in position, tap it into the crankshaft. A 1-inch, 12-point socket and extension can be used to carefully tap the bearing squarely into place (see accompanying figure). Care must be taken when installing the bearing because it is easily damaged which can lead to early failure.

6 Reinstall the clutch, pressure plate and transmission.

13 Driveshaft (all models) – general information

The driveshaft is a one-piece, tubular unit with a cardan-type universal joint installed at each end. The forward end of the front universal joint is splined and fits into the output shaft of the transmission. The rear universal joint connects to the differential through matching flanges which are bolted together. The universal joints are replaceable components.

14 Driveshaft (all models) – removal and installation

1   Park the vehicle on a level surface.
2   Place the transmission in 'Park' (automatic) or first gear (manual) and set the parking brake.
3   Raise the vehicle and support it firmly on jackstands.
4   Mark the opposing flanges on the rear universal joint and the axle pinion prior to removal so that the balance of the unit will not be disturbed on reinstallation.
5   On the rear universal joint, remove the 4 bolts securing the driveshaft to the axle pinion. Support the driveshaft so that it doesn't fall.
6   Remove the driveshaft by lowering the rear carefully and pulling it rearward, sliding the front yoke from the transmission.
7   Plug the rear of the transmission and place a tray underneath to catch any fluid leakage.
8   Prior to reinstallation, check that the front yoke is free of dirt or grit and that the splines are not cracked, rounded or burred.
9   Inspect the transmission tail extension for cracks and make sure that the seal is in good condition.
10 Lubricate the driveshaft slip yoke splines with lithium grease, remove the plug from the transmission and insert the slip yoke into the transmission.
11 Making sure that the marks are lined up, install the bolts through the flanges of the rear universal joint and pinion and tighten them to specification as shown.
12 Lower the vehicle and check the transmission fluid level before driving.

15 Universal joints (all models) – inspection

1   Wear in the universal joints is characterized by vibration in the driveline, "clunking" noises when starting from a standstill and metallic squeaking and grating sounds. Another symptom of universal joint or driveline bearing problems is a harmonic rumbling at highway cruising speeds.
2   To make a simple check of universal joint condition, park the vehicle on a level surface with the transmission in gear or 'Park'. Block the wheels and engage the parking brake.
3   From underneath the car, hold the axle pinion flange with one hand while moving the driveshaft with the other. If there is noticeable looseness in the universal joint area, the joint is worn and should be replaced with a new one.

4   Repeat this check at the front of the driveshaft paying particular attention to the universal joint condition and wear or looseness in the sliding spline section of the yoke.

16 Universal joints (all models) – removal and installation

1   Remove the driveshaft (Section 14).
2   Clean away any dirt and foreign matter from the universal joint area of the driveshaft.
3   Remove the snap-rings from the U-joint end caps (photo).
4   Refer to the accompanying figure to understand the relationship of the components of the U-joint. Use Ford tool T74P-4635 to remove the bearing caps from the U-joint yoke. If this tool or equivalent is not available, the cups may be removed as follows:
5   A vise, a selection of sockets and a quantity of bearing grease is required for this procedure. Open the vise wide enough to accommodate the U-joint and two sockets.
6   Select a socket larger than the bearing cup that will allow space for the cup to be pushed into it. Select a second socket as close as possible in size to the cup outer diameter.

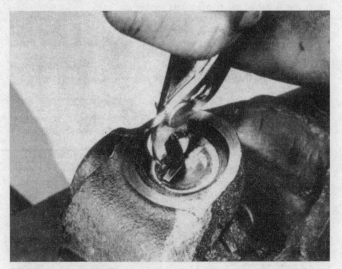

16.3 A small pair of pliers can be used to remove the universal joint bearing cup snap-ring

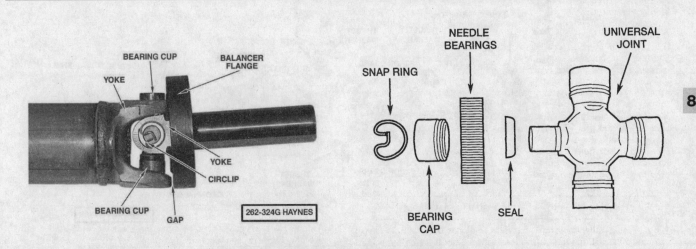

Fig. 8.6 Driveshaft and universal joint components

8

16.7 Pressing the bearing cup out of the universal joint

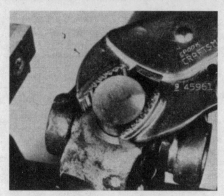

16.8 Use a vise grip or large pliers to remove the bearing cup

Fig. 8.7 Universal joint and flange marked for easier installation (Sec 16)

7   Apply pressure to the vise, forcing the bearing cup from the yoke into the larger of the two sockets (photo).
8   Remove the bearing cup from the yoke (photo).
9   Clean the yokes with a suitable solvent.
10 If the bearings are to be reinstalled, clean and re-grease them, filling the cups one-third full with grease.
11 Using new seals, start the bearing cup into the yoke and press it into position so that the cup is $\frac{1}{4}$ inch below the yoke surface.
12 Install the bearing snap-rings.
13 Check the U-joint for free movement in all directions.
14 Replace the driveshaft to the vehicle.

17 Rear axle and differential (all models) – general information

The rear axle is of the integral housing type of hypoid gear design. The centerline of the pinion is set below that of the ring gear.
The ring gear of 2.3L engine equipped models measures $6\frac{3}{4}$-in while all others use a $7\frac{1}{2}$-in ring gear. The axle and differential designs of the two rear axles used are basically the same with some slight detail differences.
The hypoid gear set is comprised of a ring gear and an overhung drive pinion supported at either end by two roller bearings. Pinion bearing preload is maintained by a crush-type spacer on the pinion

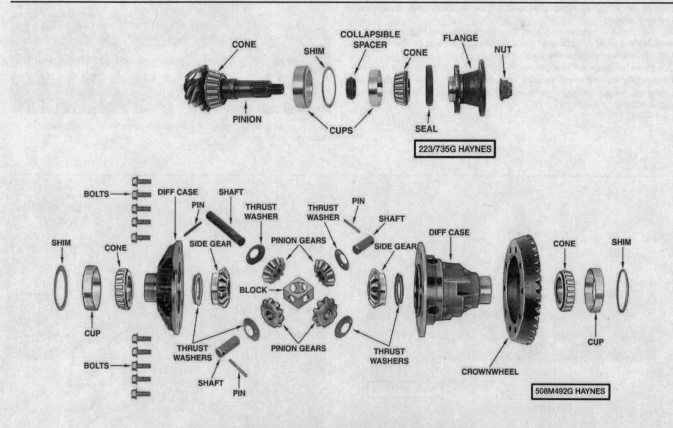

Fig. 8.8 Rear axle and components (6-3/4-in ring gear) (Sec 17)

Fig. 8.9 Axle seal removal (Secs 18 and 19)

Fig. 8.10 Axle seal installation (Sec 18)

shaft and is adjusted by tightening the pinion nut.

The housing assembly consists of a cast center section with attachment points for the rear suspension. The axle tubes are welded to either side of the center section and house the axleshafts. The semi-floating axleshafts are retained in the housing by bearing retainers at the outer ends of the axle housing on 6¾-in models and by C-locks at the inner ends on 7½-in models.

A cover on the rear of the center casting is removable to allow access to the differential. Silicone sealant is used instead of a gasket.

Due to the complexity of the differential unit and the need for special tools, it is recommended that any major work be entrusted to a local authorized dealer or a qualified repair shop.

18 Axleshaft (6¾-in ring gear) – removal and installation

1   Park the car on level ground, block the front wheels, loosen the lug nuts on the side to be worked on and jack up the rear of the car. Support the car firmly on jack stands and remove the wheel(s) on the side(s) to be worked on.
2   Release the handbrake.
3   Remove the brake drum, retaining the speed nuts.

4   Remove the nuts securing the wheel bearing retainer plate (photo).
5   Carefully withdraw the axle from the housing (photo). Place a container underneath the housing to catch any oil leakage.
6   If it is necessary to remove the bearing from the axle, take it to a dealer or machine shop as a special press is requireed for removal and installation. Do not attempt to do this job yourself by hammering or using heat on the axle. If the bearing is replaced, a new seal must also be installed.
7   The oil seal is removed with Ford tool T50T-100-A or a slide hammer and the proper jaws.
8   Inspect the axle for nicks or rough spots. If there is any sign of blueing (indicating overheating of the metal), consult a qualified repair shop. Replace any worn or damaged parts with new ones.
9   Tap the new seal into place, making sure that it is square in the axle bore. If the seal is not in straight, remove it and install a new one. Otherwise leakage could result.
10 Support the axleshaft and slide it into the housing without touching the seal.
11 Install the bearing retainer plate and tighten the nuts to specification.
12 Install the brake drum, wheel and hub cap.
13 Lower the car and check the rear axle oil level.

18.4 The wheel bearing retaining nuts are accessible through holes in the axle flange

18.5 Be careful not to hit the axle against the bearing seal during removal or installation

Fig. 8.11 Remove the pinion shaft lock bolt (Sec 19)

Fig. 8.12 Push the axle flange in, then remove the C-lock from the inner end of the axleshaft (Sec 19)

19 Axleshaft (7½-in ring gear) – removal and installation

1 Park the vehicle on level ground, block the front wheels, loosen the lug nuts on the side to be worked on and jack up the vehicle. Place the vehicle securely on jack stands and remove the wheel(s) on the side(s) requiring work.

2 Release the handbrake.

3 Remove the brake drum, retaining the speed nuts.

4 Carefully clean the differential cover of dirt and grease. Use a wire brush, solvent and clean, lint-free rags. Cleanliness is very important.

5 Remove the differential rear cover and allow all of the oil to drain from the differential into a suitable container.

6 Remove the differential pinion shaft lock screw and pinion shaft as shown.

7 Push the flanged (outer) end of the axle inward toward the center of the car and remove the C-locks from the groove in the inner end of the axleshaft (see associated figure).

8 Withdraw the axleshaft from the housing, making sure that it doesn't damage the oil seal in the end of the axle housing.

9 Inspect the axle for nicks and rough spots. If there is any sign of blueing, which indicates overheating of the axle, consult a qualified

repair shop. Replace any worn or damaged parts.

10 The bearing and seal are removed as a unit from the axle housing, using a slide hammer or Ford tool T50T-100-A as shown.

11 The new bearing should be lubricated with rear axle oil and installed squarely in the axle housing bore.

12 Install the new seal, taking care that it is not cocked in the bore. Tap the seal and bearing into place until seated squarely in the bore. If the seal or bearing are not installed square, early failure or leakage could occur.

13 Slide the axleshaft carefully into the axle housing so that the bearing and seal assembly are not disturbed or damaged. Align the axleshaft splines with the side gear in the differential and push firmly until the end of the axle can be seen in the differential case.

14 Slide the C-locks onto the button end of the axleshaft splines. Push the shaft outward until the shaft splines engage and the C-locks become seated in the counterbore of the differential side gear.

15 Insert the differential pinion shaft through the case and pinion gears, lining up the hole in the shaft with the lock screw hole. Install the differential pinion shaft lock bolt and tighten to specifications.

16 Install the rear cover as described in Section 22.

17 Install the brake drum, wheel and wheel cover.

Fig. 8.13 Measuring pinion preload (Sec 20)

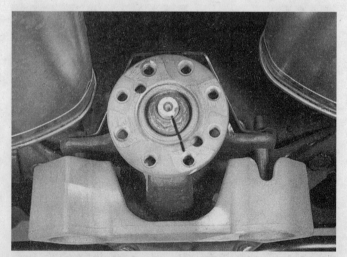

Fig. 8.14 Marking pinion and flange (Sec 20)

Fig. 8.15 Removing pinion nut and flange (Sec 20)

Fig. 8.16 Removing the pinion seal (Sec 20)

18 Lower the vehicle to the ground and if oil loss is suspected, check the rear axle oil level.

20 Pinion oil seal (all models) – removal and installation

1 Raise the vehicle and support it securely on jack stands.
2 Remove the rear wheels and brake drums.
3 Mark the driveshaft and axle pinion flange for ease of realignment during reassembly as described in Section 14 see associated figure and remove the driveshaft.
4 Install a torque wrench to the pinion nut and record the torque through several revolutions as shown.
5 Mark the relationship between the pinion and flange as shown.
6 Hold the flange to keep it from turning and remove the pinion nut and remove the differential flange as shown.
7 Pry out the old seal with a slide hammer and reversed jaws or Ford tool T65L-4851-A as shown.
8 Clean the oil seal mounting surface.
9 Tap the new seal into place, taking care to insert it squarely as shown in the associated figure.
10 Inspect the splines on the pinion shaft for burrs and nicks. Remove

any rough areas with a crocus cloth. Wipe the splines clean.
11 Install the differential flange, aligning it with the marks made during removal.
12 Tighten the pinion nut while allowing the assembly some movement to seat properly as shown in the accompanying figure.
13 Take frequent pinion bearing preload measurements as described in paragraph 4 until the original readings are obtained.
14 Reinstall the driveshaft, brake drums and wheels.
15 Check the differential oil level and fill as necessary.
16 Lower the car and take a short test drive to check for leaks.

21 Rear axle oil (all models) – draining and refilling

1 Place the vehicle on a flat surface.
2 Place a suitable container under the differential, remove the drain plug and allow the oil to drain. Allow 15 minutes for complete drainage.
3 Refill the axle through the plug located on the upper side of the housing.
4 Torque tighten the fill plug and check for leaks.

Fig. 8.17 Installing the pinion seal (Sec 20)

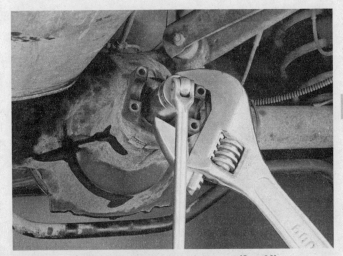

Fig. 8.18 Tightening the pinion nut (Sec 20)

8

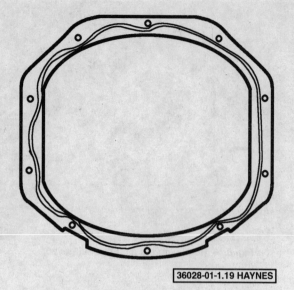

36028-01-1.19 HAYNES

**Fig. 8.19 Axle carrier cover silicone sealant bead
application (Sec 22)**

22 Differential cover (all models) — removal and installation

1   The differential cover can be removed to inspect the differential for
the cause of noise or vibration, missing or cracked gear teeth and
metal flakes in the oil.
2   Drain the oil as described in Section 20.
3   Remove the bolts securing the differential cover to the axle
housing.
4   After inspection, clean the cover and housing mating surfaces.
5   Apply a thin line of silicone sealant to the axle housing as shown.
6   Tighten the cover bolts in a criss-cross pattern to specifications.
7   Refill the axle with oil and take a short test drive.
8   Check for leaks.

Chapter 9 Braking system

Contents

Specifications

System type	Four wheel hydraulic, dual circuit. Power assist optional
System layout	Disc at front, self-adjusting drum at rear
Parking brake	Mechanical, rear brakes only

Disc brakes
Type	Single piston, sliding caliper
Disc diameter	10.08 in (256 mm)
Thickness	
Standard	0.0870 in (22 mm)
Reground	0.0810 in (20 mm)
Lining size	
Inner	4.74 x 2.32 in (120 x 59 mm)
Outer	5.92 x 1.97 in (150 x 50 mm)

Drum brakes
Drum diameter	
Sedan	9.0 in (228.6 mm)
Wagon	10.0 in (316 mm)
Maximum runout	0.007 in (0.1778 mm)
Linings	
Primary	
Sedan	1.75 x 6.12 (44 x 156 mm)
Wagon	1.75 x 8.55 (44 x 217 mm)
Secondary	
Sedan	1.75 x 8.63 (44 x 219 mm)
Wagon	1.75 x 10.45 (44 x 257 mm)
Wheel cylinder bore	0.8125 in (20 mm)

Master cylinder
Type	Tandem
Bore	0.875 (22 mm)
Brake pedal	
Free height (power brakes)	7.0 in (177 mm)
Free height (standard brakes)	8.8 (223 mm)
Pedal travel (power brakes)	2.0 in (50 mm)
Pedal travel (standard brakes)	3.0 in (76 mm)

9

Torque specifications

	ft-lb	Nm
Brake bleeder valve screw		
Disc brake	10 to 11	14 to 16
Drum brake, sedan	2.5 to 5.5	3.6 to 7.3
Drum brake, wagon	7.5 to 15	10 to 20
Hydraulic lines	10 to 18	14 to 24
Caliper bolt/locating pins	30 to 40	41 to 54
Brake hose-to-caliper	20 to 30	28 to 54
Parking brake securing bolts	13 to 25	18 to 34
Master cylinder bolts	13 to 25	10 to 18
Wheel cylinder bolts		
Sedan	9 to 14	12 to 18
Wagon	9 to 20	12 to 28
Pressure differential valve bolts	7 to 11	5 to 8
Parking brake assembly bolts	13 to 25	18 to 34
Servo unit-to-firewall	13 to 25	18 to 34
Brake pedal pivot nut	10 to 20	14 to 27

1 General description

The standard braking system is composed of disc brakes on the front wheels and self-adjusting drum brakes on the rear. A vacuum brake booster providing servo assistance is available on some models as an option.

The rear drum brake system is of the single anchor, internal expanding and self-adjusting assembly type. A dual piston single cylinder is used to expand the shoes against the drum.

The self-adjusting mechanism consists of a cable, cable guide, adjusting lever adjusting screw assembly and an adjuster spring. The cable is hooked over the anchor pin at the top and is connected to the lever at the bottom and is passed along the web of the secondary brake shoe by means of the cable guide. The adjuster spring is hooked onto the primary brake shoe as well as to the lever.

The automatic adjuster operates when the brakes are applied and the vehicle is backed up, or when the secondary brake shoe is able to move towards the drum beyond a certain limit.

The self-centering pressure differential valve assembly body has a stepped bore to accommodate a sleeve and seal which is fitted over the piston and into the large valve body in the front brake system area.

The brake light warning switch is located at the center of the valve body and the spring loaded switch plunger fits into a tapered shoulder groove in the center of the piston. When in this condition the electric circuit through the switch is broken and the warning light on the instrument panel is extinguished.

The disc brake assembly is composed of a ventilated disc and caliper. The caliper is of the single piston, sliding caliper design and is mounted to the front suspension strut. The cylinder bore contains one piston with a rubber seal located in a groove to provide sealing between the piston and the cylinder bore walls.

An independent foot-operated parking brake system actuates the rear brakes through a system of cables.

2 Bleeding the hydraulic system

1 Removal of all the air from the hydraulic fluid in the braking system is essential to the correct working of the braking system. Before undertaking this task, examine the fluid reservoir cap to ensure that the vent hole is clear, also check the level of fluid in the reservoir and top-up if necessary.
2 Check all brake line unions and connections for possible leakage, and at the same time check the condition of the rubber hoses which may be cracked or worn.
3 If the condition of a caliper or wheel cylinder is in doubt, check for signs of fluid leakage.
4 If there is any possibility that incorrect fluid has been used in the system, drain all the fluid out and flush through with methylated spirits. Replace all piston seals and cups as they will be affected and could possibly fail under pressure.
5 Gather together a clean jar, a 12 inch (304 mm) length of rubber tubing which fits tightly over the bleed valves and a container of the correct grade of brake fluid.
6 The primary (front) and secondary (rear) hydraulic brake systems are individual systems and are therefore bled separately. Always bleed the longest line first.
7 To bleed the secondary system (rear) clean the area around the bleed valves and start at the rear right-hand wheel cylinder by first removing the rubber cap over the end of the bleed valve.
8 Place the end of the tube in the clean jar which should contain sufficient fluid to keep the end of the tube submerged during the operation.
9 Open the bleed valve approximately ¾ turn with a wrench and depress the brake pedal slowly through its full travel.
10 Close the bleed valve and allow the pedal to return to the released position.
11 Continue this sequence until no more air bubbles issue from the bleed tube. Give the brake pedal two more strikes to ensure that the line is completely free of air, and then re-tighten the bleed valve, ensuring that the bleed tube remains submerged until the valve is closed.
12 At regular intervals during the bleeding sequence, make sure that the reservoir is kept topped-up, otherwise air will enter again at this point. Do not re-use fluid bled from the system.
13 Repeat the whole procedure on the rear left-hand brake line.
14 To bleed the primary system (front), start with the front right-hand side and finish with the front left-hand side cylinder. The procedure is identical to that previously described (photo).

Note: *Some models have a bleed valve incorporated in the master cylinder. Where this is the case, the master cylinder should be bled before the brake lines. The bleeding procedure is identical to that already described. Do not use the secondary piston stop screw which is located on the bottom of some master cylinders for bleeding. This could damage the secondary piston on the stop screw.*

15 Top-up the master cylinder to within 0.25 inch of the top of the reservoirs, check that the diaphragm type gasket is correctly located in the cover and then refit the cover.

2.14 Bleeding the brakes by opening the bleed screw, allowing fluid to drain into the catch bottle (arrows)

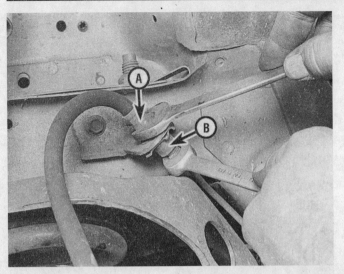

Fig. 9.1 Front brake hose installation (Sec 4)

A Back-up wrench   B Flare nut wrench

3 Pressure differential valve – centralization

1   After any repair or bleed operations it is possible that the dual brake warning light will come on due to the pressure differential valve remaining in an off-center position.
2   To centralize the valve, first turn the ignition switch to the ON or ACC position.
3   Depress the brake pedal several times and the piston will center itself again causing the warning light to go out.
4   Turn the ignition off.

4 Flexible hoses – inspection, removal and installation

1   Inspect the condition of the flexible hydraulic hoses leading to each of the front disc brake calipers and the one at the front of the rear axle. If they are swollen, damaged or chafed, they must be replaced.
2   Wipe the top of the brake master cylinder reservoir and unscrew the cap. Place a piece of polythene sheet over the top of the reservoir and refit the cap. This is to stop hydraulic fluid siphoning out during subsequent operations.

3   To remove a flexible hose wipe the union and any supports free from dust and undo the union nuts from the metal pipe ends.
4   Undo and remove the lock nuts and washers securing each flexible hose end to the support and lift away the flexible hose.
5   Refitting is the reverse sequence to removal. It will be necessary to bleed the brake hydraulic system as described in Section 2. If one hose has been removed it is only necessary to bleed either the front or rear brake hydraulic system.

5 Front disc pads – removal, inspection and installation

1   Raise the vehicle and support with jack stands.
2   Remove the wheel assembly.
3   Remove the master cylinder cap and remove approximately one-half of the fluid in the reservoir. Discard.
4   Loosen the caliper locating bolt/pins.
5   Support the caliper with a piece of wire and remove the locating bolt/pins. This will allow the caliper to move freely without putting any strain on the hydraulic brake hose (photo).
6   Lift the caliper from its mounting position (photo).

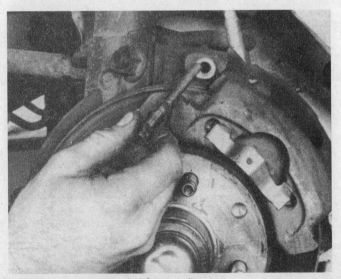

5.5 Removing the caliper bolt/locater pin

5.6 Remove the caliper by pushing it outward to collapse the piston and then slide it rearward and lift up

9

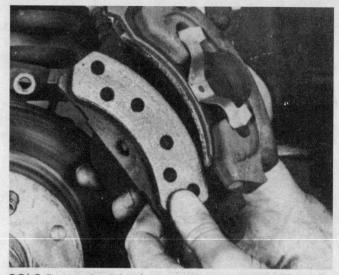

5.7A Pull outward and then forward to remove the inner pad

5.7B Remove the anti-rattle clip from the back of the inner pad and transfer it to the new pad

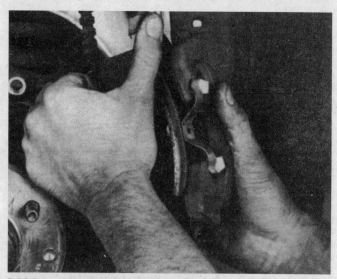

5.7C Releasing the outer pad retaining clip

5.7D Removing the outer pad

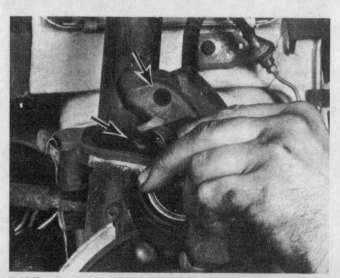

5.13 The round bottoms on the back of the pad must be securely seated in the caliper (arrows)

7   The brake pads can be unsnapped from their position in the caliper (photos).

8   Discard the locating bolt/pin insulators. They are not designed to be re-used.

9   Inspect the brake pads for cracks and missing material.

10 Replace the pads (as an axle set) if there is less than $\frac{1}{8}$ inch (0.125 in) of friction material left on any pad, measured from the metal backing plate.

11 Insert new insulator sleeves into the mounting holes as shown.

12 Depress the piston. Use a block of wood and a C-clamp if necessary to drive the piston back into the caliper casting.

13 Reinstall the brake pads. Make sure the two round torque buttons on the outer pad are solidly seated in the caliper (photo).

14 Position the caliper on the mounting ears.

15 Insert the locating bolt/pins.

16 Tighten the locating bolt/pins.

17 Reinstall the wheel assembly.

18 Remove the jack stands. Pump the brake pedal a few times and check the hydraulic fluid level; fill as needed. Test for a solid brake pedal before and during a test drive.

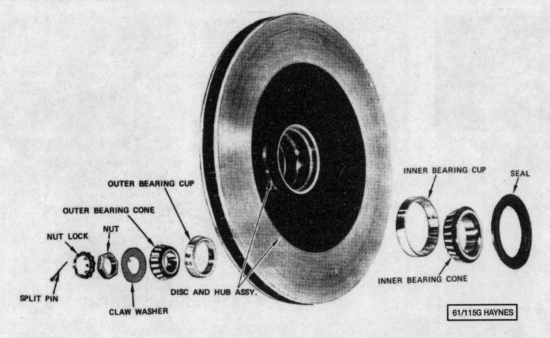

Fig. 9.2 Typical wheel and hub components (Sec 6)

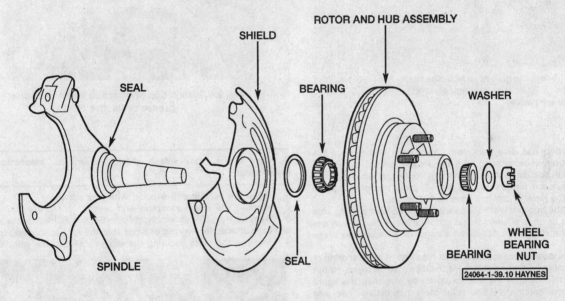

Fig. 9.3 Brake, spindle and hub installation (Sec 6)

6 Front disc brake disc and hub – removal and replacement

1   Refer to Section 5, and remove the caliper and anchor plate assembly. To save extra work and time, if the caliper and anchor plate are not requiring attention, it is not necessary to disconnect the flexible brake hose from the caliper. Suspend the assembly with string or wire from the upper suspension arm.

2   Carefully remove the grease cap from the wheel spindle (photo).

3   Withdraw the cotter pin and nut lock from the wheel bearing adjusting nut.

4   Undo and remove the wheel bearing adjusting nut from the spindle.

5   Grip the hub and disc assembly and pull it outwards far enough to loosen the washer and outer wheel bearing.

6.2 Use a large pair of pliers to remove the grease cap

9

6.6 The outer bearing and washer

6.8A Removing the inner grease seal

6.8B The inner wheel bearing

6.11 Work the grease up from the back of the race until the bearing cage and roller are packed

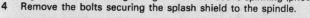

Fig. 9.4 Installation of front hub inner and outer grease seals (Sec 6)

6   Push the hub and disc back onto the spindle and remove the washer and outer wheel bearing from the spindle (photo).

7   Grip the hub and disc assembly and pull it from the wheel spindle.

8   Carefully pry out the grease seal and lift away the inner tapered bearing from the back of the hub assembly (photos).

9   Clean out the hub and wash the bearings with solvent making sure that no grease or oil is allowed to get onto the brake disc. Clean any grease from the rotor with denatured alcohol or an approved brake cleaner.

10 Thoroughly clean the disc and inspect for signs of deep scoring or excessive corrosion. If these are evident the disc may be reground but the minimum thickness of the disc must not be less than the figure given in the Specifications. It is desirable however, to install a new disc if at all possible. A new disc should be cleaned to remove its protective coating, using carburetor cleaner.

11 To reassemble, first work a suitable grease well into the bearings; fully pack the bearing cages and rollers (photo).

12 To reassemble the hub fit the inner bearing and then gently tap the grease seal back into the hub. A new seal should always be installed. The lip must face inward to the hub.

13 Replace the hub and disc assembly onto the spindle keeping the assembly centered on the spindle to prevent damage to the inner grease seal or the spindle threads.

14 Place the outer wheel bearing and flat washer on the spindle.

15 Screw the wheel bearing adjusting nut onto the spindle according to the associated figure.

16 Detach the caliper from the upper suspension arm and guide the assembly towards the disc. Be careful not to stretch or twist the brake flexible hose.

17 Start by sliding the caliper assembly onto the disc at the lower part of the caliper and continue installing the assembly as described in Section 5.

7   Disc brake rotor splash shield – removal, inspection and installation

1   Raise the vehicle and support with jack stands.

2   Remove the wheel assembly and caliper.

3   Remove the rotor assembly, refer to Section 6. Inspect the spindle bearing surfaces for scoring or signs that the race is spinning (photo).

4   Remove the bolts securing the splash shield to the spindle.

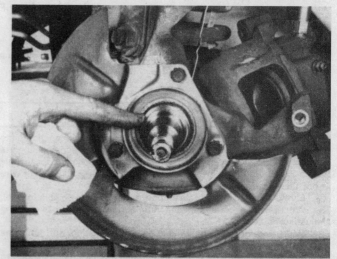

7.3 Check the area adjacent to the spindle shoulder for signs of a spinning bearing race

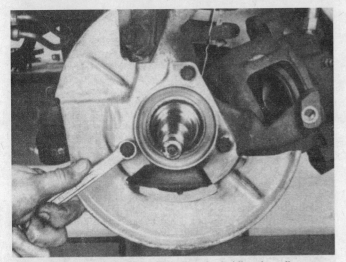

7.8 Installing the splash shield. Note the wire holding the caliper out of the way

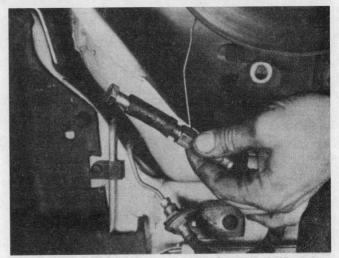

8.2 To prevent leakage, place a piece of tubing with a bolt in it over the end of the brake line

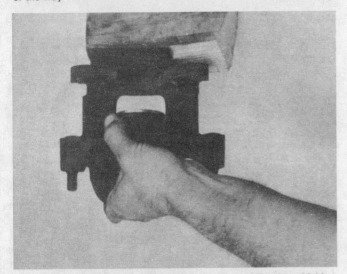

8.3A Strike the caliper on a block of wood to remove the dust shield

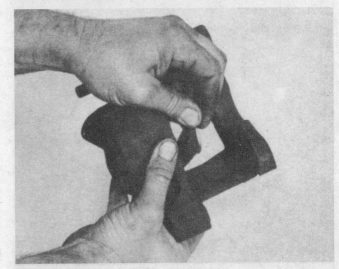

8.3B Removing the dust shield

5   Lift the shield away from the spindle and remove the gasket from the spindle mount.
6   The splash shield should be replaced if it is broken, cracked or severely bent. The mounting bolts and gasket should not be re-used.
7   To reinstall, fit a new gasket to the spindle.
8   Position the splash shield to the spindle. Secure with new bolt (photo).
9   Tighten the bolts to 9-14 ft-lb (7 to 11 Nm).
10   Reinstall the rotor assembly, caliper assembly, and wheel.
11   Check for solid brake 'feel'.
12   Check hydraulic fluid level.
13   Test drive.

8 Disc brake caliper – inspection and overhaul

1   If hydraulic fluid is leaking from the caliper seal it will be necessary to replace the seals. Should brake fluid be found running down the side of the wheel or if the master cylinder fluid level drops excessively, it is also indicative of seal failure.
2   Remove the caliper and disconnect the hydraulic line at the caliper. Plug the brake line to avoid fluid leakage (photo).
3   Remove the rubber dust boot by striking the caliper sharply against a block of wood (photos).
4   Place a rag or shop cloth over the piston bore and again strike the caliper on the block to dislodge the piston, with the cloth catching it.

Several attempts may be necessary before the piston comes out.
5   Remove the rubber piston seal from the cylinder bore (photo).

8.5 Removing the piston seal

9

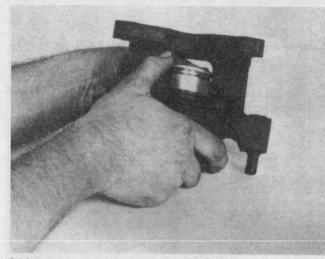

8.10 Insert the piston all the way into the bore

9.2A Unscrewing the tinnerman nut with needle nose pliers

9.2B Removing the brake drum

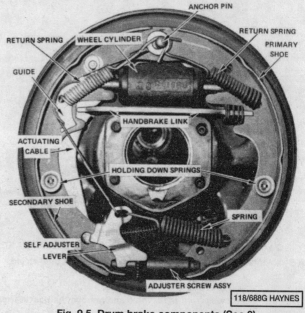

Fig. 9.5 Drum brake components (Sec 9)

6   Thoroughly wash all parts in the proper solvent or clean hydraulic fluid. During reassembly new rubber seals must be installed and these should be well lubricated with clean hydraulic fluid before installation.
7   Inspect the piston and bore for signs of wear, score marks or other damage. If evident a new caliper assembly will be necessary.
8   To reassemble, insert the new piston seal in the inner groove of the cylinder bore after lubricating with brake fluid.
9   Install the dust boot by setting it in the outer groove of the bore. Lock it in the groove with your finger while seating the boot.
10   Carefully insert the piston squarely in the boot and slide the piston into the bore. Push the piston in until it bottoms against the end of the bore (photo).
11   Reassembly is now complete and the unit is ready for installation in the vehicle.

9   Rear drum brake shoes – inspection, removal and installation

1   Chock the front wheels, jack up the rear of the car and support on firmly based jack stands. Remove the wheel.
2   Remove the three Tinnerman nuts and remove the brake drum (photos).
3   If the drum will not come off, remove the rubber cover from the brake backplate and insert a narrow screwdriver through the slot. Disengage the adjusting lever from the adjusting screw.

4   While holding the adjusting lever away from the screw, back off the adjusting screw with either a second screwdriver or shaped piece of metal as shown in the accompanying figure. Take care not to burr, chip or damage the notches in the adjusting screw.
5   The brake linings should be replaced if they are worn to within 0.03 in of the rivets or will be before the next routine check. If bonded linings are installed they must be replaced when the lining material has worn down to 0.06 in at its thinnest part.
6   To remove the brake shoes, detach and remove the secondary shoe-to-anchor spring and lift away the spring (photo).
7   Detach the primary shoe-to-anchor spring and lift away the spring (photo).
8   Unhook the adjusting cable eye from the anchor pin (photo).
9   Remove the shoe hold-down springs followed by the shoes, adjusting screw, pivot nut, socket and automatic adjustment parts (photos).
10   Remove the parking brake link and spring. Disconnect the parking brake cable from the parking brake lever (photo).
11   After the secondary shoe has been removed, the parking brake lever should be detached from the shoe (photo).
12   It is recommended that only one brake assembly be overhauled at a time unless the parts are kept well apart. This is because the brake

shoe adjusting screw assemblies are not interchangeable and, if interchanged, would in fact operate in reverse, thereby increasing the drum to lining clearance every time the car is backed up.

13 To prevent any mix-up, the socket end of the adjusting screw is stamped with an 'R' or 'L'. The adjusting pivot nuts can be identified by the number of grooves machined around the body of the nut. Two grooves on the nut indicate a right-hand thread and one groove indicates a left-hand thread as shown in the associated figure.

14 If the shoes are to be left off for a while, place a warning on the steering wheel as accidental depression of the brake pedal will eject the pistons from the wheel cylinder.

15 Thoroughly clean all traces of dust from the shoes, backplate and brake drums using a stiff brush. Excessive amounts of brake dust can cause judder or squeal and it is therefore important to remove all traces. It is recommended that compressed air is *not* used for this operation as this increases the possibility of the dust being inhaled.

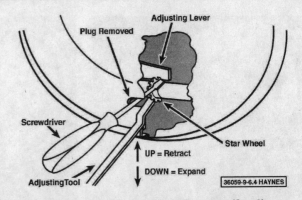

Fig. 9.6 Backing off the brake adjustment (Sec 9)

9.6 Releasing the anchor springs

9.7 Removing the anchor springs, note the brake adjustment cable (arrow)

9.8 Adjusting cable, guide and spring

9.9A Removing the hold down spring

9.9B Lifting away the brake shoes

9.10 Parking brake lever (arrow)

9.11 Disengaging the parking brake lever from the cable

9.17A The shoe support pads should be lubricated with lithium grease prior to reassembly

9.17B Lubricating the brake shoe pivot

9

9.17C Lubricating the adjuster mechanism

9.19 Installing the hold down spring

9.21 Installing the shoe guide

16 Check that the pistons are free in the cylinder, that the rubber dust covers are undamaged and in position, and that there are no hydraulic fluid leaks.

17 Prior to reassembly smear a trace of brake grease on the shoe support pads, brake shoe pivots and on the ratchet wheel face and threads (photos).

18 To reassemble, install the parking brake lever to the secondary shoe and secure with the spring washer and retaining clip.

19 Place the brake shoes on the backplate and retain with the hold-down springs (photo).

20 Install the parking brake link and spring. Slacken off the parking brake adjustment and connect the cable to the parking brake lever.

21 Install the shoe guide (anchor pin) plate on the anchor pin when installed (photo).

22 Place the cable eye over the anchor pin with the crimped side towards the backplate.

23 Replace the primary shoe to anchor spring.

24 Install the cable guide into the secondary shoe web with the flanged hole fitted into the hole in the secondary shoe web. Thread the cable around the cable guide groove. It is very important that the cable is positioned in this groove and not between the guide and the shoe web.

25 Install the secondary shoe-to-anchor spring.

26 Check that the cable eye is not twisted or binding on the anchor pin when fitted. All parts must be flat on the anchor pin.

27 Apply some brake grease to the threads and socket end of the adjusting screw. Turn the adjusting screw into the adjusting pivot nut fully and then back off $\frac{1}{2}$ turn.

28 Place the adjusting socket on the screw and fit this assembly between the shoe ends with the adjusting screw-toothed wheel nearest to the secondary shoe.

29 Hook the cable hook into the hole in the adjusting lever. The adjusting levers are stamped with an 'R' or 'L' to show their correct relationship to the left or right brake assembly.

30 Position the hooked end of the adjuster spring completely into the large hole in the primary shoe web. The last coil of the spring must be at the edge of the hole.

31 Connect the loop end of the spring to the adjuster lever holes.

32 Pull the adjuster lever, cable and automatic adjuster spring down and towards the rear to engage the pivot hook in the large hole in the secondary shoe web (photo).

33 After reassembly, check the action of the adjuster by pulling the section of the cable between the cable guide and the anchor pin towards the secondary shoe web far enough to lift the lever past a tooth on the adjusting screw wheel.

34 The lever should snap into position behind the next tooth and releasing the cable should cause the adjuster spring to return the lever to its original position. This return motion of the lever will turn the adjusting screw one tooth.

35 If pulling the cable does not produce the desired action, or if the lever action is sluggish instead of positive and sharp, check the position of the lever on the adjusting screw toothed wheel. With the brake unit in a vertical position (the anchor pin at the top), the lever should contact the adjusting wheel 0.1875 in ± 0.0313 in above the centerline of the screw.

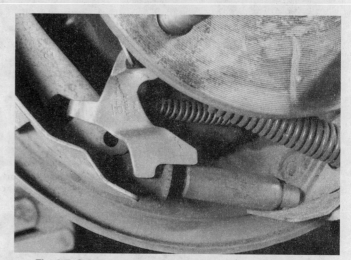

Fig. 9.7 Self-adjusting brake adjuster components (Sec 9)

36 Should the contact point be below this centerline the lever will not lock on the teeth in the adjusting screw wheel, and the screw will not be turned as the lever is actuated by the cable.

37 Incorrect action should be checked as follows:

a) Inspect the cable and fittings. They should completely fill or extend slightly beyond the crimped section of the fittings. If this is not so, the cable assembly should be replaced.

b) Check the cable length. The cable should measure 8.4063 in from the end of the cable anchor to the end of the cable hook.

c) Inspect the cable guide for damage. The cable groove should be parallel to the shoe web, and the body of the guide should lie flat against the web. Replace the guide if it is damaged.

d) Inspect the pivot hook on the lever. The hook surfaces should be square to the body of the lever for correct pivoting action. Replace the lever if the hook shows signs of damage.

e) Check that the adjustment screw socket is correctly seated in the notch in the shoe web.

38 Reinstall the brake drum and wheel, lower the car to the ground and take it for a short test run to check the operation of the parking brake and footbrake.

10 Rear drum brake wheel cylinder – removal and installation

1 Referring to Section 9, remove the brake shoes as described in paragraphs 1 thru 11.

2 On the back side of the brake backing plate, loosen the brake line fitting at the wheel cylinder. Do not try to pull the brake tube from the wheel cylinder as this could bend it, making installation difficult (photo).

9.32 The adjuster pivot hook fits into the hole (arrow) in the secondary shoe

10.2 Removing the brake line from the back of the wheel cylinder

10.3 Removing the wheel cylinder bolts

10.4 Plug the brake line with rubber tubing and a bolt

11.5 Cleaning the wheel cylinder with brake fluid

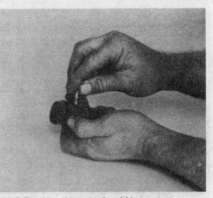

11.6 The bleed screw should be removed and checked for obstructions

11.9 Installing the seal and piston

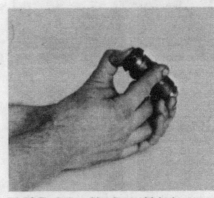

11.10 Flush the rubber boot with brake fluid for easier installation

3   Remove the 2 bolts securing the wheel cylinder to the brake backing plate and lift the cylinder away from the vehicle (photo).
4   Plug the brake line to stop hydraulic fluid leakage (photo).
5   Installation is the reverse of removal. After reinstallation it will be necessary to bleed the hydraulic system as described in Section 2.

11 Rear drum brake wheel cylinder – inspection and overhaul

1   Remove the wheel cylinder as described in the previous Section.
2   To dismantle the wheel cylinder, first remove the rubber boot from each end of the cylinder and push out the two pistons, cup seals and return spring the accompanying figure.
3   Inspect the pistons for signs of scoring or scuff marks; if these are present the pistons should be replaced.

4   Examine the inside of the cylinder bore for score marks or corrosion. If these conditions are present the cylinder can be taken to a machine shop for boring (maximum oversize 0.003 in). However the best policy is to replace it.
5   If the cylinder is sound, thoroughly clean it out with fresh hydraulic fluid (photo).
6   Remove the bleed screw and check that the hole is clean (photo).
7   The old rubber cups will probably be swollen and visibly worn. Smear the new rubber cups and insert one into the bore followed by one piston.
8   Place the return spring in the bore and push up until it contacts the rear of the first seal.
9   Reinstall the second seal and piston into the cylinder bore (photo).
10 Replace the two rubber boots (photo).
11 The wheel cylinder is now ready for reinstalling to the brake backplate.

9

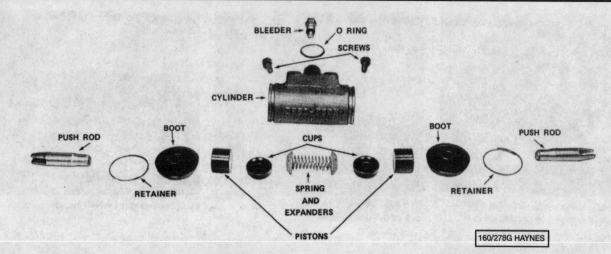

Fig. 9.8 Exploded view of rear wheel cylinder (Sec 11)

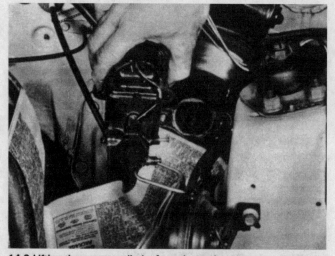

14.3 Lifting the master cylinder from the engine compartment. Note the newspapers placed below to catch leaking fluid

Fig. 9.9 When you disassemble the pistons, place them on a clean surface and organize the parts as you disassemble (Sec 14)

12 Rear drum brake backplate – removal and installation

1   Refer to Sections 9 and 10, and remove the brake shoes and wheel cylinder from the backplate.
2   Disconnect the parking brake lever from the cable.
3   Refer to Chapter 8 and remove the axle shaft.
4   Disconnect the parking brake cable retainer from the backplate.
5   The backplate and gasket may now be lifted away from the end of the axle housing.
6   Reinstalling the brake backplate is the reverse sequence to removal. It will be necessary to bleed the brake hydraulic system as described in Section 2. Do not forget to top-up the rear axle oil level if necessary.

13 Rear drum brake shoes – adjustment

Automatic adjusters are fitted to the rear drum brakes and these operate when the car is backed-up and stopped. Should car use be such that it is not backed-up very often and the pedal movement has increased then it will be necessary to adjust the brakes as follows:
1   Drive the car rearwards and apply the brake pedal firmly. Now drive it forward, and again, apply the brake pedal firmly.
2   Repeat the cycle until a desirable pedal movement is obtained. Should this not happen, however, it will be necessary to remove the drum and hub assemblies and inspect the adjuster mechanism as described in Section 9, paragraphs 33 to 37 inclusive.

14 Brake master cylinder – removal and installation

1   Unscrew the brake pipes from the primary and secondary outlet parts of the master cylinder. Plug the ends of the pipes to prevent contamination. Take suitable precautions to catch the hydraulic fluid as the unions are detached from the master cylinder body.
2   Undo and remove the two screws securing the master cylinder to the dashpanel (or servo unit).
3   Pull the master cylinder forward and lift it upward from the car. Do not allow brake fluid to contact any paintwork as it acts as a solvent (photo).
4   Reinstall the master cylinder using the reverse procedure to removal. It will be necessary to bleed the hydraulic system as described in Section 2.

15 Brake master cylinder – dismantling, inspection and reassembly

If a replacement master cylinder is to be installed, it will be necessary to lubricate the seals before installation on the car as they have a protective coating when originally assembled. Remove the blanking plugs from the hydraulic pipe union seatings. Inject some clean hydraulic fluid into the master cylinder and operate the pushrod several times so that the fluid spreads over all the internal working surfaces.

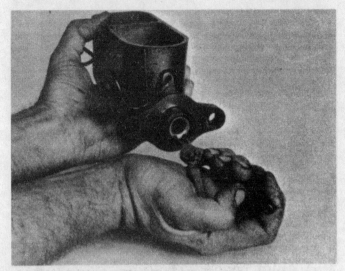

15.5 Removing the snap ring

15.6 Removing the primary piston assembly

15.8 Removing the secondary piston assembly

15.10 Using a honing tool to remove scratches from the master cylinder bore

If the master cylinder is to be dismantled after removal proceed as follows:

1   Clean the exterior of the master cylinder and wipe dry with a lint-free rag.

2   Remove the filler cover and gasket from the top of the reservoir and pour out any remaining hydraulic fluid.

3   Undo and remove the secondary piston stop bolt from the bottom of the master cylinder body.

4   Undo and remove the bleed screw.

5   Depress the primary piston and remove the snap-ring from the groove at the rear of the master cylinder bore (photo).

6   Remove the pushrod and the primary piston assembly (photo).

7   **Do not** remove the screw that retains the primary return spring retainer, return spring, primary cup and protector on the primary piston. This is factory set and must not be disturbed.

8   Remove the secondary piston assembly (photo).

9   **Do not** remove the outlet pipe seats, outlet check valves and outlet check valve springs from the master cylinder body.

10 Examine the bore of the cylinder carefully for any signs of scores or ridges. If this is found to be smooth all over new seals can be installed. If, however, there is any doubt of the condition of the bore then a new master cylinder must be installed. Minor scratches or scoring in the bore can be removed using a honing tool (photo).

11 If the seals are swollen, or very loose on the pistons, suspect oil contamination in the system. Oil will swell these rubber seals and if one is found to be swollen it is reasonable to assume that all seals in the braking system will need attention.

12 Thoroughly clean all parts in clean hydraulic fluid or methylated spirits. Ensure that the ports are clear.

13 All components should be assembled wet after dipping in fresh brake fluid.

14 Carefully insert the complete secondary piston and return spring assembly into the master cylinder bore, easing the seals into the bore, taking care that they do not roll over. Push the assembly fully home.

15 Insert the primary piston assembly into the master cylinder bore.

16 Depress the primary piston and fit the snap-ring into the cylinder bore groove.

17 Reinstall the pushrod, boot and retainer onto the pushrod and fit the assembly into the end of the primary piston. Check that the retainer is correctly seated and holding the pushrod securely.

18 Place the inner end of the pushrod boot in the master cylinder body retaining groove.

19 Install the secondary piston stop bolt and O-ring into the bottom of the master cylinder body.

20 Reinstall the diaphragm into the filler cover making sure it is correctly seated and replace the cover. Secure it in position with the spring retainer.

9

16 Brake pedal – removal and installation

1   Disconnect the negative battery cable.
2   Disconnect the stop light switch wire from the switch.
3   Remove the clutch cable clevis from the pedal on manual transmission equipped vehicles.
4   Loosen the brake booster nuts approximately $\frac{1}{4}$ inch and remove the pushrod retainer and washer.
5   Slide the stop light switch out along the brake pedal to clear the pin. Lower the stop light switch to remove.
6   Remove the black stop light switch bushing from the push rod.
7   Note the location of the pivot location and washers before removing the pedal.
8   Installation is the reverse of removal. However, during installation, coat any pivot points with a small drop of 10W30 motor oil to prolong bearing life and ease of operation.
9   Check for proper operation before driving.

17 Pressure differential valve assembly – removal and installation

1   Disconnect the brake warning light connector from the warning light switch.
2   Disconnect the front inlet and rear outlet pipe unions from the valve assembly. Plug the ends of the pipes to prevent loss of hydraulic fluid or dirt ingress.
3   Undo and remove the two nuts and bolts securing the valve bracket to the underside of the fender apron.
4   Lift away the valve assembly and bracket taking care not to allow any brake fluid to contact paintwork as it acts as a solvent.
5   The valve assembly cannot be overhauled or repaired, so if its performance is suspect a new unit will have to be obtained and installed.
6   Reinstalling the pressure differential valve assembly and bracket is the reverse sequence to removal. It will be necessary to bleed the brake hydraulic system as described in Section 2.

18 Brake pedal travel – measurement and adjustment

1   When the parking brake is fully released, measure the brake pedal free height by first inserting a needle through the carpet and sound deadening felt until it contacts the metal dashpanel.
2   Measure the distance from the top center of the brake pedal pad to the metal dashpanel. This should be within the pedal height limits given in the Specifications.
3   If the measurement obtained is not within the specified limit, check the brake pedal linkage for missing, worn or damaged brushes or loose securing bolts. Rectify as necessary.
4   If the measurement is still incorrect then the master cylinder should be checked to see if it has been correctly reassembled after overhaul.
5   To check the brake pedal travel measure and record the distance from the pedal free height position to the datum point which is the six o'clock position on the steering wheel rim.
6   Depress the brake pedal and take a second reading. The differences between the brake pedal free height and the depressed pedal measurement should be within the pedal travel Specifications.
7   If the pedal travel is more than that specified, adjust the brakes as described in Section 13.
8   Should this still not produce the desired results the drums will have to be removed to check that the linings are not badly worn and the automatic adjusters are operating correctly. Rectify any faults found.

19 Parking brake assembly – removal and installation

1   Release the parking brake.
2   Back off the parking brake adjusting nut to relieve the tension from the rear cables.
3   Disconnect the control assembly release cable or vacuum release motor (if equipped).
4   Disconnect the parking brake warning light connector.
5   Remove the 3 screws which attach the control assembly to the cowl inner panel.
6   Remove the hairpin clip retaining the parking brake cable to the assembly housing and disconnect the cable.
7   Remove the assembly from the vehicle.
8   Installation is the reverse of removal. The securing screws should be tightened according to specifications.

20 Parking brake – adjustment

1   Refer to Section 13, and adjust the brakes.
2   Chock the front wheels, jack-up the rear of the car and support on firmly based stands.
3   Release the parking brake fully and move the shift to the neutral position.
4   Slowly tighten the adjustment nut on the equalizer rod at the parking brake lever assembly until the rear brakes are just applied.
5   Back-off the adjusting nut until the rear brakes are just fully released.
6   Lower the car and check parking brake lever free-movement.

21 Parking brake cables – removal and installation

1   Block the front wheels. Jack up the rear of the vehicle and support it on firmly based jack stands. Remove the rear wheels.
2   Release the parking brake and remove the brake drums as described in Section 9.
3   Referring to the associated figure, loosen the adjusting nut to slacken the parking brake cables.
4   Disconnect the right and left parking brake cable connectors. The left cable connects to the end of the intermediate cable and the right cable connects to the transverse cable.
5   Remove the cable attaching brackets and the adjuster assembly.
6   Disconnect the rear cables from the body brackets.
7   Remove the self-adjuster springs.
8   From inside the vehicle, remove the clip which retains the cable to the parking brake control. Disconnect the cable and remove it from the control.
9   From underneath the vehicle, slide the cable from the brake backing plates and remove the cable from the vehicle.
10 To install, first connect the rear cables to the body brackets with the clips.
11 Push the front cable up through the openings in the floor pan and install it to the parking brake control assembly.
12 Insert the rear cables through the holes in the backing plates and attach them to the parking brake levers on the brake shoes.
13 Push the cables through the holes in the backing plates until the retaining prongs are securely positioned.
14 Install the self-adjuster springs and attach the forward ends of the cables to the connector.
15 Install the equalizer assembly and transverse cables and attach them to the connectors at the rear cable.
16 Install the rear brake drums and wheels.
17 Install the adjuster nut and adjust the parking brakes as described in Section 20.

22 Vacuum servo unit – description

A vacuum servo unit is installed in the brake hydraulic circuit in series with the master cylinder, to provide assistance to the driver when the brake pedal is depressed. This reduces the effort required by the driver to operate the brakes under all braking conditions.

The unit operates by vacuum obtained from the induction manifold and comprises basically a booster diaphragm and check valve. The servo unit and hydraulic master cylinder are connected together so that the servo unit piston rod acts as the master cylinder pushrod. The driver's braking effort is transmitted through another pushrod to the servo unit piston and its built-in control system. The servo unit piston does not fit tightly into the cylinder, but has a strong diaphragm to keep its edges in constant contact with the cylinder wall, so ensuring an air tight seal between the two parts. The forward chamber is held under the vacuum conditions created in the inlet manifold of the engine, and during periods when the brake pedal is not in use, the controls open a passage to the rear chamber, so placing it under vacuum conditions as well. When the brake pedal is depressed, the vacuum passage to the rear chamber is cut off and the chamber opened to atmospheric pressure. The consequent rush of air pushes the servo piston forward in the vacuum chamber and operates the main pushrod to the master cylinder.

The controls are designed so that assistance is given under all conditions and, when the brakes are not required, vacuum in the rear chamber is established when the brake pedal is released. All air from the atmosphere entering the rear chamber is passed through a small air filter.

Under normal operating conditions the vacuum servo unit will give trouble-free service for a very long time. If, however, it is suspected that the unit is faulty, ie, increase in foot pressure is required to apply the brakes, it must be exchanged for a new unit. No attempt should be made to repair the old unit as it is not a serviceable item.

23 Vacuum servo unit – removal and installation

1   Remove the stop light switch and actuating rod from the brake pedal as described in Section 16.

2   Working under the hood, remove the air cleaner from the carburetor and the vacuum hose from the servo unit.

3   On four cylinder engines only (2.3 liter), it will be necessary to remove the two screws securing the throttle cable bracket to the engine and move the bracket in toward the engine. Remove the water inlet hose from the automatic choke house and move it out of the way. Also detach the vacuum hose from the EGR reservoir if necessary.

4   Refer to Section 14 and remove the master cylinder.

5   From inside the car, remove the nuts securing the servo unit to the dashpanel.

6   Working inside the engine compartment, move the servo unit forward until the actuating rod is clear of the dashpanel, rotate it through 90° and lift the unit upward until clear of the engine compartment.

7   Reinstalling a new servo unit is the reverse sequence to removal. It will be necessary to bleed the brake hydraulic system as described in Section 2.

9

Notes

Chapter 10 Chassis electrical system

Refer to Chapter 13 for specifications and information on later models

Contents

Specifications

Battery rating .... Check battery identification stickers
Bulbs

	Number
Alternator warning indicator	194
Instrument cluster illumination	194
Dome	906
Dual brake warning indicator	194
Heater controls illumination	161
High beam indicator	194
Interior switch	906
Back-up lamp	1156
Front parking lamp	194A
Front side marker	194
Head light, high beam	4651
Head light, low beam	4652
Rear side marker	194
Rear running lamp	1157
Turn indicator	194
License plate lamp	168
Luggage compartment	89
Oil pressure/temperature warning indicator	194
Console shift PRNDL illumination	1893
Seat belt warning indicator	194

1 General information

The electrical system is of the 12 volt negative ground type.

Power for the lighting system and all electrical accessories is supplied by a lead/acid-type battery which is charged by an alternator.

This Chapter covers repair and service procedures for the various lighting and electrical components not associated with the engine. Information on the alternator, voltage regulator and starter motor can be found in Chapter 5.

Note: *Whenever the electrical system is worked on, the negative battery cable should be disconnected to prevent electrical shorts and/or fires.*

2 Battery – maintenance

1 Most models are equipped with maintenance-free batteries which do not require the addition of water or electrolyte.

2 Maintenance-type batteries should be checked every week and topped-up with distilled water so that the level is $\frac{1}{4}$ inch above the top of the plates. Be carefully not to overfill.

3 Keep the top of the battery clean and free from dirt and moisture so that the battery does not become partially discharged by leakage through dampness and dirt. The terminals should be kept free of corrosion and covered with petroleum jelly. If a felt ring is used under the battery terminals, it should be oiled periodically.

10

4   Once every three months, remove the battery and inspect the securing bolts, battery clamp plate and leads for corrosion (white fluffy deposits on the metal which are brittle to the touch). If any corrosion is found, clean it off with an ammonia or soda and water solution. After cleaning, smear petroleum jelly on the terminals and lead connectors.
5   If topping-up of the battery becomes excessive and there are no cracks in the case causing leakage, the battery is being over-charged and the alternator will have to be tested and repaired if necessary.
6   If any doubt exists about the state of charge of the battery, a hydrometer should be used to test a little electrolyte drawn from each cell.
7   The specific gravity of the electrolyte at the temperature of 80°F (26.7°C) will be approximately 1.270 for a fully charged battery. For every 10°F (5.5°C) that the electrolyte temperature is above that stated, add 0.04 to the specific gravity or subtract 0.04 if the temperature is below that stated.
8   A specific gravity reading of 1.240 with an electrolyte temperature of 80°F (26.7°C) indicates a half-charged battery.

3   Battery charging

1   In winter time when heavy demand is placed upon the battery, such as when starting from cold, and much electrical equipment is continually in use, it is a good idea to occasionally have the battery fully charged from an external source at the rate of 3.5 to 4 amps.
2   Continue to charge the battery at this rate until no further rise in specific gravity is noted over a four hour period.
3   Alternatively, a trickle charging at the rate of 1.5 amps can be safely used overnight.
4   Special rapid boost charges which are claimed to restore the power of the battery in 1 to 2 hours are most dangerous as they can cause serious damage to the battery plates. This type of charge should only be used in a 'crisis' situation.

4   Battery – removal and installation

1   The battery is located at the front of the engine compartment. It is held in place by a hold-down rod running across the top of the battery.
2   As hydrogen gas is produced by the battery, keep open flames or lighted cigarettes away from the battery at all times.
3   Avoid spilling any of the electrolyte battery fluid on the vehicle or yourself. Always keep the battery in the upright position. Any spilled electrolyte should be immediately flushed with large quantities of water. Wear eye protection when working with a battery to prevent serious eye damage from splashed fluid.
4   Always disconnect the negative (-) battery cable first, followed by the positive (+) cable.
5   After the cables are disconnected from the battery, remove the hold-down mechanism, be it a rod or bottom clamp.
6   Carefully lift the battery from its tray and out of the engine compartment.
7   Installation is a reversal of removal; however make sure that the hold-down clamp or rod is securely tightened. Do not over-tighten, however, as this may damage the battery case. The battery posts and cable ends should be cleaned prior to connection.

5   Fuses

1   The electrical circuits of the car are protected by a combination of fuses, circuit breakers and fusible links.
2   The fuse panel or fuse box is located in most models underneath the dashboard, on the left side of the vehicle. It is easily accessible for fuse inspection or replacement without completely removing the box from its mountings.
3   Each of the fuses is designed to protect a specific circuit, and the various circuits are identified on the fuse panel itself.
4   If an electrical component has failed, your first check should be the fuse. A fuse which has 'blown' can be readily identified by inspecting the element inside the glass tube. If this metal element is broken, the fuse is inoperable and must be replaced with a new one.
5   When removing and installing fuses it is important that metal

Fig. 10.1 Typical fuse panel (Secs 5 and 7)

objects are not used to pry the fuse in or out of the holder. Plastic fuse pullers are available for this purpose.
6   It is also important that the correct fuse be installed. The different electrical circuits need varying amounts of protection, indicated by the amperage rating on the fuse.
7   At no time should the fuse be bypassed by using metal or foil. Serious damage to the electrical system could result.
8   If the replacement fuse immediately fails – do not replace again until the cause of the problem is isolated and corrected. In most cases this will be a short circuit in the wiring system caused by a broken or deteriorated wire.

6   Fuse links

1   In addition to fuses, the wiring system incorporates fuse links for overload protection. These links are used in circuits which are not ordinarily fuse.
2   Fuse links are several wire gauges smaller than the circuit they are incorporated into. The fuse links are green or black and have a molded color identification tag. The tag color identifications are as follows:

    a)   *Green – 14 gauge*
    b)   *Orange – 16 gauge*
    c)   *Yellow – 17 gauge*
    d)   *Red – 18 gauge*
    e)   *Blue – 20 gauge*

3   Fuse links cannot be repaired. A new fuse link of the same gauge, length and insulation must be used to replace a blown link. This process is as follows:
4   Disconnect the battery ground cable.
5   Disconnect the fuse link or fuse link eyelet terminal from the battery terminal of the starter relay.
6   Determine which circuit is damaged and the cause of the overload.
7   Cut the damaged fuse link from the circuit and discard it. Strip the insulation from the circuit wire back from the cut approximately ½ inch.
8   Determine the proper replacement fuse link and crimp it into place in the wiring circuit. It may be necessary to cut one or both eyelets off the fuse link when installing.
9   Use a resin core solder at each end of the new link to obtain a good solder joint.
10 Use plenty of electrical tape around the soldered joint. No exposed wiring should show.
11 Connect a fuse link at the starter solenoid. Connect the battery ground cable. Test the circuit for proper operation.

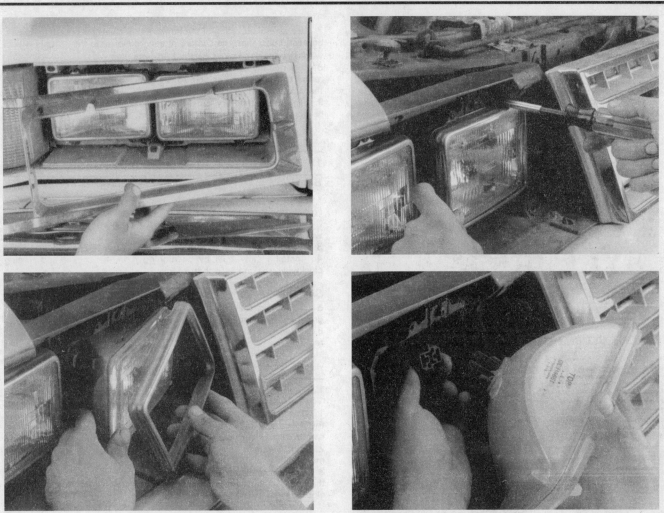

Fig. 10.2 Headlight removal details

7 Turn signal and hazard flasher – removal and replacement

1   The turn signal and hazard flasher are found on the main fuse panel which is located in the lower left of the instrument panel.
2   The turn signal flasher unit plugs into the fuse panel and is retained by a spring clip.
3   To remove, grip firmly and pull straight out, taking care not to bend the connector tabs.
4   The hazard warning flasher is located on the opposite side of the fuse panel and is removed in the same way.
5   Replacement is the reverse of removal.

8 Horn – fault testing

1   If horn proves inoperable, the first check should be the fuse. A blown fuse can be readily identified at the fuse panel in the left side of the instrument panel.
2   If the fuse is in good condition, disconnect the electrical lead at the horn. Run jumper wires from the battery positive and negative terminals to the horn terminals.
3   If the horn does not work and there is no evidence of spark at the battery terminal, turn the adjusting screw $\frac{1}{4}$ to $\frac{3}{8}$ of a turn counter-clockwise, making sure to secure the adjustment screw by clinching the housing extrusion with pliers.
4   If the horn does not sound after adjustment, replace it with a new unit.

9 Headlight sealed beam unit – removal and installation

1   Remove the headlamp screws, door and retaining ring. Make sure that the *retaining* screws and not the *adjustment* screws are removed.
2   Pull the headlight forward and support it as you disconnect the wiring plug.
3   Install the plug to the new headlight and position it by locating the glass tabs at the back in the slots in the receptacle.
4   Install the headlight retaining ring, screws and door.
5   Check the headlight alignment.

10 Headlight – alignment

1   It is always advisable to have the headlights aligned on proper optical beam setting equipment but if this is not available the following procedure may be used:
2   Position the car on level ground 10ft (3.048 meters) in front of a dark wall or board. The wall or board must be at right-angles to the center-line of the car.
3   Draw a vertical line on the board or wall in line with the center-line of the car.
4   Bounce the car on its suspension to ensure correct settlement and then measure the height between the ground and the center of the headlights.
5   Draw a horizontal line across the board or wall at this measured height. On this horizontal line mark a cross on either side of the vertical

10

center-line, the distance between the center of the light unit and the center of the car.

6   Remove the headlight rims and switch the headlights onto full beam.

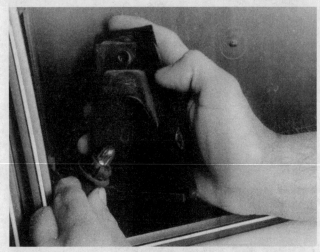

Fig. 10.3 Separate the cover from the light (Sec 11)

Fig. 10.4 Access the front turn signal harnesses and bulbs from under the bumper (Sec 11)

7   By careful adjusting of the horizontal and vertical adjusting screws on each light, align the centers of each beam onto the crosses which were previously marked on the horizontal line.

8   Bounce the car on its suspension again and check that the beams return to the correct position. At the same time check the operation of the dipswitch. Replace the headlight rims.

9   This is a temporary, emergency operation until the headlights can be adjusted using the proper equipment.

11 Bulb replacement – front end

Parking lamp

1   The parking lamp bulb is removed from inside the engine compartment.

2   Grasp the socket assembly, twist it counterclockwise and withdraw it from the lamp body.

3   Push in and twist to remove the bulb from the socket.

4   Install a new bulb by positioning it in the socket and turning clockwise, making sure that it locks.

Side marker lamp

5   To remove the front side marker bulbs, reach up under the fender, grasp the bulb socket, turning it counterclockwise as you withdraw it.

6   After replacing the bulb in the socket, installation is the reverse of removal.

12 Bulb replacement – rear end

1   The various rear lamp bulbs are accessible from inside the trunk of the coupe and sedan. It may be necessary to remove some inner trim panels in the cargo area of the station wagon to reach the lamps.

2   Pull the lamp socket from the housing with a slight twisting motion.

3   Replace the bulb in the lamp socket and align the keying slot of the lamp socket with the tab of the lamp body, press down and turn clockwise to install.

13 Bulb replacement – interior lamps

Dome lamp

1   Pull down on left side of the dome lamp assembly and remove it from its mounting.

2   Slide the bulb from its socket, using long-nosed pliers.

3   Installation is the reverse of removal.

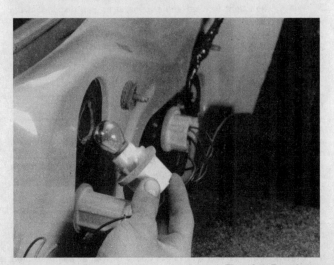
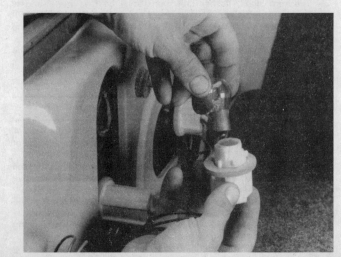

Fig. 10.5 Rear lamps and bulb removal (Sec 12)

Station wagon cargo area lamp

4   Insert a small-bladed screwdriver between the end of the lens and the lamp body and carefully pry the lens out of the body.
5   Wrap a cloth around the bulb and slide the bulb from its socket with a pair of long-nosed pliers, gripping it lightly as it could break.
6   After replacing the bulb in the socket, installation is the reverse of removal.

14   Bulb replacement – instrument panel

1   The instrument cluster and trim panel must be removed to gain access to the instrument panel bulbs (Section 18).
2   Disconnect the battery negative cable.
3   After removing the instrument cluster, remove the two screws retaining the lower access panel to gain access to the cluster bulbs.
4   To reach the instrument cluster indicator bulbs, remove the clutch trim panel.

15   Headlight switch – removal and installation

1   Disconnect the battery negative cable.
2   Pull the control knob to the ON position.
3   Reach under the instrument panel and press the release button on the switch. With the release button pushed in, pull the control knob out of the switch.
4   Unscrew the bezel nut which retains the switch to the instrument panel.
5   Detach the switch, disconnect the electrical connector and remove the switch.
6   To reinstall, connect the electrical plug to the connector, place the switch in position on the instrument panel and install the bezel nut.
7   Insert the knob and shaft into the switch, rotating it slightly until a click is heard.
8   Connect the battery ground cable and check the switch for proper operation.

16   Windshield wiper switch – removal and installation

1   Disconnect the battery negative cable.
2   Remove the steering column shroud attaching screws and separate the two halves. Push the electrical connector off the wiper switch with a flat screwdriver.
3   Remove the two wiper switch attaching screws and remove the switch.
4   Installation is the reverse of removal.

17   Cigar lighter assembly – removal and installation

1   Disconnect the battery negative cable.
2   Disconnect the lighter feed wire from the socket.
3   Remove the cigar lighter socket retainer and socket.
4   Installation is the reversal of removal.

18   Instrument cluster – removal and installation

1   Disconnect the battery negative cable.
2   Remove the steering column shroud.
3   Remove the cluster trim cover.
4   Remove the screw retaining the PRND21 cable to the steering column and detach the cable loop from the shift cane. Remove the plastic clamp from around the steering column.
5   Remove the screws retaining the instrument cluster to the instrument panel and pull the cluster away from the panel. Disconnect the speedometer cable as described in Section 19.
6   Disconnect the cluster electrical plug from the receptacle in the printed circuit.
7   Lift the cluster away from the dash panel.
8   When installing, apply a $\frac{3}{16}$ inch ball of silicone damping grease in the speedometer head drive hole.

9   Connect the electrical feed plug to the printed circuit.
10 After aligning the speedometer connector with the adapter push the cable onto the speedometer with a twisting motion until the catch is engaged.
11 Place the cluster in position to the instrument panel and engage the locating pins.
12 Install the instrument cluster retaining screws.
13 Install the plastic PRND21 cable clamp around the steering column, engaging the clamp locater pin in the slot in the column tube.
14 Start the clamp screw into the retaining clip but do not tighten it fully. Place the loop on the PRND21 cable over the pin on the shift lever.
15 With the transmission selector in the 'Drive' position, rotate the cable clamp around the column tube until the indicator pointer is centered on the 'D'. Tighten the clamp screw and move the lever through all shift positions, checking the pointer location.
16 Connect the battery negative cable.

19 Speedometer head – removal and installation

Note: *U.S. Federal law requires that the odometer in any replacement speedometer must register the same mileage as that registered in the removed speedometer.*
1   Disconnect the battery negative cable.
2   Remove the instrument cluster as described in Section 18.
3   If the cluster is equipped with a clock, remove the reset knob and retainer. Remove the 4 screws retaining the mask and lens to the backplate and remove the mask and lens.
4   Disconnect the speedometer cable at the back of the speedometer.
5   After removing the 2 attaching screws, remove the speedometer from the cluster.
6   To reinstall, place the speedometer in the backplate and install the 2 retaining screws.
7   Apply a $\frac{3}{16}$ inch ball of silicone damping grease to the speedometer head drive hole.
8   Place mask and lens in position on the backplate and install the 4 attaching screws. Install the clock reset knob and retainer (if equipped).
9   Install the instrument cluster as described in Section 18.
10 Connect the battery negative cable.

20 Speedometer cable – removal and installation

1   Disconnect the speedometer cable from the speedometer head.
2   Push the cable and grommet through the dash panel opening.
3   From underneath the vehicle, disengage the cable retaining clips.
4   Disconnect the cable at the transmission and remove the driven gear.
5   To install, connect the new cable to the driven gear and install to the transmission.
6   Engage the cable to the retaining clip at the marker tapes on the cable housing, route it through the dash panel opening and push the grommet in place.
7   From inside the vehicle, apply a $\frac{3}{16}$ in diameter ball of silicone damping grease in the speedometer head drive hole and install the cable.

21 Instrument printed circuit – removal and installation

1   The printed circuit that comprises the 'wiring' of the instrument panel should be handled as little as possible to avoid damage to the circuit sheet.
2   Disconnect the battery negative cable.
3   Remove the instrument cluster as described in Section 18.
4   Unsnap the printed circuit from the instrument voltage regulator.
5   Remove the illumination and indicator assemblies.
6   Remove the 2 screws retaining the cluster resistor and remove the resistor.
7   Remove the fuel gauge attaching nuts and remove the printed circuit.

10

8　To install, place the printed circuit over the backplate locating pins.
9　Install the illumination and indicator assemblies and fuel gauge attaching nuts.
10　Install the instrument cluster resistor.
11　Place the instrument voltage regulator in position, install the attaching screw and snap the printed circuit to the regulator.
12　Install the instrument cluster as described in Section 18.
13　Connect the battery negative cable.

22　Windshield wiper blade element – removal and installation

1　Locate the notch approximately 1 inch from the end of the blade element.
2　Stand the assembly on a firm surface with the notched end up. Be careful that the assembly is not braced against a painted surface which could be scratched.
3　Grasp the frame and push down so that the assembly is tightly bowed out and twist which will snap the element from the retaining tab.
4　Lift the wiper assembly and slide the blade element down the frame, until the notch is aligned with the locking tab. Twist the element to slip it out.
5　Installation is the reversal of removal.

23　Windshield wiper arm – removal and replacement

1　Before removing a wiper arm, turn the windshield wiper switch on and off to ensure the arms are in their normal parked position parallel with the bottom of the windshield.
2　To remove the arm, swing the arm away from the windshield, depress the spring clips in the wiper arm boss and pull the arm off the spindle.
3　When replacing the arm, position it in the parked position and push the boss onto the spindle.

24　Wiper motor – removal and installation

1　Disconnect the battery ground cable.
2　Remove the left hand wiper.
3　Remove the cowl top grille screws.
4　To gain access to the linkage drive arm, raise the forward left hand corner of the cowl guide. Remove the retaining clip from the motor output crank and disconnect the arm.

5　Disconnect the wiper motor wire connector.
6　Remove the motor-to-cowl panel bolts and remove the motor.
7　Installation is the reverse of removal.

25　Windshield washer assembly – removal, installation and adjustment

1　Use a small screwdriver to unlock the tabs and disconnect the electrical connector. Remove the retaining screws and lift the washer reservoir and motor assembly from the vehicle.
2　Drain the reservoir by disconnecting the hose with a small screwdriver.
3　Pry out the retaining ring which holds the motor in the reservoir.
4　Grasp one wall around the electrical terminals with a pair of pliers and pull the motor, seal and impeller assembly out. If the impeller and seal become separated they can be reassembled. Inspect the reservoir for foreign matter before installing the old motor in a new reservoir.
5　Prior to installation, lubricate the outside of the seal with powdered graphite for ease of assembly.
6　Position the small projection on the motor end cap with the slot in the reservoir and assemble so that the seal seats against the bottom of the motor cavity.
7　Use a 1 inch twelve-point socket to hand press the retaining ring against the motor end plate.
8　Fill the reservoir and check for leaks.
9　The cowl mounted nozzle jets can be adjusted for the proper spray pattern by carefully bending them with needle-nosed pliers, taking care not to crimp them.
10　The rear mounted (station wagon) nozzles are adjusted by inserting a paper clip into the hole and rotating the socket until the proper spray pattern is achieved.

26　Radio – removal and installation

1　Disconnect the battery negative cable.
2　Disconnect the electrical power leads, speaker and antenna lead-in cable.
3　Remove the control knobs, nuts and retainers.
4　Remove the ash tray and bracket.
5　Remove the radio rear support attaching nut.
6　Remove the instrument panel lower reinforcement and air conditioning ducts (if equipped).
7　Remove the radio receiver assembly from the bezel and the rear support, lowering it from the instrument panel.
8　Installation is the reverse of removal.

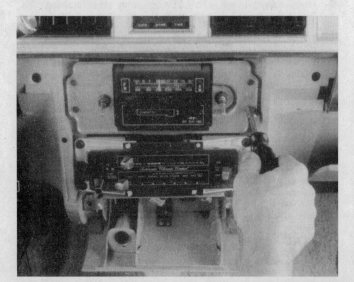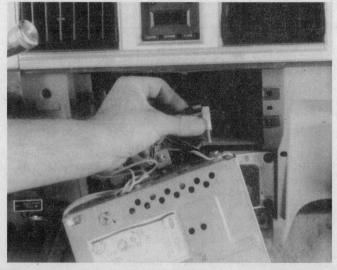

Fig. 10.6　Typical radio installation (Sec 26)

27 Power window switch – removal and installation

2-door

1 Disconnect the battery negative cable.
2 Remove the switch bezel retaining screw and bezel. Remove by pivoting the bezel outward and up.
3 Pry the switch carefully from the electrical connector which retains it, using a small screwdriver.
4 To install, position the switch in alignment with the connector and press firmly in place.
5 The rest of installation is the reverse of removal.

4-door

6 Perform steps 1 and 2.
7 Disconnect the electrical connector from the switch and bezel.
8 Installation is the reversal of removal.

28 Power window motor – removal and installation

Front door (4-door models)

1 Raise the window to the full up position if possible. If the glass cannot be raised to the up position, it must be supported so that it will not fall into the door wall.
2 Disconnect the battery negative cable.
3 Remove the door trim panel and watershield as described in Chapter 12.
4 Disconnect the motor electrical leads and move them out of the way.
5 Use a $\frac{3}{4}$ inch hole saw with a $\frac{1}{4}$ inch pilot, drill a hole at the dimple Remove the drillings from the door.
6 Grind the sheet metal interference away from the upper motor mount screw head.
7 Prior to the motor drive assembly removal make sure that the regulator arm is in a fixed position so that the counterbalance spring can't unwind.
8 Remove the mounting screws and disengage the motor and drive assembly from the quadrant gear.
9 Install the new motor and drive assembly and tighten the motor mount screws fully.
10 Connect the electrical wiring plug and install the trim.

Rear door (4-door models)

11 Perform steps 1 through 3.
12 Use a $\frac{3}{4}$ inch hole saw with a $\frac{1}{4}$ inch pilot to drill at the existing dimples in the door inner panel.
13 Before removing the motor drive assembly, make sure that the regulator arm is in the fixed position. Remove the window motor mounting screws and disengage the motor and drive assembly from the regulator. If the window glass is in the down position, use a screwdriver to disengage the drive gear from the regulator.
14 Install the new motor and drive assembly.
15 Connect the electrical wiring plug and install the door trim as described in Chapter 12.

2-door models

16 Perform steps 1 through 3.
17 Use a drift punch to remove the center pin from each of the four rivets retaining the door regulator to the inner door panel. Drill out the remainder of each rivet, using a $\frac{1}{4}$ drill, being careful not to enlarge the rivet hole.
18 Slide the regulator square from the glass bracket C frame. Make sure that the glass is supported in the full up position.
19 Move the regulator base to the inner panel access hole so that counterbalance spring can be reached for removal. Use a C clamp to clamp the regulator base to the inner door panel.
20 Obtain or fabricate a tool for releasing the tension in the counterbalance spring. This can be made by cutting a slot $\frac{1}{8}$ in wide and $\frac{1}{2}$ in deep in a $\frac{5}{8}$ in diameter socket ($\frac{1}{2}$ in drive) and using a 6 in or 10 in extension with a ratchet or breaking bar for leverage. When releasing the tension in the counterbalance spring, be very careful to check that the regulator is in the fixed position as described in Step 18.

21 Release the C clamp and move the regulator so that the motor and drive assembly retaining screws are accessible through the radio speaker opening.
22 Clamp the regulator base to the door inner panel. Remove the motor and drive assembly retaining screws.
23 Remove the C clamp and disengage the regulator motor and drive assembly from the quadrant gear.
24 Install the new motor and drive assembly.
25 Clamp the regulator in place at the large access hole and reinstall the counterbalance spring. This spring must be installed in the same poisition as prior to removal or the window travel action will be reversed.
26 Release the C clamp and engage the square slide into the glass bracket channel.
27 Place the regulator in position at the retaining holes and install $\frac{1}{4}$ in x $\frac{1}{2}$ in bolts with washers and nuts.
28 Reconnect the wiring and install the door trim.

29 Stop light switch – removal and replacement

1 Disconnect the negative battery cable.
2 Above the brake pedal near the pivot, remove the electrical wires from the switch.
3 Unclip the pushrod retainer and slide the switch, nylon washers and pushrod away from the pedal.
4 Slide the switch off the bracket.
5 Refit the stop light switch in reverse order of removal.

30 Grid-type heated rear window defogger – testing and repair

1 The rear window defogger consists of a rear window with a number of horizontal elements that are baked onto the glass.
2 Small breaks in the element system can be successfully repaired without removing the rear window.
3 To test the grids for proper operation, start the engine and turn on the system.
4 Use a strong light inside the vehicle to visually inspect the wire grid from the outside. A broken wire will appear as a brown spot.
5 From inside the car, use a 12-volt DC voltmeter and contact the broad reddish brown strips on the back window. The meter reading should be 10 to 13 volts. A lower voltage reading indicates a loose connection on the ground side of the glass.
6 Make a good ground contact with the meters' negative lead. The voltage should remain the same.
7 Ground the meter negative lead and touch each grid line at its midpoint with the positive lead. The reading should be approximately 6 volts, indicating the line is good.
8 No reading indicates that the line is broken between the midpoint of the line and the side.
9 A reading of 12 volts means that the circuit is broken between the midpoint and passenger side or the grounding pigtail on the passenger

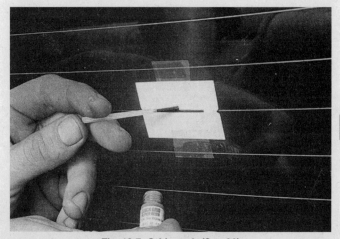

Fig. 10.7 Grid repair (Sec 30)

10

side of the glass is loose.

10 Once the area needing repair is determined, it is recommended that a grid repair kit be obtained from a dealer.

11 Clean the area to be repaired with alcohol to remove dirt, grease or other foreign material.

12 With the area clean and dry, mark the spot to be repaired on the outside of the glass.

13 Shake the bottle of grid repair compound for at least one minute and shake it frequently during use. The compound and the glass must be at room temperature.

14 Mask the area above and below the break with electrical tape so that the gap is the same as the width of the grid.

15 Apply several smooth continous strokes of the coating, using the brush applicator cap. The repair coating should extend $\frac{1}{4}$ in on both sides of the break.

16 Allow the repair to dry for at least 3 minutes and remove the tape. The repair can be energized within 3 minutes. Optimum hardness occurs after 24 hours.

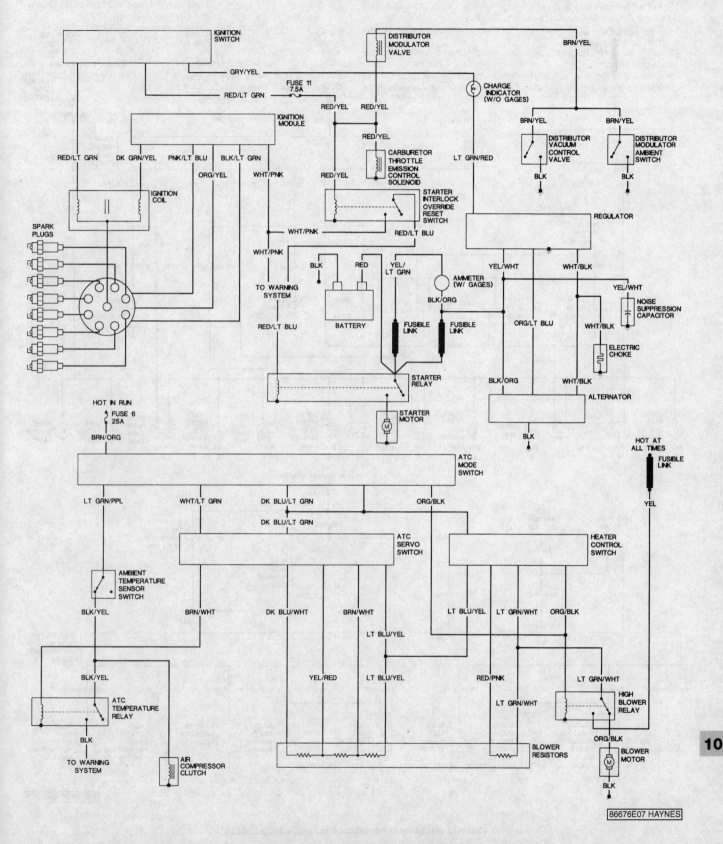

Engine control and chassis electrical schematic - 1975 V8 engine models (1 of 2)

86676E07 HAYNES

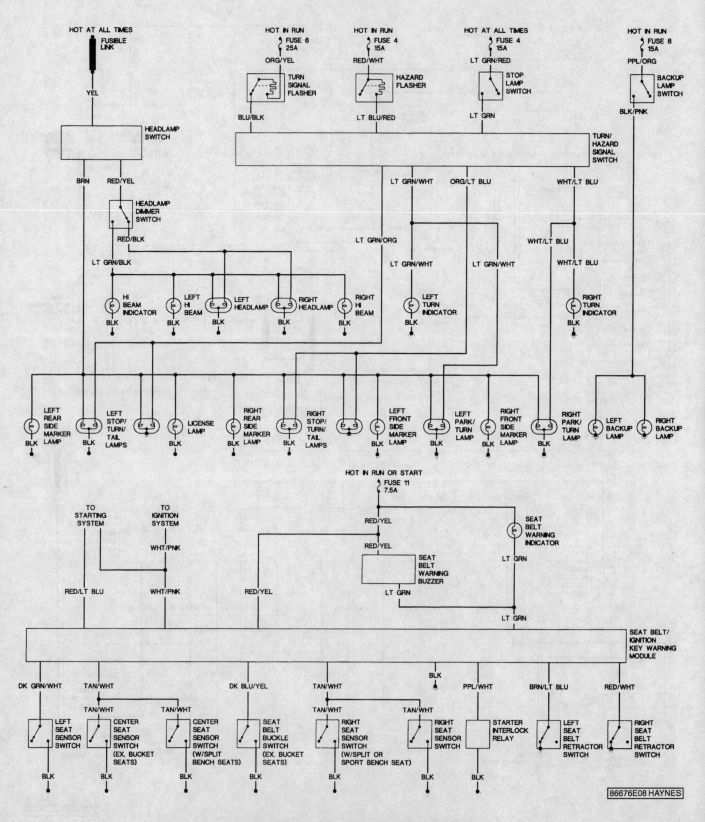

Chassis electrical schematic continued - 1975 (2 of 2)

86676E08 HAYNES

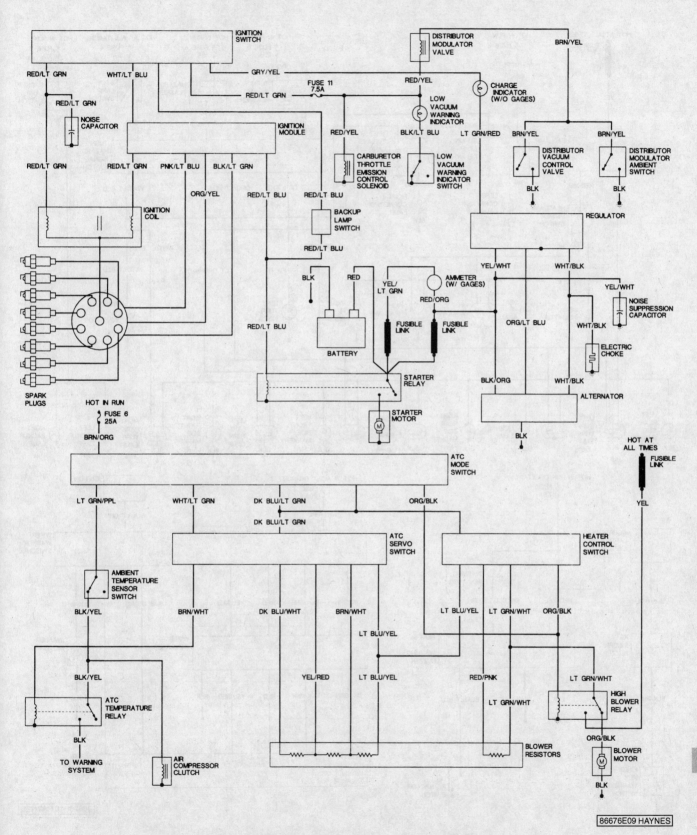

Engine control and chassis electrical schematic - 1976 V8 engine models (1 of 2)

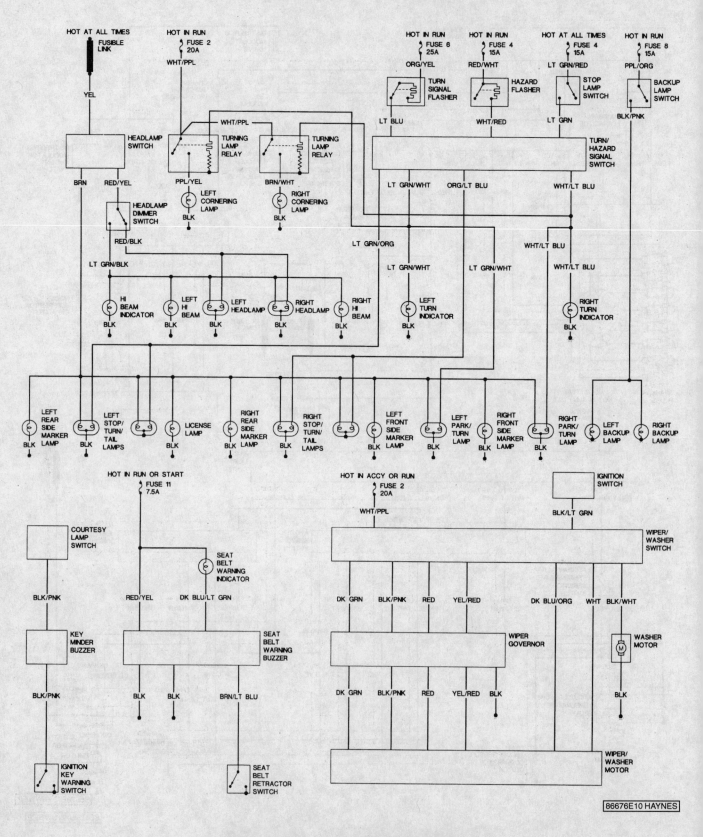

Chassis electrical schematic continued - 1976 (2 of 2)

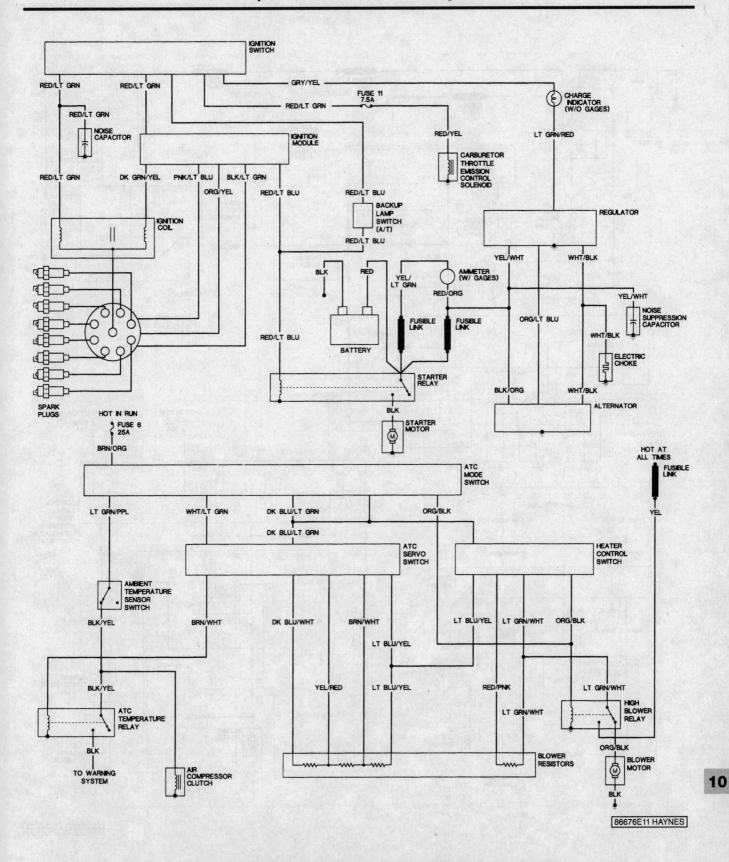

Engine control and chassis electrical schematic - 1977 V8 engine models

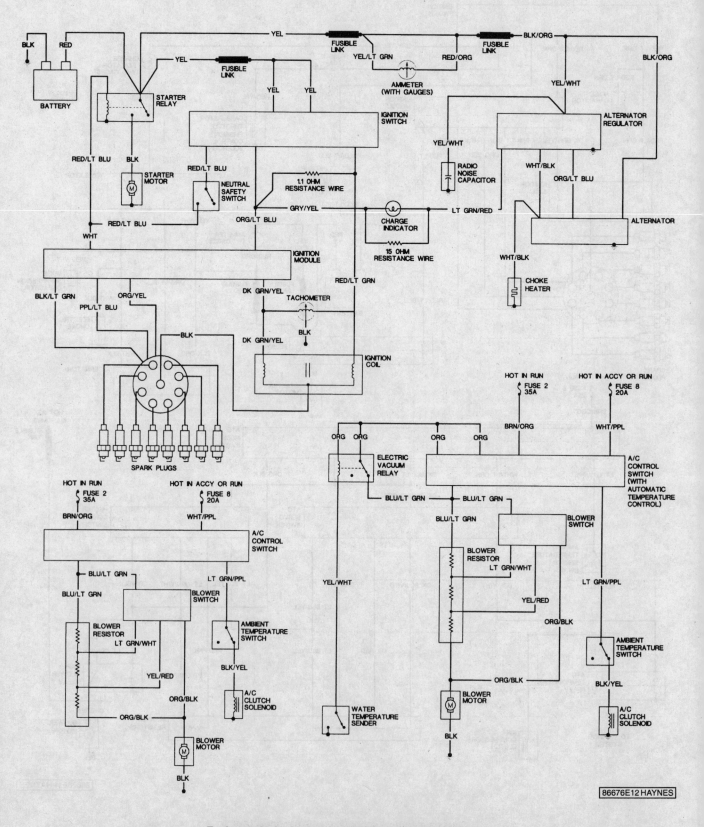

Engine control schematic - 1978 V8 engine models (1 of 3)

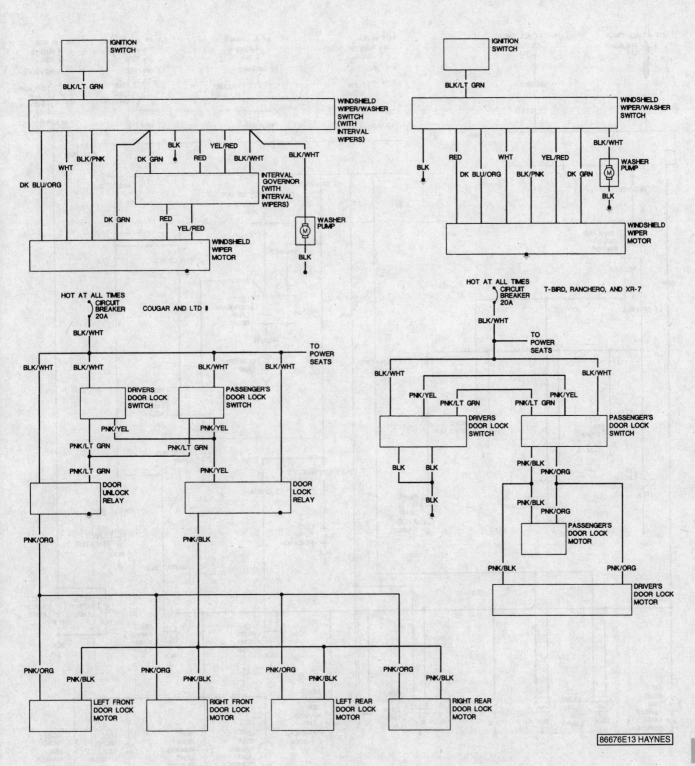

Chassis electrical schematic - 1978 models (2 of 3)

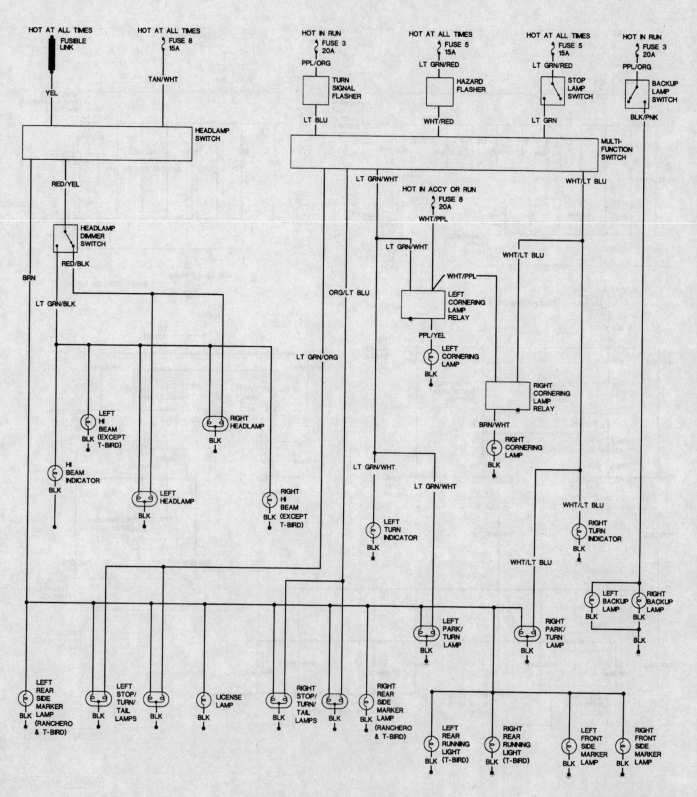

Chassis electrical schematic continued - 1978 models (3 of 3)

86676E14 HAYNES

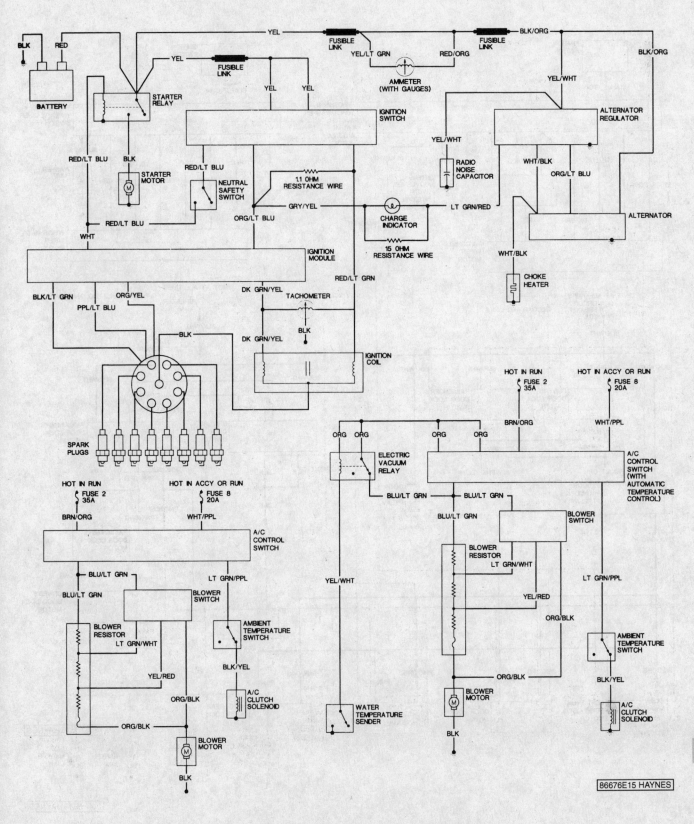

Engine control schematic - 1979 V8 engine models (1 of 3)

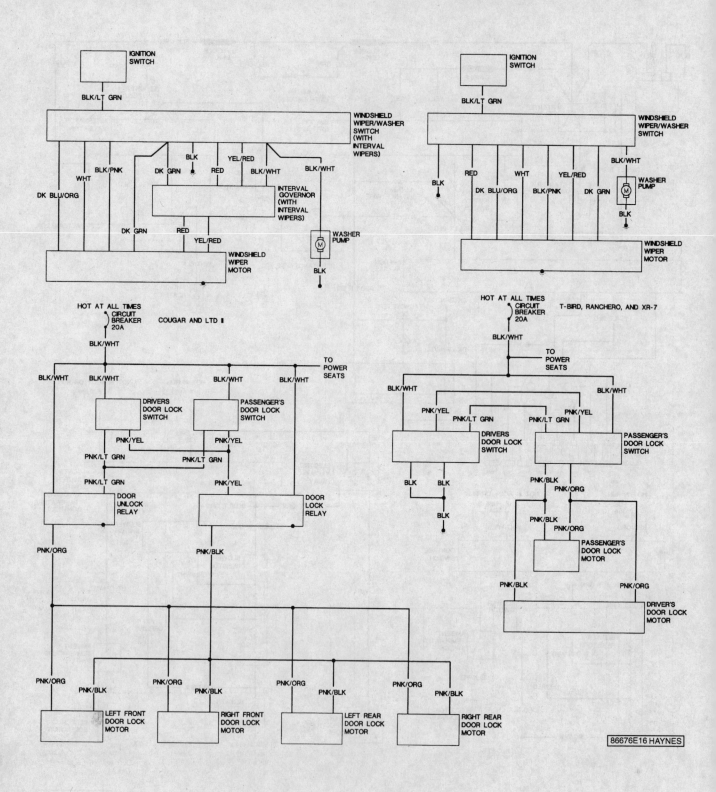

Chassis electrical schematic - 1979 models (2 of 3)

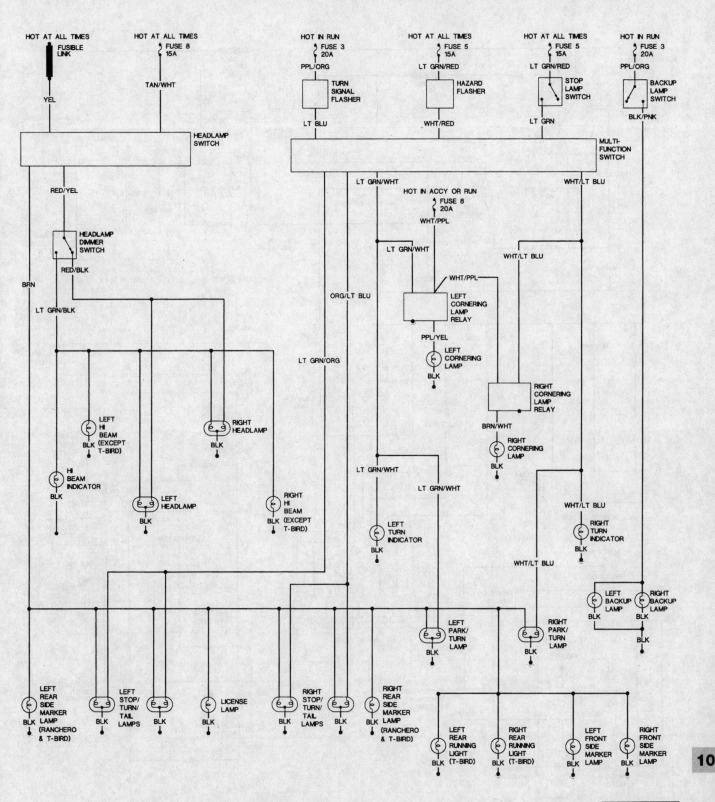

Chassis electrical schematic continued - 1979 models (3 of 3)

10

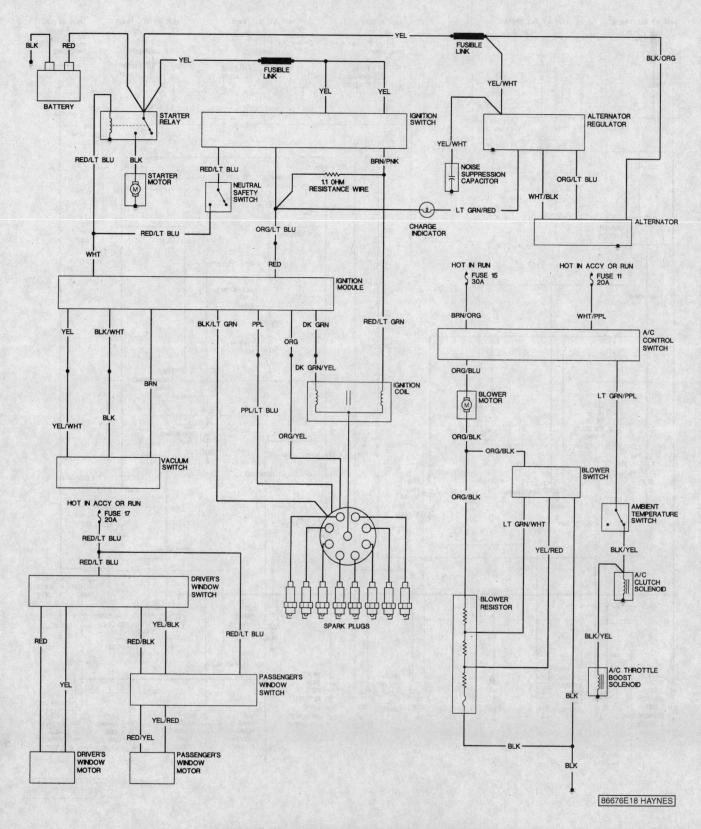

Engine control schematic - 1980 V8 engine models (1 of 3)

86676E18 HAYNES

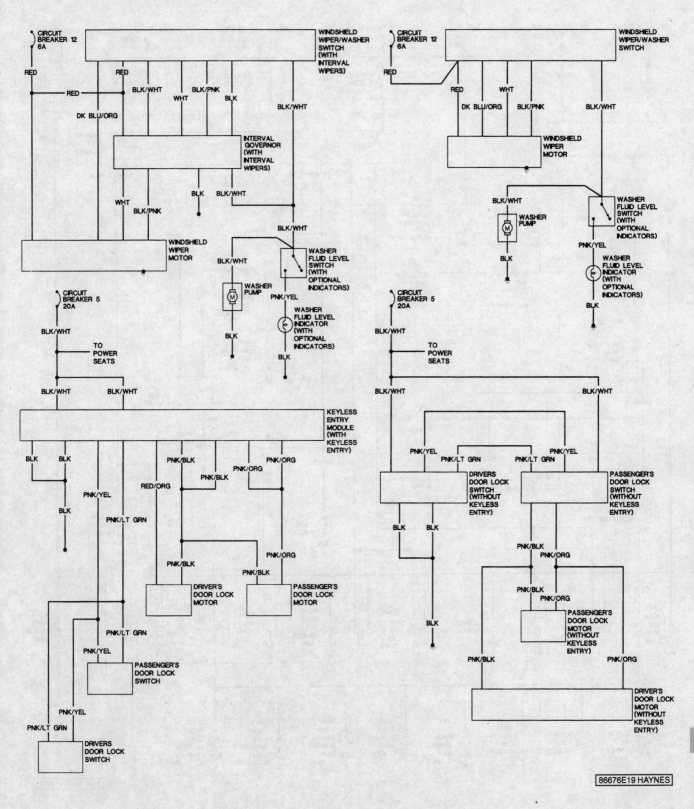

Chassis electrical schematic - 1980 models (2 of 3)

86676E19 HAYNES

10

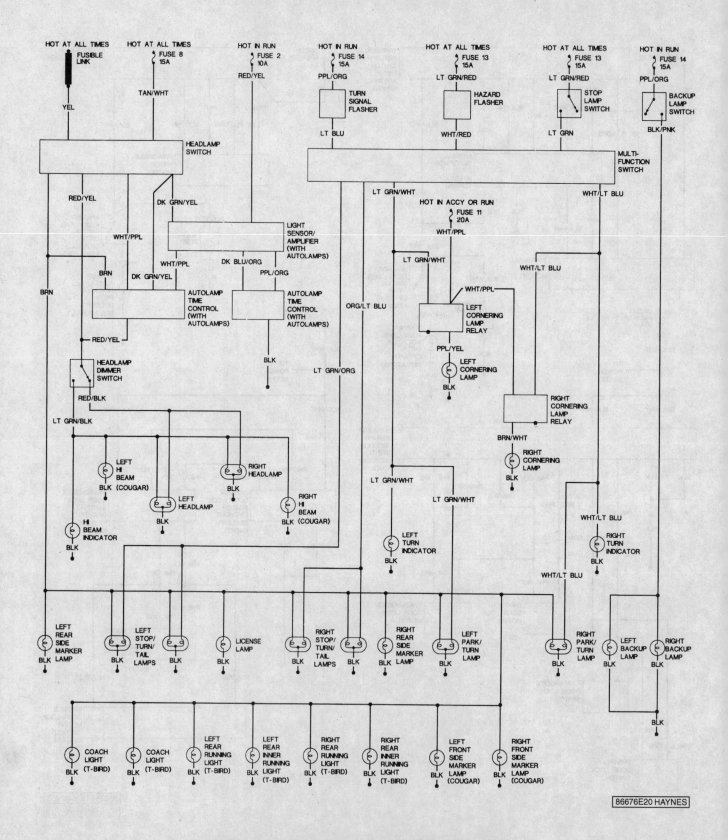

Chassis electrical schematic continued - 1980 models (3 of 3)

86676E20 HAYNES

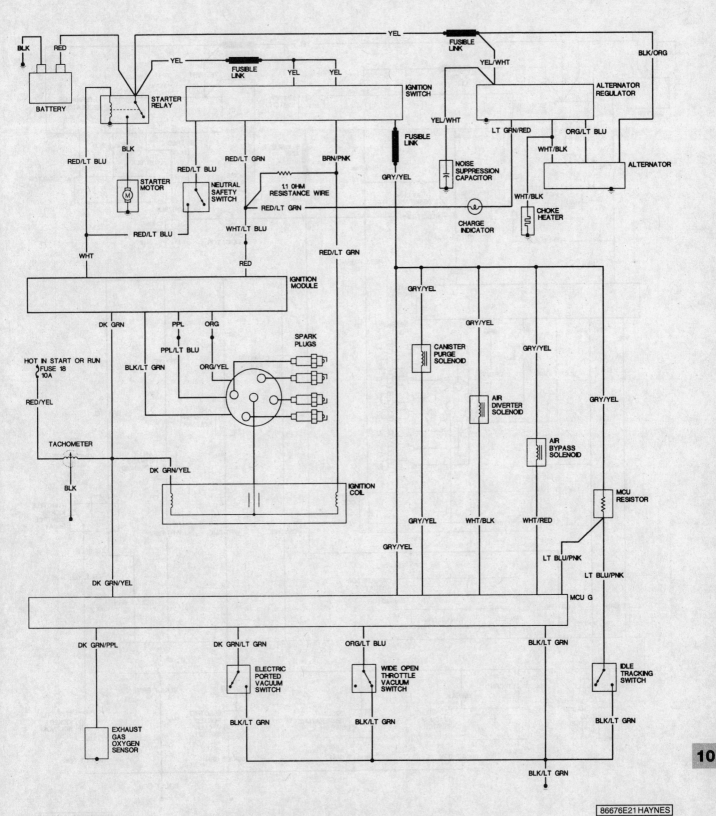

Engine control schematic - 1981 4 cylinder engine models

86676E21 HAYNES

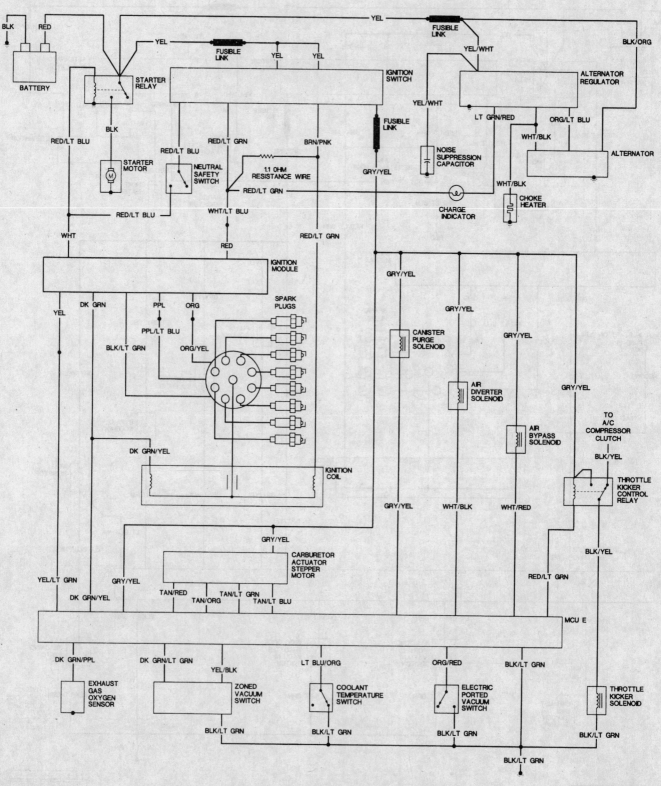

Engine control schematic - 1981 V8 engine models

86676E23 HAYNES

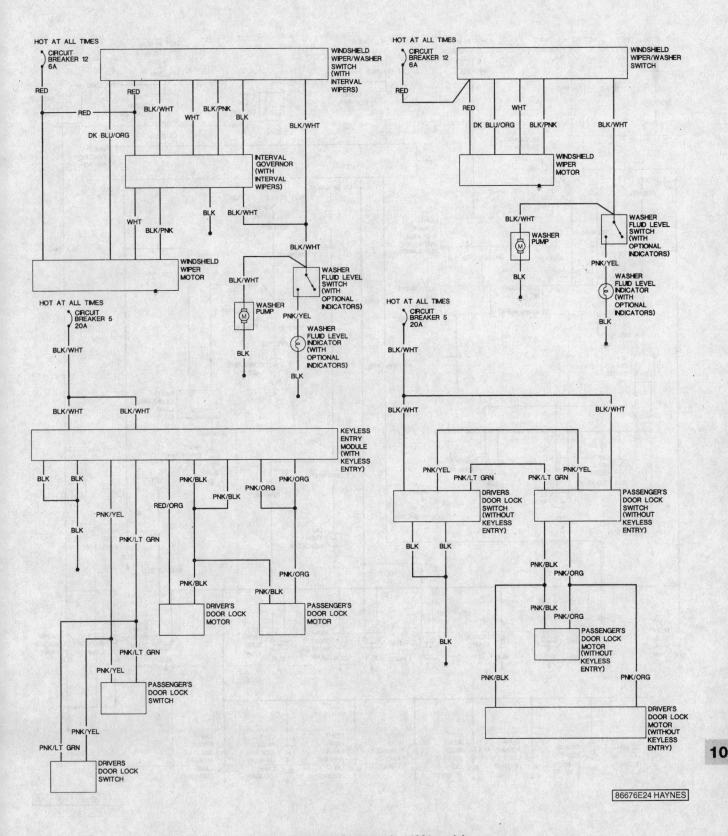

Chassis electrical schematic - 1981 models

86676E24 HAYNES

10

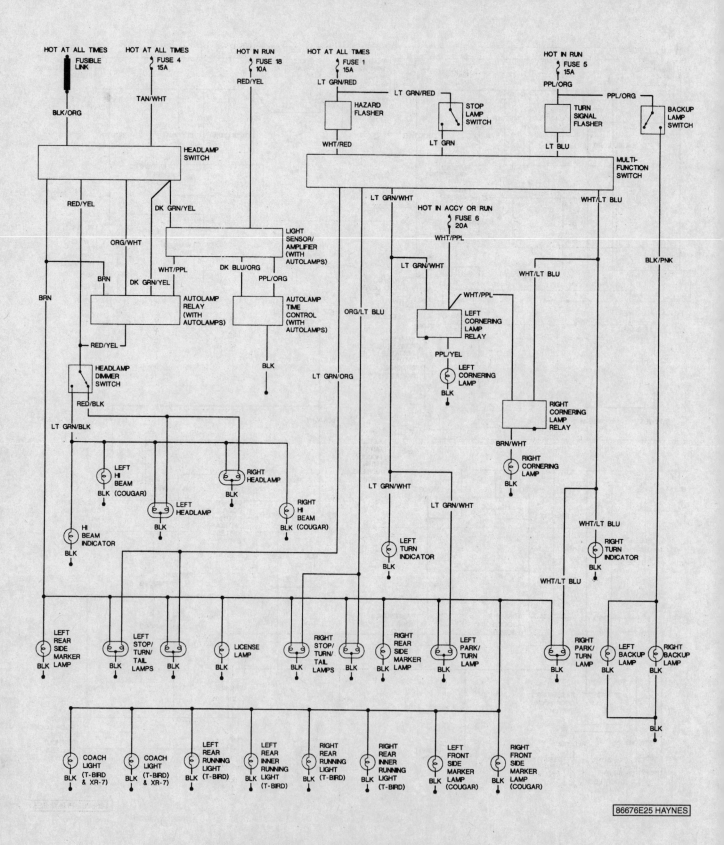

Chassis electrical schematic continued - 1981 models

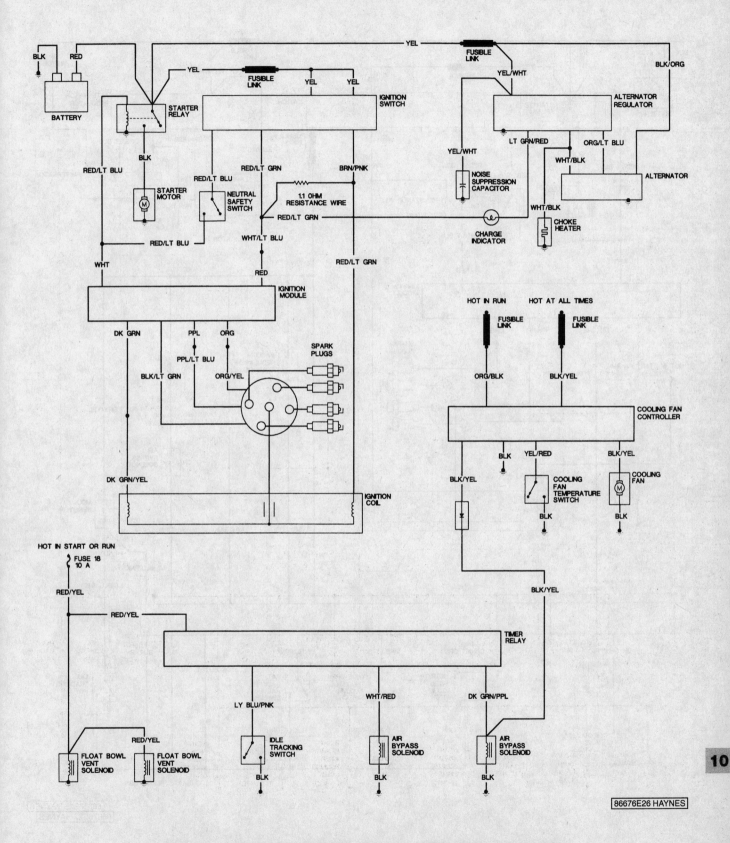

Engine control schematic - 49 states and Canada; 1982 4 cylinder engine models

86676E26 HAYNES

10

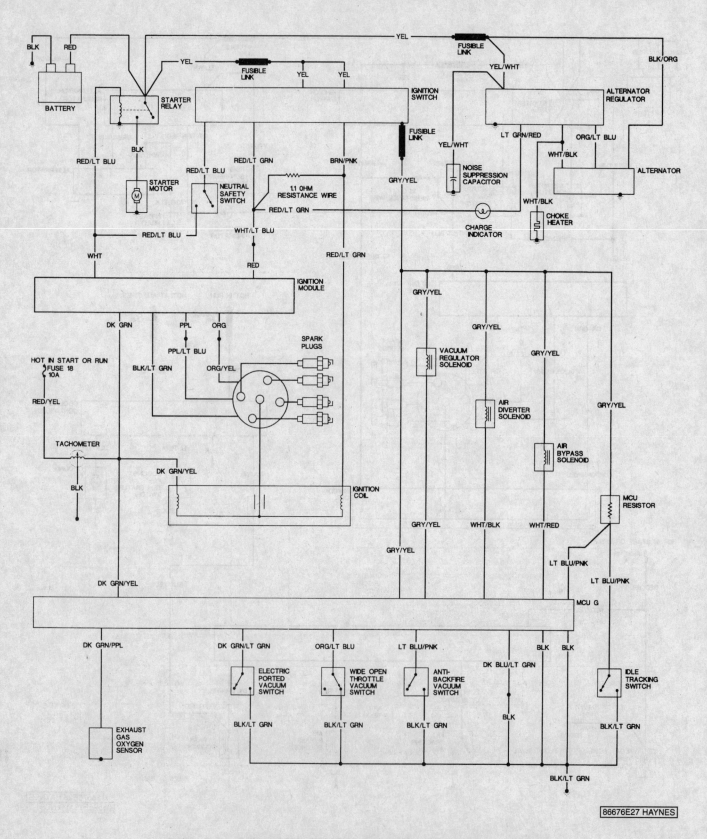

Engine control schematic - California models; 1982 4 cylinder engine models

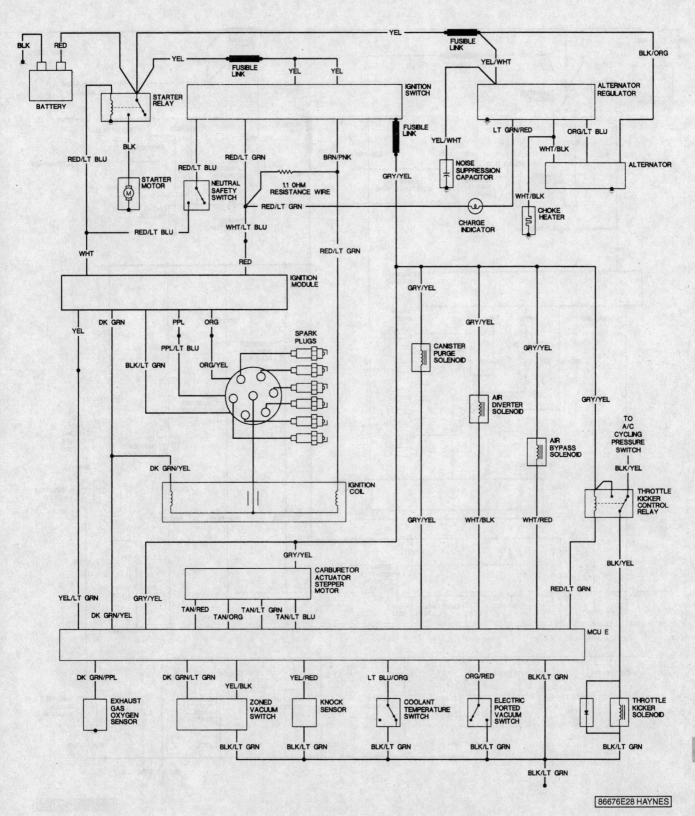

Engine control schematic - 1982 V6 engine models

10

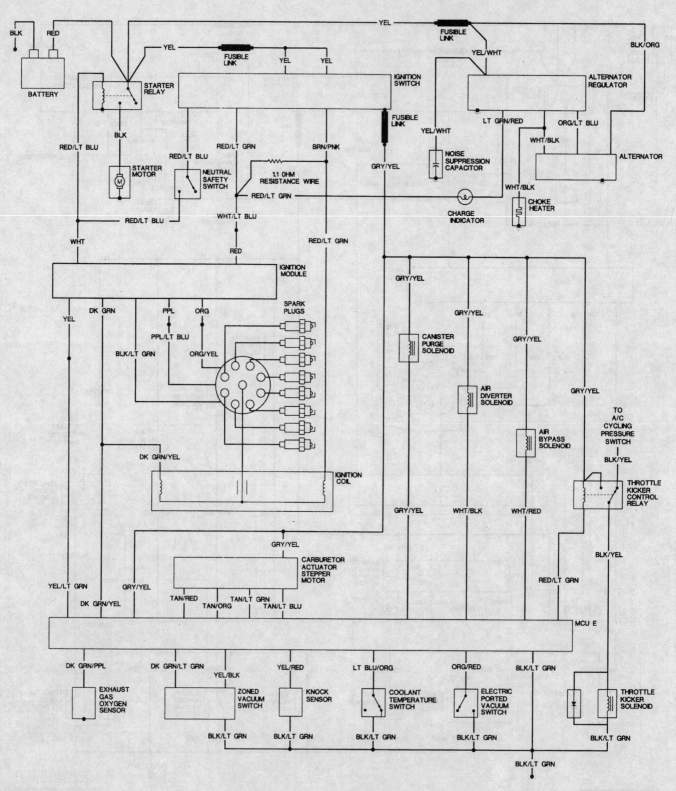

Engine control schematic - 1982 V8 engine models

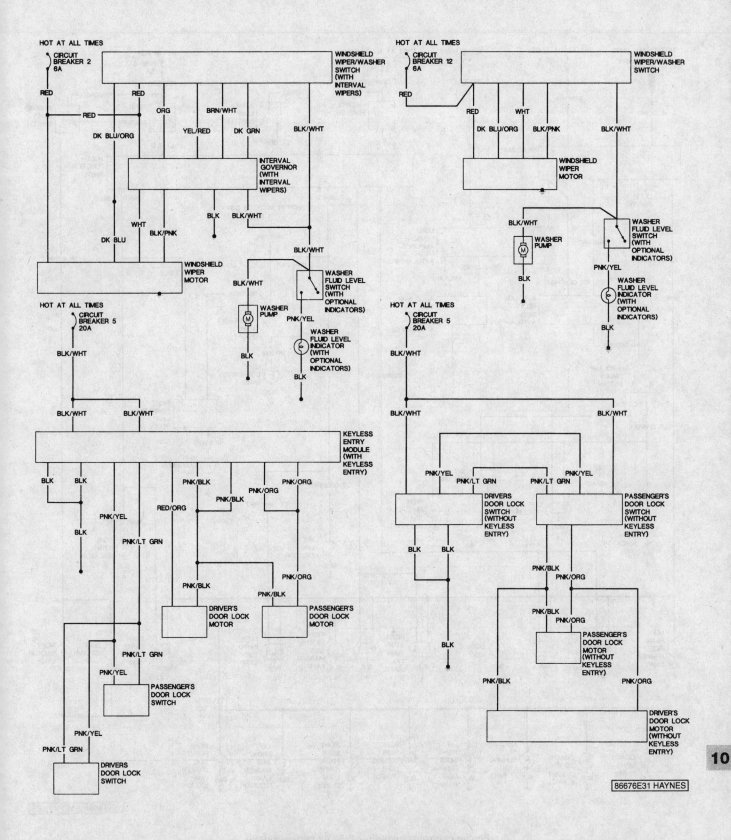

Chassis electrical schematic - 1982 models

86676E31 HAYNES

10

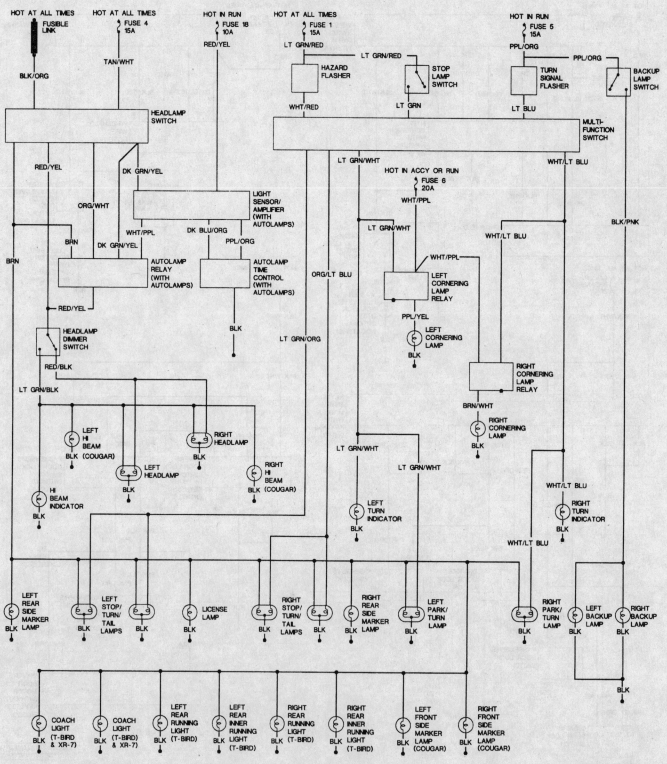

Chassis electrical schematic - 1982 models

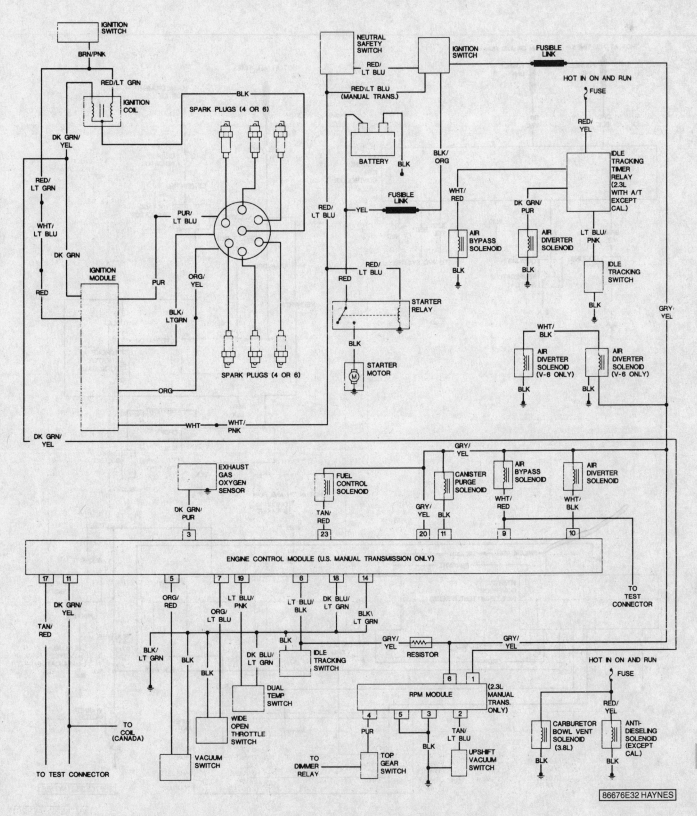

Engine control schematic - 1983 Marquis and LTD with 4 and 6-cylinder engines

10

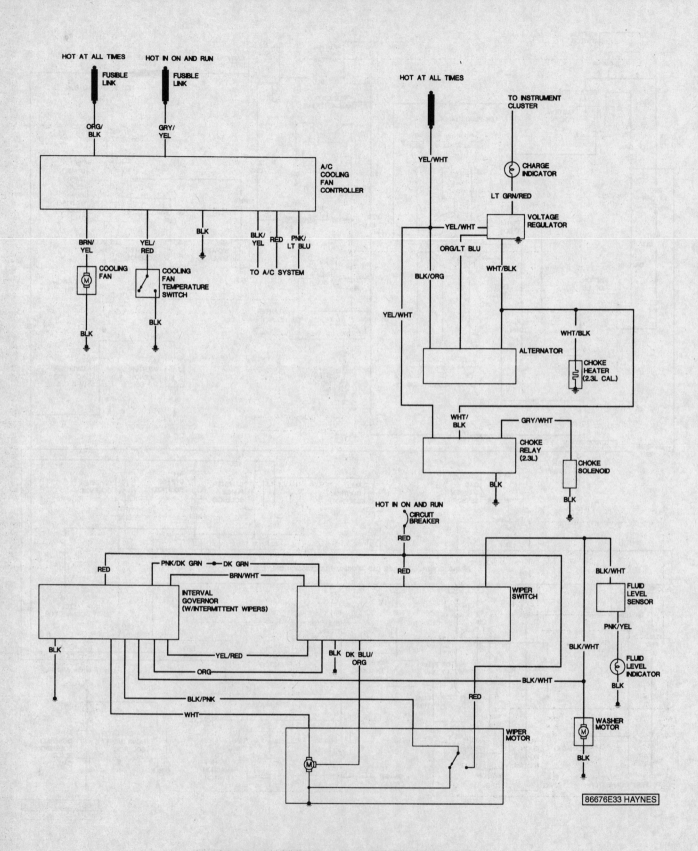

Chassis electrical schematic - 1983 Marquis and LTD

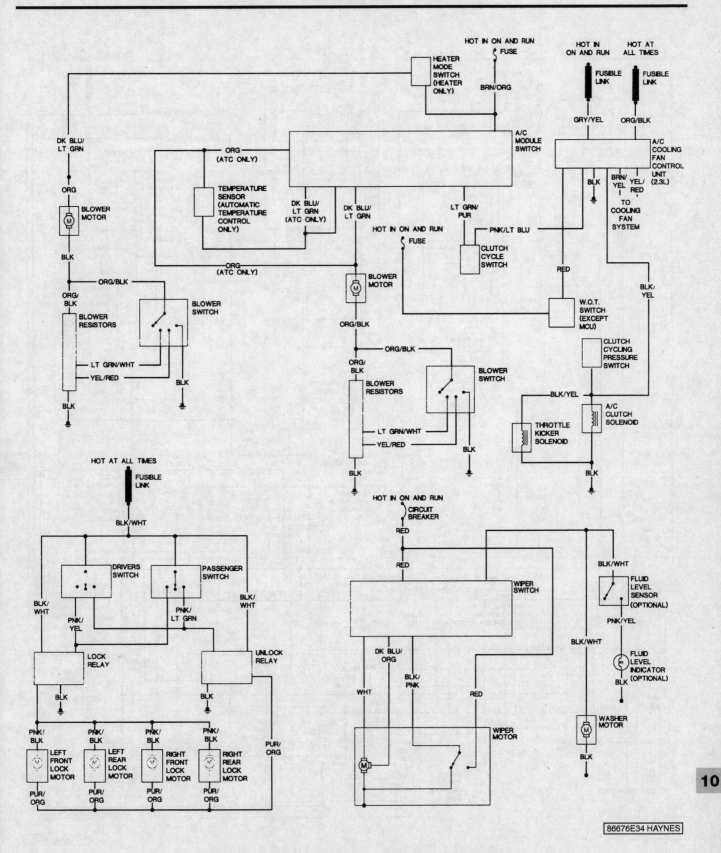

Chassis electrical schematic continued - 1983 Marquis and LTD

86676E34 HAYNES

10

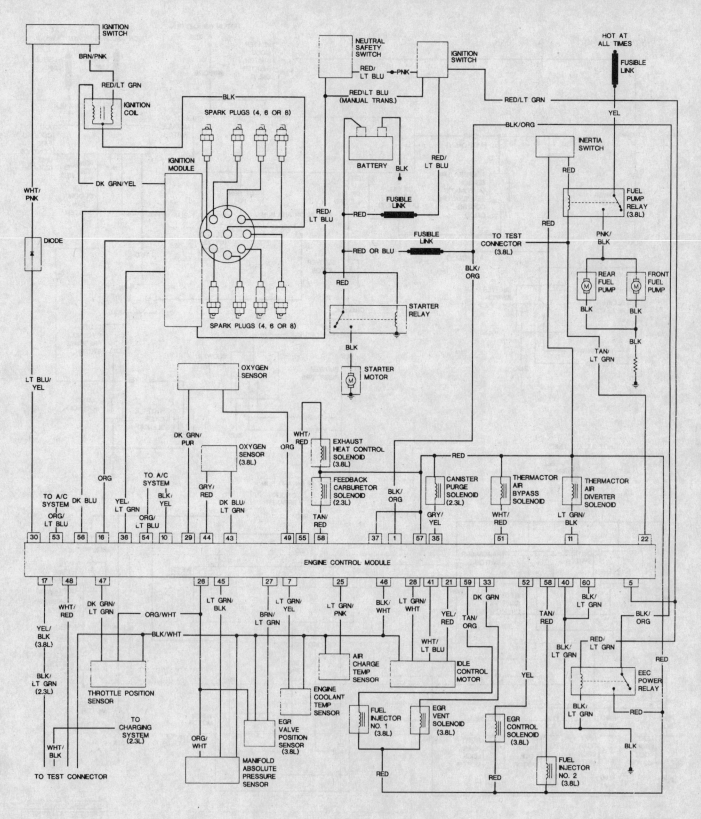

Engine control schematic - 1984 Marquis and LTD with 4-cylinder, V6 and V8 engines

86676E39 HAYNES

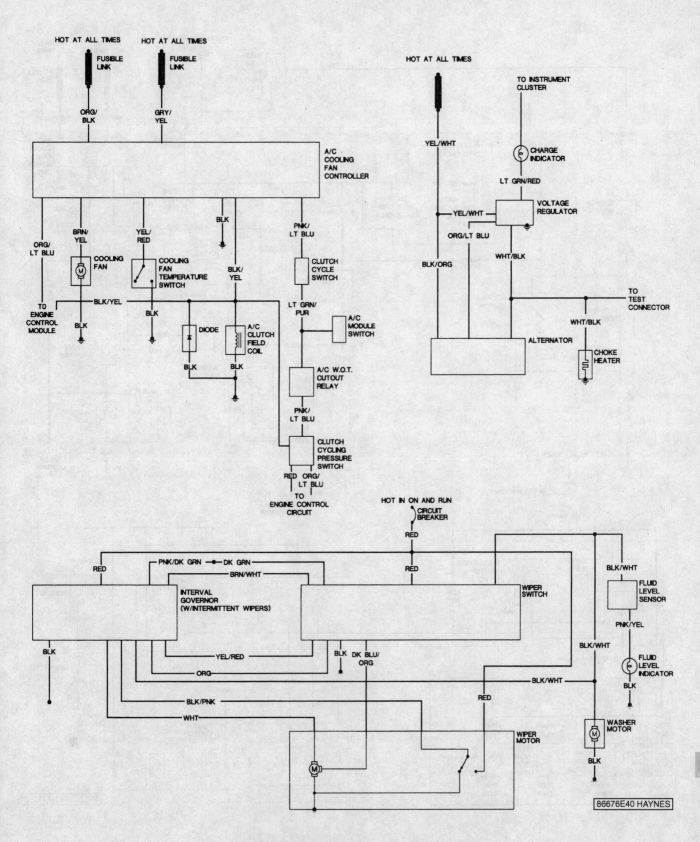

Chassis electrical schematic - 1984 Marquis and LTD

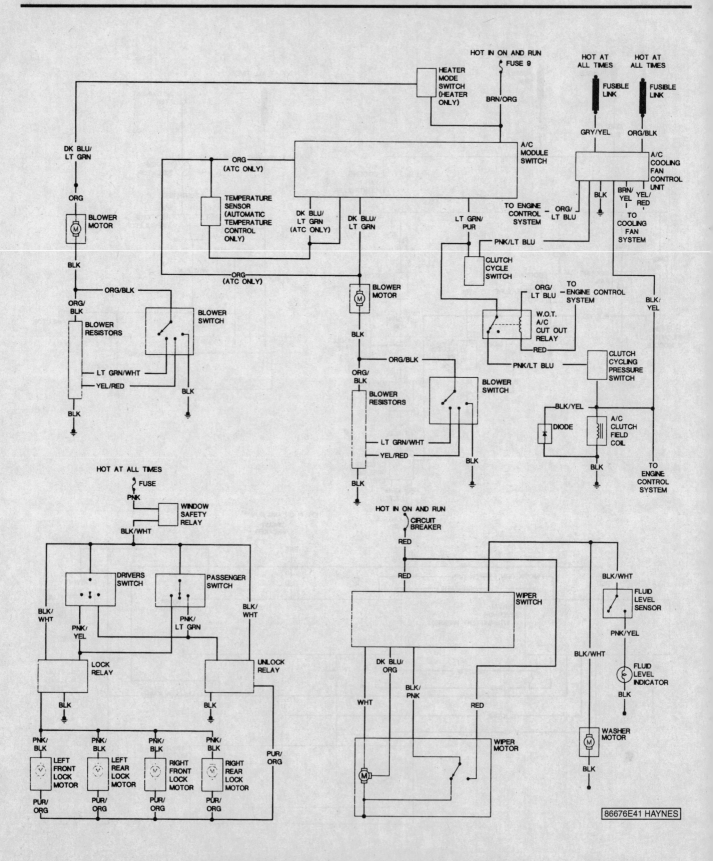

Chassis electrical schematic continued - 1984 Marquis and LTD

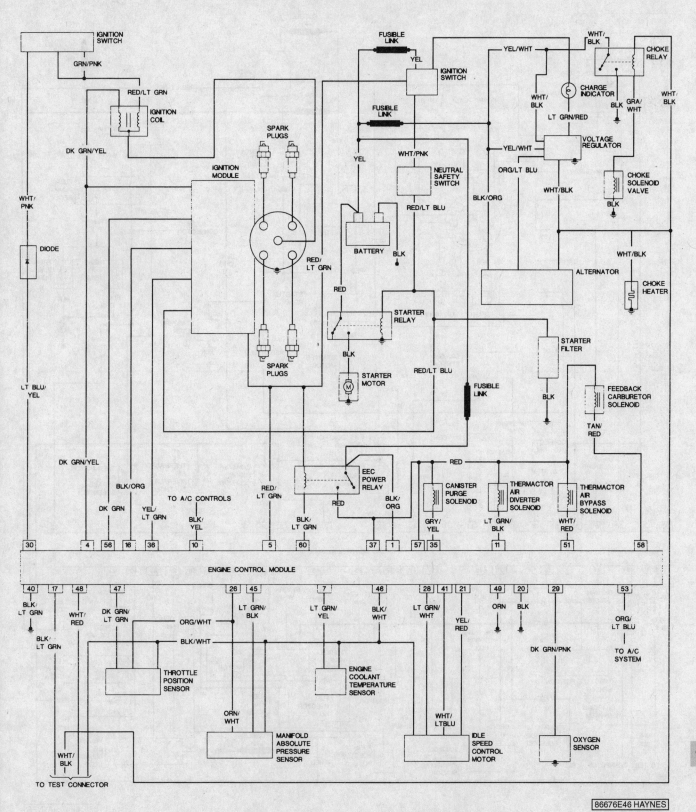

Engine control schematic - 1985 Marquis and LTD with 4-cylinder engine

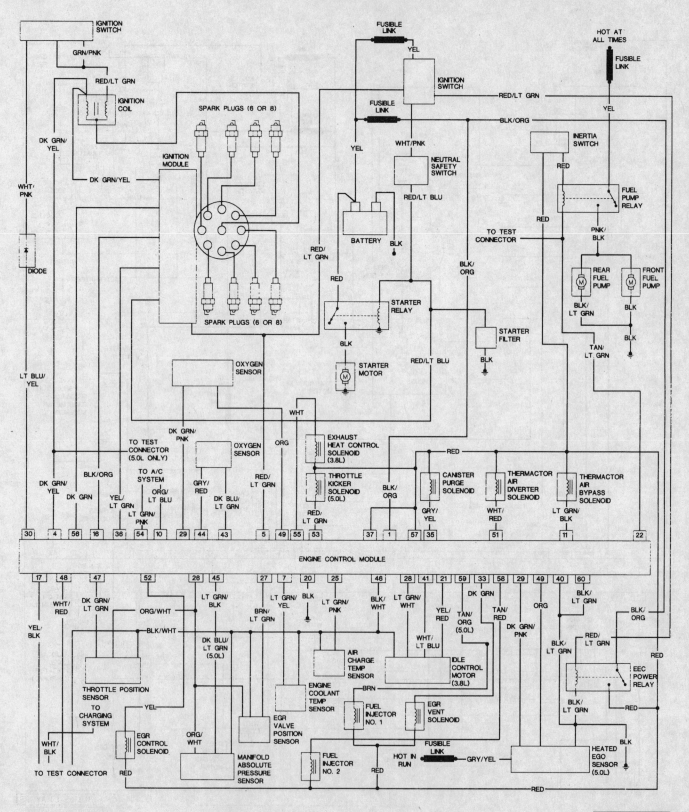

Engine control schematic - 1985 Marquis and LTD with V6 and V8 engine

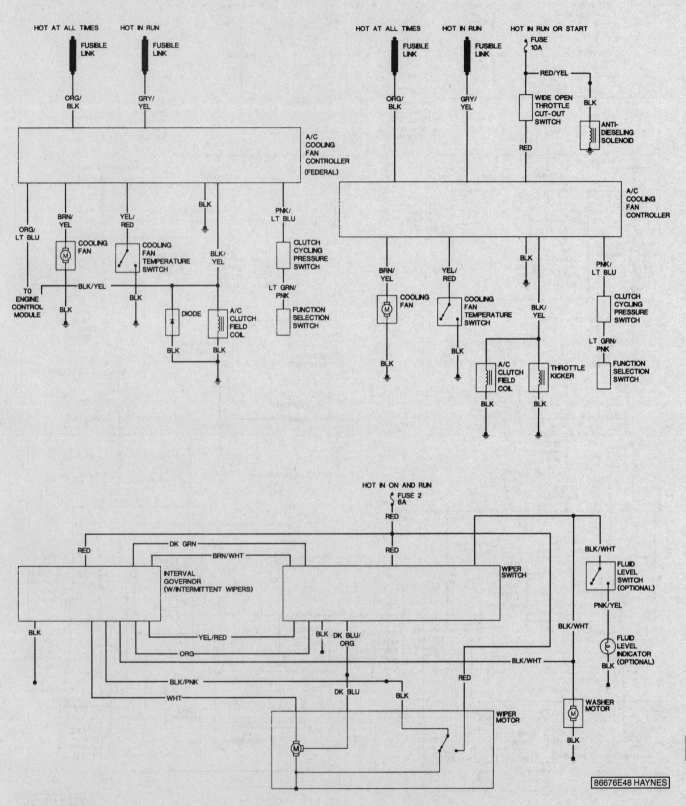

Chassis electrical schematic - 1985 Marquis and LTD

86676E48 HAYNES

10

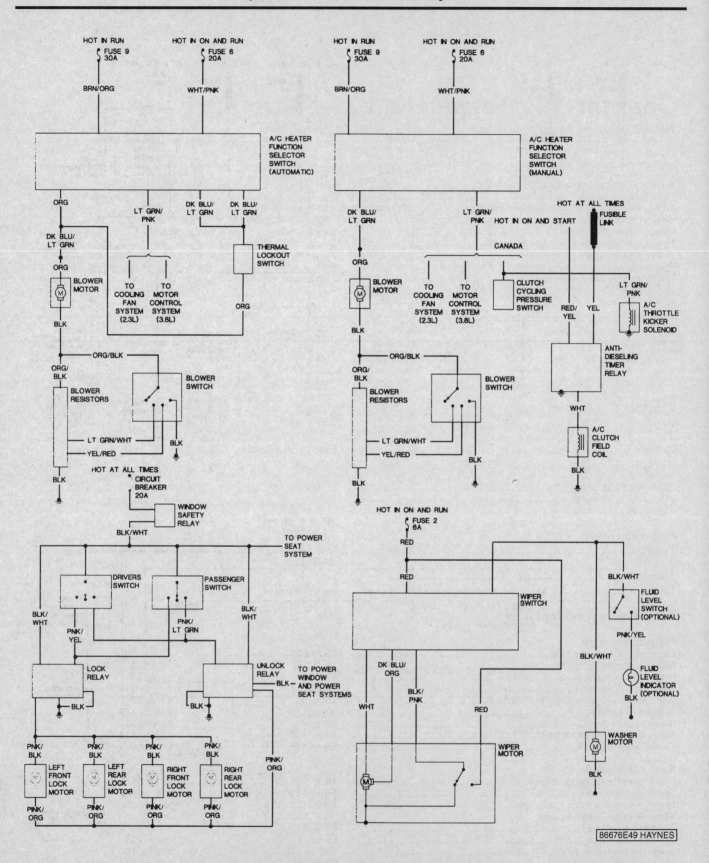

Chassis electrical schematic continued - 1985 Marquis and LTD

86676E49 HAYNES

Chapter 11 Suspension and steering

Refer to Chapter 13 for specifications and information on later models

Contents

Specifications

Front suspension
Type .... Modified MacPherson strut

Toe-in
Sedan, all .... $\frac{3}{16}$ to $\frac{5}{16}$ in
Wagon, all .... $\frac{1}{16}$ to $\frac{3}{16}$ in

Caster .... Preset, non-adjustable

Camber
1978 and 1979 sedan .... $\frac{3}{4}°$ pos.
1980 and 1981 sedan .... $\frac{7}{8}°$ pos.
Wagon, all .... $\frac{1}{2}°$ pos.

Rear suspension
Type .... Four link design with coil springs and hydraulic telescopic shock absorbers

Steering
Type .... Rack and pinion

Torque wrench settings	ft-lb	Nm
Front suspension		
Lower arm-to-crossmember	200 to 220	271 to 298
Sway bar mounting clamp	14 to 26	19 to 39
Sway bar-to-lower arm	9 to 12	12 to 16
Spindle-to-shock strut	150 to 180	203 to 244
Sway bar mounting bracket-to-underbody	35 to 50	47 to 68
Balljoint-to-spindle	80 to 120	108 to 163
Shock upper mount	60 to 75	81 to 102
Steering gear-to-crossmember	90 to 100	122 to 136
Tie-rod end-to-spindle	35 to 47	47 to 64
Rear suspension		
Shock absorber-to-upper mount	14 to 26	19 to 35
Upper arm-to-frame	85 to 120	115 to 162
Upper arm-to-axle	70 to 100	95 to 135
Shock absorber lower mount		
1978 thru 1980	40 to 45	54 to 74
1981 Torx-type	65 to 70	88 to 95
Lower arm-to-frame (bolt)	100 to 110	135 to 150
Lower arm-to-axle (nut)	90 to 100	122 to 135
Stabilizer bar to lower arm		
1978 thru 1979	30 to 40	41 to 54
1980 thru 1981	18 to 20	24 to 27

11

1   General information

The front suspension fitted to all models is modified MacPherson strut comprising a shock absorber/strut assembly, coil spring, and lower A-arm.

Each front wheel rotates on a spindle, the upper end mounted to the lower strut and the lower end to the A-arm. The lower spindle is attached with a balljoint.

The upper end of the strut is attached to the body structure through an insulator bushing.

The coil spring mounts between the front frame crossmember and the lower A-arm. To control body roll in corners a front stabilizer bar is fitted.

Each rear wheel, hub and brake drum assembly is bolted to the rear axle shaft flange and the wheel and axle shaft rotates in the rear axle housing.

The rear axle housing rests on a spring assembly suspended from hangers integral with the body. Location of the axle assembly is controlled by four pressed steel arms. Two of the arms connect the bodywork to the axle housing center, two others connect the housing at the outer ends of the axle. Rubber insulated shock absorbers are fitted at each side.

The steering gear is rack and pinion type with power assistance as optional. The steering wheel is connected to the gear through a collapsible shaft and flexible couplings.

A tie-rod is attached to each end of the rack joint which allows the tie-rod to move with any deflection in the front suspension unit. The rack and pinion assembly ends are sealed by rubber bellows.

Couplings attached to the tie-rods are retained on the rack and pinned with roll pins. The rack, housing, valve assembly and rack piston are rebuildable.

The steering column is of the safety type. A locking mechanism is actuated by depressing the button located on the steering column. This prevents inadvertent locking of the steering wheel by blocking the actuator out of the lock position.

The outer column tube terminates just below the attachment to the brake support bracket. Energy absorption is accomplished by the lower column mounting bracket. There is no shift tube in this assembly.

The steering shaft has a machined bar with grooves in the lower half designed to accept two anti-rattle clips. The lower shaft comprises an upper section that is a formed tube to fit into the upper shaft.

The column is secured to the brake support brackets bolted to the flanges on the brake support. The lower column attaching collar contains a sintered iron ring with internal protrusions. These protrusions act as a guide which deforms the outer tube as the column collapses.

2   Front wheel bearings – removal and installation

1   Chock the rear wheels, apply the parking brake, loosen the front wheel nuts, jack up the front of the car and support on firmly based axle stands. Remove the roadwheel.
2   Refer to Chapter 9 and detach the disc brake caliper.
3   Carefully remove the grease cap from the hub.
4   Withdraw the cotter pin and lift away the nut lock, adjusting nut and plain washers from the spindle.
5   Lift away the outer bearing cone and roller assembly.
6   Remove the disc from the wheel spindle.
7   Using a screwdriver or tapered drift remove the grease seal. This must not be used again but always replaced.
8   Remove the inner bearing cone and roller assembly from the hub.
9   Remove grease from the inner and outer bearing cups and inspect for signs of wear, scratching or pitting. Damage of this kind means that the bearings must be replaced, using a tapered drift. The outer bearing cups can be removed.
10 Clean the inner and outer bearing cone and roller assemblies and wipe dry with a clean lint-free rag.
11 Carefully inspect the cone and roller assemblies for signs of wear or damage which, if evident, mean that complete race assemblies must be obtained. Do not use a new cone and roller assembly in an old cup,
12 Clean the spindle and lubricate with fresh grease.
13 If the inner and/or outer bearing cups were removed the new cups

should be fitted using a suitable diameter drift. Make sure they are replaced the correct way round and also correctly seated (Refer to Chapter 9).
14 Pack the inside of the hub with fresh grease until it is flush with the inside diameter of both bearing cups.
15 With each bearing cone and roller assembly clean off old grease, pack with fresh grease taking care to work the grease well in between the rollers.
16 Place the inner bearing cone and roller assembly in the inner cup.
17 Apply a smear of grease to the lip of the grease seal and replace using a suitable diameter drift. Ensure the seal is correctly seated.
18 Reinstall the disc onto the wheel spindle taking care to keep the hub in a central position so that the grease retainer is not damaged (photo).
19 Replace the outer bearing cone and roller assembly. Follow this with the plain washer and adjustment nut.
20 Adjust the wheel bearing as described in Section 3.
21 Fit a new cotter pin and bend the ends around the castellations of the nut lock to prevent interference with the radio static collector in the grease cap (if equipped).
22 Replace the grease cap, tapping in position with a soft faced hammer.
23 Refer to Chapter 9 and replace the caliper.
24 Reinstall the wheel and secure. Lower the car to the ground. Before driving the vehicle, pump the brake pedal to restore normal brake pedal travel.

3   Front wheel bearings – adjustment

1   Front wheel bearings should be adjusted if the wheel is loose on the spindle or if the wheel does not rotate freely.
2   Chock the rear wheels and apply the parking brake. Jack up the front of the car and support on firmly based stands.
3   Remove the hub cap and ease off the grease cap from the hub.
4   Wipe the excess grease from the end of the spindle. Remove the cotter pin and nut lock.
5   Slowly rotate the wheel and hub assembly and tighten the adjusting nut to the specified torque wrench setting to seat the bearings.
6   Using a box wrench, back off the adjustment nut by one half of a turn and then retighten the adjusting nut to a torque wrench setting of 10 to 15 in-lb or finger-tight.
7   The castellations on the nut lock on the adjusting nut must be aligned with the cotter pin hole in the spindle.
8   Fit a new cotter pin and bend the ends of the cotter pin around the castellated flange of the nut.
9   Check that the wheel rotates freely and then replace the grease cap and hub cap. Lower the car to the ground.

4   Sway bar link insulators – removal, inspection and installation

1   Raise the vehicle and support with jack stands.
2   Remove the nut, washer and insulator from the top of the stabilizer bar bolt.
3   Remove the bolt, washers and spacers. Note their location for reinstallation.
4   Inspect the insulators for cracks or breakage, replace as necessary.
5   Install the stabilizer bar insulators by reversing the above procedure.
6   Tighten the attaching nut to specifications.

5   Sway bar – removal and installation

1   Raise the vehicle and support with jack stands.
2   Loosen the bolt securing the sway bar to the sway bar link.
3   Loosen the bolts at the sway bar insulator attaching clamps.
4   When all tension has been removed from the sway bar bolts, complete their removal and lift out the sway bar.
5   Check the plastic bushings for grooves or cracks. Replace as necessary.
6   Installation is the reverse of removal with the following precautions:
7   Coat any rubber/metal junction with a rubber lubricant to avoid galling.

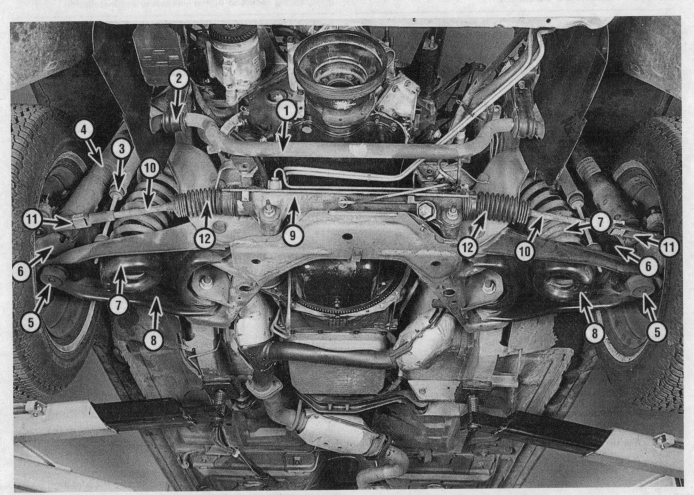

Fig. 11.1 Underside view of the front suspension and steering components

1	Stabilizer bar	5	Balljoint	9	Steering gear
2	Stabilizer bar bracket	6	Spindle	10	Tie-rod
3	Stabilizer bar link and bushings	7	Coil spring	11	Tie-rod end
4	Strut/shock absorber assembly	8	Lower control arm	12	Steering gear boots

8   Replace any bolt used either at the attaching clamp or the sway bar link.

9   Torque the attaching brackets and stabilizer link bolts to specifications.

6   Front coil spring – removal and installation

Note: *Extreme caution should be exercised during this procedure, as personal injury could result if the tension is suddenly released from the compression spring.*

1   Raise the vehicle and support with jack stands.

2   Remove the front wheel(s).

3   Disconnect the stabilizer link from the lower A-arm.

4   Disconnect the steering coupler bolts.

5   Disconnect the tie-rod from the steering spindle, using a 'pickle fork'-type wedge or bearing puller.

6   Using a spring compressor, available from most tool rental shops, insert and compress the spring. When installing the compressor, turn

the end plates so as to hold as much of the spring as possible.

7   Tighten the spring compressor until the spring is loose in the seat.

8   With an assistant's help, support the inboard end of the suspension arm and remove the 2 bolts securing it to the crossmember. A hydraulic jack is the safest method of providing support.

9   Carefully lower the jack to remove the spring.

10 If a new spring is to be installed, mark with chalk the spring compressor end plate position on the old spring so that the new spring can be marked and installed in the same position. Measure the distance between the marks so that the new spring can be compressed the same amount prior to installation. Carefully remove the compressor to relieve the spring tension.

11 Installation is the reverse of removal, with the following precautions:

12 Check that the spring is fully seated onto the spring perch before releasing the compressor. The lower end of the coil spring must be located between the 2 holes in the lower spring pocket.

13 Torque the lower A-arm bolts and the tie-rod nut to specifications.

14 Check the front suspension for binding and loose bolts before driving the car.

11

7 Strut – removal and installation

1   Raise the vehicle and support with jack stands.
2   Insert the ignition key and turn to the unlock position to allow free movement of the front wheels.
3   Inside the engine compartment on the top of the inner fender, loosen the strut mount nut. Using a screwdriver on the shaft will keep the strut from turning.
4   Remove the wheel assembly.
5   Remove the brake caliper, rotor assembly, and dust shield.
6   Remove the two lower nuts and bolts securing the strut to the spindle. Remove the upper strut nut. Lift the strut up to compress the rod, then pull down to remove it.
7   The struts are not rebuildable; should there be evidence of leakage, or rust on the shaft or cracks, they must be replaced.
8   Installation is the reverse of removal.
9   Torque the strut upper nuts to specifications.
10 Torque the lower strut mount bolts to specifications.

8 Spindle – removal and installation

1   Raise the vehicle and support with jack stands.
2   Remove the wheel assembly, rotor, brake caliper, and dust shield.
3   Remove the tie-rod end.
4   Remove the cotter pin from the balljoint nut.
5   Loosen the nut two or three turns, but do not remove the nut at this time.
6   Strike the side of the A-arm to relieve the stud pressure.
7   Position a floor jack under the A-arm and compress the coil spring until working clearance is obtained.
8   Remove the two nuts and bolts securing the spindle to the strut and the loosened balljoint nut. Remove the spindle.
9   Installation is the reverse of the removal instruction sequence.
10 Place the spindle on the balljoint stud and install the nut finger-tight.
11 Position the strut to the spindle and install the two bolts and nuts. Tighten to specifications.
12 Tighten the balljoint nut to specifications.
13 Remove the floor jack.
14 Install the stabilizer link and torque the nut to specifications.
15 Attach the tie-rod and torque the nut to specifications. Install the cotter pin.
16 Install the brake caliper, dust shield, rotor and wheel assembly.
17 Remove jack stands.

9 Steering rack and pinion – removal and installation

1   Raise the vehicle and support with jack stands. Disconnect the battery negative cable.
2   Disconnect the flexible coupling at the input shaft.
3   Remove both tie-rod ends, referring to Section 6.
4   Mark the position of the steering coupler halves. Remove the bolts.
5   Loosen the bolts securing the steering rack to the front crossmember.
6   Disconnect the two steering pressure lines. Plug the open ends to prevent contamination.
7   Remove the nuts from the mounting bolts (loosened in step 5) and lower the rack.
8   The steering rack assembly is a rebuildable unit; however, due to its complexity and need for special factory tools, any repair is best left to a qualified technician.
9   To install, position the rack unit on the front crossmember and install the mounting nuts and bolts. Do not tighten.
10 Reconnect the tie-rod ends and tighten to specifications.
11 Position the wheels in a straight-ahead position.
12 Center the steering wheel and reconnect the steering coupler. The indexing flat on the input shaft should be pointing down when inserted into the flexible coupling. Check for alignment of the marks made during disassembly. Install the bolts and tighten to specifications.
13 Torque the rack mounting bolts to specifications.
14 Connect the steering hydraulic lines. The manufacturer recommends their replacement if they are disconnected. New lines are available from your local dealer or parts store. Tighten all connections firmly.
15 Remove the vehicle from the jack stands. Turn the ignition to the OFF position and re-connect the negative battery cable.
16 Start the car operating the steering in both directions. Check for leakage from the hydraulic lines. Fill the fluid reservoir to the recommended level.
17 Because the alignment is critical for tire wear and economy, recheck the alignment. Refer to a dealer or alignment shop for this service.

10 Rear suspension coil spring – removal and installation

Note: *Springs must always be replaced in pairs. See the note in Section 6.*

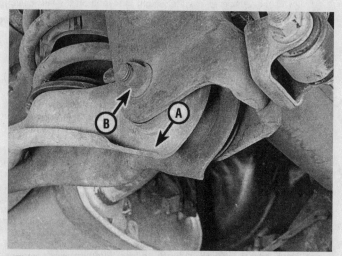

Fig. 11.2 Rack and pinion steering installation (Sec 9)

Fig. 11.3 Support the rear suspension lower arm (A) with a jack placed under the pivot bolt, then remove the pivot bolt nut (B) and push the bolt out through the bushing and axle bracket (Secs 10, 11 and 12)

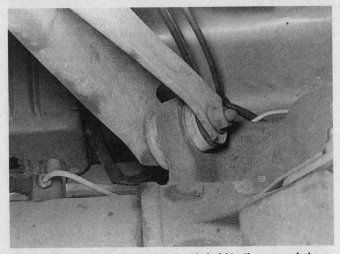

Fig. 11.4 The upper suspension arm is held to the rear axle by a through bolt - the bushing in the axle housing is replaceable, but special tools are required for the operation (Secs 10, 11 and 12)

10.5 Lowering the jack until spring pressure is relieved

1   Raise the vehicle and support it securely on jack stands under the frame so that the rear suspension is fully extended. Remove the rear wheels.
2   Remove the rear stabilizer bar, if equipped.
3   Support the axle under the differential so that the shock absorbers are compressed about one inch.
4   With a jack under the lower suspension arm pivot bolt, remove the bolt and nut.
5   Slowly lower the jack to relieve the spring pressure. Remove the spring and insulator (if equipped) (photo).
6   To install, place the upper and lower spring insulators (if equipped) in position. Tape in place if necessary. Position the spring on the lower suspension arm spring seat so that the pigtail on the lower arm is at the rear and pointing toward the left side of the vehicle.
7   Raise the jack slowly until the spring is compressed and the pivot bolt holes are in alignment.
8   Install the pivot bolt and nut with the nut facing outwards. The manufacturer recommends using new bolts and nuts. Do not tighten the nuts to torque specifications until the vehicle weight is lowered onto the suspension.
9   Install the rear sway bar, if equipped.
10 Remove the support from the pivot point and axle and install the rear wheels.
11 Lower the vehicle so that its weight is resting on the suspension and torque tighten lower suspension arm pivot bolts.

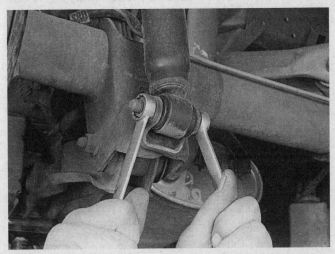

Fig. 11.5 Installation of rear shock absorber (Torx drive needed for 1981 models) (Sec 12)

11 Shock absorbers – inspection

1   The most common test of the shock absorber's damping is simply to bounce the rear corners of the vehicle several times and observe whether or not the car stops bouncing once the action is stopped by you. A slight rebound and settling indicates good damping, but if the vehicle continues to bounce several times, the shock absorbers must be replaced.
2   If your shock absorbers stand up to the bounce test, crawl beneath your car and visually inspect the shock body for signs of fluid leakage, punctures or deep dents in the metal of the body, and that the shock absorber is straight from several angles. If the piston rod is bent, you will not be able to see that it is. A bend in the shock body or signs of the upper portion of the shock body rubbing on the lower section will let you know. Replace any shock absorber which is leaking or damaged, in spite of proper damping indicated in the bounce test.
3   When you have removed a shock absorber, pull the piston rod out and push it back in several times to check for smooth operation throughout the travel of the piston rod. Replace the shock absorber if it gives any signs of hard or soft spots in the piston travel.
4   When you install a new shock absorber, pump the piston rod fully in and out several times to lubricate the seals and fill the hydraulic sections of the unit.

12 Rear shock absorber – removal and installation

Note: *Shock absorbers should always be replaced in pairs.*
1   The upper shock absorber bolt is accessible inside the trunk on sedan models or after the removal of trim panels on station wagons. Remove the rubber cap (if equipped) and remove the shock absorber nut, washer and insulator.
2   Chock the front wheels, raise the car, support it securely and remove the rear wheels.
3   From underneath the car, reach up and compress the shock absorber by pulling it down from the upper shock tower hole.
4   Remove the lower shock absorber nut and washer. On 1981 models a special Torx-type bolt is used requiring a special wrench.
5   Remove the shock absorber and inspect it (Section 11).
6   To install, compress the shock absorber. Place the lower mounting eye on the mounting stud and install the washer and nut. Do not tighten.
7   Install the inner washer and insulator on the upper attaching stud and extend the shock absorber upward into position in the upper mounting hole.
8   Tighten the lower mounting nut to specification. On 1981 models the self wrenching should be allowed to turn freely so that the wrenching tabs seat on the outboard leg of the axle bracket.

11

9   Lower the vehicle and install the insulator, washer and nut. Tighten to specification.
10 Replace the rubber caps or trim panels as necessary.

13 Power steering – general information

The power steering systems available on these cars have a pulley-driven Ford Model CII type pump. This pump delivers fuel to a servo assisted rack and pinion gear assembly.

Servo assistance is obtained through a piston mounted on the rack and running in the rack tube. The degree of assistance is controlled by a spool valve mounted concentrically with the input and pinion shaft.

The power steering pump incorporates an integral fluid reservoir.

Because of the complexity of the power steering system it is recommended that servicing etc, is limited to that given in the following Sections. In the event of a fault occurring it is recommended that repair or overhaul be entrusted to a specialist in this type of work.

14 Power steering – bleeding

1   The power steering system will only need bleeding in the event of air being introduced into the system, ie, where pipes have been disconnected or where a leakage has occurred. To bleed the system proceed as described in the following paragraphs.
2   Open the hood and check the fluid level in the fluid reservoir. Top up if necessary using the specified type of fluid.
3   If fluid is added, allow two minutes then run the engine at approximately 1500 rpm. Slowly turn the steering wheel from lock-to-lock, while checking and topping-up the fluid level until the level remains steady, and no more bubbles appear in the reservoir. Do not hold the steering wheel in the far right or left positions.
4   Clean and refit the reservoir cap, and close the hood.

15 Power steering pump – removal and installation

1   Loosen the pump adjusting bolt and retaining bolts.
2   Push the pump in toward the engine, and remove the drivebelt.
3   Disconnect the power system fluid lines from the pump and drain the fluid into a suitable container.
4   Plug, or tape over, the end of the lines to prevent dirt ingress.
5   If necessary, remove the alternator drivebelt(s) as described in Chapter 2.
6   Remove the bolts attaching the pump to the engine bracket and remove the pump. **Note:** *On some engine installations it may be necessary to remove the pump complete with bracket (photo).*

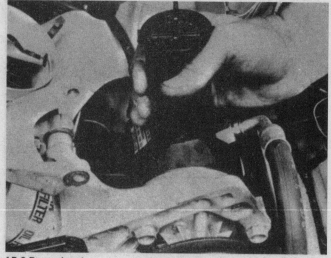

15.6 Removing the power steering pump complete with bracket

7   Replacing is a direct reversal of the removal procedure. Ensure that the fluid lines are tightened to the specified torque, top-up the system with an approved fluid, adjust the alternator drivebelt tension.

16 Steering wheel – removal and installation

1   Disconnect the battery negative cable.
2   Pull out on the steering wheel hub cover (2- and 3-spoke) or push the emblem out from behind (4-spoke).
3   Remove the steering wheel attaching nut.
4   Remove the steering wheel with a suitable wheel puller. Do not strike the end of the steering column with a hammer or use a knock-off type of puller as this will damage the collapsible steering column bearing.
5   When reinstalling align the marks on the steering shaft with those on the wheel. Make sure that the wheels are pointed straight ahead in relation to the steering wheel position.
6   Install the steering wheel nut and tighten to specifications.
7   Align the hub cover pins or springs with their holes or slots in the steering wheel and push into place.

11.6 Typical power steering pump installation (Sec 15)

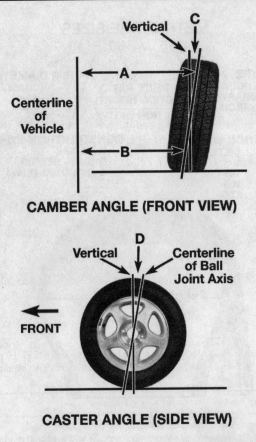

CAMBER ANGLE (FRONT VIEW)

CASTER ANGLE (SIDE VIEW)

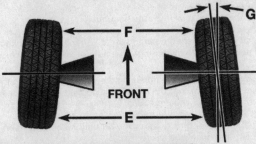

TOE-IN (TOP VIEW)

Fig. 11.7 Front end alignment details (Sec 18)

A minus B = C (degrees camber)
E minus F = toe-in (measured in inches)
G = toe-in (expressed in degrees)

17 Steering column – removal and installation

1   Disconnect the battery negative cable.
2   Remove the steering wheel as described in Section 16.
3   Disconnect the flexible coupling at the steering input flange and disengage the safety strap assembly
4   Remove the steering column trim shrouds which are held in place by self-tapping screws.
5   On column shift models, disconnect the transmission shift rod from the selector lever. Using the proper tool, remove the grommet and replace it with a new one at reassembly.

6   Remove the steering column cover and hood release which is located directly under the column.
7   Disconnect all of the steering column switches and mark their positions for ease of reassembly.
8   Remove the screws attaching the dust boot to the dash panel.
9   Remove the attaching nuts holding the column to the brake pedal support.
10 Lower the column to clear the mounting bolts. On column shift models, reach between the steering column and the instrument panel and lift the shift cable off the cleat on the shift lever. The column can now be pulled so that the U-joint assembly passes through the dash panel clearance hole.
11 Refer to Chapter 12 for removal of the ignition lock and switch.
12 When reinstalling the safety strap and bolt assembly to the steering gear input shaft, make sure that the strap is positioned to prevent metal-to-metal contact. Also, the flexible coupling must not be distorted when the bolts are tightened by prying the shaft up or down with a suitable pry bar the insulator can be adjusted so that it is installed flat.
13 The rest of reinstallation is a reversal of removal. Be sure to install the dust boot over the steering shaft before inserting the shaft through the dash panel.

18 Steering angles and front wheel alignment

1   Accurate front wheel alignment is essential for good steering and tire wear. Before considering the steering angle, check that the tires are correctly inflated, that the front wheels are not bent, the hub bearings are not worn, or incorrectly adjusted and that the steering linkage is in good order, without looseness or wear at the joints.
2   Toe-in is the amount by which the distance between the front inside edges of the roadwheels (measured at hub height) is less than the distance measured between the rear inside edges.
3   Front wheel alignment (toe-in) checks are best carried out with modern setting equipment but a reasonably accurate alternative is by means of the following procedure.
4   Place the car on level ground with the wheels in the 'straight-ahead' position.
5   Obtain or make a toe-in gauge. One may easily be made from a length of rod or tubing, cranked to clear the sump or bellhousing and having a setscrew and lock nut at one end.
6   With the gauge, measure the distance between the two inner wheel rims at hub height at the front of the wheel.
7   Rotate the roadwheel through 180° (half a turn) by pushing or pulling the car and then measure the distance again at hub height between the inner wheel rims at the rear of the roadwheel. This measurement should either be the same as the one just taken or greater by not more than 0.28 in (7 mm).
8   Where the toe-in is found to be incorrect loosen the lock nuts on each trackrod, also the flexible bellows clips and rotate each trackrod by an equal amount until the correct toe-in is obtained. Tighten the trackrod-end lock nuts while the balljoints are held in the center of their arcs of travel. It is imperative that the lengths of the trackrods are always equal otherwise the wheel angles on turns will be incorrect. If new components have been fitted, set the roadwheels in the 'straight-ahead' position and also centralize the steering wheel. Now adjust the lengths of the trackrods by turning them so that the tie-rod-end balljoint studs will drop easily into the eyes of the steering arms. Measure the distances between the centers of the balljoints and the grooves on the inner ends of the trackrods and adjust, if necessary, so that they are equal. This is an initial setting only and precise adjustment must be carried out as described in earlier paragraphs of this Section.

11

19 Wheels and tires

1   Check the tire pressures weekly (when they are cold).
2   Frequently inspect the tire walls and treads for damage and pick out any large stones which have become trapped in the tread pattern.
3   If the wheels and tires have been balanced on the car then they should not be moved to a different axle position. If they have been balanced off the car then, in the interests of extending tread life, they can be moved between the front and rear on the same side of the car and the spare incorporated in the rotational pattern.
4   Never mix tires of different construction or very dissimilar tread patterns.
5   Always keep the roadwheels tightened to the specified torque and if the bolt holes become elongated or flattened, replace the wheel.
6   Occasionally, clean the inner faces of the roadwheels and if there is any sign of rust or corrosion, paint them with metal preservative paint. **Note:** *Corrosion on aluminum alloy wheels may be evidence of a more serious problem which could lead to wheel failure. If corrosion is evident, consult your local authorized dealer for advice.*
7   Before removing a roadwheel which has been balanced on the car, always mark one wheel stud and bolt hole so that the roadwheel may be refitted in the same relative position to maintain the balance.

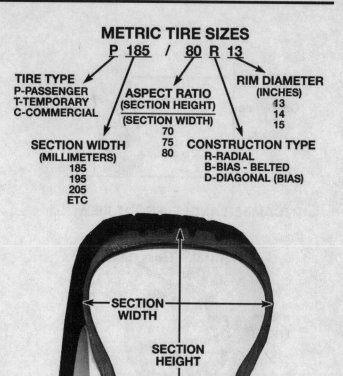

Fig. 11.8 Metric tire size code (Sec 18)

Chapter 12 Bodywork

Contents

1 General information

Models are available in 2-door coupe, 2-door and 4-door sedan and 4-door station wagon.

The body is of unitized, all-welded construction and certain components which are particularly vulnerable to accident damage can be replaced by unbolting them and installing replacement items. These include the fenders, inner fender skirts, radiator support panel, grille, bumpers and trunk.

2 Body exterior – maintenance

1 The condition of your vehicle's bodywork is of considerable importance as it is on this that the resale value will mainly depend. It is much more difficult to repair neglected bodywork than to replace mechanical assemblies. The hidden portions of the body, such as the wheel arches, fender shirts, the underframe and the engine compartment, are equally important, although obviously not requiring such frequent attention as the immediately visible paint.
2 Once a year or every 12 000 miles it is a sound idea to visit your local dealer and have the underside of the body steam cleaned. All traces of dirt and oil will have to be removed and the underside can then be inspected carefully for rust, damaged hydraulic pipes, frayed electrical wiring and similar trouble areas. The front suspension should be greased on completion of this job.
3 At the same time, clean the engine and the engine compartment either using a steam cleaner or a water-soluble cleaner.
4 The wheel arches and fender skirts should be given particular attention as undercoating can easily come away here and stones and dirt thrown up from the wheels can soon cause the paint to chip and flake, and so allow rust to set in. If rust is found, clean down to the bare metal and apply anti-rust paint.

5 The bodywork should be washed once a week or when dirty. Thoroughly wet the vehicle to soften the dirt and then wash down with a soft sponge and plenty of clean water. If the surplus dirt is not washed off very gently, in time it will wear the paint down.
6 Spots of tar or bitumen coating thrown up from the road surfaces are best removed with a cloth soaked in a cleaner made specially for this purpose.
7 Once every six months, or more frequently depending on the weather conditions, give the bodywork and chrome trim a thoroughly good wax polish. If a chrome cleaner is used to remove rust on any of the vehicle's plated parts, remember that the cleaner can also remove part of the chrome so use it sparingly.

3 Upholstery and carpets – maintenance

1 Remove the carpets or mats and thoroughly vacuum clean the interior of the vehicle every tree months or more frequently if necessary.
2 Beat out the carpets and vacuum clean them if they are very dirty. If the upholstery is soiled apply an upholstery cleaner with a damp sponge and wipe off with a clean dry cloth.
3 Consult your local dealer or auto parts store for cleaners made especially for newer automotive upholstery fabrics. Always test the cleaner in an inconspicuous place.

4 Roof covering – maintenance

Under no circumstances try to clean any external vinyl roof covering with detergents, caustic soap or petroleum based cleaners. Plain soap and water is all that is required, with a soft brush to clean dirt that may be ingrained. Wash the covering as frequently as the rest of the vehicle.

5 Body damage – minor repair

See photo sequence on pages 318 and 319.

Repair of minor scratches in the vehicle's bodywork

If the scratch is very superficial, and does not penetrate to the metal of the bodywork, repair is very simple. Lightly rub the area of the scratch with a paintwork renovator, or a very fine cutting paste, to remove loose paint from the scratch and to clear the surrounding bodywork of wax polish. Rinse the area with clean water.

Apply touch-up paint to the scratch using a thin paint brush; continue to apply thin layers of paint until the surface of the paint in the scratch is level with the surrounding paintwork. Allow the new paint at least two weeks to harden; then blend it into the surrounding paintwork by rubbing the paintwork, in the scratch area, with a paintwork renovator or a very fine cutting paste. Finally, apply wax polish.

Where the scratch has penetrated right through to the metal of the bodywork, causing the metal to rust, a different repair technique is required. Remove any loose rust from the bottom of the scratch with a penknife, then apply rust inhibiting paint to prevent the formation of rust in the future. Using a rubber or nylon applicator fill the scratch with bodystopper paste. If required, this paste can be mixed with cellulose thinners to provide a very thin paste which is ideal for filling narrow scratches. Before the stopper-paste in the scratch hardens, wrap a piece of smooth cotton rag around the top of a finger. Dip the finger in cellulose thinners and then quickly sweep it across the surface of the stopper-paste in the scratch; this will ensure that the surface of the stopper-paste is slightly hollowed. The scratch can now be painted over as described earlier in this Section.

Repair of dents in the vehicle's bodywork

When deep denting of the vehicle's bodywork has taken place, the first task is to pull the dent out, until the affected bodywork almost attains its original shape. There is little point in trying to restore the original shape completely, as the metal in the damaged area will have stretched on impact and cannot be reshaped fully to its original contour. It is better to bring the level of the dent up to a point which is about $\frac{1}{8}$ in (3 mm) below the level of the surrounding bodywork. In cases where the dent is very shallow anyway, it is not worth trying to pull it out at all. If the underside of the dent is accessible, it can be hammered out gently from behind, using a mallet with a wooden or plastic head. Whilst doing this, hold a suitable block of wood firmly against the outside of the panel to absorb the impact from the hammer blows and thus prevent a large area of the bodywork from being 'belled-out'.

Should the dent be in a section of the bodywork which has double skin or some other factor making it inaccessible from behind, a different technique is called for. Drill several small holes through the metal inside the area – particularly in the deeper section. Then screw long self-tapping screws into the holes just sufficiently for them to gain a good purchase in the metal. Now the dent can be pulled out by pulling on the protruding heads of the screws with a pair of pliers.

The next stage of the repair is the removal of the paint from the damaged area, and from an inch or so of the surrounding 'sound' bodywork. This is accomplished most easily by using a wire brush or abrasive pad on a power drill, although it can be done just as effectively by hand using sheets of abrasive paper. To complete the preparation for filling, score the surface of the bare metal with a screwdriver or the tang of a file, or alternatively, drill small holes in the affected area. This will provide a really good 'key' for the filler paste.

To complete the repair see the Section on filling and re-spraying.

Repair of rust holes or gashes in the vehicle's bodywork

Remove all paint from the affected area and from an inch or so of the surrounding 'sound' bodywork, using an abrasive pad or a wire brush on a power drill. If these are not available a few sheets of abrasive paper will do the job just as effectively. With the paint removed you will be able to gauge the severity of the corrosion and therefore decide whether to renew the whole panel (if this is possible) or to repair the affected area. New body panels are not as expensive as most people think and it is often quicker and more satisfactory to fit a new panel than to attempt to repair large areas of corrosion.

Remove all fittings from the affected area except those which will act as a guide to the original shape of the damaged bodywork (eg headlamp shells etc). Then, using tin snips or a hacksaw blade, remove all loose metal and any other metal badly affected by corrosion. Hammer the edges of the hole inwards in order to create a slight depression for the filler paste.

Wire brush the affected area to remove the powdery rust from the surface of the remaining metal. Paint the affected area with rust inhibiting paint; if the back of the rusted area is accessible treat this also.

Before filling can take place it will be necessary to block the hole in some way. This can be achieved by the use of Zinc gauze or Aluminum tape.

Zinc gauze is probably the best material to use for a large hole. Cut a piece to the approximate size and shape of the hole to be filled, then position it in the hole so that its edges are below the level of the surrounding bodywork. It can be retained in position by several blobs of filler paste around its periphery.

Aluminum tape should be used for small or very narrow holes. Pull a piece off the roll and trim it to the approximate size and shape required, then pull off the backing paper (if used) and stick the tape over the hole; it can be overlapped if the thickness of one piece is insufficient. Burnish down the edges of the tape with the handle of a screwdriver or similar, to ensure that the tape is securely attached to the metal underneath.

Bodywork repairs – filling and re-spraying

Before using this Section, see the Sections on dent, deep scratch, rust holes and gash repairs.

Many types of bodyfiller are available, but generally speaking those proprietary kits which contain a tin of filler paste and a tube of resin hardener are best for this type of repair. A wide, flexible plastic or nylon applicator will be found invaluable for imparting a smooth and well contoured finish to the surface of the filler.

Mix up a little filler on a clean piece of card or board – measure the hardener carefully (follow the maker's instructions on the pack) otherwise the filler will set too rapidly or too slowly.

Using the applicator apply the filler paste to the prepared area; draw the applicator across the surface of the filler to achieve the correct contour and to level the filler surface. As soon as a contour that approximates the correct one is achieved, stop working the paste – if you carry on too long the paste will become sticky and begin to 'pick up' on the applicator. Continue to add thin layers of filler paste at twenty-minute intervals until the level of the filler is just proud of the surrounding bodywork.

Once the filler has hardened, excess can be removed using a metal plane or file. From then on, progressively finer grades of sandpaper should be used, starting with a 40 grade production paper and finishing with 400 grade wet-and-dry paper. Always wrap the abrasive paper around a flat rubber, cork, or wooden block – otherwise the surface of the filler will not be completely flat. During the smoothing of the filler surface the wet-and-dry paper should be periodically rinsed in water. This will ensure that a very smooth finish is imparted to the filler at the final stage.

At this stage the 'repair area' should be surrounded by a ring of bare metal, which in turn should be encircled by the finely 'feathered' edge of the good paintwork. Rinse the repair area with clean water, until all of the dust produced by the rubbing-down operation has gone.

Spray the whole repair area with a light coat of primer – this will show up any imperfections in the surface of the filler. Repair these imperfections with fresh filler paste or bodystopper, and once more smooth the surface with abrasive paper. If bodystopper is used, it can be mixed with cellulose thinners to form a really thin paste which is ideal for filling small holes. Repeat this spray and repair procedure until you are satisfied that the surface of the filler, and the feathered edge of the paintwork are perfect. Clean the repair area with clean water and allow to dry fully.

The repair area is now ready for final spraying. Paint spraying must be carried out in warm, dry, windless and dust free atmosphere. This condition can be created artificially if you have access to a large indoor working area, but if you are forced to work in the open, you will have to pick your day very carefully. If you are working indoors, dousing the floor in the work area with water will help to settle the dust which would otherwise be in the atmosphere. If the repair area is confined to one body panel, mask off the surrounding panels; this will help to minimise the effects of a slight mis-match in paint colours. Bodywork fittings (eg chrome strips, door handles etc) will also need to be masked off. Use genuine masking tape and several thicknesses of newspaper for the masking operations.

Before commencing to spray, agitate the aerosol can thoroughly, then spray a test area (an old tin, or similar) until the technique is mastered. Cover the repair area with a thick coat of primer; the thickness should be built up using several thin layers of paint rather than one thick one. Using 400 grade wet-and-dry paper, rub down the surface of the primer until it is really smooth. While doing this, the work area should be thoroughly doused with water, and the wet-and-dry paper periodically rinsed in water. Allow to dry before spraying on more paint.

Spray on the top coat, again building up the thickness by using several thin layers of paint. Start spraying in the centre of the repair area and then, using a circular motion, work outwards until the whole repair area and about 2 inches of the surrounding original paintwork is covered. Remove all masking material 10 to 15 minutes after spraying on the final coat of paint.

Allow the new paint at least two weeks to harden, then, using a paintwork renovator or a very fine cutting paste, blend the edges of the paint into the existing paintwork. Finally, apply wax polish.

6 Body damage – major repair

1   Major damage must be repaired by competent mechanics with the necessary welding and hydraulic straighttening equipment.
2   If the damage has been serious it is vital that the body be checked for correct alignment as otherwise the handling of the vehicle will suffer and many other faults – such as escessive tire wear, and wear in the transmission and steering, may occur.
3   There is a special body jig which most body repair shops have and to ensure that all is correct it is important that this jig be used for all major repair work.

7 Maintenance – hinges and locks

Every 3000 miles (5000 km) or 3 months the door, hood and trunk or liftgate hinges and locks should be lubricated with a few drops of oil. The door striker plates should also be given a thin smear of grease to reduce wear and ensure free movement.

8 Door – removal and installation

1   Use a pencil or scribe to mark the hinge location for ease of reinstallation.
2   With an assistant supporting the weight of the door, remove the upper and lower hinge retaining bolts. Lift the door away and stand it on an old blanket.
3   Installation is a reversal of removal, using the marks scribed around the hinges in step 1 as a guide. If it is necessary to realign the door, refer to Section 10.

9 Door hinges – removal and installation

1   Remove the door as described in Section 8.
2   Mark the location of the hinge on the door, remove the bolts and lift away the hinges.

3   Repeat this procedure for the body mounted hinges.
4   Installation is a reversal of removal. If new hinges are installed, it will probably be necessary to align the door as described in Section 10.

10 Door – alignment

1   The door hinge bolt holes are elongated or enlarged so that hinge and door alignment can be accomplished.
2   Loosen the hinge bolts just enough so that the door can be moved with a padded pry bar.
3   After the door has been adjusted, tighten the hinge bolts and check the door fit.
4   Repeat this operation until the proper fit is obtained.
5   After the alignment is made, check the striker plate for proper closing.

11 Door opening weatherstripping – removal and installation

1   Remove the garnish moldings and pull the old weatherstripping off the welded flanges around the door opening.
2   Inspect the flanges for any bends or distortions. Use a pair of vise grips or 2 hammers to flatten any distortion.
3   Application of rubber lubricant to the new weatherstripping will ease installation. Install the weatherstripping around the door opening, taking care not to stretch it.
4   Do not trim the ends until installation is complete and then cut it $\frac{1}{2}$ to 1 in longer than necessary so that the ends can be butted together.

12 Door latch striker – removal, installation and adjustment

1   Use a pair of vise grips to unscrew the door latch striker stud.
2   Installation is the reverse of removal.
3   The striker stud may be adjusted vertically and laterally as well as fore-and-aft.
4   The latch striker must not be used to compensate for door misalignment (refer to Section 10).
5   The door latch striker can also be shimmed to obtain the correct clearance between the latch and striker.
6   The clearance can be checked by cleaning the latch jams and striker area and applying a thin layer of dark grease to the striker.
7   Close and open the door, noting the pattern of the grease.
8   Move the striker assembly laterally to provide a flush fit at the door and pillar or quarter panel.
9   Tighten the striker stud after adjustment.

13 Door trim panel – removal and installation

1   Remove the door handle and cup.
2   Remove the window crank.
3   Remove the armrest.
4   Use a screwdriver to pry the panel away from the door and remove the panel (photo).
5   Carefully peel the watershield away from the door inner panel (photo).

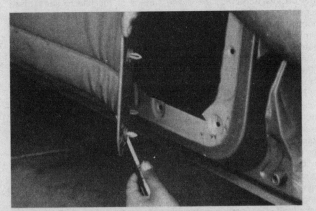

13.4 Prying the plastic retaining rivets from the inner door panel

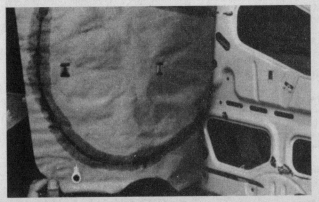

13.5 Be careful not to damage the adhesive on the watershield during removal

12

These photos illustrate a method of repairing simple dents. They are intended to supplement *Body repair - minor damage* in this Chapter and should not be used as the sole instructions for body repair on these vehicles.

1 If you can't access the backside of the body panel to hammer out the dent, pull it out with a slide-hammer-type dent puller. In the deepest portion of the dent or along the crease line, drill or punch hole(s) at least one inch apart . . .

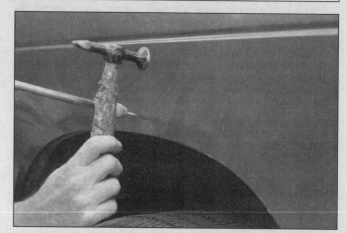

2 . . . then screw the slide-hammer into the hole and operate it. Tap with a hammer near the edge of the dent to help 'pop' the metal back to its original shape. When you're finished, the dent area should be close to its original contour and about 1/8-inch below the surface of the surrounding metal

3 Using coarse-grit sandpaper, remove the paint down to the bare metal. Hand sanding works fine, but the disc sander shown here makes the job faster. Use finer (about 320-grit) sandpaper to feather-edge the paint at least one inch around the dent area

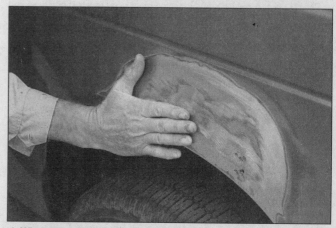

4 When the paint is removed, touch will probably be more helpful than sight for telling if the metal is straight. Hammer down the high spots or raise the low spots as necessary. Clean the repair area with wax/silicone remover

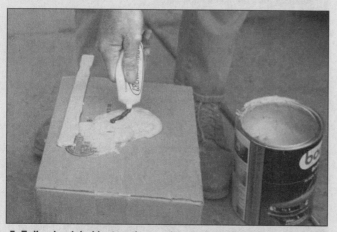

5 Following label instructions, mix up a batch of plastic filler and hardener. The ratio of filler to hardener is critical, and, if you mix it incorrectly, it will either not cure properly or cure too quickly (you won't have time to file and sand it into shape)

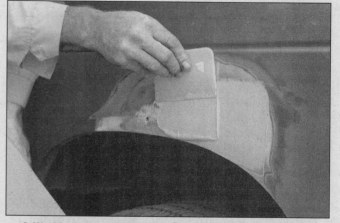

6 Working quickly so the filler doesn't harden, use a plastic applicator to press the body filler firmly into the metal, assuring it bonds completely. Work the filler until it matches the original contour and is slightly above the surrounding metal

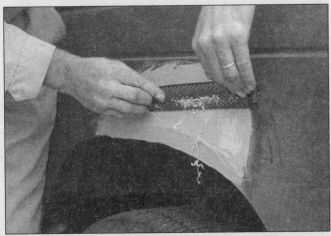

7 Let the filler harden until you can just dent it with your fingernail. Use a body file or Surform tool (shown here) to rough-shape the filler

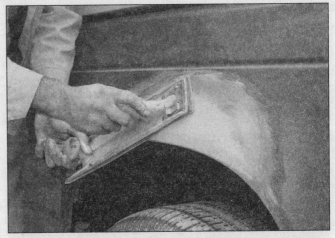

8 Use coarse-grit sandpaper and a sanding board or block to work the filler down until it's smooth and even. Work down to finer grits of sandpaper - always using a board or block - ending up with 360 or 400 grit

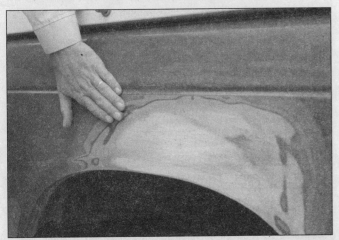

9 You shouldn't be able to feel any ridge at the transition from the filler to the bare metal or from the bare metal to the old paint. As soon as the repair is flat and uniform, remove the dust and mask off the adjacent panels or trim pieces

10 Apply several layers of primer to the area. Don't spray the primer on too heavy, so it sags or runs, and make sure each coat is dry before you spray on the next one. A professional-type spray gun is being used here, but aerosol spray primer is available inexpensively from auto parts stores

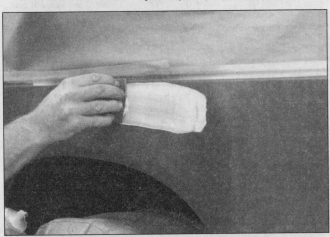

11 The primer will help reveal imperfections or scratches. Fill these with glazing compound. Follow the label instructions and sand it with 360 or 400-grit sandpaper until it's smooth. Repeat the glazing, sanding and respraying until the primer reveals a perfectly smooth surface

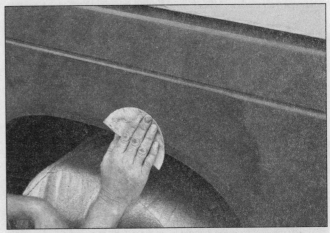

12 Finish sand the primer with very fine sandpaper (400 or 600-grit) to remove the primer overspray. Clean the area with water and allow it to dry. Use a tack rag to remove any dust, then apply the finish coat. Don't attempt to rub out or wax the repair area until the paint has dried completely (at least two weeks)

6   To install, position the watershield against the inner panel so that the adhesive on the back aligns with the adhesive on the door and press into place.

7   The rest of installation is a reversal of removal.

---

14 Door latch assembly – removal and installation

Front door

1   Remove the door trim and watershield as described in Section 3.

2   Mark the location of the rear run lower bolt and remove the bolt.

3   Disconnect the rod ends from the latch. Because of its configuration, the remote link and latch-to-lock rod cannot be removed.

4   Remove the lock cylinder rod from the cylinder lever.

5   Remove the screws attaching the latch assembly to the door and remove the latch.

6   Remove the remote link and latch-to-cylinder rods.

7   Lock the cylinder rod by installing the remote link and latch.

8   Position the latch in the door and install the attaching screws.

9   Connect the latch-to-cylinder rod to the lock cylinder lever.

10 Connect the remaining rods and check the latch operation.

11 Reinstall the rear run lower attaching bolt in the marked position.

12 Reinstall the watershield and trim panel.

Rear door

13 Remove the trim panel and watershield.

14 Disconnect the rear door latch actuating rod from the latch assembly.

15 Remove the screw which attaches the door latch bellcrank and remove the bellcrank.

16 Remove the 3 screws retaining the door latch and remove the latch.

17 To install, place the latch assembly in position and install the attaching screws.

18 Connect the door latch actuating rod.

19 Assemble the door latch bellcrank to the push button rod control link and install the bellcrank to the door inner panel.

20 Check the operation of the latch assembly.

21 Install the door watershield and trim.

---

15 Door latch remote control – removal and installation

1   Raise the window and remove the door panel as described in Section 13.

2   Disengage the remote control by compressing the locking tabs and sliding the control forward.

3   Rotate the control to remove it from the rod.

4   To install, position the remote control through the hole in the inner panel and rotate it onto the rod.

5   Actuate the remove control handle, place the remote control in position on the inner panel and slide it rearward until the locking tabs snap into the panel opening.

6   Check the remote control operation and install the trim panel.

---

16 Door outside handle – removal and installation

1   Remove the door trim and watershield.

2   Disconnect the door latch activating rod from the door outside handle.

3   Prop the door handle open with a piece of $\frac{1}{2}$ x 4 in wood to expose the 2 blind rivets which retain the handle.

4   Use a drift punch to punch out the center of each rivet. Drill out the remainder of the rivet with a $\frac{1}{4}$ in drill, taking care not to enlarge the hole.

3   Remove the door handle.

6   To install, place the handle in position with the wood underneath and the holes aligned.

7   Install $2\frac{1}{4}$ in x $\frac{1}{2}$ in blind oval head rivets or 2 $\frac{1}{4}$ x 20 x $\frac{3}{4}$ in weld studs with nuts and washers.

8   Remove the wood and check the door handle operation.

9   Install the trim panel and watershield.

---

17 Front door window glass – removal and installation

Removal on doors without pivot-type vent windows

1   Remove the door trim panel and watershield.

2   Raise the glass to gain access to the 3 rivets attaching the glass to the brackets. Drive out the center of the rivets with a drift punch and drill out the remainder with a $\frac{1}{4}$ in drill bit. During this operation, insert a suitable piece of wood between the door outer panel and glass bracket to act as a brace. Do not pry on the rivet heads as damage could result.

3   Remove the glass.

Removal on doors with pivot-type vent windows

4   Remove the vent window knob, window regulator handle, door handle, arm rest, trim panel and watershield.

5   Raise the glass to the full up position, remove the 3 vent window retaining screws and remove the regulator.

6   Remove the rubber downstop from the glass bracket and lower the glass to the full down position.

7   Remove the door glass run assembly from the vent window division bar and the top of the door frame.

8   Remove the 3 screws retaining the vent window to the door frame A post. Tilt the top of the vent frame rearward and then upward to remove it.

9   Remove the door glass.

Installation – all models

10 Install the spacer and retainer assemblies onto the glass retention holes.

11 Insert the glass between the door belt weatherstrips and into the door.

12 Place the regulator arm slide assembly in place against the glass bracket and use $\frac{1}{4}$ in x 1 in (6 mm x 12 mm) hex head bolts with nuts and washers to replace the rivets and attach the glass.

13 The rest of installation is a reversal of removal. After installation and before installing the door trim, check the window mechanism for proper operation.

---

18 Rear door window glass – removal and installation

1   Remove the door trim panel and watershield as described in Section 13.

2   Remove the center pin from the rivets securing the glass to the glass bracket. Drill out each rivet head with a $\frac{1}{4}$ in drill. Lower the glass and rest it in the door well.

3   Remove the attaching screw and washer from the retainer division bar glass run.

4   Remove the screw and washer assembly at the top of the division bar at the door frame. Tilt the division bar and main glass forward and remove the weatherstrip from the top of the door frame. Remove the stationary vent glass from the door frame (if equipped).

5   Position the glass, retainer and division bar in an upright position. Pull the main glass and division bar above and outside of the door frame. Swing the two assemblies 90° from the door frame and work the glass and division bar upward and out of the door channel.

6   Prior to installation, assemble the door glass, glass channel, division bar glass run and division bar and retainer.

7   Install the glass channel to the glass with everseal tape (0.065 in x $1\frac{3}{4}$ in x $17\frac{3}{4}$ in). Align the notches in the glass with the cutouts in the glass channel.

8   Trim the tape from the channel cutouts and install the nylon front and lower guides in the glass channel slots. Snap the mylar glass run over the glass channel.

9   Lubricate the inside of the retainer and division bar assembly with silicone lubricant. Place the retainer and division bar assembly over the nylon guides and slide them over the glass channel.

10 Install the run assembly to the front and top of the door frame, leaving the last 6 in next to the division bar hanging loose.

11 Hold the rear door glass and division bar assembly at 90° from the door. Insert the division bar between the door belt weatherstrip and swing the glass inboard to the belt and install it loosely in the door channel.

12 Lubricate the belt weatherstrip with silicone lubricant or soapy solution prior to installation.

13 Install the vent glass and weatherstripping into the rear of the door frame.

14 Place the glass, retainer and division bar in position and install the top screw and washer, making sure that the sealer at the screw head covers the hose so that there is a tight seal.

15 Install the loose 6 inches of the run assembly into the door frame and division bar.

16 Install the retainer and division bracket screw.

17 Install the glass to the bracket with $\frac{1}{4}$ in x 1 in (6mm x 24mm) hex head bolts with nuts and washers.

18 Install the door trim panel and watershield.

19 Front door window regulator – removal and installation

1 Remove the door trim and watershield.

2 Support the glass in the full up position.

3 Use a drift punch to remove the center pin from the rivets attaching the regulator to the door. Drill out the remainder of the rivet with a $\frac{1}{4}$ in drill, taking care not to enlarge the holes.

4 Disengage the regulator arm from the glass bracket and remove the regulator assembly from the door.

5 When installing the regulator assembly, use $\frac{1}{4}$ in x $\frac{1}{2}$ in (6 mm x 12 mm) hex head bolts with nuts and washers to replace the rivets.

6 The rest of installation is a reversal of removal.

20 Rear door window regulator – removal and installation

1 Remove the door trim panel and watershield.

2 Support the glass in the full up position.

3 Drive out the center pin of the regulator retaining rivets with a drift punch and then drill out the head of the rivet with a $\frac{1}{4}$ in drill.

4 Disengage the regulator arm from the glass bracket and remove the regulator assembly from the door.

5 Lubricate the window mechanism prior to installation.

6 Install the regulator through the access hole in the inner panel.

7 Place the regulator arm roller into the glass bracket channel.

8 Install $3\frac{1}{4}$ in x $\frac{1}{2}$ in hex head bolts with nuts and washers and attach the regulator to the door channel.

9 The rest of installation is reversal of removal.

21 Door window glass – adjustment

1 Since the window glass on these models is contained within the door weatherstrip run, minimal adjustment is possible or necessary.

2 The glass can be adjusted fore and aft by loosening the upper run and bracket assembly forward or rearward.

3 On 2-door models the top edge of the glass can be moved inboard or outboard for better fit by loosening the lower glass bracket guide. On all other models this can be accomplished by adjusting the lower attaching nut on the run and bracket assembly.

22 Windshield, stationary quarter window and rear glass – removal and refitting

The windshield, stationary quarter window and rear glass on all models are sealed in place with a special butyl compound. Removal of the existing sealant requires the use of an electric knife specially made for the operation and glass replacement is a complex operation.

In view of this, it is not recommended that stationary glass removal be attempted by the home mechanic. If replacement is necessary due to breakage or leakage, the work should be referred to your dealer or a qualified glass or body shop.

23 Hood – removal and installation

1 Open the hood and support it in the open position.

2 Protect the fenders and cowl with old blankets to prevent damage to the paint.

3 Scribe round the hinges for ease of reinstallation.

4 Have an assistant support the weight of the hood and remove the hinge-to-hood bolts.

5 Lift the hood over the front of the car.

6 Installation is a reversal of removal, taking care to align the hinges with the previously scribed marks.

24 Hood hinges – removal and installation

1 Open the hood and support it in the open position.

2 Remove the hood as described in Section 3.

3 Scribe around the hinge housing with a pencil for ease of installation.

4 Remove bolts and washers securing the hinge to the body and remove the hinge.

5 Installation is the reverse of removal.

25 Hood latch – removal, installation and adjustment

1 Open the hood and support it in the open position.

2 Remove the hood latch cable retainer plate and disengage the cable from the hood latch assembly.

3 Remove the latch attaching screws and remove the latch.

4 Installation is the reverse of removal. Do not fully tighten the latch screws until adjustment is made.

5 The hood latch can be adjusted from side-to-side to align it with the hood latch hook. It can also be adjusted up and down to obtain a flush fit between the hood and fenders.

6 Move the hood latch from side-to-side until it is properly aligned with the opening in the hood inner panel.

7 Loosen the hood bumper lock nuts and lower the bumpers.

8 Move the latch up and down until the proper fit is obtained when the hood is pulled up. Tighten the hood latch screws.

9 Raise the hood bumpers to eliminate any hood looseness and then tighten the bumper lock nuts.

26 Hood support rod – removal and installation

1 Open the hood and support it in the open position with a long piece of wood.

2 Remove the support rod from its stowed position.

3 Remove the bolt which attached the support rod mounting bracket to the left side of the radiator support.

4 Remove the rod and bracket.

5 Installation is the reverse of removal.

27 Trunk lid (sedan and coupe) – removal and installation

1 Open the trunk lid and support it in the open position.

2 Remove the screws securing the hinges to the trunk.

3 Lift the trunk from the car.

4 Installation is the reverse of removal. It may be necessary to adjust the position of the trunk lid after installation.

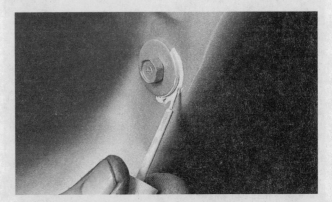

Fig. 12.1 Scribe or paint alignment marks on the trunk lid mounting flange to insure reinstallation in the same position (Sec 27)

28 Trunk lid (sedan and coupe) – adjustment

The trunk lid can be moved fore-and-aft by loosening the hinge-to-door securing screws. The up-and-down adjustment is obtained by adding or subtracting shims between the hinge and door.

29 Trunk lid weatherstrip (sedan and coupe) – removal and installation

1 Open the trunk and carefully pull the old weatherstrip from around the opening.
2 Clean off any old adhesive from the weatherstrip mounting area.
3 Place the new weatherstrip in position and cut to required length, leaving 1 or 2 inches extra at one end.
4 Apply a bead of adhesive around the entire weatherstrip mounting area.
5 Fit the weatherstrip to the body opening with the joint at the rear center.
6 Close the trunk lid and leave closed until the adhesive has at least partially dried.

30 Trunk lid and lock (sedan and coupe) – removal and installation

1 Open the trunk.
2 Remove the latch attaching screws and remove the latch.

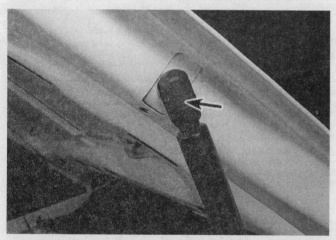

3 Remove the support and bracket.
4 Remove the lock cylinder retainer and the lock cylinder.
5 Installation is the reverse of removal.

31 Station wagon liftgate latch and lock – removal and installation

1 Open the liftgate and support.
2 Remove the trim panel.
3 Remove the license plate holder.
4 Remove the nut and washer and remove the shield.
5 Remove the latch and cover assembly.
6 Remove the retainer which holds the lock cylinder in place and remove the lock cylinder.
7 Installation is the reverse of removal. It may be necessary to adjust the components after installation for proper action.

32 Station wagon liftgate – adjustment

1 Remove the upper rear interior garnish molding and loosen the hinges-to-roof headliner slightly to gain access to the header roof panel attaching nut and washer.
2 Adjust the hinge as necessary to obtain proper closing and fit and reinstall the headliner and garnish molding.

33 Station wagon gas cylinder liftgate assist rod – removal and installation

1 Open the liftgate and support it.
2 Use a small screwdriver to push the locking wedge out of the ball socket or unsnap the locking spring of the lift assembly, depending on design.
3 Detach the opposite end of the rod in the same manner.
4 Remove the assist rod.
5 To install, place the rod in position onto the ball socket and push the locking wedge or ball socket at first one end, then the other.
6 Close the liftgate and check for proper operation.

34 Front and rear bumpers – removal and installation

1 On front bumpers, it will be necessary to remove the lower splash guard (photo).

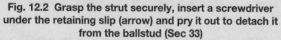

Fig. 12.2 Grasp the strut securely, insert a screwdriver under the retaining slip (arrow) and pry it out to detach it from the ballstud (Sec 33)

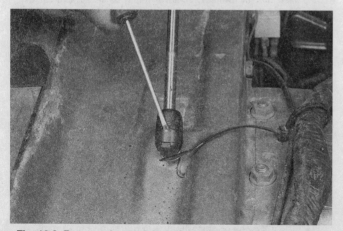

Fig. 12.3 Remove the retaining clip and detach the lower end of the strut (Sec 33)

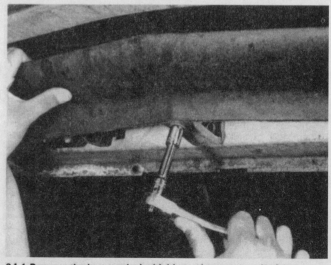

34.1 Remove the lower splash shield to gain access to the front bumper bolts

2   Mark the bolt location for ease of installation.
3   Remove the bolts retaining the bumper to the reinforcement plate (photo).
4   Lift the bumper away from the vehicle.
5   When installing, have an assistant hold the bumper in place so that the bolts can be installed at the marked locations.
6   Install the front splash guard.

35 Radiator grille – removal and installation

1   Open the hood.
2   Remove the left headlight door.
3   Remove the screws retaining the grille.
4   Slide the grille out of the right side headlight door and remove.
5   Installation is the reverse of removal.

36 Instrument panel trim pad – removal and installation

1   Remove the retaining screws from the instrument cluster and finish panel.
2   Remove the instrument panel pad retaining screws from the front and ends of the pad.
3   Remove the pad retaining screws from the top defroster openings and lift the pad away from the instrument panel.
4   Installation is the reverse of removal, making sure that all screws are reinstalled.

37 Steering wheel – removal and installation

1   Disconnect the battery negative cable.
2   Pull out on the steering wheel hub cover (2- and 3-spoke) or push the emblem out from behind (4-spoke).
3   Remove the steering wheel attaching nut.
4   Remove the steering wheel with a suitable wheel puller. Do not strike the end of the steering column with a hammer or use a knock-off type of puller as this will damage the collapsible steering column bearing.
5   When reinstalling align the marks on the steering shaft with those on the wheel. Make sure that the wheels are pointed straight ahead in relation to the steering wheel position.
6   Install the steering wheel nut and tighten.
7   Align the hub cover pins or springs with their holes or slots in the steering wheel and push into place.

34.3 Unbolt the bumper at the reinforcement plate

38 Ignition switch lock cylinder – removal and installation

1   Disconnect the battery ground cable.
2   Remove the horn pad, steering wheel and column trim shroud.
3   Move the selector lever to the Park position (automatic transmission) or the reverse position (manual transmission) and turn the ignition switch to the RUN position.
4   Insert a wire pin or small drift punch of $\frac{1}{8}$ in (3 mm) diameter in the casting hole halfway down the lock cylinder housing.
5   To remove the lock cylinder, press the wire pin while pulling up on the lock cylinder.
6   To install the lock cylinder, turn it to the RUN position and depress the retaining pin. Insert the lock cylinder into its housing, making sure that the cylinder is fully seated and aligned in the interlocking washer. Turn the key to the OFF position which will extend the cylinder retaining pin into the hole in the lock cylinder housing.
7   Turn the key to all positions to check for proper operation.
8   Install the steering wheel, pad and column shroud trim and connect the battery ground cable.

12

Notes

Chapter 13 Supplement:
Revisions and information on later models

Contents

1 Introduction

This supplement contains specifications and changes applying to models produced from 1982 through 1983. Also included is information related to previous models that was not available at the time of original publication of this manual.

Where no differences (or very minor differences) exist between 1982 and 1983 models and earlier models, no information is given. In those instances, the original material included in Chapters 1 through 12 should be used.

2 Specifications

Note: *The specifications listed here include only those items which differ from those listed in Chapters 1 through 12. For information not specifically listed here, refer to the appropriate Chapter.*

Engine

2.3L engine (1982 and 1983)

Piston pin bore diameter .... 0.9012 to 0.9096 in

4.2L V8 engine (1982)

Valve stem diameter (0.015 in oversize) .... 0.3573 in
Crankshaft main bearing journal taper limit .... 0.004 max.
Main bearing oil clearance
   Desired .... Number 1, 0.0004 to 0.0025 in
      Others, 0.0004 to 0.0015 in
   Allowable .... Number 1, 0.0001 to 0.0004
      Others, 0.0004 to 0.0021 in
Connecting rod piston pin bore diameter .... 0.9096 to 0.9112 in

Cooling, heating and air conditioning systems

Cooling system capacities

1982   US qts
2.3L engine (standard cooling) 8.6
2.3L (air conditioning) 9.4
3.3L engine (standard cooling) 8.4
3.3L (air conditioning) 8.5
4.2L engine (all) 15.2

1983
2.3L engine (standard cooling) 8.6
2.3L (air conditioning) 9.2
3.3L engine (all) 8.5

Torque specifications

	Ft-lb	Nm
Fan clutch-to-fan	12 to 18	16 to 24
Electric fan motor-to-shroud	6 to 8	8 to 11
Electric fan shroud-to-radiator	6 to 8	8 to 11

Fuel and exhaust systems

Carburetor (1982)

2.3L
    49-state ....   Holley 5200 2-V
    California ....   Holley 6500 2-V
3.3L ....   Holley 1946 1-V
4.2L
    49-state ....   Motorcraft 2150 2-V
    California ....   Motorcraft 2700 VV 2-V

Carburetor (1983)

2.3L
    49-state ....   YFA 1-V
    California ....   YFA 1-V Feedback
3.3L ....   Holley 1946-V

Torque specifications (YFA carburetor)

	Ft-lb	Nm
Air horn-to-main body	1.5 to 3.0	3.1 to 4.2
Main body-to-throttle body	4 to 4.4	5.4 to 6.0
Accelerator pump housing screws	6 to 11 (in-lb)	0.7 to 1.2
Choke pulldown diaphragm housing screws	3	4
Feedback or altitude solenoid screws	3.7 to 4.4	5 to 6
Fast idle cam retaining screw	3.7 to 4.4	5 to 6
Choke plate-to-choke shaft	9 to 11 (in-lb)	1.0 to 1.3
Throttle plate-to-throttle shaft screws	4 to 5 (in-lb)	0.5 to 0.6
Main metering jet	2	3
Choke cap retaining screws	17 to 20 (in-lb)	1.9 to 2.3
Carburetor-to-intake manifold	13 to 14	17.7 to 19
Bracket screw	5.2	7
Throttle control bracket nut	2.2	3

Automatic transmission

Application (1982 and 1983)

2.3L and 3.3L C3
3.3L and 4.2L C5

Fluid capacities (refill from dry)

                                                        US qts
C3 (2.3L and 3.3L) 8.0
C5 (3.3L and 4.2L) 7.5
C5 (3.3L, clutch-type converter) 11.0

Fluid type

C3 ....   DEXRON II
C5 ....   ESP-M2C166-H, Type H

Torque specifications (C5)

	Ft-lb	Nm
Oil pan-to-case	12 to 10	16 to 22
Torque converter-to-flywheel	20 to 34	27 to 47
Converter cover-to-housing	12 to 16	17 to 21
Neutral start switch	4.4 to 6.6	6 to 9
Transmission-to-engine	40 to 50	55 to 67
Band adjusting screws-to-case	10	13.5
Intermediate and Reverse band adjusting screw locknut	40	54
Converter drain plug	15 to 18	20 to 24
Speedometer clamp bolt	3 to 4.4	4 to 6
Filter assembly retaining bolt	2.2 to 3	3 to 4.5

Suspension and steering

Steering angles

Toe-in (all)	3/16 to 5/16 in	
Camber (all)	7/16° pos	
Caster (all)	1° pos	

Torque specifications

	Ft-lb	Nm
Front suspension		
Lower arm-to-crossmember	150 to 180	203 to 244
Sway bar mounting clamp	20 to 25	27 to 37
Stabilizer bar-to-lower arm	9 to 12	12 to 15
Spindle-to-shock strut	150 to 180	203 to 224
Balljoint-to-spindle	100 to 120	136 to 163
Shock upper mount	62 to 75	84 to 102
Upper shock strut nut	55 to 92	75 to 125
Steering gear-to-crossmember	90 to 100	122 to 136
Tie-rod end-to-spindle	35 to 47	47 to 64
Rear suspension		
Shock absorber-to-upper mount	14 to 26	19 to 35
Upper arm-to-frame	100 to 105	135 to 142
Upper arm-to-axle	90 to 100	122 to 135
Shock absorber lower mount	55 to 70	75 to 95
Lower arm-to-frame	100 to 105	135 to 142
Lower arm-to-axle	90 to 100	122 to 135
Stabilizer bar-to-lower arm	45 to 50	60 to 70

3 Cooling, heating and air conditioning systems

General note

1   The cooling systems of 1982 and 1983 models are nearly identical to the cooling systems of previous models. The procedures outlined in Chapter 3 apply.

2   Beginning in 1982, temperature-activated clutch-type and electric fans were installed on some models, in addition to the direct-drive-type fans described in Chapter 2.

3   The clutch-type fan uses a temperature-activated fluid coupling to regulate fan speed. Air passing through the radiator core and over the bi-metal spring activates the fan in accordance with temperature. Symptoms of failure are the fan operating all of the time, even when the radiator is cold or the fan not turning at all, even at high temperatures.

4   The electric fan is of the same design as that described in Chapter 3. The fan is activated by a temperature switch located in the heater hose tube which closes when the coolant temperature reaches 221° F (105° C), thus completing the relay ground circuit and starting the fan. When the coolant temperature drops below 201°F (87°C), the relay opens and the fan stops. On air conditioned models the Wide Open Throttle (WOT) switch, throttle kicker solenoid or air conditioner cycling switch can also activate the fan.

Clutch-type fan removal and installation

5   Disconnect the negative battery cable and remove the shroud attaching screws.

6   loosen the drivebelt, unbolt the drive clutch and remove the clutch, fan and shroud as an assembly.

7   To install, place the fan on the drive clutch, install the retaining bolts and tighten to the specified torque. Place the drive clutch, fan and shroud in position and install the drive clutch and fan retaining bolts, tightening to specification.

8   Install the shroud and attaching screws and connect the negative battery cable.

Fig. 13.1 Clutch-type cooling fan component layout (Sec 3)

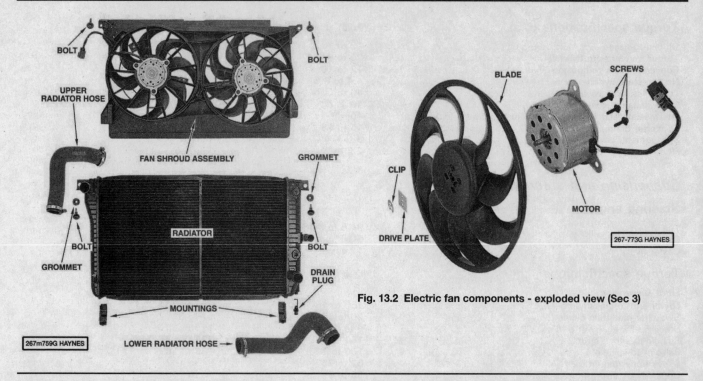

Fig. 13.2 Electric fan components - exploded view (Sec 3)

Electric fan removal and installation

Caution: *Because the electric cooling fan is activated by temperature, it may start at any time, even when the ignition is off. Always disconnect the battery negative cable when working in the vicinity of the fan.*

9   Disconnect the negative lead from the battery.

10   Remove the fan wiring harness from the routing clip and then push down on the two lock fingers and disconnect the harness from the fan motor connector.

11   Remove the four mounting screws and lift the fan and shroud assembly from the vehicle.

12   Slide the retaining clip off and remove the fan. Inspect the fan for cracks or separation of the blades, particularly at the roots.

13   Remove the attaching nuts and lift the motor from the mounting bracket.

14   To install, place the motor in position in the bracket and install the attaching nuts, tightening to the specified torque. Slide the fan onto the shaft and retain it with the clip. Place the bracket and shroud assembly in position and install the retaining screws. Plug the wiring harness into the motor connector making sure the locking fingers snap into place.

15   Connect the negative battery cable.

Fan motor testing

16   If it is necessary to work in the vicinity of the fan when power is applied to the motor, remove the retaining clip and slide the fan from the shaft.

Fan motor does not run

17   Disconnect the motor lead and connect a jumper wire between the negative-to-ground and positive-to-B +. If the motor still does not run, it is defective and must be replaced with a new one.

18   If the motor runs, unplug the coolant switch connector and connect a jumper between the connector and ground. Turn the ignition switch on. If the motor runs, check the switch ground for a short circuit. If there is none, replace the coolant temperature switch with a new one.

Fan motor operates when the engine over-heats but not when the air conditioner clutch engages

19   With the air conditioner selector switch in the A/C position, turn the ignition switch on. If the air conditioner clutch does not engage, check the fuse panel for a blown fuse, replacing as necessary. If the fuse is good and/or the clutch engages, check for voltage on the 347 circuit at pin 6 of the cooling fan controller.

20   If there is no voltage at pin 6, check for an open in circuit 347. If there is voltage, ground circuit 57 at pin 4 of the controller with the controller connected. If the fan motor runs, check for a fault in the ground circuit. If the motor does not run, replace the controller with a new one.

21   To test the air conditioner clutch pressure switch, unplug it and connect a jumper wire across the connector. If the clutch engages, check the air conditioner system for a low refrigerant charge. Have the system charged and serviced as necessary. Check the Wide Open Throttle (WOT) cut-out switch for continuity. If there is continuity, replace the air conditioner compressor clutch pressure switch with a new one.

22   If the compressor clutch does not engage when the test in Step 21 is performed, check for voltage on the 348 circuit of the clutch cycling pressure switch. If there is voltage, check for and repair as necessary an open in the 347 circuit leading to the clutch.

---

4   Fuel and exhaust systems

General note

1   The YFA 1-V carburetor is used on 1983 models equipped with the 2.3L engine. Models sold for use in California use a feedback version of this carburetor.

YFA 1-V carburetor removal and installation

2   Remove the air cleaner assembly and disconnect the throttle lever from the linkage. Disconnect the vacuum lines and the fuel filter tube.

3   Disconnect any electrical connections from the throttle control, idle tracking switch and (if equipped) the Wide Open Throttle air conditioning cut-off switch and feedback solenoid.

4   Disconnect the wire from the electric choke.

5   Remove the retaining nuts and lift the carburetor from the manifold.

6   Remove the mounting gasket, spacer (if equipped) and lower gasket. Carefully clean the mounting surfaces of the spacer and carburetor and inspect for nicks or damage which could cause an air leak. Prior to installation, place the spacer between two new gaskets and position it on the intake manifold.

7   Place the carburetor in position and install the retaining nuts. Tighten the nuts in a criss-cross fashion to the specified torque.

8   Connect the fuel filter, vacuum lines and throttle linkage.

9   Attach the electrical connections to the throttle control, idle tracking switch, Wide Open Throttle air conditioning cut-out switch, feedback solenoid and electric choke.

10   Install the air cleaner assembly.

YFA 1-V carburetor dismantling and reassembly

11 Drill out the rivets, remove the retaining screw and lift the choke assembly and fast idle link away from the carburetor.

12 Remove the Wide Open Throttle air conditioning cut-out switch (if equipped), throttle control device and fuel filter inlet.

13 On feedback carburetors, remove the choke pulldown motor and link and disengage the link from the shaft.

14 Remove the air horn retaining screws and the Solevac or solenoid and lift the air horn off. On feedback carburetors, remove the feedback solenoid which is retained by two Torx-type screws.

15 Invert the air horn assembly and remove the float pin, followed by the float and lever assembly. Turn the assembly over and be prepared to catch the needle pin, spring and needle. Remove the needle seat and gasket.

16 Remove the choke plate retaining screws and remove the plate, link lever and choke shaft. It may be necessary to file the burrs off the shaft to facilitate removal.

17 Remove the spring retainer from the mechanical fuel bowl vent flapper valve, followed by the vent shaft rod, spring and flapper valve. Be sure to note the position of the ends of the torsion spring on the vent rod for easier installation.

18 Turn the carburetor main body over and catch the accelerating pump check ball and weight.

19 Remove the throttle shaft mechanical fuel bowl lever retaining screw from the end of the throttle shaft, followed by the operating lever spring washer, vent rod, actuating lever and E-clip.

20 Loosen the set screw on the throttle shaft and remove the arm and pump connector link.

21 Remove the fast idle cam and screw.

22 Remove the accelerating pump diaphragm housing screws and pump transfer tube and then lift the diaphragm assembly, pump lifter link and metering rod as one unit, followed by the lifter link seal.

23 Disengage the metering rod arm spring from the rod and remove the rod from the arm assembly. Make sure to note the location of any shim washers so they can be reinstalled in the same position. Compress the upper pump spring and remove the retainer and cup, followed by the upper spring, metering rod arm assembly and the pump lifter link.

24 Compress the pump diaphragm spring and remove the spring retainer, spring and pump diaphragm assembly from the housing.

25 On feedback carburetors, use a sharp punch to remove the temperature compensated accelerator pump bleed valve plug from the main or outside main body casting. If equipped, loosen the bleed valve screw and remove the valve.

26 Use the proper size jet tool or screwdriver to remove the main metering rod jet and low speed jet.

27 Remove the retaining screws, separate the throttle body flange assembly from the main body and remove the gasket.

28 File off the ends of the staked throttle plate retaining screws. Slide the throttle shaft and lever assembly from the throttle body flange assembly, making sure to note the location of the ends of the spring on the shaft for reinstallation in the same position.

29 If it is necessary to remove the idle mixture screw adjustment cap and cup assembly, proceed as follows: Turn the carburetor assembly over and cover all fuel and vacuum openings with tape to make sure no metal filings can enter. Carefully saw a lengthwise slot through the cup with a hacksaw as shown in the accompanying illustration. Insert a screwdriver into the slot and twist it to spread the cup apart sufficiently for removal. After removal, count the number of turns necessary to seat the mixture screw needle lightly on its seat. Record this information for use during reassembly. Remove the screw and cup and clean the carburetor of metal shavings.

30 The carburetor is now completely disassembled and should be cleaned and inspected for wear. After the carburetor components have been cleaned in the proper solvent of dirt, gum and carbon deposits, they should be rinsed in kerosene and dried, preferably with compressed air. **Caution:** *Do not immerse or clean the air horn in cleaner or solvent, as this could damage the vent shaft seal. Do not use a wire brush to clean the carburetor or wire or drills to clean any passages, as this could enlarge them.* Inspect the throttle and choke shafts for grooves, wear or excessive looseness. Check the throttle and choke plates for nicks and smoothness of operation. Inspect the carburetor body and components for cracks. Check the floats for leaks by submerging them in water which has been heated to just below the boiling point. Leaks will be indicated by the appreance of bubbles. Check the float arm

needle contact surface for grooves and wear. If the grooves are light, polish the needle contact surface with crocus cloth or steel wool. Replace the floats if the shafts are badly worn. Inspect the gasket contact surfaces for burrs or nicks. Replace any distorted springs, screws or bolts which have stripped or damaged threads.

31 To begin reassembly, install the throttle shaft and lever assembly in the throttle body flange. Install the throttle return spring and bushing. Place the throttle plate in position and install the screws snugly but do not tighten them fully at this time.

32 Check the throttle plate to make sure it does not bind in the bore by moving the shaft back and forth and rotating it. Make sure the adjusting screw is backed out sufficiently so the plate does not close tight in the bore. Tighten the retaining screws fully and stake them in position.

33 Install the idle mixture screw and spring and a new limiter cup, making sure to turn the screw the same number of turns out recorded at removal.

34 Install the throttle body to the main body, using a new gasket. Install the low speed and main metering jets, using a thread-locking compound.

35 Install the pump diaphragm in the pump housing and place the diaphragm spring in position on the shaft and housing assembly. Install the shim washers in the previously noted locations, followed by the spring retainer and pump lifter link. Install the throttle shaft arm and pump lifter link, metering rod arm and spring assembly and the upper spring onto the diaphragm shaft. Press down on the spring and install the upper pump spring retainer.

36 Install the metering rod onto the metering arm with the looped end of the spring on the rod. Make sure the pump diaphragm housing holes are aligned and install the retaining screws.

37 Install the pump housing, lifter link, metering rod and baffle plate assembly in the main body casting, making sure the vacuum passages are aligned. Engage the pump lifter link with the lifter link seal and main body and insert the metering rod in the main jet. Install the pump retaining screws snugly and press down on the diaphragm shaft to compress the diaphragm. Tighten the screws fully. Connect the pump transfer tube and adjust the metering rod.

38 On feedback carburetors, place the temperature compensated pump bleed valve and washer in position and install the retaining screw. Install a new welch plug (if equipped).

39 Install the fast idle cam and screw.

40 Install the throttle shaft arm and pump connector link onto the throttle shaft and pump lifter link. Tighten the lock screw and install the E-clip vent rod actuating lever, spring washer, operating lever and retaining clip onto the end of the throttle shaft. Tighten the retaining screw.

41 Install the choke shaft assembly into the air horn.

42 Place the choke plate in position on the shaft and install the screws snugly. Check the plate movement to make sure there is no binding and tighten the screws. Install the choke lever link and screw.

43 Install the needle seat and gasket into the air horn and invert the horn assembly. Install the needle, pin, spring, needle pin, float and lever assembly and the float pin.

44 With the bowl vent flapper valve aligned with the vent rod and the spring in place on the rod shaft, install the spring retainer.

45 Install the pump check ball and weight in the main body castings.

46 Place the new air horn gasket, air horn assembly, Solevac or solenoid bracket in position on the main body and install the attaching screws, tightening to the specified torque. Make sure the mechanical fuel bowl vent rod is engaged with the forked actuating rod.

47 Install the choke assembly, making sure the thermostatic spring engages the choke lever tang properly and retain it with two new rivets and the screw.

48 Install the air cleaner bracket and the fast idle link.

49 Connect the choke pulldown link with the choke shaft lever and the pulldown diaphragm rod. Place the diaphragm bracket in position on the air horn and install the retaining screws. Connect the throttle body pulldown vacuum hose to the diaphragm housing.

50 Install the feedback solenoid (if equipped).

51 Install the Solevac or solenoid kicker and Wide Open Throttle air conditioning cut-out switch (if equipped).

YFA 1-V carburetor Wide Open Throttle (WOT) air conditioner cut-out switch checking and adjustment

52 The WOT cut-out switch is normally closed, which allows current

13

to flow at any throttle setting other than wide open. The switch is located on the left side of the carburetor and an actuating lever on the throttle shaft contacts the switch arm so the air conditioner clutch is de-energized during wide open throttle operation.

53 To check the switch, unplug the wiring harness and connect battery power and a test lamp. With the throttle closed, the test light should be on and if it is not, replace the switch with a new one.

54 Open the throttle fully and check that the test light then goes off. If the light does not go off, turn the adjusting screw clockwise until it does. Rotate the adjusting screw an additional four turns. If the lamp does not go off after the screw has been turned to it's maximum travel, replace the switch with a new one. After the switch has been replaced, turn the adjusting screw counterclockwise until the lamp remains on at the wide open throttle position. Turn the adjusting screw clockwise until the test light goes off and then turn it the four additional turns.

55 Remove the test lamp and plug in the connector.

YFA 1-V carburetor metering rod adjustment

56 Remove the air cleaner assembly followed by the carburetor air horn and gasket.

57 Use a side cutter to remove the tamper-proof cap covering the adjusting screw.

58 Push down on the top of the pump diaphragm shaft until the assembly bottoms. Hold the assembly in place and turn the rod adjustment screw in a counterclockwise direction until the metering rod just bottoms in the body casting.

59 Turn the screw one turn clockwise for the final adjustment.

60 Install the air horn, using a new gasket.

61 Turn the adjusting screw clockwise until it contacts the casting to reset the closed plate adjustment. Turn the screw one additional turn clockwise and install a new tamper-proof cap.

62 Install the air cleaner assembly.

YFA 1-V carburetor mechanical fuel bowl vent adjustment

63 Prior to adjustment, the idle speed must be set to the specification on the emission label. The engine must be at normal operating temperature.

64 Referring to the accompanying illustration, open the throttle lever until the throttle lever actuating lever does not touch the fuel bowl vent rod.

65 Return the throttle lever to the idle set position and measure the travel of the fuel bowl vent rod at point A. This measurement should be 0.100 to 0.150 in (2.54 to 3.81 mm). If it is not, bend the actuating lever at the notch until the travel is within specification.

---

5 Automatic transmission

General note

1   Some models equipped with 3.3L and 4.2L engines use the C5

Fig.13.3 If the old filter grommet or gasket remains attached to the transmission, be sure to remove it before installing the new filter (Sec 5)

automatic transmission. The C5 is very similar to the C4, which it replaces, although some maintenance procedures are different. The C5 transmissions use a different fluid, designated Type H. **Note:** *Type F or DEXRON II fluid specified for the C3 and C4 must not be used.*

2   Some models of the C5 transmission use a clutch-type torque converter which, when engaged, provides a direct connection between the engine and rear wheels for improved economy. The vehicle will respond in a manner similar to one with a manual transmission when the clutch is in operation.

C5 transmission removal and installation

3   Open the hood, install protective covers on the front fenders and disconnect the battery negative cable.

4   Remove the fan shroud bolts and place the shroud over the fan.

5   Raise the front of the vehicle and support is securely.

6   Remove the driveshaft as described in Chapter 8.

7   Disconnect the muffler pipe from the catalytic converter and use a piece of wire to support the muffler and pipe assembly.

8   Remove the exhaust pipe-to-manifold retaining nuts, pull the catalytic converter back from the hangers and release the hangers from the mounting bracket.

9   Remove the speedometer from the extension housing and unplug the Neutral start switch harness connector.

10 Disconnect the kickdown rod from the transmission lever.

11 Disconnect the shift linkage from the bellcrank. On floor-shift equipped vehicles, unbolt the shift cable routing bracket and disconnect the cable from the transmission lever.

12 Remove the converter dust shield for access and remove the converter retaining nuts. Rotate the crankshaft pulley nut with a suitable wrench to gain access to all of the nuts.

13 Remove the starter.

14 Loosen the rear support-to-number three crossmember nuts.

15 Place a jack under the transmission and secure it with a chain, if possible.

16 Lower the transmission sufficiently to gain access and disconnect the cooler lines. It may be necessary to use Ford tool T82L9500-AH.

17 Pull back on the jack to disengage the converter studs from the driveplate and then lower the transmission from the vehicle.

18 To install, raise the transmission into position and rotate the torque converter to align the studs and drain plug with the holes in the driveplate.

19 Move the converter and transmission assembly forward against the back of the engine and make sure the converter studs engage with the driveplate and transmission dowels engage the bellhousing.

20 Connect the cooler lines, raise the transmission and install the number three crossmember through-bolts.

21 Remove the jack and tighten the rear support attaching nut to the specified torque.

22 Install the starter.

23 Install the torque converter nuts and tighten them to the specified torque.

24 Install the dust shield and on column shift models, place the linkage in position on the bellcrank. Install the attaching bolts and tighten to the specified torque.

25 Connect the shift linkage to the bellcrank. On floor-shift equipped vehicles, connect the cable to the shift lever and install the routing bracket attaching bolt.

26 Connect the kickdown rod to the transmission lever and plug in the Neutral start switch.

27 Install the speedometer cable.

28 Install the catalytic converter to the exhaust manifold, using new seals.

29 Install the exhaust pipes to the manifold with the nuts finger tight.

30 Remove the supporting wire and connect the pipe to the converter outlet with the nuts finger tight.

31 Align the exhaust system and tighten the retaining nuts.

32 Install the driveshaft.

33 Check the shift linkage operation, adjusting as necessary.

34 Lower the vehicle.

35 Install the fan shroud and connect the negative battery cable.

36 Lower the hood.

37 Start the engine and make sure that it cranks over only when the selector is in the Neutral or Park positions.

38 Check the transmission fluid level.

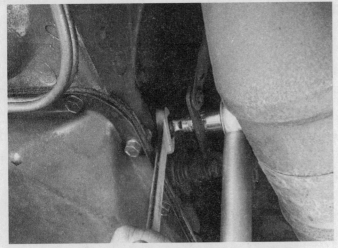

Fig.13.4 Adjusting the C5 intermediate transmission band (Sec 5)

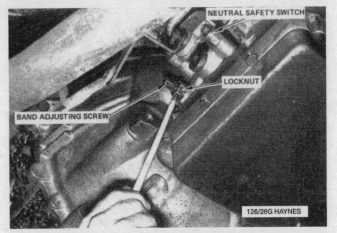

Fig.13.5 C5 transmission Low and Reverse band adjustment (Sec 5)

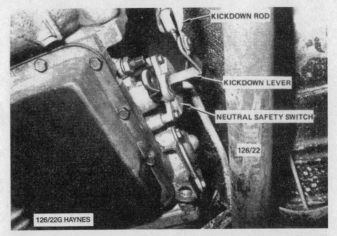

Fig.13.6 C5 transmission Neutral start switch adjustment (Sec 5)

C5 transmission filter replacement

39 Remove the transmission oil pan and drain the fluid as described in Chapter 7.
40 Remove and discard the oil filler shipping plug which is located in the transmission case.
41 Unbolt and remove the filter screen assembly.
42 Place the new filter assembly in position, making sure to seat the seal properly. Install the retaining bolt and tighten to specification.
43 Install the oil pan and new gasket and refill the transmission as described in Chapter 7.

C5 transmission intermediate band adjustment

44 Clean the dirt from around the adjusting screw and loosen the locknut.
45 Tighten the adjusting screw with a torque wrench to 10 Ft-lb (13.5 Nm).
46 Back the screw off exactly 4-1/4 turns.
47 Hold the adjusting screw so that it cannot turn and tighten the locknut to 40 Ft-lb (54 Nm).

C5 transmission Low and Reverse band adjustment

48 Clean the dirt from around the adjuster screw and loosen the locknut.
49 Tighten the adjuster screw to 10 Ft-lb (13.5 Nm) and then back it off exactly three (3) full turns.
50 Hold the adjusting nut to keep it from turning and tighten the locknut to 40 Ft-lb (54 Nm).

C5 transmission Neutral start switch adjustment

51 Make sure the shift linkage is properly adjusted and loosen the two Neutral start switch attaching bolts.
52 With the lever in the Neutral position, rotate the switch and sert a number 43 drill. The drill must pass through all three holes in the switch to a depth of 15/32 in (11.91 mm).
53 Tighten the switch attaching screws to the specified torque and remove the drill.
54 check the switch operation to make sure the engine will start only when the shift lever is in the Neutral or Park positions.

C5 transmission cable-type floor linkage adjustment

55 Place the transmission selector lever against the rearward stop of the Drive position. The lever must be held in this position during the adjustment procedure.
56 Raise the vehicle, support it securely and loosen the manual lever shift rod retaining nut. Place the transmission selector lever in the Drive position, which is the second detent from the back of the transmission.
57 With both the selector lever and the shift lever in the Drive position, tighten the retaining nut to 15 Ft-lb (19 Nm).
58 Lower the vehicle and check the operation of the shift lever in each position.

Notes

Index

Notes

Notes